BEDFORD
ANORVM
CANT ABRI
GI Æ
PARS
HART
FORDIÆ
PARS
Potton
Shefforde
Baldock
Royston
Hichin
Luton
Eaton
Temsforde
Sutton
Dunton
Edworth
Afhwell
Radwell
Norton
Stanton
Holewell
Peirton
Hexton
Scala
Miliarium
Christophorus Saxton descrip

IN THE STEPS OF JOHN BUNYAN

An Excursion into Puritan England

"It was a distinguished Christian minister who said that 'all our liberties are due to men who, when their conscience has compelled them, have broken the laws of the land'."

Dr. HARRY ROBERTS: *British Rebels and Reformers*. (BRITAIN IN PICTURES).

"None of the people who talk about 'art for art's sake' and 'the distracting influence of a moral purpose in art' have ever yet produced art on a par with Milton's and Bunyan's, and they never will. The greatest artists are even more interested in life than in art. Art seems to them a something given, by which to interpret the significance of life."

G. M. TREVELYAN: *Bunyan's England*. (REVIEW OF THE CHURCHES, July 1928).

JOHN BUNYAN IN 1673

Reproduced from the Plimpton Collection by kind permission of the owner, Mrs. George A. Plimpton, and of the Frick Art Reference Library, Columbia University, New York.

IN THE STEPS OF JOHN BUNYAN

An Excursion into Puritan England

by

VERA BRITTAIN

With 56 Illustrations

by

CYRIL HARGREAVES

and Others

RICH AND COWAN

London New York Melbourne Sydney Cape Town

"Wherever I have seen the print of his Shooe in the Earth, there I have coveted to set my Foot too . . ."
JOHN BUNYAN: *The Pilgrim's Progress*, Part II.

To the Town and People of
BEDFORD
where John Bunyan lived
and his spirit survives

First Published	1950
Reprinted	1970
This Reprint	1987

ISBN 1-85351-022-X

This reprint is published by Bedfordshire Leisure Services with the agreement of Vera Brittain's Literary Executors

Printed by Stanley L. Hunt (Printers) Ltd. Rushden, Northants

CONTENTS

LIST OF ILLUSTRATIONS

* A hamlet in the parish of Elstow.

Line Drawings in the Text:

AUTHOR'S ACKNOWLEDGMENTS

I AM deeply grateful to Mr. Thomas Cooper, F.L.A., and his colleagues in Bedford Public Library for their assistance in my research on John Bunyan's life and work.

It is especially difficult to find adequate words in which to acknowledge my debt to Mr. Cyril Hargreaves, who as Deputy Borough Librarian in charge of the John Bunyan Library has not only kept me constantly supplied with the information that I required, but has also given so much of his free time and skill as an amateur photographer to making the majority of the pictures for this book. I am equally indebted to him for reading and checking the manuscript. Throughout my work he has acted as my Interpreter, and if I have failed to make the best use of his interpretations, the fault is not his.

Sincere thanks are also due to Mr. Joseph Whiting and the Trustees of the Bunyan Meeting, Mill Street, Bedford, for the inspection of their treasures and permission to photograph their property; to Mr. Whiting personally for reading the manuscript; and to the custodian of Bunyan Meeting, Mr. F. T. Wells, for accompanying me to the site of Bunyan's birthplace and the scenes of his mission.

I owe another debt of gratitude to Mrs. Audrey Samet, of the De Parys Hotel, Bedford, who kindly allowed me to use my petrol allowance in her own car, with herself as the patient and resourceful driver.

Grateful thanks are also due to His Worship the Mayor of Bedford, and Mr. G. D. Gilmore, Assistant Solicitor to Bedford Corporation, for their help with the Borough Records and the legal aspects of Bunyan's story. For assistance with the County records I am greatly indebted to Miss Joyce Godber, the Bedfordshire County Archivist, whose generous help in relation to recent Bunyan discoveries is more adequately acknowledged in the Introduction; and to Mr. Eric J. Davis and Mrs. Joan Varley, County Archivists of Buckinghamshire and Lincolnshire. I also owe thanks to Mr. H. G. Tibbutt for lending me the manuscript of his forthcoming book *Colonel John Okey*, and for making available to me his own historical researches and other material which less generous writers are apt to keep to themselves.

I wish to express my gratitude to the following for help and information, often involving considerable expenditure of their valuable time: The National Book League, and especially Miss Joan Stevenson, who supplied me with a list of essential books; Dr. E. C. Walker, Bedfordshire Divisional Education Officer; the Rev. S. V. Hartley, Vicar of the Abbey Church, Elstow, to whom I am also indebted for permission to photograph the Church and its surroundings; the Rev. R. D. Guinness, Rector of St. John's Church, Bedford; Mr. D. A. Bungey, of St. Mary's Church, Bedford; Mr. Horace Gale, Treasurer of the Bedfordshire Union of Baptist and Congregational Churches; the Rev. E. Victor Whittle, of the Baptist Meeting, Stevington; the Rev. W. H. Redfern, of the Old Meeting Baptist Church, Gamlingay; the Rev. R. G. Martin, Newport Pagnell Congregational Church; the Rev. B. J. Tidball, Bocking End Congregational Church, Braintree, Essex; the Rev. S. G. B. Weston, Vicar of Keysoe; Mr. John L. Nickalls, Librarian to the Society of Friends, Friends' House, Euston Road, London; Mr. F. M. Gardner, Borough Librarian, Luton; Miss Margaret Beattie, Borough Librarian, Aylesbury; the Chief Librarian, Manchester Central Library (for permission to read the only copy in England of Bunyan's *A Confession of my Faith*); Mr. G. K. Wilkie, Librarian, Central Reference Library, Leicester; Mr. A. W. Janes, Editor of the *Bedfordshire Times and Standard*; Mr. C. E. Freeman, Curator of the Luton Museum and Art Gallery, and Editor of *The Bedfordshire Magazine*; Mr. H. O. White and the Leagrave Press Ltd., Publishers of *The Bedfordshire Magazine*; Mr. Henry Darlow, Town Clerk, Bedford; Mr. Anthony Pickford, Town Clerk, City of London Corporation, who kindly permitted me to obtain photographs of Bunhill Fields; Mr. Cherry Kearton, Manager, Messrs. Rich and Cowan; The London News Agency Photos Ltd.; the Director, The Royal Botanic Gardens, Kew, for expert information on seventeenth-century trees; Mrs. G. M. Tabor, the present owner of Harlington Manor; the Bedfordshire Historical Record Society; Mr. R. S. R. Fitter, Author of *London's Natural History*; Mr. Basil Blackwell; Mr. Stephen Hobhouse; M. Henri Talon, author of *John Bunyan, L'Homme et L'Oeuvre*; Mlle Cecile

Chevreau; the Rt. Hon. Sir Geoffrey Shakespeare, Bt.; Mr. H. F. Rubinstein; and Professor L. C. B. Gower.

I should also like to express my thanks to the authors and publishers of the books and articles upon which this work is based, many of which are included in the Bibliography at the end. I am especially indebted to Sir G. M. Trevelyan, O.M., and the late Rev. John Brown, D.D. I also owe thanks to my husband, Professor George Catlin, Ph.D., whose books include *Thomas Hobbes: An Introduction*, and other works dealing with the seventeenth century, for reading and checking the manuscript.

Last, but perhaps first in importance, I must mention my debt to the late Dr. Frank Mott Harrison and to Mrs. Harrison for the John Bunyan Library given by them to Bedford. I am, I believe, the first British biographer of Bunyan to have the privilege of using this Library.

If any name has been inadvertently omitted from this list I trust I may be forgiven, owing to the very large number of those to whom I owe gratitude and appreciation.

V. B.

NOTE ON THE FRONTISPIECE

The portrait of John Bunyan which appears at the beginning of this book was painted by an unknown artist in 1673, the year after Bunyan's long imprisonment ended. It came into the possession of Robert Louis Stevenson's father, and was greatly valued by both him and his son. When the younger Stevenson settled in Samoa, he had the picture sent out to him.

After Robert Louis Stevenson's death, the portrait was purchased by the late Mr. George A. Plimpton of New York, and became part of the Plimpton Collection. Owing to its American ownership, it has not previously been used by a British biographer of Bunyan. It is here reproduced by the courtesy of Mrs. George A. Plimpton and the Frick Art Reference Library, Columbia University, New York. I am greatly indebted for help given me in tracing it to Mr. Francis T. P. Plimpton, son of Mr. George A. Plimpton, and to the Macmillan Company of New York.

A copy of the portrait made in Mr. George A. Plimpton's lifetime, and presented by him to the late Dr. Frank Mott Harrison, hangs in the John Bunyan Library which Dr. Harrison gave to Bedford a few years before his death in 1945.

The only contemporary portraits of John Bunyan hitherto familiar to British readers are the pencil sketch by Robert White, bequeathed by the Rev. Clayton M. Crackerode to the British Museum in 1799; the portrait made in 1685 by Thomas Sadler, son of John Sadler, Master of Magdalene College, Cambridge, which hangs in the National Portrait Gallery, Room VII (No. 1311); and the engraving by Sturt, prefixed to the first folio edition of Bunyan's works in 1692 and taken from a painting which has not been discovered.

The Advocateship of Jesus Christ, published by Dorman Newman in 1688, contained a steel-engraved portrait of John Bunyan executed by Van Hone. It is not known whether a further portrait owned by the late John Beagarie of Hitchin was an original or a copy.

Robert White's drawing is smooth and slick, though done with a sure and elegant touch. White had a considerable reputation as an accomplished artist, but his sketch was a rapid picture made on a strip of vellum about six inches by four as a preliminary to the engraved sleeping portrait prefixed to the third edition of *The Pilgrim's Progress*, published in 1679. It presents Bunyan with a completely unlined face at the age of fifty; he does not appear to be a man upon whose head the storms and stresses of life had often descended.

Sadler's picture may have correctly depicted the external man, but it seems to be even further than White's from conveying his spirit. The crude Puritan peasant of the National Gallery portrait might have produced *The Life and Death of Mr. Badman*; he could not possibly have written *Grace Abounding* or *The Pilgrim's Progress*.

I have chosen the portrait that belonged to Robert Louis Stevenson because it seems to me to capture the essential John Bunyan. The artist painted the date clearly on his picture, and though he did not leave us his name, it is obvious that he followed the Rembrandt tradition and understood his craft.

He shows us a Bunyan tense and puffy of countenance, as he would have appeared after long confinement, with hair cut short, and deep lines under the eyes. Those eyes, at times, had looked on terrible things.

John Bunyan went into Bedford County Gaol a hot-headed young rebel just thirty-two years old. He came out a mature and experienced man of forty-three, in whose presence other prisoners had died. On the face of this portrait his story is written. It speaks to us of the suffering and fortitude which unite through all time the men and women who are moved by the power of the spirit.

INTRODUCTION

THE AUTHOR TO THE READER

"I found my condition, in his experience, so largely and profoundly handled, as if his Book had been written out of my heart."
JOHN BUNYAN: *Grace Abounding.*

WHEN I started work on this book, a friend said to me: "I'm not sure whether I'm glad about your story of Bunyan. His magnificent *Pilgrim's Progress* is enough for me; I don't want to know about his life."

No doubt many readers feel the same as my friend. They are satisfied with the allegorical Christian in whom each one of us can find his own soul, and imagine a gulf between the author and his creation which does not exist.

The immortal figure with a Book in his hand and a Burden on his back, crying, "What shall I do?" is John Bunyan himself, though he is more than Bunyan. As Professor G. M. Trevelyan has shown in his essay on *Bunyan's England,* this lonely Puritan traveller symbolizes the unique contribution of the seventeenth century to our turbulent past.

He is the individual who established, through political confusion and religious persecution, the right to maintain a direct relationship between himself and God. To him we owe that freedom of worship which the English-speaking world, unlike other nations of our day, has never forfeited.

The epic story of Christian's creator is hence not merely dramatic and absorbing in itself. The fact that it is a mirror of seventeenth-century England in the quality and direction of its spiritual adventure gives it a special relevance for our own epoch, in which the same struggle is taking place in a different form. It brings the challenge of hope and courage to all who are fighting for the integrity of the human soul against totalitarian philosophies and spiritual demoralization.

The popular failure to realize the significance of John Bunyan's life apart from his books is due, I am afraid, mainly to his biographers. Some of them, good conscientious men who were more interested in his theology than his prose, have turned him into a bloodless moral abstraction instead of the elemental peasant, terrific in his earthy vitality, who became a man of sorrows and human understanding.

They have analysed *The Pilgrim's Progress* until, if it were not indestructible, it would have perished from analysis. Throwing a mantle of piety over its author, they have all but reduced him to the semblance of worthy mediocrity. They have pointed morals and adorned tales until the real John Bunyan, with his salty tongue, keen wit, and strong primitive emotions, has assumed the character of a Madame Tussaud's waxwork, strangely attired in the combined garb of Puritan minister and Victorian Sunday School teacher.

It would be as logical to transform Joan of Arc into a hospital almoner or police-court probation officer. Puritan preacher or Catholic saint, the prophetic child of nature speaks a different language from that of the earnest educator and the trained social worker.

A few critics have gone to the other extreme, for the great will always have their detractors among the small. Inspired by a comprehensible reaction against the moralists, they have endeavoured to present John Bunyan as a species of village idiot.

One danger inherent in modern psychology is a tendency to regard inspired departures from the average as forms of psychopathic aberration. Individuals who pride themselves upon their own normality are liable to be baffled by exceptions.

We should not begrudge these attempts to explain away genius by those who do not possess it; they serve as a goad to the critical faculty, a useful challenge in the task of assessment. But they must not blind us to the resplendent quality of the prophetic soul, nor to the fact that, though human values and practices change, the spirit of man has been essentially the same throughout history in its loves, joys, sorrows, aspirations, and above all in its quest for truth.

From time to time, in this excursion into seventeenth-century England, I shall refer to the twentieth-century survivals from

John Bunyan's experience, and to the memorials of his life and work as you can still see them in Bedfordshire and London. Occasionally, too, I shall tell you of my own adventures as I sought to follow his footsteps through his countryside. But this story of a seeking is not mine, but his. Though the author of *The Pilgrim's Progress* has led me into a pilgrimage, my purpose is to recreate for you his own pilgrimage through "the wilderness of this world".

One thing only I want to do which for him was impossible. I shall try to show you this journey of his in a perspective denied to him and his contemporaries by those limitations of time, space, and knowledge which we have largely overcome, though in overcoming them we have sacrificed much of the tranquillity, the time to think, and the contact with Nature at its best, which men and women enjoyed in more isolated and deliberate communities.

We cannot get back to that slower, quieter world, but we can seek to understand it in terms of the "consciousness" by which we estimate the significance of any society, whether John Bunyan's or our own.

In Bunyan biography as a whole (though there are brilliant exceptions, such as Lord Macaulay's *Essay* on *The Pilgrim's Progress* and Sir Charles Firth's Introduction to the edition of 1898), I have missed this awareness of what was happening in the world as he knew it. Too often he appears as a lay figure with no roots in his time or environment.

No doubt this isolation is a true picture of John's own consciousness, particularly in his earlier years. But even in an age of radio, films, and cheap newspapers, we are moulded by influences of which we become only gradually aware. Such influences, because not immediate, were realized even more slowly when means of communication were primitive and long delayed. Nevertheless, they existed.

This presentation of John Bunyan, while introducing nothing of which he would not have known into his own awareness, seeks therefore to show him in relation to the England of his day, and his England in relation to contemporary Europe. His life is fully comprehensible only in terms of his age. At the end of his story, we can consider its relevance to our own.

The individual struggle for freedom of conscience, which

carried John into prison for over a decade, mirrored in personal terms the national struggle for liberty of thought, speech, and worship which brought seven years of Civil War to England, and reached its climax in the execution of a king. Two conclusions have been forced upon me in seeking to reconstruct John Bunyan's spiritual conflicts and physical odysseys.

The first is that the truth about him cannot be discovered, however conscientious the worker, only within the walls of a library. Some Bunyan biographies smell more of midnight oil than of Bedfordshire air. They appear to have been written far from the places and people that John knew.

To recapture the life of seventeenth-century Bedfordshire, it is necessary to visit the scenes where it was lived; to seek out the remote villages and secret woods to which the Nonconformists were driven by the series of repressive Acts known to history as the Clarendon Code.

The story is still there to be uncovered, none the less dramatic because it is so often hidden beneath changes which are not always improvements. Sometimes it lies disregarded, to be retrieved without difficulty once the clue is found.

Villages such as Stevington and Millbrook are still some distance from modern highroads and railways. They are easily accessible only to the owners of private cars, though the second gives its name to a station on a small branch line nearly two miles away.

Tiny hamlets of the type of Harrowden and Edworth have hardly altered since John Bunyan's time, though the one, close to Cardington Aerodrome, incongruously lies beneath the shadow of a weather balloon, and the other is situated within a mile of the great Roman road which runs from Biggleswade through Baldock to Stevenage.

My second conclusion has been that an adequate study of John Bunyan cannot be made in less than a lifetime. In that lifetime the student should come to know the Bible, as John knew it, so intimately that at every turn of every road its words are a lamp unto his feet and a light unto his path.

The material is so vast and so elusive that something more than mere industry is required to track it down. Often the pointers to the meaning of events are concealed beneath masses of documentary verbiage, to be found only by that type of intuition known as a flair.

Many such documents have still to be retrieved from local archives and parish records. Two were discovered so recently that this book was half finished before the research workers who traced them fully realized their significance. To the foremost of these, Miss Joyce Godber, the Bedfordshire County Archivist, I am deeply indebted, not only for her work, but for the generosity with which she placed its results at my disposal.

These are now embodied in her article *The Imprisonments of John Bunyan*, published in *The Transactions of the Congregational Historical Society* for April 1949.

The most comprehensive and scholarly of John Bunyan's biographers was Dr. John Brown, pastor at the Bunyan Meeting in Bedford from 1864 to 1903; the greater part of his Bunyan studies are unlikely to be superseded. Miss Godber's work, interpreting the chance findings of others, has added knowledge which Dr. Brown did not possess to the story of John Bunyan's second imprisonment and the writing of *The Pilgrim's Progress*.

Since the publication of John Brown's biography in 1885, it has been taken for granted that this second (short) imprisonment was spent in the old Town Prison on Bedford Bridge from 1675–6, and that the First Part of *The Pilgrim's Progress* was written or at least begun during this period.

Dr. Brown's arguments in favour of the Bridge Prison were largely based upon "the old tradition, which has come down from most reliable authorities". This very reliable tradition had already been disproved for the first (long) prison period by the research work of two Bedford townsmen, Messrs. Blower and Wyatt, subsequently confirmed by the discovery in 1934 of many assize records for the old Norfolk circuit. These showed John Bunyan's name on the list of prisoners in Bedford County Gaol, a totally different building which formerly stood in the High Street, for various years between 1661 and 1672.

Bedford has cherished its Town Prison tradition, and Dr. Brown was reluctant to abandon it altogether. His theory appeared to be proved when a Warrant, dated 4 March, 1675, for John Bunyan's arrest under the Conventicle Act of 1670 was rediscovered in 1887.

This document has been greatly valued in the belief that it was the instrument responsible for the imprisonment which produced *The Pilgrim's Progress*. In 1904 Mr. Pierpont Morgan, of New York, purchased it for his library. Some time before the Warrant left England a number of facsimiles complete with seals had been made, and one was accepted by Queen Victoria.

In an article entitled *Bunyan's Imprisonments*, published in the *Transactions of the Baptist Historical Society* during 1918, a legal expert, Mr. W. T. Whitley, first cast doubts upon the importance of the Warrant in John Bunyan's history. It referred, he said, to teaching at a conventicle, or private religious meeting, and the Conventicle Act of 1670 which forbade such meetings imposed only fines, not imprisonment.

Mr. Whitley therefore concluded that some other form of legislation was responsible for John's second prison period. He referred to a vague and confused assertion in Asty's *Life of Owen* (John Owen, 1616–1683, the Nonconformist divine) that "Mr. John Bunyan had been confined to a gaol for twelve years upon an Excommunication for Nonconformity", and regretted that no document existed to verify the statement. Such a document is now available. It is the copy of a bond, relating to John's release, in Aylesbury Museum.

Besides mentioning the cause of the second imprisonment, though he was wrong about both its date and duration, Asty described an intervention on John Bunyan's behalf by John Owen with the Bishop of Lincoln. He went on to say: "Now there was a law that if any two persons will go to the bishop of the diocese and offer a cautionary bond that the prisoner shall conform in half a year, the bishop may release him upon that bond."

This bond, discovered in Aylesbury Museum, is the main subject of Miss Joyce Godber's article. It is dated 21 June, 1677, and the sureties who undertook that John should conform within half a year were two London Nonconformists, Thomas Kelsey and Robert Blaney. They knew, of course, that he would not conform, but were evidently prepared to take the risk that once he was released nothing further would happen.

The bond was discovered by the late Edwin Hollis, Curator of Aylesbury Museum, and it was probably through him that a copy of it came into the possession of the late Dr. G. H. Fowler, Editor of the Bedfordshire Historical Record Society. Here it was seen by the late Frederick Gurney, who drew Miss Godber's attention to it in 1944.

None of the three individuals concerned had quite decided what the bond meant, though they all realized its importance. Mr. Gurney, who thought it indicated a third imprisonment, was preparing an article on it when he died. Miss Godber has continued and completed his work.

On mentioning this piece of research to Miss Kathleen Major, formerly Diocesan Archivist in Lincoln, she learned that confirmatory evidence existed in a volume giving details of the Proceedings at the Visitation of the Archdeaconry of Bedford in 1674. There it was reported that "John Bunnion, tinckar", of the town of Bedford, then in the diocese of Lincoln, stood excommunicated, having been "presented" by the church workers for refusing to come to church and receive the sacrament.

A copy of the relevant extracts from this document, in the original Latin, has kindly been supplied to me by the present Lincolnshire County Archivist, Mrs. Joan Varley.

The Aylesbury and Lincolnshire documents, put together, create a new picture which alters four important facts hitherto taken for granted in the life of John Bunyan.

First, it changes the date of his second imprisonment. The bond in Aylesbury Museum is dated 21 June, 1677; if we accept the evidence of the various authorities who state that this second imprisonment lasted less than a year, he could not have been in prison before the autumn of 1676 instead of half-way through 1675.

This new date leaves, in the second place, a gap of eighteen months between the issue of the Warrant for his arrest in March 1675, and his second prison period. To avoid being served with this Warrant he must, for that year and a half, have been either in hiding or on the run.

A third question is raised by Miss Godber herself; in what gaol, she asks, did this second imprisonment occur?

> "A man taken on a writ *de excommunicato capiendo* was the King's prisoner; the writ was executed by the sheriff; though as the offender remained in prison till absolved, the

Bishop had the power of indirectly releasing him. It is difficult to resist the conclusion that the sheriff would commit Bunyan to the county gaol."

Without evidence other than tradition that *The Pilgrim's Progress* was written in the Town Gaol, this conclusion is indeed difficult to resist. There is still an element of doubt failing definite proof which may yet be forthcoming, and no writer could be other than reluctant to forego describing the romantic surroundings of the Bridge Prison. But at present ninety per cent of the available evidence seems to be on the side of the County Gaol.

The new documents finally modify opinions, hitherto accepted, regarding not only the place but the date at which *The Pilgrim's Progress* was written.

We know from John Bunyan himself that his allegory was a prison book. Its first sentence runs: "As I walked through the wilderness of this world I lighted upon a certain place where was a Den, and I laid me down in that place to sleep; and as I slept I dreamed a dream." In the third, which was the first complete, edition published in 1679, he wrote in the margin against this sentence, "The Goal" (i.e. gaol).

He also tells us, in his rhymed "Author's Apology for his Book" which precedes the text of *The Pilgrim's Progress*, that the idea of it came to him when he was engaged on another work.

> I writing of the way
> And race of saints in this our Gospel day,
> Fell suddenly into an Allegory . . .

Dr. John Brown, working on his theory that John was put into the Bridge Prison during 1675, assumed that this book was *The Strait Gate*, a treatise published in 1676. The treatise does not satisfactorily fulfil John Bunyan's description, for it says little about the "race of saints", and a great deal about the shortcomings of "many great Professors". In any case it is now ruled out by the new sequence of dates.

There is, however, a book, written during John's first long prison period, which fits this description more closely; it is called *A Confession of my Faith: And a Reason for my Practice, or with who, and who not, I can hold Church-Fellowship, or the Communion of Saints*. This is the treatise in which John explained those Christian principles that were for him "the way".

Because it was published in 1672 and refers in its "address to the reader" to eleven years of prison, Dr. Brown assumed that this book was written "in the early part of 1672". But there is nothing to show how long John took to write it, since his previous book was his spiritual autobiography, *Grace Abounding*, published in 1666.

It has always been difficult, in view of his energy as an author, to explain John's almost complete silence from 1666 to 1672. This silence is accounted for if he was absorbed, as I believe, in beginning *The Pilgrim's Progress*.

Though John Bunyan's minor works, mainly based on sermons, were usually written very fast, his major books show signs of being composed over long stretches of time. He pondered for ten to twelve years on the personal story related in *Grace Abounding* before finally committing it to paper, and even then made many changes in later editions. The influence of *Paradise Lost*, published in 1667, on the theme of *The Holy War* was certainly exerted upon John's mind long before he wrote the book in 1682. It seems probable that the same process of long contemplation occurred with *The Pilgrim's Progress*.

John Bunyan never took this book seriously until its success astonished him, but it always absorbed him, as his rhymed Apology shows. It was his relaxation, about which he felt periodically guilty, from work that he regarded as more important. In writing it he had not the sense of urgency which caused him to rush through controversial treatises, and to publish sermons to souls in peril. He returned to it constantly, polishing and simplifying it. Even after it was published some of its best-known scenes and characters, such as the encounters with Mr. Worldly Wiseman and Mr. By-ends, were added to the second and third editions.

I believe that, as soon as he had written his direct personal history out of his system, the idea of an allegorical version of the story occurred to him. It may well have originated in an actual dream, such as he would be likely to have after dwelling upon his own experiences for many years.

The puzzling break which occurs in Part I of *The Pilgrim's Progress* after Christian and Hopeful leave the shepherds on the

Delectable Mountains: "So I awoke from my Dream", has been taken to mean that at this point John was released from his second imprisonment and finished the story at home. But it might equally well mean, and I believe it does mean, that the narrative had reached this point when his first imprisonment ended; that it was banished from his mind during the three or four years of evangelistic activity which followed his release; and that he finished it and discussed its publication with friends during his second imprisonment.

According to the newly discovered documents this imprisonment ended in late June or July 1677, while we know that Part I of *The Pilgrim's Progress* was entered at Stationers' Hall on 22 December, 1677, and licensed for publication on 18 February, 1678. This interval of barely six months would hardly leave time for the final third of the book to be written, in addition to the pastoral duties and family problems which would await John's attention on his release.

For this reason I believe that the "break" in the story occurred at the end of the first, not the second, imprisonment.

I have described the new Bunyan discoveries in some detail, not only because in my Chapters 13, 14, and 15 the relevant parts of his story embody them, but also in order to show how, even after the lapse of centuries, history has sometimes to be rewritten in response to the patient, perceptive work of those whose task is the establishment of truth. Mankind owes them a great debt for its enlightenment which is too seldom realized.

A third problem confronting every writer on John Bunyan's life is that of deciding how far tradition and probability may be employed when direct evidence is lacking. For the sake of presenting a continuous narrative which would be halted by constant qualification, I have used some probabilities and accepted some traditions while discarding others.

The Bridge imprisonment tradition has been abandoned for the reasons already given. I also agree with the Vicar of Elstow that the present daub-and-wattle "Bunyan Cottage" in Elstow village is not the original, despite the anxiety of many visitors to believe in its authenticity. It merely stands on the same site, a target for oncoming traffic in the widened road, and probably incorporates some of the original materials, including the strong internal cross-beam.

Another tradition which seems to me untenable is the legend that John spent the night following his arrest at Lower Samsell in a small room, still known as "Bunyan's cell", at the top of the magistrate's residence, Harlington House (now Harlington Manor). In *A Relation of the Imprisonment of Mr. John Bunyan,* his own account of the episode states quite clearly: "So on the next morning we went to the constable, and so on to the justice."

Conversely, the belief that John served on the Parliamentary side in the Civil War seems to me to be established beyond dispute, and not only by the discovery at the Record Office in March 1898 of the name "John Bunion" on the Muster Rolls of the Newport Pagnell garrison for 1644 and 1647.

Some Bunyan students who still wish to believe him a Royalist rightly argue that the name was not uncommon in the wide area from which the garrison conscripts were drawn. But to the inconclusive evidence of the Muster Rolls must be added John's long friendship with John Gibbs and Matthias Cowley of Newport Pagnell, the familiarity with garrison fortifications shown in *The Holy War,* and the Bunyan anvil inscribed 1647 which suggests his demobilization in the year that much of the Parliamentary Army is known to have been disbanded.

Finally, if he served with the King's forces, it is difficult to believe that a fact so likely to commend him to the Restoration authorities would not have been put forward, by his wife or his friends if not by himself, at some stage of his many attempts to obtain release from prison between 1660 and 1672.

While following the majority of biographers on this question of military service, I cannot however share their pious determination to present a lusty young tinker and reprobate as the incarnation of moral purity. Though John Bunyan definitely asserted in Paragraph 315 of *Grace Abounding* that he was never guilty of adultery or fornication, the same book, in Paragraphs 8 and 9, clearly states his acquaintance with carnal sin.

I have therefore departed from the wishful whitewashing of the young John by religious historians in attributing to him the type of conduct with which all armies are familiar. I do not believe that he would have been regarded as a conspicuous sinner by the drinking, swearing, gambling and wenching young hooligans of Elstow if Sunday sports, bell-ringing and profanity had been the whole story. Once we accept his early indulgence in the lusts of the flesh, the intensity of his spiritual conflict and the sense of guilt against which he struggled become far more credible, and less the product of inexplicable neuroses.

Much authentic evidence exists regarding John Bunyan's family, friends and contemporaries, but the identity of his first wife is still unknown. Characteristically he does not, in *Grace Abounding*, ever mention her name or the names of his children. I have followed convention in assuming that she was called Mary because this was the name given to their elder daughter, while their elder son was called John. Her copy of *The Plain Man's Pathway to Heaven*, subsequently destroyed in a library fire, is known to have had the name "M. Bunyan" at the foot of its title-page.

Perhaps the greatest difficulty in assessing the value of tradition lies in the number of Bedfordshire villages and buildings which claim a Bunyan contact. John Bunyan was an extremely active evangelist, and in thirty years of preaching he probably did visit every neighbouring village, meeting-house, farm and barn where Nonconformists congregated.

His visits to a few, such as Yelden, are confirmed by references in contemporary documents. In others, such as Stevington, Keysoe, and Gamlingay, the existence of strong Nonconformist groups in his lifetime leaves little doubt that the tradition is true. The story that he preached in the old church at Ridgmont is rendered probable by the residence in this village of Colonel John Okey, a good friend to the Bedford Dissenters. At Toft, in Cambridgeshire, the building confidently shown as "Bunyan's barn" can at least claim the supporting fact of a visit confirmed by a contemporary publication.

There remain the traditions based upon internal evidence from John's own writings, particularly *The Pilgrim's Progress*. Typical of these are the belief that the original of "House Beautiful" was the Earl of Ailesbury's mansion on Ampthill Heights, and the legend that the ancient Cross in Stevington village suggested the "place somewhat ascending" where Christian lost his burden.

While John Bunyan, as a working tinker, must have entered

many aristocratic houses, there can have been few others which gave him a southward view of the "Delectable Mountains", or contained those "Records of the greatest Antiquity" that the Earl, a collector and antiquary, had assembled in his country palace. This mansion with windows looking towards the Chilterns was then known as Ampthill House, though time and the hostile neglect of a father who lost his son have transformed it into the exotic ruin now familiar as Houghton Towers.

The reader of this story will find the Stevington Cross tradition not only accepted, but repeatedly endorsed. Any traveller to Stevington who walks up the hill from the Holy Well ("the Sepulchre") between the walls of the village to the Cross at its centre, and then studies the passage from *The Pilgrim's Progress* quoted on page 306 of this book, can hardly escape the conclusion that he is reading of his own surroundings.

This village Cross becomes a main *motif* in my version of John Bunyan's history because I believe that the place where he first became conscious of divine forgiveness would play, in both his life and his allegory, the significant part that I have given it.

In some areas of Bedfordshire the Bunyan tradition is still so strong that John remains not only a vital but a controversial figure. I met one country vicar who regarded my investigation of a seventeenth-century incident in his parish with as much indignation as though John Bunyan were a local Baptist minister with whom he lived in perpetual feud. In his view, the creator of Mr. Great-heart and Mr. Valiant-for-truth had done "great harm" to the Church of God.

This clergyman overlooked the fact that the nonconformity of the seventeenth-century Dissenters, like the contemporary "recusancy" of the Roman Catholics, was a form of opposition to the State rather than the Church. It was a refusal to accept the orders of a monarchial authority identifying itself with one religious denomination, and claiming, in the name of that denomination, powers which we should today describe as totalitarian.

Through their opposition to the assumption of despotic control by political and denominational rulers in close alliance, the Catholics and Nonconformists—so dissimilar in their form of worship and their attitude to authority—were alike in their refusal to regard belief and ritual as part of the State's field of operations. Together they played a grand historic rôle in the establishment of English liberty and religious toleration—for Anglicans as for the members of other denominations.

The fact that the one contribution was mainly passive and dictated by tradition, while the other was active, aggressive, and determined by new conviction, should not cause us to under-rate our gratitude to the English Catholics for their unshaken resistance to self-interested despotism.

In his personal story as in his writings, John Bunyan typified that conflict between the individual and the State with which, in its many varieties, we are familiar today. Conspicuous among the Independents, he was so independent that he would never accept a denominational label.

The Congregationalists, the Anabaptists, and the Society of Friends, founded by George Fox in 1652, made up the majority of these Independents. (The Methodists came a century later with John Wesley.) In that age of intolerance, even their minor mutual disagreements were magnified into controversial dog-fights. John Bunyan himself, as we shall see, was in perpetual conflict with the Quakers during the years following his conversion. In the last resort there was little difference between Quaker aims and those of other Independents, but the Friends were persecuted under Cromwell, though not by him, almost as ruthlessly as they had been under Archbishop Laud.

Whatever their internal conflicts, the various Dissenting bodies were alike in resisting the attempts of the State to impose a particular religious system upon the people. During John Bunyan's lifetime, three such attempts were made.

Under Charles I and Charles II, the State and the ecclesiastical authorities sought to impose a reactionary form of Anglicanism. In the Civil War the Anglican Church was so closely linked with the King's cause that it became virtually a political organization.

During the Commonwealth, religious orthodoxy identified itself with a Presbyterianism based upon the Scottish Calvinistic model. It was sometimes oppressive enough to justify Milton's comment that "New Presbyter is but Old Priest writ large". A Presbyterian tract, written in 1641 after the Grand Remonstrance and quoted by the Rev. C. F. Farrar in *Old Bedford*, put religious toleration firmly into its place:

> "Under these fair colours and handsome pretexts do sectaries infuse their poison, I mean their pernicious, God provoking, truth defacing, church ruinating, and state shaking Toleration."

The last three years of John Bunyan's life, which coincided with the reign of James II, saw an attempt by the King and his associates, in secret collusion with Louis XIV, to carry England back to Roman Catholicism.

This policy was unpopular even with the English Catholics, who knew their country and its people too well to believe that a century of history could be erased in a year. Its beginnings under Charles II came immediately after the publication of John's second-best allegory, *The Holy War*, which was a remarkable instance of political perspicacity justified by subsequent events.

The Independents opposed all three forms of authoritarianism, each of which tried to regulate speech, worship and assembly in the name of the State. They were closer in spirit to the Presbyterian orthodoxy of the Commonwealth than to Anglicanism or Catholicism, and because their political sympathies were also involved in the parallel struggle of Republicanism versus Monarchy, many of them served, like John Bunyan, in the Parliamentary Army.

The leading officers of this Army strongly resented the resistance to Presbyterian orthodoxy put up by the Independent officers and men. We shall read in Chapter 4 how Sir Samuel Luke, the Parliamentary Governor of the Newport Pagnell garrison, arrested two officers for holding an Independent conventicle in a nearby village, contrary to his orders to the troops to attend the official celebrations of the victory of Naseby in the parish church.

It has sometimes been alleged by Anglican authors, such as the Rev. C. F. Farrar in *Old Bedford*, that the Nonconformist writers on this period, and particularly Dr. John Brown, have underrated the extent to which "the Puritans", while in power, persecuted the ejected priests of the Church of England whose wrongs were so graphically described in Walker's *Sufferings of the Clergy*. A conspicuous Bedford example was Dr. Giles Thorne, the Rector of St. Mary's in John Bunyan's youth.

As a Quaker-inclined Anglican married to a Catholic, and hence, I hope, free from the impulse to grind any denominational "axe", it does seem to me that Dr. Brown and others have perhaps insufficiently emphasized the reasons which some of John's persecutors had for their hostility against the Dissenters. Sir John Kelynge, for instance, had been in prison throughout the Commonwealth before he sentenced John Bunyan, at the January Quarter Sessions of 1661, to the period of imprisonment which was to last for nearly twelve years.

But this criticism, partly justified as it is, fails to distinguish between the orthodox Presbyterians and the always unorthodox Independents. It is possible that, in days when Toleration was regarded with much the same contempt by the Long Parliament of 1640–53 as Appeasement by the Long Parliament of 1935–45, the Independents, had they been given the chance, would have penalized their opponents with the same animosity that was visited on them. But except in the person of Cromwell, who was much closer to the modern concept of Toleration than his associates in the Commonwealth Government, they were never in power as a party, and the opportunity did not arise.

From time to time the various political pressure-groups attempted, as such groups have done throughout history, to use the Independent minority in support of their programme. Towards the end of this book we shall see how James II tried to pack the Corporation of Bedford with Nonconformists as part of his attempt to persuade one religious minority to support the repeal of the penal laws for the benefit of another.

The Nonconformists allowed themselves to be so used only when the expedient furthered their own purpose, which was freedom of conscience, worship, speech and assembly. A few were ready to accept the positions offered them as "stooges" in Bedford's local government. Most of them preferred, like John Bunyan, to remain independent members of an unpopular minority until the Bill of Rights declared "their undoubted Rights and Liberties" as the loyal citizens of a free country.

Between the accession of Charles I in 1625 and the Toleration

Act of William and Mary in 1689 (a period extending at both ends beyond the span of John Bunyan's life), thousands of Independents suffered death, exile or imprisonment rather than violate their conscience. Not again until the twentieth century would there come a time when so many men and women, resisting in its different aspects the totalitarian trend of their day, would be slaughtered, imprisoned and persecuted for conscience's sake.

The acknowledgments on a previous page make it clear, I hope, that this attempt to discover and reconstruct the story of an Englishman who still speaks with a living voice has been a rich and rewarding experience.

My pursuit of him seemed to evoke so much kindness from those whom I approached for help, that John Bunyan himself might well have lent some heritage of his own imagination and good-humour to the quest. And the country in which he lived, the immemorial England of small farms and cultivated fields, added throughout a sunny autumn its peculiar stimulus to the smallest item of research.

In Bedford they tell me with sorrow that a member of the Brains Trust, asked which English county was the most beautiful, replied that he did not know, but Bedfordshire was the ugliest. Can this really be the reputation of the still essentially unchanged countryside of John Bunyan and John Howard?

What traveller will believe it who knows the brick-and-timber villages of north Bedfordshire, with their ancient churches folded into the fertile valley of the Ouse? What visitor will agree who has seen the wooded Greensand Ridge, which sweeps across the centre of the county from Woburn through Ampthill to Potton? Which country-lovers will feel more sceptical than those familiar with the southern section, where the chalk downs rise proudly to the heights of the Icknield Way curving over their rim, and a dozen varieties of wild orchis grow in the early summer?

If Bedfordshire is in fact our ugliest county, then England must be Paradise indeed.

In recording so much pleasure and gratitude I have two protests to register, mildly but firmly, though they do not concern the people of Bedfordshire alone.

My first is addressed to parish clergy and Nonconformist ministers throughout this country. Their churches and chapels contain so much of England's history, that I wish they were as conscious of their obligation to discover and record it as of their duty towards foreign missions.

In most of the churches and chapels that I visited leaflets abounded describing the conversion of the heathen, but the conversion of England, which has not yet been accomplished, appeared to be relegated to the background.

There were exceptions, of course. Amongst them I include, with thankfulness, the Abbey Church of Elstow; the parish Church of St. Mary's, Bedford; the Church of St. Mary the Virgin at Eaton Socon; and the Nonconformist Churches at Stevington and Gamlingay. The attractive booklet on its own history made available for visitors to St. Mary's, Bedford, deserves imitation on the widest possible scale.

Turning from indoor to outdoor memorials of the past, I must register a second grievance against the farmers and other proprietors who stretch five-barred gates, plentifully reinforced by barbed-wire entanglements, across ancient footways still trustfully marked on survey maps. My protest includes the local authorities which not only permit them to do so, but issue prohibitions rather than guides to the traveller in pursuit of historic survivals.

At Harrowden my search for the site of John Bunyan's long-vanished birthplace, marked by no memorial, involved an undirected waist-deep plunge through a field of Brussels sprouts. At Stevington, the technically illegal attempt to locate the old Nonconformist baptizing-place in The Holmes wood beside the Ouse meant a battle with briars and brambles in which my clothes were the losers, though I found the place in the end.

I should be sorry to put on record how often I disregarded the severe warnings to trespassers put up by the Bedfordshire County Council, and hurried, impeded by the heavy clay soil which is not conducive to rapid movement, through the forbidden meadows where occasional concentrations of bulls glowered menacingly at the unexpected intruder.

The pedestrian in search of history or geography still has his rights; he should not be compelled to risk breaking his limbs, tearing his flesh, and incurring the indignation of surprised animals, in this inoffensive social pursuit. Bedfordshire needs a Society for the Protection of Ancient Footways to reinforce the national policy of preserving the countryside. Many of its footpaths are ancient indeed, and their conservation is one method of record-keeping for England's story.

But these things said, and I hope not discourteously, it is on the note of appreciation that I want to end this foreword. I owe it to many attractive places and kindly people, for never once did I wish that my book had taken me to the hillsides of Italy or the ancient cities of Greece.

The ugliness in Bedfordshire may be there for the eyes of the captious critic, but I did not see it. Even the industrialized districts to the south and west of Bedford lie beneath the same wide-open skies as the level fields and lovely villages, and enjoy the same panoply of sunset splendour that the men and women who made our country saw in Bunyan's day and in the vanished centuries before he lived. Such a sunset turned the sky to flame one October evening as I was going home from the John Bunyan Library to my room in north Bedford, and the red glow above the darkening roofs caused the commonplace main road between the High Street and the railway station to resemble the approach to the Celestial City itself.

This England of John Bunyan is the England of us all; it is yours and mine. We are the privileged inheritors of the green mellow land, rich in traditions and memories, which neither war nor revolution has yet destroyed.

If it is spared by the amoral progress of science it will retain its spirit for centuries more, and contribute its new generations of men and women who will seek, as John Bunyan sought, to understand and fulfil the love of God.

CHAPTER I

VILLAGE CHRISTENING

"They said moreover, That he had made many Pilgrims Princes, though by nature they were Beggars born, and their original had been the Dunghill."

JOHN BUNYAN: *The Pilgrim's Progress,* Part I.

ONE mild afternoon in the late autumn of 1628, a young woman of twenty-five came out of a roughly built cottage standing beside a stream at the corner of a large open field.

Carrying the metal can reserved for drinking-water, she walked across the field to a spring hidden beneath the damp grass of a tussocky bank. As the wet turf squelched beneath her feet and the heavy Bedfordshire mud clogged her wooden shoes, she moved slowly and carefully owing to the weight of the unborn child whose birth she expected in a few days.

Some scattered yellowish-brown leaves still clung to the boughs of the oaks, but from most of the trees these sad reminders of the bygone summer had fallen. The wild flowers had all vanished except for the withered clumps of fever-few and the tiny "clocks" of the damp groundsell growing between them.

Through the bare branches of an elm in the meadow beyond the spring, Margaret Bunyan could see the distant steeple of Elstow Church. Its super-imposed spire resembled a small candle-extinguisher turned upside down upon the massive stone of the tower. Behind her, at the bottom of the rutted lane bordering the field, lay the hamlet of Harrowden which marked the eastern end of Elstow parish. Its handful of farms and cottages huddled close together beneath the low ridge of Harrowden Hill.

Beyond Harrowden the placid acres of Stuart England stretched into the unplumbed distance, their green tranquillity oddly at variance with the passions and prejudices already tearing the hearts of the men who tilled them. And beyond Stuart England extended the wider world of which Margaret, for all her natural energy and intelligence, knew almost nothing; a world which had been so effectively divided by the Reformation that to learn its religion was to know its politics.

Her own small island, with its evenly spread population of five million inhabitants, appeared to her a vast unknown territory; its little towns seemed crowded and unfamiliar. Even London, fifty miles from Elstow, was a long way off, for in late autumn the roads became channels of mud, and communications were slow. They were slower throughout Europe than they had been under the Romans, who kept the roads much better.

Winter travellers tended to avoid the highways of north Bedfordshire owing to their clay foundation. Once the ground became damp, deep ruts and pot-holes developed which filled with water until the spring sun grew strong enough to dry them.

The winter moisture drained more quickly from the southern chalk hills and the central Greensand Ridge, said to be formed from the sand laid down by an ancient sea. But even those hills were unfamiliar to Margaret Bunyan, who had passed all her life in the neighbourhood of Elstow, with the small borough of Bedford, dominated by its five churches, as her only metropolis.

In London, the real metropolis which her unborn son was to know so well, three hundred thousand people lived close to a swiftly developing drama. Already these Londoners were playing a significant rôle in an age of change without precedent. Earlier epochs had provided the inhabitants of England with no such turning-point in their national history; the parallel was to come later, after three more centuries had passed over their fields and hills.

In that year 1628, the revolutionary spirit was capturing not only politics and theology; literature, science, and society were all infused with it. Orthodoxy, represented by priest and monarch, was being challenged from below. Each new claim made by the representatives of tradition had evoked a rising murmur, which swelled until, in the Petition of Right, it became a shout.

Three years earlier, Charles I had succeeded to the throne, inheriting from his predecessors an England which had grown firmly Protestant during the reign of Elizabeth. Within the Church the advanced Protestants, desiring a purer and freer form of worship, had earned the nickname of "Puritans".

The men and women described by this epithet had little more in common than their love of liberty and revulsion against gaiety and extravagance. They might have remained, like modern Christian pacifists, an idealistic influence within the Church had not persecution turned them into a religious sect and a political party.

Some disliked a State Church and put religious independence as the chief purpose of reform. A few believed in toleration; many more regarded persecution as a legitimate method of enforcing their opinions. One section desired a Calvinistic system even more rigidly dogmatic than that of Archbishop Laud; others looked upon all systems as forms of unjustified interference with the relationship between the Creator and His creature.

Elizabeth had not regarded with favour the belief of these fervent Bible-readers that sin alone can separate the soul of man from God. Its logical outcome in resistance to forms and ceremonies seemed to her a species of disloyal eccentricity, liable to weaken the national unity which her relentless statesmanship had managed to create. But it was her successor James I, with less hold on the affections of the people, who had caused some of his best subjects to vanish rather than protest.

Two movements had risen simultaneously from the struggle for religious liberty; one involved resistance at home, the other escape abroad. Each demanded equal courage, for the escapists left their country to encounter the hostility of Nature instead of the prejudices of man. They preferred to face the unknown as independent pioneers rather than accept oppression in their own homes and towns.

Quietly they raised the flag of their faith beside frozen rivers and tropical swamps. Fugitives in adventurous pursuit of freedom, they had begun almost unnoticed to occupy the far-off Bermudas, Barbadoes, and Bahamas; the Lesser Antilles and British Honduras. On the American continent the Pilgrim Fathers, who sailed in the *Mayflower* in 1620, had started a chain of English settlements which by the reign of James's grandson was to stretch from Canada to the Carolinas, and to represent almost every variety of religious dogma and political creed.

In 1634 and 1635, the Pilgrim Fathers were to be joined by two inhabitants of Bedfordshire, one being "Mr. Peter Bulkeley,

BUNYAN'S BIRTHPLACE

From an old drawing. The rough cottage in the fields near Harrowden disappeared over a hundred years ago.

THE AUTHOR AT THE SITE OF THE BIRTHPLACE

On 30 November, 1948, the 320th anniversary of John Bunyan's baptism. A thick fog made photography difficult.

rector of Odell, suspected for Puritanisme", and therefore suspended by Sir Nathaniel Brent, the Vicar-General of Archbishop Laud. Sent by his master to visit the diocese of Lincoln, Sir Nathaniel reported that he found Bedfordshire the "most tainted of any part". Following Zachary Symmes, minister of the Priory Church of Dunstable who had departed a year earlier, the suspect Peter sailed for New England, and making his way "thro' unknowne woods", founded with appropriate symbolism the town of Concord on the banks of the Musketaquid River.

The men and women who remained at home saw the Puritan Revolution clearly assuming a double character. On the political side it had become a contest between King and Parliament for power; as a religious movement it was a struggle between orthodox Anglicans and unorthodox Puritans for the establishment of their respective forms of worship.

In a nation with a genius for politics rather than theology, the Puritans as a party might have gained little influence had not the High Churchmen under Charles I adopted a political rôle and identified themselves with the unpopular absolutism of the Stuarts. The handsome, reserved, and dignified Charles believed, like his father James, in the Divine Right of Kings, and saw no reason to seek popular support.

His religion was that of a convinced High Anglican; he supported William Laud, who in 1628 became Bishop of London, in his attempt to enforce uniformity of worship. With Sir John Eliot as leader of the Opposition in the House of Commons, and John Pym and John Hampden amongst its Members, the dynamite which later exploded into the Civil War was already being stored.

Earlier in the year, the Puritan squires in the House had presented the Petition of Right, drawn up by Eliot, Coke, and Selden. On 7 June they compelled the King to accept that famous protest against martial law, compulsory billeting, arbitrary taxation, and arbitrary imprisonment. Margaret Bunyan had seen in the distance one of the bonfires which London and all England had lighted to celebrate the victory of the people, though she did not understand what it meant.

There was no radio then to carry to her the speech, so prophetic in its relation to the future history of her son, with which

Sir Robert Phelips, M.P., had passionately challenged the decision of the Royalist judges who favoured arbitrary imprisonment:

> "I can live, although another without title be put to live with me; nay I can live though I pay excises and impositions more than I do; but to have the liberty which is the soul of my life taken from me by power, and to be pent up in a gaol without remedy by law, and to be so adjudged to perish in gaol; O improvident ancestors! O unwise forefathers! . . . If this be law, why do we talk of our liberties!"

It would have surprised Margaret Bunyan to know that the legendary London of tensions, quarrels, and long-continued debates had any relation to the still more belligerent Europe in which the Thirty Years' War had broken out after the Bohemian Revolution of 1618.

Even in its early stages, that war had become so cruel that in 1625 the Dutch jurist, Huig van Groot—better known to European scholars by his latinized name of Grotius—had made, in his book *The Right of War and Peace,* one of the first historic pleas for an international law.

That Europe of villages sacked and populations massacred in the name of religion was moving rapidly in one political direction. Its uniform drift was to be arrested, in the last resort, only by events in small and primitive England, and in more cultured Holland. There the young Rembrandt, aged twenty-two, was already painting pictures in Amsterdam.

Within many European countries, despotic monarchs were slowly increasing their stranglehold. Amongst them attractive personalities such as Gustavus Adolphus of Sweden were the exception rather than the rule. Four years earlier, in 1624, Cardinal de Richelieu had become the first Minister of France. A year later, he used ships lent him by England against the Protestant Huguenots in La Rochelle. Thirty-seven years after that siege, Louis XIV, assuming personal control of French destinies on the death of Cardinal Mazarin, was to show that he had learned Richelieu's lessons only too well.

Louis would find those half-French Stuart sovereigns, the

second Charles and the second James, as ready as himself to accept his dictum, *"L'état, c'est moi"*. The fact that their England was eventually to give to Europe the pattern of democracy and constitutional monarchy was due to the political and religious struggle now going on at Westminster and beyond.

In that struggle Margaret Bunyan's son, the sturdy antagonist of submission and uniformity, would play a not unworthy part. To his successors it seems symbolic that he was born in the year of the Petition of Right, and was destined to die in the same twelve months that saw the Declaration of Rights and the Toleration Act.

As she returned to the cottage with her overflowing can, Margaret hurried a little across the stubbly field where the corn stood gold in full summer. She had still much to prepare for the few days in which she would be laid aside. The beef and bacon were waiting to be salted for Michaelmas, and she had not yet finished the coverings for the rough wooden cradle which would hold her baby. Like every working mother of every worker's child, she wished that she could have provided something better.

The dwelling-place into which she carried the drinking-water was a crude brick shanty, with two tall chimneys and a thatched roof that overhung the tiny windows on the upper floor. The thatch was getting old; only that autumn, part of it had slipped down across the windows to the small front porch. A wooden gate and some palings divided the door from the field path, which led past the cottage and the low forge where her husband, Thomas Bunyan, carried on his trade. Beyond the forge a tough hedge of wild rose and hawthorn made a screen against the prevailing east wind.

The stream behind the cottage ran along the dene or valley at the foot of Harrowden Hill, where it joined a wider stream known as Cardington Brook. Rising in the Greensand Ridge this brook passed through Elstow, and skirted the northern boundary of the broad strip called Pesselynton Furlong which included the Bunyan fields. Two or three miles further east the combined rivulet meandered into the Ouse at Willington, where the great clash with the Danes had occurred during their attack on Bedford.

Looking south in fine weather from the bank behind the cottage when she had finished the household washing, Margaret Bunyan could see the distant blue of the Ampthill heights rising from the Bedford plain. Thomas had described to her the majestic houses, built on those hills, in which he mended pots and kettles for the aristocratic inhabitants; they were even more impressive than Elstow Place, the stone mansion where the local squire lived beside the Abbey Church.

There was one called Ampthill House in Dame Ellensbury Park above Houghton Conquest, which was like a king's palace with its glowing red walls and tall pinnacles of richly carved stone.

Between Harrowden and the Greensand Ridge stretched the unenclosed ploughlands, broken at intervals by tracts of heath, marsh, and primeval forest. Bedfordshire, like the rest of sparsely populated England, was not yet a cultivated garden. Hedges were still few, and the planted trees introduced by the Tudors decorated only parks and churchyards. There was lavish summer wealth in the great open fields of corn cultivated by the common effort of the Bedfordshire villagers, but a beauty less dependent on warm air and sunshine dignified the gabled red-brick cottages with their high chimneys and latticed windows.

These, like the Bunyans' dwelling, usually had roofs of thatch, but some were made of stone-slab or tiles. One cottage never precisely resembled another, for in their homes as in their religion the natives of the eastern Midlands were robust independents who disliked uniformity. Free labouring men by law, they saw as yet no reason for social agitation; the 30,000 political pamphlets issued under the Commonwealth would roll over their heads like an invisible sea.

Divided by an almost impassable gulf from the great landowners holding feudal sway within their parklands, the young peasants of the Bunyans' class either lived at home, or boarded on terms of pleasant well-fed inequality with the farmer or craftsman who employed them. Only when they married did they set up, like Thomas Bunyan, a home of their own, putting their animals out to pasture on the common land if they owned no private fields, and collecting their fuel from the moors or thickets seldom further than a short walk from the gate.

When the Bunyans' son was born, they were very proud of him. He was a big, strong child, and the fair hair on his downy head had a reddish tinge. Later on people credited him with a gipsy origin because his father was a tinker or whitesmith, usually an itinerant occupation favoured by gipsies.

But whether or not a gipsy strain mingled with young John's blood, he came of an ancient lineage. He had risen straight from the soil of England; the circumstances of his birth and upbringing, added to the long record of his ancestry, were to make him, in a day that his mother would never see, the most English author who ever wrote.

In one of his greatest books, *Grace Abounding to the Chief of Sinners*, John was to tell the world that he came from "a low and inconsiderable generation; my father's house being of that rank that is meanest and most despised of all the families in the Land". But this comment was an instance of that exaggerated humility which is really a form of inverted pride.

John's father Thomas was not a roving but a landed tinker, the social equivalent of a twentieth-century ironmonger, whose family had owned property in the Harrowden neighbourhood for many generations. As early as 1542 the Court Roll of the Manor, preserved in the Augmentation Office, had described this eastern extremity of Elstow parish as "Bonyon's End".

Today the field between the site of the old cottage and the lane leading to Harrowden is still called "Bunyan Field", and the farm across the stream which borders it is known as "Bunyan's Farm". If there were no other evidence, the persistence of the name would indicate that the family owning this land, however humble, had long been dwellers there.

John Bunyan's very name, which the poet Cowper a century later rejected as too mean to be permitted to spoil his verse, had an aristocratic origin, the Norman-French "Buignon". In a lecture on *The Pilgrim's Progress* given in 1924, Professor J. W. Mackail excused Cowper's depreciation on the ground that "Bunyan" was an awkward name to fit into poetry. But a century and a quarter after Cowper, Rudyard Kipling, without apparently finding any difficulty, brought it into five verses of a seven-verse poem entitled *The Holy War*.

Whether adapted to poetry or not, the name gave scope for much ingenuity; no fewer than thirty-four ways of spelling it may be found in Bedfordshire records. The John Bunyan Library at

Bedford contains a letter from the Secretary of the Suffolk Institute of Archaeology and Natural History, which explains these and other variations.

"There is no occasion for perplexity in (H)Elstow. Spelling was in a fluid state. In fact scholars proved their learning by exhibitions of their ability to spell their own and other names, in many various ways. Shakespeare came out top with a record, I believe, of thirty-two variants" (in fact two fewer than Bunyan). "It was a prevalent form of pedantry now called swank."

Spelt in one way or another, there were Bunyans in north Bedfordshire at least as early as 1199. In that year a certain William Buniun was engaged in a lawsuit with the Abbess of Elstow at the Court of King's Bench. Its purpose was to determine the ownership of half a virgate of land, claimed by the Abbess, which John Bunyan's ancestor held from William of Wilsamstede (the modern Wilshamstead or Wilstead).

Another ancestor, Ralph Bungnon of Dunstable, "hanged 1219", was less respectable.

Thomas Bunyan, John's father, owned both "Bunyan Field" and the large cornfield west of it, at the corner of which his cottage stood. In the Court Roll of the Manor under Henry VIII, the whole area from Elstow to Harrowden lying between the two streams had been described as "the furlong called Pesselynton". Later, when thirty windmills were scattered through Bedfordshire, where the flat agricultural lands resemble parts of Holland, Thomas Bunyan's acres of corn were to be known as "Windmill Field".

Tinkering was not a traditional occupation with the Bunyans; John's father, who called himself a "braseyer", was the first member of the family to follow the craft. His own father, another Thomas, had described himself in his Will as a "pettie chapman", or small trader. Not only did he own the nine acres of land at Harrowden, but by 1607 also possessed property in Kempston.

Thomas Bunyan, junior, was therefore a man of considerable hereditary substance. He was also a Royalist. His son's first biographer, Charles Doe, the comb-maker of Southwark who became a gentle Boswell to Bunyan's Johnson, recorded in 1692 that Thomas was "of the national religion as commonly men of that trade are". Four years before the King's execution, Thomas was to christen his third son Charles.

Margaret, whose own widowed mother, Mary Bentley, occupied a well-equipped brick-and-timber cottage in Elstow village street, had no reason to be ashamed of her husband. He was now a vigorous young man nearing twenty-six, nine months her senior. Though he was her first husband she was not his first wife; he had been married when only twenty to Anne Pinney, who died childless after four years of wedlock.

Thomas's vigour was attested by his unusual ability in tree-climbing, an occupation which attracted him, as games on the village green were to attract his son, even after he became a married man. One exploit of his had already been recorded by Thomas Archer, the old rector of the next parish, Houghton Conquest.

This elderly cleric, who was a king's chaplain, kept a diary in which he amiably registered the more surprising events of his miniature world. Three years before John Bunyan's birth, he had been moved to note an achievement by the youthful Thomas:

> "Memorandum.—That in Anno 1625 one Bonion of Elsto clyminge of Rookes nests in the Bery wood found 3 Rookes in a nest, all white as milke and not a blacke feather on them."

Strange hands clasp each other across the centuries. On 11 December, 1940, at the height of the London air raids, Helen Grosvenor of Eaton Place wrote to *The Times* to report that she had seen "a white blackbird (hen) without a black feather on it" in a garden behind a house in Regent's Park.

In the first half of the seventeenth century, the Church exercised a strict control over the private life of every English man and woman. He or she was compelled by ecclesiastical law to be baptized, confirmed and married in the parish church, to attend divine service on Sundays and saints' days, and to receive communion at least three times a year. One of the duties of a churchwarden was to "present" offenders against these rules at the ecclesiastical courts, and to report their local cleric to the bishop of the diocese if he did not perform his obligations.

Being good orthodox parishioners, Thomas and Margaret

Bunyan had made arrangements for the baptism of their son. The Reverend Thomas Kellie, Vicar of Elstow, had agreed to christen him on 30 November. It is the first recorded day in his life; we do not know the exact date of his birth.

When the time came they wrapped him up warmly before starting on the muddy trip across the meadows, for the morning was humid and grey. Thin patches of mist hung like white veils above the sodden fields, blotting out the steeple of the Abbey Church a mile away, and turning to shadowy ghosts the elms that grew at the Elstow end of Pesselynton Furlong. The rooks, black or white, which lived in them were now silent, but a heron rose suddenly in the mist, flapping his wings in protest against disturbance as he flew away towards the east.

Thirty miles further in the same direction, a grave and scholarly young man, John Milton, was then in his third year at Christ's College, Cambridge, the predecessor by eighteen months of Jeremy Taylor, a sizar of Caius. At Oxford, Milton's incongruous contemporary and virtual twin, Edward Hyde—born ten weeks after him in February 1609, and destined to die in the same year, 1674—had graduated from Magdalen College in 1626, and was now a member of the Middle Temple.

By the work of the first, the child going to his baptism was to be influenced and inspired. Under the legislation of the second, then promoted to the status of Lord Clarendon, he was to be penalized and imprisoned.

Yet another Cambridge college, Emmanuel, the stronghold of Puritanism, held a future Master of Gonville and Caius who was studying theology. As Rector of Yelden, near the Bedfordshire-Northampton boundary, he too was to be connected with the boy born at Harrowden. His name was William Dell.

To the south of Elstow, on the hither side of the Greensand Ridge, a contemporary younger than the bearers of these distinguished names was also in his cradle. Two months earlier, the occupants of a country squire's nursery had been increased by the birth of Francis Wingate.

Born at Harlington House, near the thriving market town of Toddington, this baby was the third child of John Wingate by his wife Alice, and would be the first to survive till manhood. At Whitehall and in the House of Commons, the fate which would

THE NORMAN FONT WHERE BUNYAN WAS CHRISTENED
It still stands in Elstow Church.

THE NORTH DOOR OF ELSTOW CHURCH
The Norman stonework has survived for nearly a thousand years.

bring Francis Wingate and John Bunyan together was already at work.

Carrying his son in his arms, Thomas Bunyan helped his wife across the damp stubble of the spacious cornfield. At the spring where she had filled her can, they turned north along a rough bank which in April was blue with dog violets. It ended at a stile leading into a marshy meadow; already the first evidence of the winter floods was to be seen in many shallow pools surrounding clumps of rushes. In places the path, skirting the edge of a deep reedy pond, had almost disappeared beneath the slough of water and mud. The young man and woman were used to it; they knew how to find the few firm footholds which led to the stepping-stones across Cardington Brook.

Soon this wide stream, flowing between high banks over its green bed of weeds and moss, would become a hostile torrent, but in November the short cut across the stepping-stones could still just be managed. Passing the sleeping baby carefully from the one to the other, Thomas and Margaret crossed the water, scrambled up a high bank to another stile, and found themselves on the footpath which accompanied Cardington Brook all the way from Harrowden to Elstow.

Never once during their journey did John's parents, anxious for the warmth and safety of their son, look back at the rude cottage across the fields, or speculate about the destiny of the child whom they carried. When we are young, we seldom project ourselves into a far-off future; the insistent present blots out the vision of a day when we shall no longer be there, and everything that is now familiar to us will be changed.

Like all parents, Margaret and Thomas Bunyan meant to do better by their first-born than their own forbears had done by them. Already they had made up their minds that he should be taught to read and write. Since this was still a rare accomplishment among working men's children, they would not have thought it improbable that their boy might come to know ministers of the gospel, and even university professors.

But the idea was inconceivable to them that one day scholars armed with guide-books and maps would seek the site of their humble dwelling. Most surprising of all, perhaps, would have appeared the difficulty that these pedants would experience in finding the place, for every inch of the land was known to the Bunyans and they could have made their way to Elstow blindfold.

Should you too wish to visit the site of that birthplace which sank into rubble a century and a half ago, you will not find your search troublesome if you study the sketches on the next two pages that I have made for you. The first is roughly enlarged from the one-inch Survey Map of Bedford and Luton; the second is an unscientific "close-up" drawn on the spot with the aid of tradition.

In this instance tradition seems likely to be right, for at the corner where the Elstow-Harrowden boundary meets the southern stream you will find a mound of long grass and nettles, half hidden by a rough tangle of briar and hawthorn. Just so the place would appear if a heap of bricks and stones had lain there, resisting the operations of plough and harrow, for year after year.

Today, if you want to save your time, you can take a Shortstown bus from the Omnibus Station just beyond the north end of Bedford High Street, and be carried in ten minutes to a large railway bridge where the London Road joins the Harrowden Road at the fringe of the southern suburbs. If you follow the Harrowden Road for a hundred yards or so, a sharp turn to the right down a narrow lane of the ancient type known to Americans as a dirt track will take you over a smaller railway bridge, and thence almost due south past the stile which marks the old field path to Elstow.

Beyond the stile the lane crosses Cardington Brook and, still further south, passes over the narrower stream which flows into the Brook at Harrowden and becomes the small tributary running past Cardington Cross into the Ouse at Willington. Shortly after you have passed the second stream, the lane turns abruptly east and follows the watercourse of the combined streams through Harrowden hamlet towards Cardington.

The land between the streams is still known locally as Pesselynton Furlong. But nowhere will you find any sign-post or other indication that you are treading historic ground; your only guide to the site of John Bunyan's birthplace is a field gate on the right-hand side of the lane about midway between the two streams as you walk south.

From the gate a rough track leads for quarter of a mile between

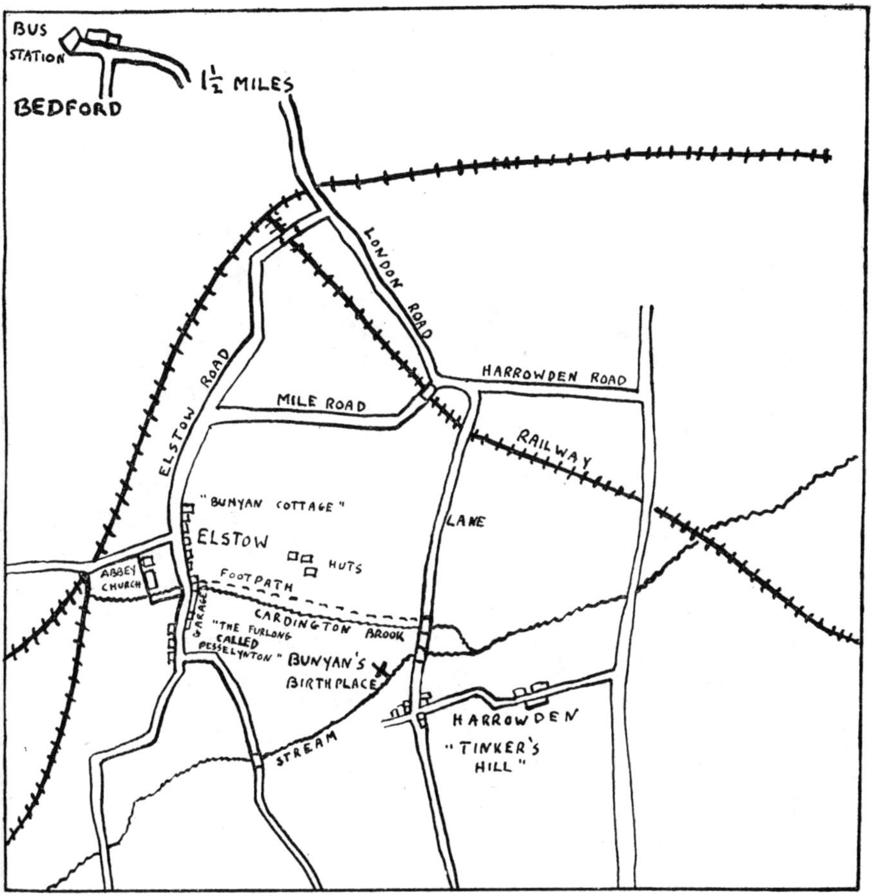

MAP OF ELSTOW AND HARROWDEN SHOWING BUNYAN'S BIRTHPLACE.

ROUGHLY ENLARGED FROM THE ONE-INCH SURVEY MAP OF BEDFORD AND LUTON WITH ACKNOWLEDGMENTS TO THE EXACT COPY OF AN OLDER MAP PUBLISHED IN *JOHN BUNYAN* BY DR JOHN BROWN.

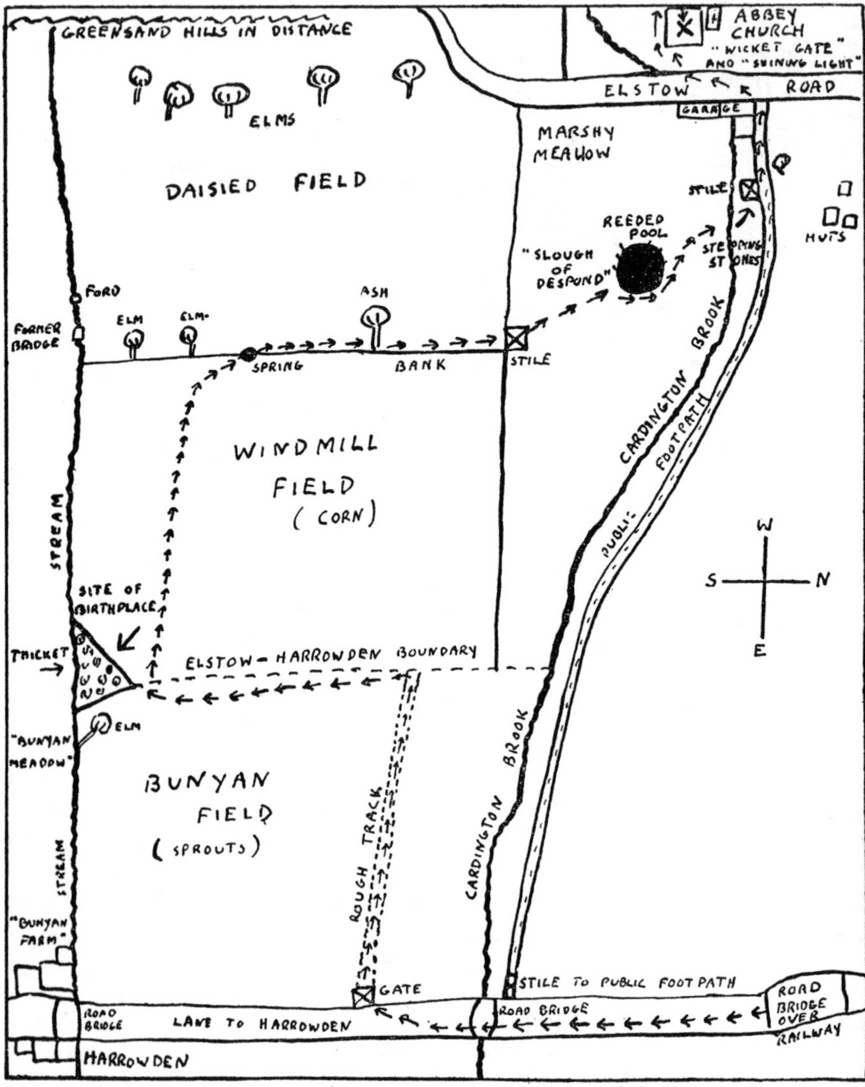

ROUGH SKETCH ("CLOSE-UP") OF BUNYAN'S BIRTH PLACE. (NOT TO SCALE). JOURNEY SHOWN BY ARROWS

rows of Brussels sprouts across Bunyan Field to the Harrowden-Elstow boundary, which divides it from Windmill Field. The change of crops from sprouts to corn makes this boundary easy to find; it is further marked by the stumps of three or four large elms which grew there until a few years ago, but have now been cut down. Another quarter of a mile along this boundary towards the southern stream brings you to the mound of tangled bushes on its bank.

In summer you can walk pleasantly back to Elstow along the footpath which follows for a mile or so the course of Cardington Brook, reaching the village from behind the filling-station of the local garage. In spite of this garage, which has replaced a blacksmith's forge, and of the massed huts and bungalows belonging to the workers from Cardington Aerodrome which you pass on the right as you come to the end of your journey, the old footway still feels like the heart of the country.

Sparrows and finches twitter in the elders and hazels which cluster beside the stream; brown dragon-flies dart in elusive zig-zags from bank to bank; white cabbage butterflies suddenly spring from the yarrow and convolvulus in the long grass at the meadow's edge. Occasionally a small fish leaps from the deep green water; at the Harrowden end, where the brook becomes shallower, minnows rest lazily in the shadows on its sandy bottom. Across the stream lies the open stretch of ploughland and green fields which have hardly changed since John Bunyan saw them through the little leaded panes of his bedroom window.

Now and again the footpath runs under tall trees, sometimes ash but usually elm, which look tattered and shaggy as though shaken by innumerable storms. Time immemorial has indeed stolen their youth, for there are elms in Bedfordshire reckoned to be a thousand years old. As you walk beneath them towards Elstow, you know that you look on the same twisted boughs which Thomas and Margaret Bunyan saw as they carried their son to his christening.

Inside the Abbey Church, the Reverend John Kellie was waiting for them beside the Norman font. Its carved octagonal bowl rested upon a stone base, where four crouching figures grotesquely represented the vices cast out by Holy Baptism. In the centre of one moulded rose, the anonymous twelfth-century sculptor had gratified his sense of humour by subtly inserting a puckered baby's face, its mouth wide open as though in process of emitting a roar.

When young John showed signs of imitating the carven baby, the Vicar hastened to begin the ceremony, but without perturbation since he was a father himself. One of the eighteen infants whom he had already christened that year was his own daughter Ann. Her entry on 2 September was distinguished by his description as "Mr. Kellie", the humbler parishioners being entered under their Christian names. The worthy cleric was more prolific than the tinker whose son he now took in his arms. Ann, the second daughter to whom he had given that name, was his fifth child since 1621, and within the next six years he was to record the births of three more.

He named the protesting infant "John", and signed him with the sign of the Cross—"in token that hereafter he shall not be ashamed to confess the faith of Christ crucified, and manfully to fight under his banner, against sin, the world, and the devil; and to continue Christ's faithful soldier and servant unto his life's end. Amen."

In the parish register, when the brief ceremony was over, the Vicar entered the baby's name.

"John the sonne of Thomas Bonnionn Jun., the 30th of November."

Then he closed the book, his mind untroubled by the remote contingency that the name he had written would become immortal.

For him it was only another village christening.

CHAPTER II

A PILGRIM GROWS UP

"He moreover objected the base and low estate and condition of those that were chiefly the Pilgrims of the times in which they lived; also their Ignorance, and want of understanding in all natural science. . . . And I thought again, this Shame tells me what Men are, but it tells me nothing what God or the word of God is."

JOHN BUNYAN: *The Pilgrim's Progress*, Part I.

UNTIL the Dissolution of the Monasteries a century earlier, the Church at which John Bunyan was christened had been part of a Benedictine convent. Countess Judith, niece of William the Conqueror, had founded it in 1078—as an attempt, the villagers believed, to quieten her troubled conscience.

Three years before, she had inadvertently betrayed her husband Waltheof, the Saxon Earl of Northampton, who had secretly taken part in a plot against the Normans. Her endeavours to atone for his judicial murder were apparently unsuccessful, for long after Elstow Abbey had risen to wealth and fame, stories were told of a lady in white who, century after century, haunted the nunnery or flitted, disconsolate, across the village green.

By the time of John's birth, Elstow was already an old village which had seen much history. Tradition said that it had been a camping place for Offa, King of Mercia; and even before the Saxons it was known to the Romans. Its very name recalled the saintly Helena, mother of Constantine the Great, who was reported to have discovered in Palestine the Cross on which Christ was crucified.

The Saxons, adding her name to their own word "Stowe", or "station", produced the combination "Helenstowe", which was later abbreviated—sometimes with the aspirate, and sometimes without—to the name generally used in John's day.

Ancient as the village was, it had never known such splendour as the Abbey brought to it. For nearly five hundred years the Abbess, exercising the despotic power of an unopposed local magistrate, held sway in Elstow. The Abbey Church, dedicated to St. Mary and St. Helen, soon overwhelmed the Saxon church which had stood there when the Normans came.

A hundred years before John Bunyan's parents carried him to his baptism in the Norman font, the end of that long magnificence was in sight. In 1530, a convenient slackness of discipline amongst the nuns had caused the convent to be officially censured by John Langland, Bishop of Lincoln.

His long list of injunctions against questionable conduct finally insisted that "Katheryne Wingate the said lady abbesse her chapleyn do not suppe ne breke her faste in the buttry with the stuard nor eny other secular person". It also enjoined that the "gownes and kyrtells" of the religious sisters "be closse afore and not soo depe voyded att the breste and noo more to use rede stomachers but other sadder colers in the same".

When John was growing up in the Harrowden cottage, the villagers had forgotten whether it was the gay and suggestive garments of the nuns, or the Abbess's habit of supping with her chaplain and steward in the buttery, which had been used as the final excuse to dissolve the Abbey. It was only known to have been surrendered to King Henry VIII in 1539, when its twenty-four inhabitants were pensioned off at £50 a year for the Abbess and £2 a year for each of the nuns.

According to Burton, the Antiquary of Leicestershire, the Priory had been valued at £325 2*s.* 1¾*d.* But the Monasticon, which was the official record, put it at only £284 12*s.* 11¾*d.*

In John's childhood the "ladies" of Elstow were already a legend. Gradually, in his fancy, they came to have names borrowed from the Puritan women of his later experience, such as Piety, Prudence, Charity, and Discretion—though the last would hardly have applied to the sisters who wore red stomachers and gowns deep voided at the breast.

Since the time of Henry II, one of the rights possessed by the Abbess of Elstow had been that of holding annual fairs on the 15th and 16th of May and the 5th and 6th of November. When the Abbey lands and buildings, in the year of Queen Mary's accession, were granted by the Crown to Sir Humphrey Radclyff, brother to the Earl of Sussex, the rights transferred included "all those our fairs at Elnestowe annually held and to be held".

The scene of these fairs was Elstow village green, linked to the village street by a narrow lane which turned west opposite the half-timbered red-brick hostelry above the arch where travellers' horses passed into the courtyard. Two other inns, the Red Lion and the Swan, brought customers to the village, together with a general shop replenished at intervals from Bedford. A local "character" named John Newall kept the Red Lion. When John Bunyan was ten years old, a new series of restrictions were placed on brewing. These did not please the independent-minded tavern-keeper, who continued to brew as though they did not exist.

At the eastern end of the village green stood the Moot Hall, a barn-shaped brick-and-timber structure decorated with curious carvings. Its Saxon origin was lost in the legendary past, but most of its workmanship belonged to the fifteenth century. In the great days of the Abbey it had been used as a "hospitium" or hostel for visitors to the convent, and the Court of Pie Powder was said to have been held there.

John Bunyan knew the building as the Court House of the manor, a glorified village hall which had become the centre for local entertainments. The hue of the terra-cotta tiles on its roof was already deepened by many-coloured lichens, gold, green, purple, orange, and brown. In the sunlight the bricks glowed with a peculiar radiance which the vanishing years would only intensify.

West of the Moot Hall the market cross stood in the centre of the large green, enclosed on three sides by brick-and-timber cottages. Not one of these duplicated its neighbour, yet all achieved a harmonious colour-picture of russet and bronze. The grey stone cross, one day to be strangely associated with John's conversion, was the centre of the village games and periodic Elstow fairs.

Long after John became a man, he would remember those fairs; the crowds buying and selling; the horse-fairs and cattle-fairs in the paddocks adjoining the green; the booths round the Moot Hall, which was then used as a Court of Justice to settle disputes and try delinquents attempting to steal; the village stocks for the punishment of offenders found guilty. At the fairs, and also on May Day and sometimes at Candlemas, the morris dancers, dressed in gilt leather, silver paper, and white coats of spangled fustian, performed round a maypole set up on the green.

The Queen of the May was always amongst them, and the

piper, and the fool with his bladder and a fox's brush at the tail of his tunic. Robin Hood and Little John usually took part, with Maid Marion and Friar Tuck, and sometimes they brought a hobby horse and a dragon. Besides the maypole dancers there were jugglers at the fair, and fire-eaters, acrobats, and performing animals. Occasionally marionettes and dancing dolls took the place of human actors. The children crowded round a new show called "Punch and Judy", played in a tall booth with scarlet trimmings, and depicting in a debased form those unpopular New Testament characters, Pontius Pilate and Judas Iscariot.

At the day's end, dancers, jugglers, and show-men sat down to a lavishly spread table on the ground floor of the Moot Hall. Long afterwards, when John had to be content with prison diet for year upon year, he was to picture those feasts seen in his childhood; the huge tankards of ale and loaves of bread, the meat, cheese, custards, cracknells, cakes, flans, and tarts piled with cream.

Twelve years before John's birth, Sir Humphrey Radclyff, whose licence included the right to hold these fairs, had sold his property to Sir Thomas Hillersdon for £700. Sir Thomas, now lord of the manor, found plenty of material left from the dismantled Priory to build himself a stately stone mansion, which he called Elstow Place, beside the Abbey Church. Its mullioned windows looked out upon a small elm-shaded park, with richly stocked fish-ponds which had once been part of the enclosed Abbey grounds.

From the high road through the village a short carriage drive swept across the park to a tree-shaded porch crowned by the Hillersdon arms. When the famous architect, Inigo Jones, came to Bedfordshire in the reign of James I, Sir Thomas had taken the opportunity to add an impressive entrance to his manor. Visitors from the neighbourhood regarded the elegant stone structure with awe and pride, admiring the graceful masques and arabesques which decorated the *intrados* of the arch, and the Italian-style panels in the pediments of the four pilasters.

It was said in Elstow that Henry VIII, persuaded by Bishop Gardiner, had once intended to retain the original Abbey Church as a Cathedral for Bedfordshire. Forty years passed and nothing came of the plan, so in 1580 the old tower and chancel were pulled down, and the flanking-tower of the nunnery, separated by several yards from the body of the church, was enlarged to contain the bells.

The truncated church, never joined to the new steeple, now became the place for village worship, and was rededicated to the Holy Trinity. In 1628 the ruins of the former choir, transept, and central tower still lay strewn east of the nave. Little remained of the nunnery except the small chapter-house between the church and Elstow Place, which served as a schoolroom and vestry. Its heavy vaulted roof rested incongruously upon a fragile-looking pillar of fluted Purbeck marble, shaped like the upturned flower of an arum lily.

When John was a small boy, he and his sister Margaret, fifteen months his junior, found the isolated steeple very frightening. There was something mysterious about the narrow shadowy space between its sheer east wall and the little postern-gate at the west end of the church. He used to imagine the Devil sitting up there, like a wicked king in his castle, shooting arrows at the people going to the gate. It was all he could do not to run headlong through the postern, as though Beelzebub himself were after him.

But even within the grey stone walls he never felt really safe, for the church had its terrors too. He was always afraid to look at the image of the man in a tight-fitting thirteenth-century tunic on the corbel beyond the Radclyff Memorial, for it just showed you what hostile walls could do. John's father had told him the local legend about this man, who was said to have been creeping towards the altar with sacrilegious intentions when the walls of the doorway through which he was passing suddenly closed and held him there for ever as a warning to other offenders.

Sometimes John would dream about the strange little figure on the corbel, with leafy branches growing out of its ears. He himself was always in scrapes, often being punished for lying and swearing, and the image became an uncomfortable symbol of divine vengeance for boyish misdeeds. Once he thought that they were running together in headlong flight from the Devil in the tower who was pursuing them, when the brass Abbess, Elizabeth Hervey, who had died in 1524, suddenly rose from her place on the floor of the south aisle and chased him away.

It was the beginning of those "fearful dreams" and "dreadful visions" which were to terrify John intermittently from the time that he was nine or ten until his twenty-fifth year. Sometimes they came even in the daytime, seizing him with such an anguish of apprehension that he was obliged to stop in the midst of his games with Margaret and their companions on the village green, and run behind a hedge or into a ditch where he could be quite alone.

Long afterwards, in his *Book for Boys and Girls*, published when he was a man of fifty-eight, John wrote some verses called "The Awakened Child's Lamentation" which showed that he still remembered those excruciating dawns when he lay huddled beneath the bed-clothes in terror of Satan and hell.

As sin hath me infected,
I am thereof detected:
Mercy I have neglected,
I fear I am rejected.

Sometimes the agony of that supposed rejection was so great that his naturally gay, exuberant nature became warped and twisted. Then he would give way to the frantic childish prayer that, since Hell certainly awaited him, he might himself be a devil and one of the tormentors, rather than endure for eternity this ordeal of the damned.

If you wish to revisit those early scenes of John Bunyan's games, prayers, and terrors, you can still use the narrow lane which turns west from Elstow village street, and takes you in a moment past the Moot Hall to the village green and the Abbey Church.

Today it is startling to travel along the wide suburban road from Bedford in the bus which stops at the Red Lion and, walking down the short lane, find yourself back in the Middle Ages.

You will feel, I believe, as regretful as myself when you see the graceful shape and glowing colours of the old Moot Hall, and then perceive that it is reaching its final stage of dilapidation and decay. Inside, the dusty staircase to the ancient courtroom and its worm-eaten floor have become so dangerous, that the outer door is locked against the many travellers who visit the village.

As my picture shows you, this ancient building is still the centre of games on the village green. The people of Elstow believe that the green is smaller now than in John Bunyan's time, but it is still a great open space where the Vicar tethers his goats and village festivities are held in summer. Palings were once put round the Moot Hall to protect it, but the section which prevented its use as goal or wicket soon disappeared. The constant impact of balls flung with the vigour of village youth shakes the mouldering structure and causes further damage to the withered timbers within.

In 1936, the Bedford Arts Club opened a public subscription in order to buy the ruins of Houghton Towers on Ampthill Heights. Handing their purchase over to the Ministry of Works, they preserved the crumbling, ivy-festooned palace for posterity. It is to be hoped that, by the time these words are read, a similar initiative will have saved the Moot Hall.

In spite of its threatened dissolution, you will be well rewarded on a Sunday morning by the short walk from Bedford to Elstow. In the Abbey Church you will find a remarkable Vicar who has lived in Elstow for thirty years without either boring his parishioners or becoming bored himself.

A small, caustic, inspired man with a beautiful voice which will renew for you the meaning of the Scriptures, he preaches short impressive sermons that draw congregations from all over Bedfordshire. If you ask him foolish questions he will not suffer you gladly, but if he finds you interested and intelligent, his time and courtesy may be yours.

The last time that I heard him preach he expressed the belief that a great change is coming over the people of this country, who have so vainly put their trust in the government of men, but now, brought by that grave error to the verge of chaos, are turning once more to the things of God.

As he spoke I watched the patterns which John Bunyan saw, made by the brief December sunshine upon the grey walls above the deep arches of the nave. The sudden illumination seemed symbolic; a hope, a promise. "Let there be light."

. . . . .

Before he was sixteen, John never went far from home. Since early impressions are the most vivid and last the longest, the scenes of mankind's symbolical drama were laid for him in the small county which to his boyhood's eyes appeared enormous.

Its neat, homely villages were vivid with wonder and adventure. Fairies lived in its woods, or hid themselves under the marsh marigolds and yellow irises growing on the banks of its slow-moving streams. Hobgoblins and foul fiends lurked in the valleys darkened by dense thickets; menacing giants waited in secret caves beneath the hills; ghosts walked in the churchyards on All Hallows' Eve.

Every year, during haytime and harvest, John turned out cheerfully with the village population to work in the fields. From the green and pleasant land lying immediately beyond his parents' doorstep, he was to draw—like so many contemporary writers whom he never knew and who never knew him—the imaginative strength which gave vitality to his books and preaching.

Not until he became a full-grown man and started travelling to London, would John find a city in which the countryside lay more than a few steps from the central market cross. Even today, after three centuries of modernization, the inhabitants of Bedford can reach lanes and open fields by ten minutes' walking. The industrial "developments" which have swept over Elstow and Harrowden surround these villages as the shell of a nut surrounds the kernel, concealing but not destroying the country life that John and his sister knew.

In that level land of boundless horizons, each man watching the sun rise and set over the quiet fields felt himself to be alone with God, and became part of the great solitude of God's creation which is totally different from loneliness. Almost before he could speak and long before he could read, John was observing from his window at Harrowden those morning and evening skies. In his last years he recalled his observations for the benefit of the children whom he addressed in his book of Country Rhymes.

> Look yonder, ah! Methinks mine eyes do see
> Clouds edg'd with silver, as fine garments be!
> They look as if they saw that golden face
> That makes black Clouds most beautiful with grace!

John Bunyan's Elstow was the home of swallows, cuckoos, and larks; he watched "all sorts of Birds fly in the Firmament", tumbling pleasantly through "the wholesom Air". In the farmyards he listened to "kackling hens" whose noisy self-advertisement was later to seem comparable to the pretentious claims of "some professing men". Less agreeable forms of livestock than swallows and even hens crawled about the fields—frogs, moles, spiders, and snails. Once, in a mood of foolish bravado, he stunned an adder crossing the highroad with his stick, and forcing open its mouth, plucked out what he believed to be its sting with his fingers.

This was one of the many narrow escapes which he afterwards saw as evidence of God's mercy. Another occurred when he accompanied his father on a river trip all the way from Bedford to the coast at Lyn (the future King's Lynn), where Thomas obtained imported metals for his trade. John had always been fascinated by the traffic along the Ouse, and often spent hours watching the bales of wool and huge baskets of fruit and vegetables being landed at Great Barford, six miles east of Bedford.

This time his excitement nearly cost him his life, for at Lyn he fell into a creek of the sea, and was half drowned when they pulled him out.

He was almost as rash when, like all Bedfordshire boys, he went fishing. One afternoon when he and Margaret were out in a boat near Bedford on the deepest part of the Ouse, he overbalanced into the river and only managed with great difficulty to clamber back from the clinging weeds. But it was worth-while going to Bedford or Kempston to catch the pike, roach and bream which hid in the calm green waters. Cardington Brook, though conveniently near the cottage in the fields, provided only an occasional perch apart from the numerous minnows which Margaret caught in her bucket.

Never again was John to know such a placid, procrastinating stream as the Ouse, which wound between reeds and willows for thirty miles in order to cross the seven of open meadowland that lay between Bedford and Turvey.

"This river," wrote Thomas Cox, the geographically-minded Vicar of Broomfield, Essex, who made a survey of Bedfordshire some years after John Bunyan's death to supplement the work of

William Camden, "seems to be sensible of the Pleasantness of the Place, and unwilling to pass into the fenny Parts of the next County." He added, with pardonable exaggeration, "It runs almost ninety miles in this Shire, in less than nineteen by land."

With Margaret beside him and a hunk of bread and cheese in his fish-basket, John passed long summer days amid the scented meadow-sweet on the banks of the shallow stream. Earlier in the century the poet Michael Drayton had also known those banks, and in the first part of his *Poly-Olbion,* published in 1613, had recorded his own impression of Bedfordshire's wandering river:

> Ouse having Olney past, as she were waxéd mad,
> From her first staider course immediately doth gad,
> And in meandering gyves doth whirl herself about,
> That, this way, here and there, back, forwards, in and out;
> And like a wanton girl, oft doubting in her gait,
> In labyrinth-like turns and twinings intricate,
> Thro' those rich fields doth run.

In spite of its lazy loiterings through the verdant pasture-lands where clumps of willow and poplar shaded deep mill-pools, the tranquil Ouse had some disconcerting habits in winter. Its sluggish flow, due to the very slight fall which it met on its way to the sea, made it liable to sudden and extensive floods. In Cambridgeshire they had a proverb, "The Bailiff of Bedford is coming", for the flooded river was apt to distrain upon the hay and cattle of their "fenny Parts".

The Fens were then a wild waste of soggy marsh, where gentlemen adventurers, attracted by the promise of a share in the salvaged land, undertook the work of reclamation. Their activities never became popular with the local inhabitants, who later found in the Civil War an excellent excuse to demolish the embankments. They preferred the immemorial company of their ducks and waders, which sometimes flew into Bedfordshire to inhabit the landowners' lakes, or to float past John and his fishing-rod beside the majestic swans on "Bedford river".

Long after his sister had been laid in her grave and the Civil Wars with their opportunities for bank-destroying Fenmen were over, John was to recall for generations of readers in the Introduction to *The Pilgrim's Progress* his exploits as an amateur Isaak Walton before he became a fisher of men.

> You see the ways the Fisher-man doth take
> To catch the Fish; what Engines doth he make?
> Behold! How he engageth all his wits;
> Also his snares, lines, angles, hooks, and nets:
> Yet Fish there be, that neither Hook nor Line,
> Nor Snare, nor Net, nor Engine can make thine:
> They must be grop'd for, and be tickled too,
> Or they will not be catcht, what e'er you do.

As soon as John had learned to ride, the fishing expeditions were varied by trips on horseback with his father across the county. He soon came to know the rough highways, crowded with waggons, pack-animals, riders, pedestrians, flocks and herds, which led in and out of the small and prosperous market towns.

The riders carried out their longer journeys on relays of horses, which could be hired or exchanged by travellers at fixed points on the main roads in exactly the same way as their descendants would pick up taxis at railway stations. The strong, well-trained horses were then the mainstay not only of private travellers and traders, but of the postal services which under Charles I were being taken over by the State from the common carrier and established throughout England.

To the favoured few, the news now came not only through letters but broadsheets, started in 1621 and printed in Holland. Three years after John's birth, Richelieu founded the first official newspaper, *La Gazette de France*. England was to imitate him under Charles II in the *London Gazette* of 1666.

Before he was old enough to read or understand broadsheets, John's longest ride had taken him to the Chilterns in South Bedfordshire. Here the Icknield Way, following the line of the chalk hills, led from Buckinghamshire through Dunstable and Luton into Hertfordshire.

The soft dry chalk delighted him, reared as he had been upon the heavy mud of north Bedfordshire's clay. In his later years he likened it to "the Child of God . . . White in his life, easily wrought upon", and wrote a rhyme about it:

This Stone is white, yea, warm, and also soft,
Easy to work upon, unless 'tis naught.
It leaves a white Impression upon those
Whom it doth touch, be they it's Friends or Foes.

One escarpment of the Chilterns, rising more than 600 feet, ran from Dunstable Downs to Warden Hill; the other, slightly lower, passed from Tottenhoe through Sundon to the Barton heights. There, from the wild fir-covered summit of Beacon Hill, John could look north to the wooded sandstone ridge sweeping from west to east, or south to the pleasant little market town of Luton.

The white road which spanned those hills was a link between his own turbulent age and the half-forgotten Romans, who had made a fine highway from a prehistoric track. On the Chilterns life had moved for thousands of years, before men could ride horses or shape their tools.

Over them had passed the Stone Age, the Bronze Age, and the Iron Age, all leaving, like the later Romans, Saxons, and Normans, their roads, tombs, and workshops to be their memorials. Thomas Bunyan could still identify for John the hut-circles of the earliest inhabitants; the camps of the warring British tribes who set their little fortress-mounds on the summits of hills; the rectangular enclosures of the Romans who had seized those camps and changed them; and the rounded barrows where the Saxons buried their leaders.

It was especially the Saxons who had impressed upon Bedfordshire the features of their civilization. Theirs were the compact villages, the spreading greens, and the high church towers in which their builders and craftsmen had found an anonymous immortality.

Scattered far and wide across the county were traces of that later past when men began to keep records. Bedfordshire was rich in the abbeys and priories established by the wealthier disciples of Christianity; in Norman keep and Plantaganet fortress; and more recently in the handsome Tudor and Stuart mansions set in their parks beneath oaks, elms, the uncommon sycamores, or the still rarer horse-chestnuts brought into England under James I.

In spring-time the grass beneath those dignified trees was spangled with primroses, celandines, wood-anemones, and wild hyacinths. As long as they could remember, John and Margaret had searched the April woods round Elstow for the more elusive daffodil and lily-of-the-valley. Now, as he moved further afield, he discovered the maiden-pinks growing near the Roman camp at Sandy, and observed the deep-blue woad which was sown in March, cropped in May, and afterwards taken to the woad-mill where it was prepared for dyeing.

When summer was over, rare autumnal gentians could be found on the Barton Hills. Above them hovered skylarks and long-legged stone curlews; occasionally a pair of buzzards cast their shadows across the short grass as they wheeled over the Downs. In hedgerows and copses, chiff-chaffs, willow-warblers, and black-caps twittered loudly from dawn till sunset, rivalling the chaffinches and reed-warblers in the valley of the Ouse.

Towards the fall of the year, large flocks of lapwing and golden plover gathered on the meadows surrounding the market gardens. In the winter woods, blue tits, gold-crests, and nut hatches flitted from tree to tree searching for food. Once John saw a couple of ravens at Woburn, and heard the bitterns booming across the fields.

But he learned more about his county than its trees, birds, and flowers, for he soon began to perceive the significance of social distinctions. Bedfordshire, as the lord-loving Thomas Cox could still record eighty years afterwards, was "well-inhabited, especially by gentlemen". It was also abundantly supplied with newly created baronets, such as Sir William Gostwick of Willington and Sir Robert Napier of Luton. They and their social contemporaries lived in those Tudor mansions which later generations would convert into farm-houses, or in the more magnificent country palaces of rose-red brick, with carven stone porches and long approach-avenues of exotic trees.

The lives led by these gentlemen and their richly dressed ladies were obviously quite different from those of the men labouring in fields or market gardens, and the women making bone-lace at their cottage doors. In winter, crowded together in small rooms, these lace-makers became sickly from the foetid air and sedentary work, which brought them only a shilling for an average day's output. They never complained, but their pale faces impressed upon John the fact that human society, rather than divine law, had made men high or lowly, and ordered their estate.

This contrast between rich and poor seemed greater in the country than in Bedford town. First his brief education, and later his work as apprentice to his father, took John constantly along the bridle path which passed from Wilstead through Medbury beneath a line of willows near the Harrowden cottage, and ended in Bedford a mile further north at the leper hospital of St. Leonard's close to St. John's Church.

John had known this walk since he was four years old, and could still remember seeing the former Vicar of St. John's, old Andrew Dennys, who died when John was five. Long before that day, in 1601, Andrew Dennys had become Vicar of St. Paul's, the big church with the soaring spire which dominated the south end of the High Street on the north side of Bedford Bridge.

In 1606 Andrew Dennys, who was uncle to Sir Thomas Hillersdon of Elstow, had been promoted to the Rectorship of St. John's Hospital and Church. This well-endowed institution, enlarged in 1280 by Robert De Parys, had long been regarded as the "plum" of Bedford livings, but it gave Andrew Dennys neither peace nor prosperity. Perpetually involved in law-suits brought by a local claimant, Edward Williams, who sought to establish a right to the possession of church and hospital, he died, worn out by litigation, at the age of sixty-three. John recalled him as an elderly man in a flowered cap, with a ruff round his neck and a staff in his hand, walking slowly up St. John's Street.

The Bunyans seldom saw but often spoke of another Bedford clergyman, who was to become a source of more ferocious controversy than the unhappy Andrew Dennys. In 1630, at the age of thirty-five, Dr. Giles Thorne had been collated by the Bishop of Lincoln to the Rectory of St. Mary's and St. Peter de Dunstable. The second church had been demolished in 1545, but the two parishes continued under one Rector. It occupied the site of the present St. Mary's Square, opposite St. Mary's Church.

The Reverend Doctor, an outspoken partisan of Archbishop Laud, lost no time in citing his Puritan neighbours before the

Archbishop's Court for various ecclesiastical offences, and was soon marked down for trouble by the local Puritan M.P.s. During John's childhood he continued to qualify for the same type of treatment by the authorities under the Commonwealth as his own Church party, twenty years afterwards, was to inflict on them.

Seventeenth-century religion might be a moral and intellectual influence, but its most fervent apologists could not have called it humane. They would, indeed, have been surprised to learn that humaneness would ever come to be regarded as an essential part of the religious life, which then tended to be an exercise in ferocity rather than conciliation. Their instruments were the rack, the pillory, the stake, the gibbet; on the Continent they slaughtered helpless populations in the name of God with a wholesale ruthlessness never to be exceeded until their successors, three centuries later, exterminated a new series of victims in the name of the State.

At every large cross-roads throughout England the gibbets stood, symbols of both secular and ecclesiastical vengeance. From his earliest years John had seen the corpses that hung from them, tarred for preservation, swinging in the breeze. They entered horribly into his ever more frequent nightmares, increasing the fear of some terrible danger that haunted him all through his schooldays.

Born long before the era of psychologists who were to diagnose such suppressed apprehensions as "anxiety neuroses", he was destined to become one of the best-known historic examples of that temperamental malady which so many intelligent and imaginative persons are condemned to endure. Like the best of them he would teach himself to overcome it, but the years of conflict were to be long and intense.

For John, the Bible was both the origin of that conflict and the means by which it would ultimately be resolved. He was growing up in an age of self-conscious literary elegance; an epoch of salons with fashionable hostesses, of writers who sought to establish themselves by means of royal or aristocratic patrons. But these decorative and ambitious figures would mean no more to John than he ever meant to them. Even the Titans who died shortly before his birth—Shakespeare and Cervantes in 1616, Bacon in 1626—lacked reality in comparison with those biblical characters whose adventures represented literature to the simple and humble circles in which he moved.

His parents were not religious enthusiasts or conspicuous Puritans, but like all their working-class contemporaries they had been trained from early youth in the habits of Bible-reading and private prayer. For many other English families, the prohibition of independent religious meetings was making their own homes the only tolerable place of worship.

Of that worship the Authorized Version of the Bible, published in 1611, had become the centre. Popular knowledge of it was exact rather than profound, but as a book it had no rival in many poor households. Its literal interpretation was responsible for a universal sense of the nearness of God and the reality of Satan. From the lovely simplicity of its language came the direct, apposite, poetic speech which the characters in *The Pilgrim's Progress* were to borrow from the plain men and women whom its author knew.

During John's boyhood the Scriptures, later to prove so disconcerting, found successful competitors in popular publications which achieved a wide circulation amongst the common people, though literary "professors" ignored them. In his third book, a treatise on the story of Dives and Lazarus entitled *A Few Sighs from Hell,* John described his own early absorption in "merry books"—the "thrillers" of his youth.

> "I remember he the preacher alleged many a Scripture, but those I valued not; the Scriptures, thought I, what are they? A dead letter, a little ink and paper, of three or four shillings price. Alas! What is the Scripture? Give me a ballad, a newsbook, George on Horseback or Bevis of Southampton; give me some book that teaches curious arts, that tells of old fables, but for the holy Scriptures I cared not."

The stories to which John referred came from the chap-books and "emblem books" beloved for a century before his time by the uneducated classes throughout Western Europe. Amongst Puritans the most popular was Francis Quarles's *Emblems, Divine and Moral,* published when John was seven years old. Later this volume of little pictures illustrating moral and religious truths, with didactic verse as a running accompaniment, became the model for his own book "for Boys and Girls".

"George on Horseback" and "Bevis of Southampton" were heroes from another favourite, Richard Johnson's *The Seven Champions of Christendom*, of which a new edition was published in 1607. Deaf to all interruptions from his family or playmates, John read how the gallant St. George slew a man-eating giant thirty feet high. Later his hero also overcame an Egyptian dragon, and was healed of his wounds by leaves from a miraculous tree.

Like his predecessor, Edmund Spenser, John absorbed these romances drawn from chivalry until they became part of his own imaginative equipment. For him his native Midlands, already the haunt of highwaymen who lay hidden in moors and woods waiting for travellers, were also peopled with the giants and dragons of those early stories and the virtuous champions who overcame them.

Years afterwards he was to combine the actual landscape with the romantic stories in such a fashion that the improbable giants became for his readers more real than their neighbours, and the homely roads and fields of Bedfordshire acquired the strange glory of a legendary kingdom.

In 1641, when John was twelve years old, he found himself caught up into the mysterious tensions of that eventful year.

On Tuesday, 16 March, Sir Roger Burgoyne, one of the four Parliamentarian M.P.s. sent by Bedfordshire to the Long Parliament, carried to the House of Commons a petition asking for the displacement of all evil councillors, the punishment of all delinquents, and the complete removal of all burdensome and scandalous ceremonies and all corrupt and scandalous ministers.

These requests referred particularly to the Earl of Strafford and Archbishop Laud, now prisoners in the Tower of London awaiting their trial. The petition was one of many carried during those spring months on the rising tide of excitement which followed the General Election and piled London's bookstalls with revolutionary pamphlets.

At Elstow, then on the highroad to London, John and Margaret, with their seven-year-old brother William, watched the large contingent of petitioners from Bedford riding past with their "protestations" in their hats. On arrival, they would raise to two thousand the number of Bedfordshire gentlemen who assembled at Finsbury Fields in support of their petition, and carried it thence to the sympathetic House at Westminster.

They rode four abreast through the City while the psalm-singers in its Gothic churches drowned the Prayer Book services, and excited mobs yelled for spiritual freedom against clerics and courtiers. Two months afterwards the echoes of Strafford's execution on Tower Hill reached even to Bedfordshire, intensifying the perpetual rumours of war which stirred and bewildered the countryside.

John Bunyan was even more puzzled than his elders, for the events of that year had their roots in happenings older than his conscious memory. His mother was unable to explain them, and even his father could only tell him that from 1629, when John was a few months old, England had been without a parliament until 1640. Ever since the new House of Commons was elected one sensation had followed another, and where it was all going to end Thomas Bunyan couldn't tell.

During those eleven years of despotic government by Charles I, the society in which John's parents moved had never attempted to protest against the unorthodox constitutional position imposed upon his country by their king. Though they were now free men, the more ignorant of the elder Bunyans' contemporaries were satisfied with bare subsistence and crude enjoyments, while the more serious-minded put into their religious practices the energy that their descendants would begin, two centuries afterwards, to expend on social reform.

Between 1630 and 1640, the old corporations in which common interests united masters and men had entered upon a period of decline. Already a gulf divided the socially conservative yeoman-farmers and the labourers who worked for them, while the trade union movement lay far in the future. The opportunities for expressing corporate indignation which that future would bring did not yet exist; religious vitality took their place.

But the workers, though unaware and inarticulate, had representatives who were both conscious and eloquent. Throughout the years of unconstitutional government, a group of peers and

THE ABBEY CHURCH, ELSTOW

The picture shows how the steeple is separate from the main building.

HARROWDEN FIELDS IN SUMMER

The site of Bunyan's birthplace is on the extreme left. Just visible in the centre of the horizon is the tower of Elstow Church.

commoners had met continually and even lived under the same roof for months on end, watching events and preparing for future action.

Amongst them was William Russell, the Earl of Bedford from Woburn, who afterwards became General of the Horse under the Earl of Essex before he moved over to the King's side in 1643. Others included John Pym, John Hampden, Lord Mandeville, and the Earl of Warwick. Sir John Eliot now belonged to this group only in spirit. Resolute to the last he had died a prisoner in the Tower in 1632, the first conspicuous martyr of the English Revolution.

These peers and commoners opposed with equal determination the King's methods of raising money without summoning Parliament, and his supposed sympathy with the "popish" practice of placing the communion table at the east end of Anglican churches and using it as an altar.

After William Laud's appointment as Archbishop of Canterbury in 1633, he had ordained that every clergyman who resisted this practice, or refused to conform to the Prayer Book service and bow at the name of Jesus, must be tried by the King's special Court of High Commission, and if convicted be deprived of his benefice. Laud thus succeeded in rousing, amongst both "conformist" and nonconformist Puritans, that passion for freedom of conscience which is a major emotion of the English people.

His episcopal censorship of the Press caused secret publications to circulate amongst the discontented populace until the Revolution turned the pent-up trickle into an angry flood. Those exasperated and illegal books and pamphlets symbolized the failure of Laud's war on Puritanism. Had it succeeded, young John Bunyan growing up in his father's cottage could never have written *The Pilgrim's Progress*, nor George Fox, four years his senior, have founded the Society of Friends.

At the Court Charles I, husband of a French queen and judicious patron of Rubens and Van Dyke, took no interest in the bloody survival of Protestantism on the Continent. The tragedies of the Thirty Years' War had left him unmoved, even when they reached an abyss of horror in the destruction of Magdeburg by the Catholic League on 10 May, 1631. Strange and terrible rumours reached England of homes and families perishing in the flames which swept through the town. It was said that the survivors, who took refuge in the Cathedral, had implored the cities further downstream to give Christian burial to the corpses of their relatives flung into the Elbe.

Since 1635, French, Swedish, Spanish, and German troops had been ravaging the exhausted countryside of Central Europe, keeping constantly on the move to avoid starvation. But the agonies of the Continent affected England's self-centred King only in so far as they offered him an opportunity to recover the lost Palatinate for his Protestant relative the Elector Frederick, who had married his sister Elizabeth in 1612.

With the year 1637 came a series of events that showed which way the English wind was blowing.

In Palace Yard, the people of London demonstrated with angry sympathy round the pillory on which Prynne, Burton and Bastwick were punished for libelling the Bishops. They supported Lilburne, the gentlemanly republican, for declining to take the Star Chamber oath, and Hampden for refusing to pay Ship-money. That same year John Milton wrote *Lycidas* before turning, for two decades, to political pamphleteering on the grand scale.

Away to the north, Scotland rose against Laud's attempt to substitute the Prayer Book for John Knox's Book of Common Order. Nobles, lairds, clergy, burghers and peasants entered into a National Covenant to defend their religion, and increased Charles's need for money by involving him in the First and Second Bishops' Wars.

At Westminster, Strafford's experiment in tyranny was thwarted by the Short Parliament before the Long Parliament took its place. During the elections Pym and Hampden travelled over England, urging the voters to choose recognized Puritans as their political leaders. Six months before the young Bunyans watched Bedford's contingent of petitioners riding through Elstow to Finsbury Fields, Bedfordshire had responded by electing Sir Oliver Luke of Cople as Parliamentary Knight of the Shire, and Sir Oliver's son, Sir Samuel, and Sir Beauchamp St. John of Bletsoe, as Parliamentary Burgesses for Bedford town.

When Sir Roger Burgoyne of Sutton replaced the one Royalist, Lord Wentworth of Toddington, the "tainted" county was appropriately represented in the House of Commons by four stalwart opponents of the King. It was one of only three throughout England in which the Members for county and borough alike were all supporters of Parliament.

During the autumn which saw John Bunyan's twelfth birthday, a new England was in process of creation. The Royalist leaders who had silenced their opponents were now silenced in turn, and they, too, produced their martyrs. Aged William Laud, a conscientious man by his own standards, lay for four years without trial in the Tower. In 1642 the Fleet Prison was to receive another determined Anglican, Dr. Giles Thorne of St. Mary's, arrested by Lord St. John's troopers as he left the pulpit of St. Cuthbert's Church on a Sunday morning, and carried a prisoner to the Swan Inn at the corner of Bedford Bridge.

Outside the walls of the Fleet and the Tower, excited groups were discussing whether Bishops should be reformed or abolished. In December 1640, a petition signed by 15,000 names for the abolition of episcopacy, "root and branch", was presented to the Commons. The Members debated it the following February in St. Stephen's Chapel, where Lambeth's green fields and the barges moving up and down the blue-grey waters of the Thames were framed, like a pastel-tinted water-colour, in the great Gothic window behind the Speaker's Chair.

That summer a visitor from Europe, the Moravian teacher Comenius, arrived in London to join the Commission which Parliament had meant to set up to reform English education. But when the time came, the Commons were so busy abolishing the Star Chamber and making Ship-money illegal that the Commission was never appointed, and within a few months Comenius departed to the quieter shores of Sweden.

In November the Commons, drawing up a list of the nation's wrongs and putting forward suggestions for reform, appealed to the people in the Grand Remonstrance. The Petition which accompanied it showed the desire of the House to absolve the King and lay the responsibility for national turmoil upon evil counsellors.

> "The duty which we owe to your Majesty and our country, cannot but make us very sensible and apprehensive, that the multiplicity, sharpness and malignity of those evils under which we have now many years suffered, are fomented and

cherished by a corrupt and ill-affected party, who amongst other their mischievous devices for the alteration of religion and government, have sought by many false scandals and imputations, cunningly insinuated and dispersed amongst the people, to blemish and disgrace our proceedings in this Parliament . . . For preventing whereof, and the better information of your Majesty, your Peers and all other your loyal subjects, we have been necessitated to make a declaration of the state of the Kingdom . . . which we do humbly present to your Majesty, without the least intention to lay any blemish upon your royal person, but only to represent how your royal authority and trust have been abused, to the great prejudice and danger of your Majesty, and of all your good subjects."

But Charles, living far from reality in an isolated world of self-created standards, lacked more disastrously than any other English monarch the capacity to see where his own interests lay. Turning, exasperated, to the attack, he entered the House in the New Year and attempted to impeach and arrest five of its leading Members, Pym, Hampden, Holles, Haselrig, and Strode. The five Members escaped, to find refuge and protection in the City of London. Lords, Commons and City entered into a triple alliance, and compelled Charles to flee to York.

Then, suddenly, drums and trumpets began to sound all over England, and men were riding post-haste to battle. Half the combatants, rallying to the King's standard at Nottingham, wore feathered hats and long curls falling over the collars of the rich cloaks that covered their armour. The other half were distinguished only by their close-cropped heads, and the sober hue of doublet and hose.

Without their will and almost without their knowledge, war had come upon them. "We intended not," wrote the Parliamentary chaplain, Richard Baxter, "to dig down the banks, or pull up the hedge and lay all waste and common, when we desired the prelate's tyranny might cease."

Both sides believed, as all warriors have persuaded themselves to believe in all wars, that they were fighting for the welfare of their country. But this time the enemy came from no foreign land; he sprang from the heart of England herself. Neither national greed nor national security, but the deep conflict between an old political tradition and a new political principle, drove each group of antagonists to take up arms, and sometimes separated brother from brother and father from son.

Perhaps because its roots lay in these baffling ideologies the war was never popular with the common people, who as always had nothing to gain and everything to lose. The seizure of horses and requisitioning of picks and mattocks, added to the conscription of men, disturbed the traditional routine of seed-time and harvest by which the country lived.

Adverse or indifferent, but compelled reluctantly to take sides by the persistent propaganda with which both parties bombarded them, the inhabitants of Bedfordshire looked on apprehensively at this struggle of minorities as the battle shifted inconclusively from north to south, and from east to west. When Parliament began to ask for money, its demands were received with no greater enthusiasm than the earlier claims of the King.

To John Bunyan, now regularly at work in his father's forge, it seemed improbable that this strange, uneasy conflict would affect him personally. He regarded it as remote even when the tide of war flowed right into Bedfordshire, in which, as Edward Hyde was to record years afterwards, "the King had not any visible party nor one fixed quarter".

Among the documents filed by Bedford Corporation were four State letters from Charles I, written in 1626 and 1627. Numbers 1, 3, and 4 had demanded money or complained of its non-receipt; Number 2 announced the dissolution of the King's Second Parliament. After these interchanges Bedfordshire escaped the Royal attention until the county was assessed, in 1635, at £3000 for Ship-money, and Bedford Corporation complained that the town was rated at too high a figure.

So vigorous was the opposition to this unconstitutional tax, that in 1638 Bedfordshire became one of the five chief defaulting counties by collecting only £389 out of an assessment of £1100. Its choice of four Parliamentarians in 1640 was the measure of its protest.

In spite of the local influence of these Members of Parliament, a number of Bedfordshire Royalists followed the King to Oxford; they included the widow of John Wingate of Harlington, and Francis, his son. Others joined Charles's army and prepared for war against their revolutionary neighbours. The most conspicuous of them, Sir Lewis Dyve of Bromham Hall, was attacked by troops under Sir Samuel Luke, M.P. for Bedford, in July 1642, and escaped only by swimming the Ouse which flowed past his house.

Fifteen months later, when John Hampden had been killed at Chalgrove Field and John Pym, his life work accomplished, lay dying in London, Sir Lewis, now an officer under Prince Rupert, returned to Bedfordshire to take his revenge.

Coming first to Ampthill with 400 horse, he and Sir John Digby surprised the Bedfordshire Committee which was meeting there to consider the sequestration of Royalist estates. Subsequently entering Bedford, Sir Lewis made prisoners of Sir John Norwich and other Parliamentary officers whom he discovered in an ale-house. Thence he went on to Sir Samuel Luke's house at Cople, "and served *that* as Sir Lewis Dyve himself was served in the same county by the sequestrators".

Shortly after this exchange of neighbourly visits, Colonel Montague with some of the Parliamentary Army entered Bedford pretending to be Royalists under Sir Lewis, and took away horses and money intended for the King. When the excitement which spread to Elstow and Harrowden had died down, John Bunyan believed that his war was vicariously over. He forgot all about it —until the bitter summer of 1644.

In June a strange sickness swept over the village, as such sicknesses often did when rules of health and cleanliness were little understood, and no scientifically trained body of medical men and women existed to combat disease. Before the end of that month his mother, with her keen tongue and busy hands, lay in her grave. A month later fourteen-year-old Margaret, his playmate as long as he could remember, was carried to the same plot of anonymous earth in Elstow churchyard.

Lonely and stricken, too old at fifteen-and-a-half to find a new companion in his young brother William, John wandered through the desolate summer fields, or sat grieving beside Cardington Brook where he and Margaret had fished for tiddlers. His ears were deaf to the cries of triumph with which Bedfordshire's Parliamentary enthusiasts had greeted the victory of Cromwell's Ironsides on 2 July at Marston Moor. He neither knew nor cared that by this battle the supporters of Independency, with which his life was to be associated, had celebrated their first triumph over their Presbyterian allies.

When Thomas Bunyan took a third wife that very August, John found his home intolerable. He could hardly be expected to remember that his lusty, practical father, who saw no purpose in needlessly prolonging the period of disconsolate widowerhood, had married his mother, in May 1627, with as little delay after the death of his first wife earlier that year.

The summer before the two Margaret Bunyans passed for ever from the lives of sons and brothers, a number of warrants had been issued by Sir Samuel Luke, now Governor of the Parliamentary Garrison at Newport Pagnell, and by Richard Edwards of the County Committee. These warrants required all able-bodied men between sixteen and sixty years of age to report at Leighton Buzzard on 3 June.

The poor response provoked Sir Samuel into exasperated threats. No echo then reached John Bunyan's preoccupied ears of the words in which three years of his life were to be involved.

> "These are to signify that it is Sir Samuel Luke's desire that it be published in your parish with all speed, that he will no longer dally with, or by more fair ways and means claw his countrymen, seeing that it is altogether vain and fruitless; but he is resolved that if all persons in every parish between sixteen and sixty, being able to carry arms, shall not severally appear at Leighton on Monday morning next, by seven of the clock, with all provisions with them, and arms and weapons for the service of the State and their own safety, he will proceed against such cold and insensible persons and parishes of this county with that vigour and severity as is done in other places, that the good may not always remain scoffed and derided at, but that they may receive such care and comfort by such his proceedings as is agreeable to all manner of equity and good conscience . . . Fail you not therefore, and to bring a list of the names of every man at your peril."

When Sir Samuel's recruiting-officers came to Elstow in that autumn of 1644 to gather Bedfordshire's proportion of men required for the defence of the Newport garrison, John Bunyan, now nearing his sixteenth birthday, was the only boy in the village who was glad to see them.

CHAPTER III

THEN A SOLDIER

"Here . . . were Judgments and Mercy, but neither of them did awaken my Soul to Righteousness; wherefore I sinned still, and grew more and more rebellious against God, and careless of mine own Salvation."

JOHN BUNYAN: *Grace Abounding.*

JOHN BUNYAN was now a tall, vigorous youth with large bones, a long stride, and a heavy tread. Even as a conscript amid other conscripts, his dynamic energy, keen blue eyes and abundant auburn hair made the sober Parliamentary officers look at him twice.

It had proved easy to persuade the recruiting-officers that he was already sixteen; the lie had been more useful than any other in his long record of lying. He felt no remorse for the simple subterfuge which had enabled him to leave home and join the Army. Though most of his companions were tired and some had deserted, he was hardly fatigued by the twelve-mile march from Bedford to Newport Pagnell in Buckinghamshire on that October day of 1644.

The company of pressed men had come by an ancient road, the Roman Akerman Street, which passed from Bedford through Newport to Stony Stratford. From the top of Sherington Hill a mile away, they first saw their destination. Beyond the flat, swampy meadows which lay before them, the church and town, then larger than Bedford, conspicuously climbed another hill on the opposite side of the waterlogged plain.

With its two rivers, the Ouse and the Lovat, forming a natural moat to the north and east of this hill, Newport Pagnell was exceptionally well-placed for a garrison town. From the encompassing rivers, trenches had been dug with drawbridges and sluices. The artificial half of the moat, passing behind a long white water-mill, circled the town on the south, and then joined the slow, reedy stream of the Lovat.

In a Parliamentary Ordinance, Newport Pagnell had been

ELSTOW MOOT HALL AND VILLAGE GREEN

Here the famous fairs were held, and Bunyan heard the voice which led to his conversion. The village boys still play games on the green as they did in his day.

THE RUINS OF HILLERSDON MANOR, ELSTOW

Behind Elstow Church, showing the porch reputedly designed by Inigo Jones. In Bunyan's day the Manor was called Elstow Place.

described as "geometrically situate" between the Associated Counties in the East and the Royalist districts to the West. This political and geographical accident was responsible for its importance; it was also mid-way between London and Nottingham, where Charles had rallied his supporters. Three celebrated inns—the Swan and the Saracen's Head side by side in the High Street, and the George near by—testified to Newport's use as a half-way house for travellers.

As John marched towards the town along the flat road which crossed the marshy meadows, he saw to his left a dignified building in a grove of trees on the banks of the Ouse which recalled the ruins behind Elstow Church.

The recollection was appropriate, for Tickford Abbey stood on the site of an older Priory. Founded by Faulk Paganell in the time of William Rufus as a cell for Cluniac monks, it had shared the fate of Elstow Abbey. After its suppression in 1525 its revenues had been converted to the use of Cardinal College, Oxford, later to be known as Christ Church. Four stone arches from the original gateway and the remains of a barred window still made their silent protest from the past against spoliation.

The small company of recruits crossed the Ouse by a brick bridge with three large arches, and entered Newport. On the brow of the hill the square grey tower of the church, crowned by a weather-vane of exceptional height, dominated the town like a solitary oak set in a thicket of hazels. The houses beside it clustered so closely together that from the river bank they appeared to be piled on the top of one another.

Owing to the Sunday services imposed on the soldiers by their Presbyterian command, the conspicuous church soon became tediously familiar. The walls of its great nave were over five feet thick; rebuilt in the fourteenth century, it had probably incorporated an earlier cruciform church.

John always preferred its outside to its inside; whenever he could escape from the wearisome services, he made his way to the natural terrace above the churchyard which sloped down to the River Lovat. From the south end of this terrace, a narrow alley called Church Lane curved downhill into St. John's Street. Over its low brick wall a dark yew peered at the red tiled roof and dormer windows of the Swan Tap.

St. John's Street took its name from the old hospital of St. John the Baptist and St. John the Evangelist, founded in 1240. In 1615 this ancient Newport charity, for three men and three women over fifty, had been refounded as Queen Anne's Hospital in honour of Anne of Denmark, the consort of James I. Its gabled buildings with their towering red chimneys stretched almost to the banks of the Lovat.

John, being a scholar, was able to read to his unlettered fellow privates the appeal for alms inscribed on a wooden beam:

> "Alyou good Chrystianes that heere dooe pas by, give soome thynge to thes poore people that in St. John's Hospital doeth ly An° 1615."

The Vicar of Newport for the time being traditionally became the Master of this hospital. In that year 1644 the post was held by Samuel Austin, an adherent of the old regime uncongenial to the garrison. He was to be "thrust out" in 1646, and owing to a shortage of suitable Puritan candidates replaced by a very young man. This youthful cleric, John Gibbs, was destined to become a lifelong friend of John Bunyan.

Marching up the hill past the church into the High Street, the conscripts dispersed to their several billets. In the long road running north-east and south-west through the town, John noticed eight butchers' shambles and the hanging sign outside the Swan Inn. It resembled the one at Bedford Bridge, and gave him a sudden feeling of homesickness.

His loneliness would hardly have been mitigated had he known that another contemporary with whom his name was to be linked had recently left Newport, for strangely little sympathy ever existed between John Bunyan and the followers of George Fox. In his dairy Fox had recorded his months at Newport Pagnell, where he stayed at the Waggon and Horses near Cannon Corner. When he left the town in June 1644, Buckinghamshire was already a stronghold of the Quakers, and Newport the home of several Friends.

At the time of John Bunyan's arrival, the garrison had been a Parliamentary fortress only for a year. Its story was part of the chequered history of the Eastern Midlands during the Civil War.

By an Ordinance of 15 December, 1642, Bedfordshire had been included in the Midland Association with the counties of Northampton, Leicester, Derby, Rutland, Nottingham, Huntingdon, and Buckingham.

The total population of Bedfordshire was then under 40,000, yet it had supplied Parliament with 500 trained bands, as well as 500 volunteers and a regiment of dragoons. Out of England's population of five million, 140,000 men were now under arms.

In 1643, after his raids on Ampthill and Bedford, Sir Lewis Dyve occupied Newport and put up fortifications. When he issued warrants requiring the local population to work on these defences and supply money and provisions, they complained that he was bringing "all the quietest part of the kingdom into combustion and distraction". Parliament therefore determined to regain Newport, and thus make sure that supplies for London were not interrupted.

The Earl of Essex, advancing to St. Albans with his Parliamentary contingent, sent forward a large detachment to Dunstable, and ordered Major-General Philip Skippon to enter Newport with a company of horse and foot. One of the strangest incidents of the War occurred when Sir Lewis Dyve, though his forces were superior, evacuated Newport on the night of 26 October and retired with all his baggage to Stony Stratford. Sir Frederick Cornwallis at Oxford, mistaking some orders from the King, had directed Sir Lewis to retreat; Skippon therefore marched in without opposition, and was astonished to see how strong a place the Cavaliers had deserted.

For the rest of the War, the garrison remained in the hands of Parliament. Sir Samuel Luke, the official Scoutmaster to the Army, was appointed Governor, and the fortunes of Bedford and Newport became closely linked.

Although Roundheads had replaced Royalists, the district did not wholly escape "combustion and distraction". By contemporary standards the morale of the Parliamentary Army was high, but many of its soldiers were not reluctant to indulge their fanatical zeal.

The parish register of Maids Moreton recorded how the

"reverend and religious Rector" had died in March 1643, "almost heartbroken with the insolence of the rebels against the church and the King"; he had seen the windows of his church broken, the Cross torn off the steeple, and the gilt desk, shaped like a spread eagle, "doomed to perish as an abominable idol". Other soldiers stationed at Aylesbury broke into the church, defaced the stained glass windows, and burned the altar rails.

Such excesses were typical of soldiers precipitated into wars of religion. John Bunyan took part in them with the rest, and never forgot the scenes that he witnessed. They came back to him in after years, to counsel restraint when he was himself a victim of intolerance.

The New Model Army, of which John was one small unit, had been formed by incorporating the remnants of armies led by Essex, Manchester, and Waller. But these forces were so much reduced by the Battle of Marston Moor and other campaigns of 1644, that they could not supply even half the 14,000 men demanded by Sir Thomas Fairfax.

Parliament therefore resolved to raise 8500 men from London and the South-east by the unpopular but familiar method of "impressment". The quota from each county was fixed, and the local authorities were ordered to send their men by a given date. Hardly more than half the number required actually arrived, so at the end of June 1644 it became necessary to raise another 4000. That was how John Bunyan, though barely sixteen, found himself on the road from Bedford to Newport Pagnell in the autumn of 1644.

Among men thus forcibly conscripted, enthusiasm for any cause whatsoever was hardly to be expected. John was almost unique in having no inclination to desert; many of his companions ran home with complete immunity, since there was nobody to chase them. But physically most of them might have been described as "good military material", and after the first few months in the New Model Army, their tendency to quit had almost disappeared.

The officers under whom John and his comrades served were relatively well-dressed. Usually bearded, they wore high plumed hats, armoured breast-plates, short knee breeches, and high leather boots. The red coats typical of Cromwell's officers were supplied to them in 1645 when the New Model Army was officially complete, and uniforms, replacing the motley clothing and colours hitherto worn by both sides, became part of the common soldiers' equipment.

John's own uniform was less decorative than that of his leaders, and he had to wait for it a long time. When it came, it consisted of a plain brown doublet and coat or "cassock", short breeches, two shirts, stockings of "good Welsh cotton", and low shoes tied with laces. For these serviceable but undistinguished garments he was obliged to pay, giving 17*s.* for his coat and breeches, 6*s.* for his doublet, 2*s.* 9*d.* each for his shirts, 1*s.* for each pair of stockings, and 2*s.* 3*d.* a pair for his shoes. He also wore a Monmouth cap, knitted, blocked, and tasselled, and carried a short musket.

The heavy bullets required for his musket were fastened, with twelve charges of powder, into a leather bandolier worn over his shoulder and fitted with small pouches. This item of equipment was both inconvenient and dangerous. Had John ever seen active service, he would have found that the loud rattle of his bullets extinguished the words of command, while the powder-charges, though enclosed in small tin cases, had a disconcerting tendency to ignite on their own.

At the head of the garrison, Sir Samuel Luke presided over his resentful collection of country bumpkins like a Presbyterian Baden-Powell over an unruly troop of raw Boy Scouts. He was a voluminous correspondent; his Letter Book, written in virile prose during his period as Governor, filled four manuscript volumes.

Unfortunately for Sir Samuel, his claim to immortality was not to rest on his governorship of the garrison or his conscientious activities as Member for Bedford, but on his identification with the derided hero of Samuel Butler's *Hudibras*. Tradition and Butler between them endowed him with a long grizzled beard in fulfilment of some legendary vow, but a contemporary portrait, reproduced in the *Buckinghamshire Record* during 1862, showed him as clean-shaven.

By a coincidence attractive to literary historians, Samuel

Butler, as his secretary at Cople, and John Bunyan, as a conscripted soldier at Newport, were both in Sir Samuel's service at the same time. Whether or not he had grievances to resent, John made no retaliation against his Commander in *The Holy War*. Butler, untroubled by similar scruples, designed *Hudibras* to satirize the military Presbyterian.

We grant, although he had much wit,
H'was very shie of using it,
As being loath to wear it out,
And therefore bore it not about,
Unless on Holy-Days or so,
As Men their best Apparel do.

Towards the end of the first Part of Canto I the satirist, uninhibited by twentieth-century libel laws, identified his pretentious hero more boldly.

'Tis sung, There is a valiant Marmaluke
In foreign land, yclep'd—
To whom we have been oft compared
For Person, Parts, Address and Beard:
Both equally reported stout,
And in the same Cause both have fought.

During the War, before his embarrassing literary title became the source of public hilarity, Sir Samuel was alternately praised and blamed by his contemporaries. One was humorous about his diminutive stature; another called him a "scarecrow", but added: "I cannot let this noble commander passe without a just ceremony as to his valour and activity, who watches the enemy so industriously that they eat, sleep, drink not, whisper not, but he can give an account of their darkest proceeding."

In spite of such praise, Sir Samuel's last years were to be embittered by Butler's satire, which became so fashionable that Samuel Pepys, who decided at the first reading that the book was "so silly an abuse of the Presbyter Knight going to the warrs that I am ashamed of it", and sold his copy, found himself compelled to buy another—"it being certainly some ill-humour to be so against that which all the world cries up to be an example of wit".

At Newport Sir Samuel lived comfortably in a house on the Green, using the Saracen's Head in the High Street as his headquarters. Like all military commanders, he had his share of anxieties. Not only did recruits disappear on their way to the rendezvous, but supplies in general were far from lavish. The pay of the troops was perpetually in arrears, causing them to become demoralized and liable to mutiny. Sir Samuel complained that his men were forced to lie three in a bed, while some had even more primitive needs which he laid before the High Command.

> "The wants of the soldiers are such that they are not fitting to be put on paper, only I shall beg your Excellency's pardon if I acquaint you with one particular. There were 2 in my Company that had but one payre of Britches betweene them soe that when one was up the other must upon necessity be in his bed."

In a final outburst of indignation he added later: "All the complaints and petitions I have poured out could neither procure me money to buy nor order to take up anything."

As a strict Presbyterian, the Governor made himself responsible for the religious education of his miscellaneous conscripts. In a letter written in October 1644, he mentioned that there were no fewer than seven "able divines" in Newport Pagnell. Two sermons were preached to the troops every Sabbath and one every Thursday, while prayers, with the reading of a Bible chapter, were held every morning before the placing of the guards. No soldier was allowed out of his billet after nine o'clock at night, for in Sir Samuel's opinion the local families were "most Papists or Atheists and extreme averse to the Parliament party".

These attempts to improve the morals of his young men met with set-backs typical of all such worthy efforts in all armies throughout history. An outburst of despair to Cornelius Holland on 18 March, 1645, acknowledged the measure of the Governor's defeat.

> "Impiety is growne to such a height in this towne that myne eyes can no longer indure the sight of it nor myne eares the hearing. Truely Sir they may have a forme of Godlyness

> but I shall pray God to send the power of it into their hearts. If I stay here I must have liberty to free the Towne of them Least God in his wrath deale with us as hee did with Sodom and Gomorrah, for here woemen can be delivered of Children without knowing men (if they belye not themselves) and men and woemen can take one anothers words and lye together and insist it not to be Adultery."

Sir Samuel was hardly more successful in suppressing conventicles; his endeavours to celebrate the victory of Naseby in orthodox fashion were to reveal the measure of his failure. Though individual preaching had also been forbidden when the New Model was formed, the soldiers continued to interrupt sermons, hold public disputes with official preachers, and thrust themselves into pulpits.

Thomas Edwards, the contemporary author of *Gangraena* who complained bitterly of unlicensed preaching by presumptuous soldiers at Oxford, recorded an argument in its favour put to him by a young man "all in scarlet", who met him at the foot of the pulpit in Christ Church:

"Sir, I assure you, if they have not leave to preach they will not fight: and if they fight not, we must all fly the land and be gone."

This anonymous claim represented a genuine demand for freedom of speech. The preaching of the seventeenth century resembled the Hyde Park oratory of the twentieth; it was a favourite method of letting off steam. Thomas Edwards's objection to it partly explains why John Bunyan remained so long unaccepted by writers and scholars. Edwards voiced the jealous disapproval of the evangelist, the inspired preacher, felt by those who depend on learning rather than genius for their contribution to the legacy of their day.

The idea of such a contribution being made by a soldier of the Newport Garrison never occurred to the High Command. In 1645 Colonel Venn at Northampton was lamenting the quality as well as the quantity of the conscripted men.

"Most counties press the Scum of all their Inhabitants . . .

Men taken out of prison, Tinkers, Pedlars, and vagrants that have no dwelling . . . it is no marvel if such run away."

There was one young tinker who still had no wish to escape. Occasional messages from his father at Harrowden reported the birth and death of John's half-brother Charles in May 1645, and the birth of another brother, Thomas, a year or so later.

He also learned that, four weeks after Charles's burial, Oliver Cromwell himself had been in Bedford with 600 horse. Two months later, 300 Royalist horse assembled on the Ouse meadows at Great Barford, whence they plundered the village of Goldington on the outskirts of Bedford. Next day the King in person had entered the town, but Lieutenant-Colonel Richard Cokayn fought a brilliant rearguard action at Bedford Bridge and compelled Charles to move on to Woburn.

Learning to drill, standing on guard, fulfilling police duties in Newport, taking part in manœuvres on field-days, John was rapidly becoming an adult in a town which his Commander had likened to Sodom and Gomorrah. Sometimes small companies of soldiers, chosen by lot, were sent by the Governor on marauding expeditions, or ordered to besiege fortified castles and manors belonging to the Royalists in the neighbourhood.

The New Model Army reduced many such strong points within a few weeks. On one of these occasions, John had another escape from death. In *Grace Abounding* twenty years later, he recorded this chance with thanksgiving and remorse:

> "When I was a Soldier, I, with others, were drawn out to go to such a place to besiege it; but when I was just ready to go, one of the Company desired to go in my room; to which, when I had consented, he took my place; and coming to the Siege, as he stood Sentinel, he was shot into the head with a Musket-bullet, and died."

After unceasing education by the Parliamentary officers, the lawless recruits became a disciplined body which behaved well so long as they had plenty to do. The commonplace vices of swearing, plundering, and drunkenness were so far kept under control that even the die-hard Clarendon later commended the courage and sobriety of Cromwell's Army. During a speech in Parliament on

13 September, 1660, he acknowledged that its members lived "like good husbandmen in the country and good citizens in the city".

But the Civil War was a conflict not only of parties but of creeds; religious observances came even before military and social duties. Essex's *Articles* charged all commanders "to see Almighty God reverently served, and sermons and prayers duly frequented". The national religion remained Presbyterian, but Cromwell found that without his Independents he would have no army. Parliament overlooked the heresy, since he won his battles.

For nearly three years, John Bunyan lived in a religious atmosphere created by the standards of the Old Testament. Whenever possible, battles were preceded by some form of religious service. After Marston Moor, the victors sang a psalm of thanksgiving, and arranged a solemn celebration for the following Sunday.

Fast Days and Days of Humiliation were kept at intervals; on 29 August, 1645, a fast was observed throughout the Army "to seek God for a blessing upon the design against Bristol". It was apparently taken for granted, as always in war, that the other side would not seek to divert the Deity's attention by a similar claim.

The Articles did not mention chaplains but each army was equipped with them, largely chosen from clergy ejected from their livings by Archbishop Laud. Between 1645 and 1647 the Independent minority gradually obtained control of the New Model Army, though the precise shade of theology preached in any particular regiment depended upon the views of its Colonel.

The growth of different creeds and political opinions in the various armies paid by Parliament foreshadowed the military interference in politics which marked the Commonwealth. Some of the Presbyterian officers left and were replaced by Independents; a few stayed and became converts.

This theological ferment inevitably affected the seven or eight thousand young conscripts in the garrison, who like John Bunyan had joined the Army with vague, undeveloped opinions. At that formative period which succeeds adolescence, they unconsciously absorbed with each day's routine both the democratic spirit which the character of the Civil War was developing in the Parliamentary soldiers, and the religious fervour by which the Independent army chaplains atoned for their own scarcity.

These chaplains included the celebrated Hugh Peters, for whom in the future a scaffold waited. Another, William Sedgwick, described by the Rev. Thomas Cox as "a conceited preacher in the Parliament Army", came to be known as "Domesday Sedgwick" owing to his belief that he could foretell the Day of Judgment.

A third was William Dell, the future twenty-first Master of Gonville and Caius. He had taken Holy Orders after leaving Emmanuel College, Cambridge, in 1631, and ten years later had been presented to the Rectory of Yelden, in north Bedfordshire, by the Puritan Oliver St. John, Viscount Bolingbroke.

The enthusiasm which greeted the sermons of these chaplains inspired the contemporary account of a Sunday during the siege of Oxford: "Mr. Dell preached in the forenoon and Mr. Sedgwick in the afternoon; many soldiers were at each sermon, divers of them climbing up the trees to hear, for it was in the orchard before his Excellency's tent." Echoes reached Newport Pagnell of Dell's famous sermon, on "The Building and Glory of the Truly Christian and Spiritual Church", preached "at the Head-quarter at the Leaguer, before Oxford", on 7 June, 1646.

"There hath been," he declared, "a very sensible presence of God with us; we have seen his goings, and observed his very footsteps, for he hath dwelt among us, and marched at the head of us, step by step." A year later he added a Preface to the published version, praising the unity, humility and faith of Cromwell's soldiers and their "spirit of prayer":

> "This the Lord hath poured upon many of them in great measure; not only upon many of the chief commanders, but on very many of the inferior officers and common troopers, some of whom I have by accident heard praying with that faith and familiarity with God, that I have stood wondering at the grace."

William Dell's eloquence was soon rewarded. On 15 June, 1646, he officiated at the marriage of Cromwell's daughter Bridget with General Ireton, and five days later entered Oxford with the Army on the surrender of the city. Carrying the news of this triumph to London, he received fifty pounds from Parliament as his reward. He was to be one of the Puritans who offered his services to Charles Stuart in his last hours, and received from him a message:

> "The King sent him thanks for his love of his soul, hoping that he would be mindful of him in his addresses to God, but as he had made choice of Dr. Juxon he would have no other."

John Bunyan's friendship with this remarkable man was still many years ahead, but in Newport Pagnell he met another "clerk" much nearer his own age.

The Rev. Samuel Austin was removed from the living of St. Peter and St. Paul by Sir Samuel Luke in 1646, but John Gibbs did not replace him until the following year. The delay was comprehensible, for young Gibbs had been baptized only eighteen months before John Bunyan, on 15 June, 1627. Like the younger John he was a native of Bedfordshire, being the son of Samuel Gibbs, a cooper, of St. Mary's parish, Bedford.

After his education at a Bedford school John Gibbs had become a sizar at Sidney Sussex College, Cambridge, where he matriculated in 1645. One day a long flat stone with a plain lead inscription would mark his grave near the outside wall of Newport Pagnell Church behind the Chancel, but now he was a boy of nineteen rejoicing in the premature authority given him by the strange vicissitudes of politics. In 1647 he became involved in a public theological controversy with Richard Carpenter, a native of Newport and so versatile an Independent that he was three times alternatively Protestant and Papist, and died a Catholic.

Carpenter subsequently printed a record of this dispute, entitled *The Anabaptist washt and washt and shrunk in the Washing; or a Scholasticall Discussion of the much agitated Controversie concerning Infant Baptism.* In this work he described young Gibbs as

> "a heady enthusiast, a lean lone Pagnell saint . . . and somewhat vexatious to the protestant ministers in the circle about him, and says that his friends and allies fixed all their eyes upon him, as the Carry castle or Behemoth of the county."

With so congenial a spirit in charge of the Church, John Bunyan found the services less tedious. Their growing friendship, added to the agreeable company of the Newport bookseller,

Matthias Cowley, began at last to fill the emotional void left by his mother and Margaret.

Part of John's off-duty time during his years at the garrison was spent with less scholarly companions than Gibbs and Cowley. Like all towns, Newport had areas in which even a praying and preaching army could shed its puritanism. Here John became familiar with the taverns and brothels which provoked Sir Samuel Luke's complaint to Cornelius Holland.

John was now an adult, who shared with his contemporaries the normal impulses of young male adulthood. The tankard and dice-box no longer offered sufficient outlet to his precocious physical energy; reacting against the severe admonitions of the strait-laced officers, he gave rein to his natural desires "in all manner of vice and ungodliness".

This behaviour increased the habit of swearing which had grown upon him since childhood; it also caused the concealments habitual to soldiers, whose chief crime is to be found out. He did not foresee the heavy burden of guilt which these experiences would lay upon him, nor realize that he was among those who, sowing the wind, inevitably reap the whirlwind. Years later, in *Grace Abounding*, he faced and recorded the depths that he had known.

> "A while after, these terrible dreams did leave me, which I soon also forgot; for my pleasures did quickly cut off the remembrance of them, as if they had never been: Wherefore with more greediness, according to the strength of nature, I did still let loose the reins to my lust, and delighted in all transgression against the Law of God: So that until I came to the state of Marriage, I was the very ringleader of all the Youth that kept me company, in all manner of vice and ungodliness.
>
> Yea, such prevalency had the lusts and fruits of the flesh, in this poor Soul of mine, that had not a miracle of precious Grace prevented, I had not only perished by the stroak of Eternal Justice, but had also laid my self open, even to the stroak of those Laws, which bring some to disgrace, and open shame before the face of the world."

Even at Newport, John knew occasional hours of misgiving and self-disgust. In these he would escape from the too congenial indulgences of his full-blooded youth to the willow-shaded bank above the meeting place of the Ouse and the Lovat, where the two rivers encircled the fortified mound known as "the battery".

This green hump of earth beyond the north end of the churchyard marked the spot where the Paganells, and their successors the de Somerys, had owned a castle before the reign of King John. From time immemorial, the field on the opposite bank of the Lovat had been known as Castle Mead.

Beyond the meeting of the rivers two flat swampy meadows, known as Port Field and Bury Field, stretched north to the low ridge of Sherington Hill. In late autumn its chequer-work of green pastures and ochre-shaded corn-stubble climbed to the sky-line crowned with the familiar elms.

Across the meadows deep trenches had been dug and filled from the two rivers. Between the older reed-fringed streamlets, willows and poplars cast afternoon shadows over the fields. A tangle of convolvulus clung to the roadside hedges; even in November the pale green of hops and deep crimson of hawthorn berries lent patches of vivid colour to the landscape. Occasionally a couple of magpies bustled in a black-and-white flurry across the sodden grass.

Sitting on the bank above the rivers, half fascinated and half tormented by tumultuous reflections, John remained, as always, indifferent to external surroundings when preoccupied by the turmoil within. Keen angler though he was, he did not even notice the circles made on the water by the fish springing from the Ouse, here closer to its source and narrower than at Bedford but as slow and reedy as he had always known it. Could he have formulated his remorseful speculations, he might have cried in the words of Augustine:

"And what was it that I delighted in, but to love and be loved? but I kept not the measure of love, soul to soul, friendship's bright boundary: but out of the muddy concupiscence of the flesh, and the bubblings of youth, mists fumed up which beclouded and overcast my heart."

Sometimes, when his thoughts threatened to become intolerable, John took from his coat pocket two small octavo volumes, bound in sheepskin and sewn with black cord. Though he knew their contents by heart, he tried by re-reading them to divert his mind.

These little books, *The Souldiers' Pocket Bible* and *The Souldiers' Catechism*, had been designed by their compilers to help the overworked official chaplains. Many Puritans who fought against Charles I struggled with conscientious scruples which had to be soothed and convinced; this was the work of the *Catechism*, compiled by Robert Ram, Minister of Spalding.

It answered in a fashion satisfactory to the Parliamentary leaders such awkward questions as "Is it lawfull for Christians to be souldiers?" and "Is it not against the King that you fight in this Cause?" (Answer: "No surely . . . Wee take up armes against the enemies of Jesus Christ, who in His Majesties name make warre against the Church and People of God.")

The *Souldiers' Bible*, bearing the "imprimatur" of Edmund Calamy, the eminent non-juror, similarly consisted of appropriate and reassuring texts arranged under various headings:

"A Souldier must not doe wickedly.

"A Souldier must be valiant for Gods Cause.

"A Souldier must love his enemies as they are his enemies, and hate them as they are gods enemies."

Those years 1640 to 1660 were the golden age of pamphleteers, who provided John and his few literate companions with alternative reading in the form of political tracts, black-letter ballads, and the allegorical trials which were a popular polemical device used by propagandists on both sides. When the Presbyterians in the Parliamentary party endeavoured, like Sir Samuel Luke, to suppress the individualistic worship of the sectaries, a bold Independent published *The Trial of Mr. Persecution*, and an occasional copy found its way to Newport.

John read with far greater interest the sensational crime-recording broadsheets which were sometimes pasted on the walls of the town, and the newsbooks and popular chap-books, with crude woodcuts, sold by "flying stationers". These wares, as usual, caused religious instruction to become "grievous" to him; they left him with little inclination to study the theological works commended by the garrison chaplains, Captain Paul Hobson and the Presbyterian divine, Thomas Ford.

Neither he nor they suspected that, years afterwards, the ballads, fables, trials, and theological volumes would fuse through the power of John's imagination into an allegory which would make his name the only one from all the garrison to win the affection of mankind.

In Matthias Cowley's shop, famous contemporary books sometimes appeared with which John never dreamed that his own work would be compared. One, published in 1644, was the *Areopagitica* of John Milton, whose prophetic phrases carried his demand for uncensored printing to its logical conclusions. In his pages the plea for toleration became a general argument for freedom, in which freedom of speech was the most precious of civil rights. "Give me the liberty to know, to utter, and to argue freely according to conscience, above all liberties."

John Bunyan did not then spend his leisure in studying his learned older contemporary, but such writings contributed to the enormous vitality which inspired him and his companions. In that age of spiritual ferment, it seemed that all things were being revalued, and changed, and made new. The young soldiers would have regarded with bewildered astonishment any instructor who explained to them that they were in the Army in order to help decide where sovereignty lay in the British Constitution, but they responded instinctively to the revolutionary atmosphere which encompassed them in that seed-time of a new social and political order.

Even the idea that it was not intrinsically wrong to oppose a King or a Government began to seem less fantastic. Subconsciously they were adapting themselves to the stature of the cause in whose name their world was being remade, though the freedom of discussion and speculation in the Parliamentary Army produced beliefs of unlimited diversity and wild extravagance.

In 1649, the rising of the Levellers—the seventeenth-century "Left"—sprang from a purely political and social movement, but extreme views in politics and religion were then seldom separated. There were, however, opinions which no soldier could publicly maintain without risking expulsion from the Army, and after the Levellers had been suppressed, some of the more extravagant sectaries were sent away.

Among such fanatics, and others known as Fifth Monarchy

men who dreamed of the establishment of a theocratic republic in seventeenth-century England, the later Protectorate seemed a direct challenge to all their principles. Cromwell, they said, "had taken the Crown from the head of Christ and put it on his own". But even these visionaries, with whom John Bunyan was later to disclaim association, did not exhaust the list of those who would today be described as "the lunatic fringe".

One captain, Francis Freeman, whom Colonel John Okey of Bedfordshire drove out of his regiment because he disliked his strange theological views, was a mystic with an incomprehensible though blissful creed of his own. Neither Presbyterian, Independent, Anabaptist nor Seeker, the saintly captain endeavoured to explain his opinions to his exasperated superior by insisting that "there is nothing but mirth in them, there is a continual singing of birds in them, chirping sweetly, in a sweet harmony of soul-ravishing, delightful music".

We have no evidence that John Bunyan came into contact with Francis Freeman at Newport Pagnell, but in such an army even Freeman's dulcet mysticism was not unique. Similar "Saints'" helped to create the climate of speculative fervour which led to spiritual conflicts of the kind described in *Grace Abounding*. For one such set of experiences put down on paper, others less conscious and coherent existed among the semi-articulate, and contributed to the atmosphere of religious excitement.

Writers who state that John Bunyan was not influenced by his service in the Civil War can only have forgotten the formative years of their own youth, or declined to enter, even in imagination, into its turmoils, indulgences, reticences, resentments, loves, hopes and despairs.

CHAPTER IV

A SOLDIER GOES HOME

"As for my own natural life, for the time that I was without God in the world, it was, indeed, according to the course of this world, and the spirit that now worketh in the children of disobedience."

JOHN BUNYAN: *Grace Abounding*.

THE surrender of Leicester to the Royalists on 1 June, 1645, caused a minor panic at Newport Pagnell.

Sir Thomas Fairfax, raising the siege of Oxford and marching by way of Marsh Gibbon, Great Brickhill and Newport, reached Sherington, between Newport and Olney, six days later.

Here he was joined by Cromwell himself, but Sir Samuel Luke, giving want of accommodation as his excuse, did not prepare a feast for the General. He limited his hospitality to showing Oliver round the works of the garrison, giving him a "peale of ordnance", and providing him and his followers with wine.

The overwhelming Roundhead victory at Naseby on Saturday, 14 June, exorcized the fears of the garrison, and Sir Samuel ordered a public thanksgiving to be celebrated at Newport the following day. To him the parish church, purified of all ornaments and "superstitions", was still the proper official meeting-place for religious exercises. But when the time came he found many places vacant, and on inquiry discovered that Captains Hobson and Beaumont, Independent officers in Fairfax's Army who had "passes" for London, were staying in Newport on their way. Instead of attending the official thanksgiving they had delivered, as Hobson subsequently explained, "a treatise to some friends in a quiet and peaceable manner".

This private conventicle, which had drawn a crowd of men and women to the nearby village of Lathbury, so infuriated the Governor that he had the two captains arrested under a Parliamentary Ordinance for the apprehension of stragglers. He sent them back to Fairfax with an irate letter, referring to the unfortunate outcome of a recent engagement, which clearly showed the growing tension between the Presbyterian and Independent sections of Cromwell's Army.

> "For you to draw my parishioners away and so leave the church empty I could no longer endure. If they return back again to me I shall send them up to your Assembly, and then I hope you will take order that such Anabaptistical companions trouble us no more. I hear the praying and preaching regiments, as they term you, trusted more to earth than to heaven for their heels were their chiefest refuge . . . most of you found four legs under you."

Not unnaturally Fairfax resented the addition of insult to the initial injury of arresting his officers, whom he had no wish to lose in the midst of a campaign. He compelled Sir Samuel to release them from arrest at once, and the ensign and provost-marshal who had apprehended them were subsequently cashiered.

On 26 June Sir Samuel Luke's governorship ended owing to the recent passage of the Self-Denying Ordinance, by which Members of either House undertook to resign all military commands. He therefore returned to London to attend to his duties as Member for Bedford. Whatever might happen to the ill-paid troops, he managed to collect successfully his own arrears of pay, and in January 1647 became the triumphant owner of £4482 13*s*. 6*d*. due to him as Colonel of a troop of horse and Governor of the Newport Garrison. He continued to represent Bedford for some years, being nominated as a Member of the Little Parliament in 1653, but he retired before the Restoration and died at Cople in 1670.

John Bunyan and his fellow foot-soldiers found themselves with a new Governor, Captain Charles D'Oyley, appointed on Fairfax's recommendation. By the end of that summer the garrison had been reduced to 800 foot and 120 horse.

During the autumn and winter of 1645–6, discipline became very lax; John and the rest of the troops had nothing to do, and the majority amused themselves by lawless exploits. Throughout 1646 the King's cause declined so rapidly that on 6 August an

Ordinance of "the Lords and Commons Assembled in Parliament" laid down that

> "the severall garrisons of Newport Pagnell, Cambridge, Huntingdon, and Bedford be forthwith sleighted and demolished . . . and . . . all the officers and Souldiers both Horse and Foot . . . be forth with entertained and imployed for the service of Ireland . . . and it is further ordered that such common Souldiers as shall refuse to go for Ireland shall be forthwith disbanded."

The purpose of this proposed expedition was "the reliefe of the Protestants". On 16 October the Committee of both Houses of Parliament for Irish Affairs asked the House of Commons to order the army at Newport to be sent to Chester. John Bunyan, still in no hurry to return to Elstow, volunteered for Ireland; he was therefore put into Colonel Robert Hammond's regiment under one of his captains, Charles O'Hara.

O'Hara's company was not part of the Newport garrison; he had been a captain in Hammond's foot regiment since 1645. This regiment, which was to be sent in advance of the rest to secure Dublin, marched to Chester. John went with it and, across the estuary of the Dee, saw mountains more sheer and grim than he had dreamed of in his Bedfordshire boyhood.

Colonel Hammond's regiment never actually crossed the sea; in April 1647, it returned to Army Headquarters. Here the larger section refused to serve in Ireland, but a minority of six officers and 400 men was willing to go. As one of the minority John Bunyan remained with his Company Commander, marched under O'Hara to Newport Pagnell, and thus appeared in the Muster Roll of O'Hara's Company on 17 June.

The journey to Ireland was eventually cancelled, and John, disbanded late in July, found himself a tinker once more.

He arrived home just after Bedford had been, for one week, the headquarters of Cromwell's Army, packed tight with the 20,000 men whom Fairfax had brought from Reading. Cromwell, Fairfax and Ireton paced the Bedford streets during that period in which they were negotiating with the King, who went to Woburn after the Scots surrendered him to Parliament.

THE MEETING PLACE OF THE RIVERS OUSE AND LOVAT AT NEWPORT PAGNELL

Bunyan served in the garrison here for three years during the Civil War.

NEWPORT PAGNELL CHURCH AND CHURCH PASSAGE

In the seventeenth century this by-way was known as Church Lane.

The Parliamentary party had now finally split into two sections, the Presbyterians aiming at uniformity of worship, and the Army Independents who stood for toleration and freedom of conscience. In the hope of restoring the King to the throne with strictly limited powers, both sides were endeavouring to come to terms with Charles, who was himself trying to play the one off against the other.

When nearly two months of negotiation had produced no results, the Army occupied London on 1 August and drove the Presbyterian leaders into exile. The irritation of the Army with the Long Parliament was no new emotion, for the Parliamentary leaders, supported by the City mob, had foolishly and ungratefully begun to persecute their Independent allies. They had initiated Bills imposing prison or death on Baptists, Unitarians, and "free-thinking heretics", in a last-moment attempt to conciliate the King and his more moderate supporters.

After the death of Hampden and Pym, the Commons had lacked constructive statesmen who understood that if a peace settlement is to last, life must be made tolerable by the conquerors for their defeated enemies, whether they be South Africans, Germans, or British Royalists. Had the trials of William Laud and Charles I been better than a travesty of justice, had Anglican clergymen been less summarily expelled from their livings and the fines for "delinquency" imposed on Cavalier estates been smaller, the Puritans would have suffered less severely from reaction at the Restoration.

John Bunyan would then, perhaps, have been spared the twelve years' imprisonment by which he and his fellow victims expiated the sins of intolerance for which others had been responsible.

Before the negotiations with the King began, Fairfax and the Army Council had drawn up their scheme for the settlement of the Kingdom in "The Heads of the Proposals", which they now tendered to the Parliamentary Commissioners. Though Clarendon characteristically described this plan as "full of fantastic giddiness", it was a wise and potentially permanent arrangement which aimed at restricting the authority of both King and Parliament. Needless to say, it was for this reason anathema to both.

Throughout that autumn the Army remained the centre of political ferment. The agents called "Agitators", appointed by the troops to represent their interests, were in perpetual and explosive contact with John Lilburne and other leaders of the Levellers. One of them, Colonel Rainborough, put into famous words the principle that inspired them.

> "The poorest he that is in England hath a life to live as the greatest he . . . Everyman that is to live under a Government ought first by his own consent to put himself under that Government."

Not only democrats but opponents of force, these Levellers or "Diggers" were ideological first-cousins to the Quakers. A contemporary song, "Stand Up Now, Diggers All!", probably written by Gerald Winstanley, enlarged upon the possibility of countering the reactionary influence of gentry and clergy by the mystical power of non-violence.

> To conquer them by love, come in now, come in now,
> To conquer them by love, come in now
> To conquer them by love, as it does you behove,
> For He is King above; no power is like to love.
> Glory here, Diggers all.

To John Bunyan, working again at his trade in Elstow, these exhausting political agitations seemed already far away. Active politics never attracted him, and he was now concerned with the possibility of setting up a home of his own.

The bitter disapproval roused in him by his father's prompt third marriage had been mitigated by three years of military moral standards, and he found that he and Thomas could sometimes discuss impersonal topics while working over their forge. But his stepmother and her young children had made the cottage a different place from the home in which he and Margaret had grown up together, and he was anxious to leave it.

Increasingly his mind was haunted by thoughts of Mary, the gentle, fragile girl whom he had met as a soldier.

Before he could marry and start business on his own, it was necessary to make or collect his own set of the tools required for his trade. He needed a hammer, a pair of pliers, snippers for cutting tin, a soldering iron, and a roundhead for shaping the lids of kettles and saucepans. More costly than these smaller tools would be a T iron, or anvil, and John decided that, after the day's work was over, he would forge this heavy instrument himself with the help of a moulder whom he knew in Bedford.

Gradually the roughly-hewn anvil took shape; he added a spear-point to hold it firm in a metal or wooden base. When the tool was finished, it resembled an inverted obelisk and weighed sixty pounds. To distinguish it from his father's equipment he carved his name on it—"J. BVNYAN"—and turning it over added the date "1647" and the word "H ELSTOWE".

Owing to the tough metal from which it was made, this anvil had a high survival value. It has in fact survived, though not without adventures.

In 1905 William Rowlett of St. Neots, Huntingdon, who collected curios and sold them to museums, was searching through a heap of old iron in Carters' Marine Store in St. Neots' High Street, when he came across an object which he thought bore an inscription. He purchased the object, cleaned it, and rubbed the letters with oil until they became legible. Considerably excited, he asked a St. Neots business man, John Beagarie, to inspect his purchase, which was found to be a "stake" or brazier's anvil.

Mr. Beagarie then endeavoured to trace the history of the tool. He found that it had been sent to the Marine Store with other old iron by a man named Chasty, who had purchased it in 1865 from his employer, an ironmonger called Fisher. It had remained in his possession for forty years until some alterations in his premises involved the clearing out of his stock of old iron.

In the early part of the nineteenth century Mr. Fisher's business had been carried on by John Carrington, a member of a Biggleswade family, who described himself in a *Cambridge Chronicle* advertisement in 1810 as a "Manufacturer of Braziery and Tin Ware". He had been in St. Neots for some time when he purchased the ironmonger's business from a man called Gurry. It was next owned by George Bower, and then by his successor, Mr. Lanning, who sold it to Mr. Fisher. The business had thus a history of more than a century.

This story, related in the *Bedfordshire Times* for 26 December, 1924, has perhaps a prelude in another published by *The Cambridge Press and News* for 10 February, 1933.

At that time a collection of tinker's tools came into the possession of a man named Evans, who explained to his local newspaper the tradition which identified them with John Bunyan.

> "Bunyan, who was a rogue and a great drinker in his youth, got into debt with an inn-keeper in Elstow, and gave the tools to the inn-keeper to pay the debt. My great-grandfather, who was a tinker, as was his father before him, bought the tools from the landlord. Both my grandfather and father were tinkers, and the tools were handed down from father to son, having been in the family over a hundred years."

If there is any truth in this tale, which seems to be confirmed by the story of the tavern-frequenting apprentice in *The Life and Death of Mr. Badman,* the inn-keeper probably disposed of the anvil—by far the most valuable tool—long before his successor at the Elstow tavern sold the other tools to Mr. Evans's great-grandfather. It may have passed from one owner to another until eventually it arrived at Mr. Gurry's store in St. Neots.

The signature has been compared with other John Bunyan signatures known to be genuine; the "V" in Bunyan agrees with the same letter in John's copy of Foxe's *Book of Martyrs*. On the reverse side the "H" in "HELSTOWE" recalls the Saxon form "Helenstowe". Experts who have examined the anvil have testified to its seventeenth-century workmanship.

A few years ago it was purchased by the late Sir Leicester Harmsworth and presented to Bunyan Meeting in Mill Street, Bedford, where it can now be seen.

Absorbed in his domestic preoccupations and the problem of finding a cottage which a twenty-year-old tinker could afford, John took little part in the village talk about the revolutionary scheme of settlement, drawn up by the democratic party leaders, known as "The Agreement of the People".

It was worth discussing, for it went to the length of demanding manhood suffrage, equal electoral divisions, biennial Parliaments and, by implication, the abolition of the monarchy and the House of Lords. But the virtual mutiny which produced it was soon quelled by Cromwell and Ireton, who restored discipline and thus extinguished a premature attempt to establish representative government in the Army.

John hardly realized the outbreak of the Second Civil War, which continued until August 1648, and finally crystallized the Army's determination to put Charles to death for stirring up civil strife. Still less was he aware that the continent of Europe was moving in an opposite direction to the road on which the rulers of England had set their venturesome feet.

A year after John went back to Elstow, the Treaty of Westphalia, signed at Münster Town Hall on 24 October, 1648, officially ended the Thirty Years' War. For some time the interminable strife had been petering out, owing to the number of the participants and the confusion of their aims. Now at last the fighting was over, but Europe had still to reckon with its results.

In Germany the depths of misery and depopulation had reached a nadir never to be exceeded until three more centuries of progress had passed over Europe. Compared with the brutal armies of Tilly and Wallenstein, the soldiers on both sides in England's Civil War appear as a collection of archangels.

England might still be burning witches at home and making slaves of the coloured peoples abroad, but in the perspective of history she ranks as a humanitarian country. The tortures inflicted on Guy Fawkes in 1605 had been declared illegal twenty years later, and two heretics burned in the reign of James I for denying the doctrine of the Trinity were the last martyrs to suffer death at the stake for their convictions.

Central Europe was not so fortunate. The population of Augsburg had fallen from 80,000 to 16,000; hundreds of villages were annihilated; wolves roamed Saxony, and the suffering people, barbarized by privation, had become the victims of superstition and terror.

"It was a period when misfortune meted crushing measure," Wilhelm Raabe has written in his story, *Elsa of the Fir*; "when no terror and no pain which could strike mortal man were so great, that they were not likely to be out-horrored by calamity yet more monstrous".

The thin fabric of civilization had proved too fragile to sustain three decades of relentless war. With exhausted Germany unable to contribute to European culture for a century and a half, the way was left open for the long domination of Louis XIV. He had come to the throne in 1643, when internal strife stained England's green fields with blood. By his own wars of aggression he was destined to keep Europe in turmoil for half a century, and to build up the very type of absolutism successfully denied to Charles I by Parliament, by the Army, and by the resistance of Recusants and Independents.

For the forty years of life still before him, John Bunyan as one of them would struggle against hostility and persecution to solve the religious problem of his century: How were free churches to exist beside a State church without surrender of principle or violation of conscience by the supporters of both?

"Why else," Milton had asked in his *Areopagitica*, "was this Nation chosen before any other, that out of her, as out of Sion, should be proclaimed and sounded forth the first tidings and trumpet of Reformation to all Europe? . . . God is decreeing to begin some new and great period in His Church, even to the reforming of Reformation itself: what does He then but reveal Himself to His Servants, and as His manner is, first to His Englishmen?"

Those Englishmen, led by a group of high-minded extremists, were now preparing to execute their King. On 6 and 7 December, 1648, the Army, by means of "Pride's Purge", expelled the Presbyterian M.P.s who favoured reconciliation between Parliament and King. With them went Sir Samuel Luke, John Bunyan's old Commander.

Cromwell himself, the military saint guided by "the dark lantern of the spirit", fearlessly accepted the burden of a deed which outraged both Royalists and Presbyterians, and postponed for forty years the setting up of a democratic constitution supported by all the people.

The King's execution extinguished any immediate hope of such a settlement, and yet, perhaps, made its coming more certain by violently setting men free from their superstitious reverence for "the Lord's Anointed". Whether England's true interests were served or retarded by the illegal sacrifice of Charles I is a question which historians will argue for ever.

When Charles, under protest, surrendered his life, the groan of the huge multitude which gazed on his bleeding head carried even to Elstow the shock of horror and fear. A strange story began to circulate among the people of Bedfordshire. In whispers they related how, a few weeks earlier, the River Ouse had suddenly stood still, "so that Men walked on foot in the very Depth of the Chanel . . . while the Waters upward swelled to a great height".

It was a poet usually accounted a Puritan, Andrew Marvell, who found words to describe the dignity with which Charles redeemed in death his blind and self-interested life:

He nothing common did or mean
Upon that memorable scene,
    But with his keener eye
    The axe's edge did try;

Nor called the gods, with vulgar spite,
To vindicate his helpless right;
    But bow'd his comely head
    Down, as upon a bed.

And, as strangely, it was a Royalist poet and favourite, James Shirley, last of the Elizabethan dramatists, who sadly recorded the deeper significance of that "equality" demanded by Lilburne and the Levellers:

There is no armour against Fate;
Death lays his icy hand on kings:
    Sceptre and Crown
    Must tumble down,
And in the dust be equal made
With the poor crookéd scythe and spade.

CHAPTER V

CONVERSION OF A TINKER

"Suddainly this conclusion was fastned on my spirit . . . That I had been a great and grievous sinner, and that it was now too late for me to look after Heaven; for Christ would not forgive me, nor pardon my transgressions."

JOHN BUNYAN: *Grace Abounding.*

WHEN John Bunyan became a householder with a garden of his own, he found "the poor crooked scythe and spade" almost as useful as his hammer and anvil.

During the period between demobilization and marriage, he seemed to his friends to be a strong, cheerful young man of enormous energy, with no problem more complex than that of earning a living to shadow his prospect of happiness.

For a time he gave himself up, without misgivings, to the pursuits which attracted his natural high spirits. Regularly he joined in the various sports—wrestling, jumping, pitching the bar, ninepins, and dancing—which were held on Elstow Green. Sometimes on holidays he took part in the rude masques and allegorical processions organized by the village.

The thoughts and practices of religion were still tedious to him: "I could neither endure it myself, nor that any other should." He did not guess in those carefree days how soon he was to condemn himself, in an agony of remorse, for his "sad and sinful state".

John was now twenty; apart from the three years at Newport Pagnell he had been working with his father ever since he was ten. He could therefore claim the seven years' apprenticeship without which, under the Statute of Apprentices, he was not permitted to set up as a craftsman on his own account.

He had been successful in finding a small cottage suited to his means, for Elstow was a village of modest householders. Twenty years later, in 1670, its records showed that it had only sixty-one houses, eight with three hearths, eighteen with two, and twenty-five with one. The last group of householders still included Thomas Bunyan at the Harrowden end of the parish.

Neither then nor at any later period could John afford a dwelling with more than one hearth. The cottage of his choice stood at the entrance to the village on the right-hand side of the main road from Bedford; it was cheaply built of timber and pebble stucco, with a lean-to workshop against its southern gable. A small garden, its one apple-tree growing amid a wild tangle of poppies and marigolds, surrounded the workshop.

From the long grass and weeds which bordered the muddy road, John could step straight down into a low room with a large kitchen fire. Across the ceiling a huge beam supported the one bedroom. Above this was the gabled roof, with its tall chimney and tiny dormer windows surrounded by thatch. Conveniently opposite the unobtrusive entrance, a well fringed with hart's tongue fern would provide John and his future wife with water. At the end of the village street, which was shaded by substantial trees, the grey tower of Elstow Church stood guardian.

Having now a home and the tools of his trade, John decided to marry Mary without the further delay required by the collection of suitable furniture. He recorded frankly that "this woman and I . . . came together as poor as poor might be (not having so much house-hold-stuff as a dish or spoon betwixt us both)". But this young, impatient venture into matrimony proved more successful than many marriages prepared with greater prudence and calculation, for John's wife was gentle, affectionate, and religious.

Her father, now dead, had been "counted godly", and Mary, though hardly more than a child, was tactful. Unobtrusively she upheld parental standards instead of reproving her robust and ebullient husband for behaving like an undisciplined adolescent.

Mary's father had left her two devotional books, which represented the only dowry that she brought to John. One, *The Plain Man's Pathway to Heaven,* a small square-shaped book bound in sepia-coloured vellum, had been published in 1601 by Arthur Dent, "Preacher of the Word of God" at Shoebury in Essex. In his "Epistle to the Reader" he described this work, which had reached its twenty-fourth edition by 1637, as "my little Sermon of Repentance", and assured his readers that "this book medleth not at all with any controversies in the Church, or anything in the

State Ecclesiasticall, but onely entreth into a controversie with Sathan and sin".

The "Little Sermon" amounted to 423 pages of substantial discourse, "set forth Dialogue-wise for the better understanding of the simple". The simple were not, however, let down too lightly, for the dialogue, ranging widely over such topics as original sin, worldly corruption, Salvation and Damnation, was carried on between four "Interlocutors"—Theologus, a Divine; Philagathus, an Honest Man; Asunetus, an Ignorant Man; and Antilegon, a Caviller.

Thirty years afterwards, when John was writing *The Life and Death of Mr. Badman*, the influence of this technique upon his subject and style showed how much more deeply it had impressed him than he realized at the time.

The second book which John and Mary sometimes read together, *The Practice of Piety*, had become as popular with devout readers as the first. Published in 1612 by Lewis Bayly, later Bishop of Bangor, it was another small, thick book, in gold-embossed brown leather, written for the purpose of "directing a Christian how to walke, that hee may please God". Two hundred and fifty-four pages of involved "Meditations" followed, modestly described by their author as "A plaine Description of the Essence and Attributes of God, out of the holy Scripture".

When John studied this book alone, he found himself drawn, by a morbid fascination which defied analysis, to the gruesome "Meditations of the misery of a man not reconciled to God in Christ when he faces death":

> "O what a ghastly sight it is to see him then in his bed, when death hath given him his mortall wound! what a cold sweat over-runs all his body! what a trembling possesseth all his members! the head shooteth, the face waxeth pale, the nose blacke, the nether jaw-bone hangeth down, the eye-strings break, the tongue faltreth, the breath shortneth, and smelleth earthly, the throat ratleth, and at every gasp the heart-strings are ready to break asunder."

This grim picture of ungodly dissolution was contrasted with "the blessed estate of a regenerate man in his death", but John always turned with relief from both examples of realism to the final prayer:

> "Keep me for ever, O my Saviour, from the torments of hell, and tyrannie of the Devil. And when I am to depart this life, send thy holy Angels to carry me, as they did the soule of Lazarus, into thy Kingdome."

At twenty the hour of departure seems comfortably distant, and though the gloomier "Meditations" aroused in John some qualms of uneasy remorse, he felt pleased with himself because both books "did beget within me some desires to Religion". He was still far from the tempestuous anguish which his peculiar form of conversion was to involve, but the conjugal readings stirred in him an impulse towards external conformity. He began to read the Old Testament, and to go twice a day to Elstow Church.

The Vicar of Elstow was then Christopher Hall, who had succeeded John Kellie in 1639, and was to hold the living undisturbed by the resounding political and ecclesiastical revolutions which raged between 1640 and 1666. Appointed by Archbishop Laud, he managed throughout the Commonwealth to maintain the practices described by John as "the High Place, Priest, Clerk, Vestments, Service, and what else", and be ready to jump on the band-waggon at the Restoration. Unless he was a man of exceptional charm, he must have possessed in unusual measure those gymnastic qualities ascribed by John to Mr. Facing-both-Ways.

But the newly-married tinker, his zealous nature expanding with the consciousness of virtue, was not prepared to be over-critical. Sometimes his fellow-worshippers did divert his attention from the preacher; in this period of assiduous church-going he first realized those shortcomings of congregations, not confined to the seventeenth century, which in 1674 he was to recall with asperity in his *Treatise of the Fear of God*:

> "Some come into the worship of God to sleep there; some come thither to meet with their chapmen, and get into fellowship with their vain companions. Some come thither to feed their lustful and adulterous eyes with the flattering beauty of their fellow-sinners."

These fleshly failings did not diminish John's pleasure in the pealing bells, the impressive Radclyff and Hillersdon memorials, the gleaming Madonna-like faces of the Abbesses perpetuated in brass above their tombs, and the warriors' helmets and coats of mail which always recalled his years as a soldier. His enthusiastic reverence extended even to the "superstitions" practised in the Church. As for the priest he was a veritable Elijah, wholly worthy of love and reverence from a young disciple.

One Sunday the compass-boxing Vicar, who though an Anglican never overlooked the militant Puritanism of his new masters, elected to preach a sermon against Sunday sports. John, sitting beside Mary on his unvarnished bench near the high oak pulpit with carven panels, felt a cold conviction of guilt creeping over his spirit.

Sports of all kinds, especially on the Sabbath, were still his great delight. Robert Southey, the Bristol-born man of letters, commented two centuries later that it was "remarkable to find a married man engaged in games which are now only played by boys". John, like other persons of genius, was young for his years, but the games beloved of rural areas are preserved as much by age as by youth.

He went home conscience-stricken and crestfallen, believing with youthful egotism that the Vicar had preached this sermon "on purpose to show me my evil-doing". Mary, distressed by his evident unhappiness, used all her skill in cooking their Sunday dinner, and John, like other penitents of a similar age, soon found that the satisfaction of his healthy appetite took the edge off his remorse. Immensely relieved to find how readily it could be conquered, "he shook the Sermon" out of his mind, and returned with increased zest to the village green.

Undeterred by the incongruous symbolism of the grey stone cross, he joined his noisy comrades in a game of "cat". This game is still played in Bedfordshire. The player strikes a small piece of wood into the air from a hole in the ground; as it rises, he hits it again as far as he can.

On this Sunday afternoon, John struck his "cat" out of the hole. He was about to give it a second blow, when suddenly he thought that he heard a Voice. Its severe accents seemed to address him personally.

"Wilt thou leave thy sins and go to Heaven; or have thy sins, and go to Hell?"

All John's physical strength ebbed away; he let the tapered stick fall to the ground and looked fearfully at the sky. And there he seemed to see the face of Jesus gazing down upon him, "as being very hotly displeased with me, and as if he did severely threaten me with some grievous punishment for these and other my ungodly practices".

Since John's knowledge of the world had been confined to Bedfordshire and Newport Pagnell, he could hardly have been expected to realize how far he was a victim of contemporary theology. The God of the Puritan chaplains had been the stern Jehovah of the Old Testament, their Devil a real and evil spirit who tempted men to wickedness by direct intervention.

At times strange resemblances appeared between the behaviour of their God and the habits of their Satan. Though the purposes of this menacing couple were different, they both seemed to be anxious, like malevolent policemen, to catch human beings napping and trip them up. The Jesus of Sir Samuel Luke would never have told the woman taken in adultery to go and sin no more; he would have hauled her before the magistrates and handed her over to the ecclesiastical authorities.

On Elstow Green John Bunyan, overwhelmed by a sense of sin, stood helpless and aghast before his terrible Judge. His thoughts went back to the shameful hours in Newport Pagnell; his conscience insisted that he had been too great a sinner for any hope of pardon. His mind was still captive, his spirit not yet free. Only after great suffering would the meaning of the Cross come to him with its message of love and forgiveness, and cause his burden, like Christian's, to fall from his shoulders.

"If my case be thus," he thought in despair, "my state is surely miserable; miserable if I leave my sins, and but miserable if I follow them. I can but be damned; and if it must be so, I had as good be damned for many sins, as be damned for few."

His companions, he noticed, were looking at him curiously, but he could not explain to them the sudden trance into which he had fallen. He returned desperately to his game, and, as he played, his distraught mind seemed to make itself up. His hope of Heaven, he believed, was gone, so he would take his fill of sin; he would satisfy his earthly desires lest he die before he had fully sampled the sweetness of indulgence.

So, for a month, he continued "in sin with great greediness of mind", but now the vengeful demon of remorse pursued him more relentlessly than ever. One day, as he stood before a neighbour's shop-window, "belching out oaths like the madman that Solomon speaks of", the woman owner of the shop, though a notorious loose-liver, came out and reproved him.

"Verily, John," she chided, "you're the ungodliest fellow for swearing that ever I heard in all my life! This way you'll be able to spoil all the youth in the whole town, if they come but in your company."

He hung his head and remained silent; sinner as she was, he knew that she spoke the truth of him before the God of Heaven. If only, he thought, suddenly losing his relish for tasting sin to the full, I could be a little child again and learn to speak without all these oaths, for I shall never break myself of the habit!

Yet somehow he found, though he went on taking part in village games, that his boastful swearing gradually ceased. Consciously he felt no closer to his Master, but an intuition deeper than reason told him that his heedless, exuberant life would never again be the same. Unaware as he still was of its true significance, the Voice that he heard on the village green had heralded the moment of spiritual birth.

Like that other Voice heard by Saul on the road to Damascus, it called upon him to leave the old careless, lascivious ways. It summoned him to a hard life of self-discipline and service, where persecution and imprisonment were privileges, and death was the great reward.

At first John thought that the necessary response to his experience was merely an increase of outward reformation. He cultivated the company of a poor man who professed to be religious and discoursed pleasantly of the Scriptures; he studied the historical books of the Bible, and did his best to keep the Commandments. His success was measured by the astonishment of the neighbours, who "did marvel much to see such a great and famous alteration in my life and manners".

During this period of external conformity, their first child, a daughter, was born to Mary and John. On 20 July, 1650, the Vicar christened her "Mary" also. Afterwards John could never remember exactly when he and his wife finally accepted the fact that she was blind. It had first been a shocking suspicion, then a nightmare dread, and at last a certainty; a certainty that made him ask himself in anguish whether the sins of the reprobate father had been visited by divine vengeance upon the innocent child.

"Had I then died," he subsequently reflected, "my state had been most fearful. I was nothing but a poor painted hypocrite, yet I loved to be talked of, as one that was truly godly!"

Before his vision on the village green John had enjoyed ringing the bells of Elstow steeple, where he had once imagined the Devil sitting aloft to shoot arrows at passers-by. Now, because he had admired his own prowess as a bell-ringer, he felt that bell-ringing, like dancing, was one of the vanities unsuited to a religious man that the Lord Jesus had summoned him to abandon.

It was so hard to give up ringing the bells that, even though he forced himself to relinquish them, his longing for the vigorous exercise and cheerful chimes impelled him to stand inside the tower and watch the ringers at work. Immediately some inner revulsion seemed to prompt a conscience-stricken inquiry: "How if one of the bells should fall?"

To protect himself from this imaginary accident he took refuge under a large beam, only to picture the bell rebounding from the wall and killing him. He then tried standing outside the belfry door, thinking that if the bell should come down, he would no longer be near it. But now a new and worse dread came into his mind. How if the steeple itself should fall, burying him beneath it? The thought recurred until, shaken with fear, he fled in terror from the tower altogether, and hurried back to his cottage.

Only when, in writing *The Pilgrim's Progress*, he made all the bells of the Celestial City ring to welcome Christian and Hopeful, was this curious conflict resolved. Some nostalgic stanzas in his *Book for Boys and Girls*, composed when he was nearly sixty, revealed his lifelong hankering after a favourite pastime so strangely sacrificed.

Bells have wide mouths and tongues, but are too weak,
Have they not help, to sing, or talk, or speak,
But if you move them they will mak't appear
By speaking they'll make all the Town to hear.
When Ringers handle them with Art and Skill,
They then the ears of their Observers fill,
With such brave Notes, they ting and tang so well
As to outstrip all with their ding, dong, Bell.

The long set of verses ended with an obvious self-reference:

O Lord! If thy poor Child might have his will
And might his meaning freely to thee tell,
He never of this Musick has his fill,
There's nothing to him like thy ding, dong, Bell.

Today John's vehement self-condemnation for innocent occupations seems disproportionate and absurd. Some of the practices for which he blamed himself so unmercifully would, in Macaulay's words, "have passed for virtues with Archbishop Laud". Even in youth, he was neither cruel nor dishonest; though his conduct had not always been strict, his conscience was sensitive. When he assumed responsibilities he took them seriously, and became a kindly, affectionate husband and father.

Lord Macaulay's life and work lay in smooth pastures; it is difficult to imagine him as the ringleader of wanton companions or to picture him as subsequently involved in frantic spiritual remorse. The phase into which John Bunyan was now passing can have touched no chord of reminiscent suffering. But in his indignation with Robert Southey, the refined High Anglican poet who meant to do his best for John but ventured to call him a "blackguard", Macaulay was right to emphasize the harsh theological yardstick with which John measured his own offences. To him, unlike some of his biographers, they were never merely social.

Throughout this period of mounting travail, John Bunyan's work as a tinker carried him into different parts of Bedfordshire.

BUNYAN'S COTTAGE AT ELSTOW
From an old print.

BUNYAN'S COTTAGE ON THE SAME SITE TODAY

The village street gives a good view of Elstow Church. "Bunyan's Cottage" is on the right of the picture.

He had now a wife and child to support and, like many others whose souls are battered by a sense of sin, he was obliged to maintain the standards of competent craftsmanship by which he and his family lived.

During 1650 one of his jobs took him to Willington, a village four miles east of Bedford on the road to Sandy and Potton. Here he worked for the proud and prolific Gostwick* family, who lived in a sumptuous new house built of timber and brick. For three centuries their predecessors had been carried after death into the grey square-towered church, founded by Sir Robert Gostwick who died in 1315.

The church had already acquired a Puritan tradition. Sitting there to rest after a morning's toil, the visiting tinker observed the plain tomb of Sir John Gostwick, Master of the Horse to King Henry VIII, who helped Thomas Cromwell to suppress the monasteries. In order to commemorate Squire Gostwick's profession, the stars had been taken from his coat of arms and replaced by horses' heads.

Above his grave hung the helmet which he had worn at the Field of the Cloth of Gold. Beside him the effigy of his son, Sir William, lay in armour lined with gold and scarlet. A crimson hybrid, half chanticleer, half gryphon, perched at Sir William's feet.

The village was proud of its history, as old as any in Bedfordshire. Willington Vicars went back to 1066, and on the banks of the Ouse were the remains of harbours constructed by the Danes to protect their ships. At the further end of the village, the surviving remnant of moat and ditches marked the spot where the castle of the Mowbrays, Earls of Norfolk, had once dominated the river.

Within the Gostwick estate, two conspicuous outbuildings had been erected under Henry VIII; it was for repairs to the metalwork on these century-old structures that John had been summoned. One, an ornate stone dovecot with stepped gables and small openings in the roof, had been built to supply pigeons for pies, popular when fresh meat was difficult to obtain even by the rich. Inside the much-decorated building, the 1400 holes where the doves roosted formed a chequered pattern on the ochre-shaded walls.

* Sometimes spelt Gostwyck in Bedfordshire records.

The second building, in similar style, was an embellished cow-house of the same buff-grey stone. Like the dovecot it had a roof of vermilion tiles, and was still known as "King Henry's Stable". On the upper floor with its finely moulded windows, a large open fireplace offered to John the tempting opportunity, which he seldom missed, of inscribing his name. On the chimney-piece he carved it roughly with his tinker's tools:

IOHN BVN
YAN
1650

His hands were busy, but his thoughts were absorbed by the struggle to give up dancing; he saw no glimpse of a distant future in which students of his life and work would borrow ladders from neighbouring farmers in order to see the inscription made inaccessible by the perilous mouldering of the wooden floor. He was more concerned with the life everlasting than with the human posterity which would visit the dovecot and stable maintained by that unpredictable body, the National Trust.

Long after he was dead his successors would still see the golden glow of ancient stone with its soft growth of lichen, flanked by a twentieth-century market garden. In autumn the yellow and bronze of massed chrysanthemums would reflect the colours of the old tiles, ranging indescribably from pale chrome to the deep purple of a ripened grape.

More fascinating to John than this pleasant village were his visits to Ampthill House* on the slope rising steeply from Houghton Conquest to Ampthill Heights. Years ago, his father had often described to his mother this half-legendary palace. In summer John could walk to it by a path which crossed the fields from the lane linking Houghton Conquest Church and Rectory, but in winter he was obliged to take the main road from Bedford to Ampthill. It climbed Ampthill Ridge so steeply that he mentally christened it "Hill Difficulty", for in wet weather he often had to scramble up on his hands and knees.

At the foot of the slope was a spring, which overflowed into a trickle of water running down the wooded bank on the left-hand

* Now known as Houghton House or Houghton Towers.

side of the road. In the flat clay-land of north Bedfordshire no such springs were to be found; the small rill indicated a different geological formation from that of the swampy plain. Between the great oaks to the east of the roadway ran a steep, winding path; on its way up the hill it passed through a pleasant glade which seemed to John's fancy like an arbour where a tired traveller could forget his feverish speculations in sleep.

On the top of the hill stood the remains of a fortified house, built by Sir John Cornwall whose fortune had come from the spoils of Agincourt. In this house two wives of Henry VIII had sought refuge, Katharine of Aragon and Catherine Howard. Years later, a Gothic cross carrying a shield with the arms of Aragon was to mark the spot.

The two Queens, robbed of their dignified status, had each looked sorrowfully down upon the Vale of Bedford, stretching with its meadows, cornfields and elms to the level horizon till its outline was lost in a haze of blue. Immediately below the terrace, brown and golden fields lay side by side in the complex pattern imposed on English agriculture by the Anglo-Saxon strip system.

From the summit the road dipped down into Ampthill, an elegant, sleepy little town with the battlemented tower of its fourteenth-century church looking across the valley of the River Flit, and its central cross-roads passing beneath the placid face of a wooden clock tower. But John did not go on into Ampthill; his work took him to the rich rose-red mansion standing half a mile to the east of the hill-top in Dame Ellensbury Park. The park had been named after Dame Alianor, the second wife of a fourteenth-century land-owner and crusader, Sir Almaric de St. Amand.

This ornate jewel of Jacobean architecture, standing in proud isolation on the hill-top, had been built in 1615 for Mary, Countess of Pembroke, the sister of Sir Philip Sidney. Local rumour said that John Thorpe, the architect of those climbing turrets and classic colonnades, had called in a greater master to decorate the central section of the north front facing Bedford plain, and to embellish the west front with its Doric columns. To John Bunyan, Inigo Jones was still an unknown name. He only knew, as he walked past the north front to the servants' entrance in the east wing, that the intricate friezes and arabesques reminded him of the handsome familiar portal of Elstow Place.

The majestic house which he now entered was a rectangular brick building, with ornamental stone facings and high square towers crowned by double gilded pinnacles at each of the four corners. It covered a large area of the northern Ampthill slopes, and its windows, in style both Elizabethan and Jacobean, looked towards the Bedfordshire countryside across the great park, with its pleasure gardens, which surrounded the house.

From the main north entrance, a long avenue of elms stretched downhill to join the road from Houghton Conquest. To the south a second avenue of rare Spanish chestnuts, brought to England only in the year that the house was begun, linked the estate with the summit of Ampthill Ridge. Above a secluded bower in the pleasure garden, another exotic tree, the Cornelian Cherry known to southern Europe, put forth each spring its abundant blossoms like a fall of celestial snow.

Long afterwards, in John's creative imagination, this Jacobean palace would become something even greater than itself. For him it was to be a symbol of loveliness both human and divine, a House Beautiful in which earthly pilgrims might receive inspiration and refreshment on their way to a heavenly city still more glorious.

After the Countess of Pembroke died in 1621, her son, the Earl of Montgomery, was not attracted by the magnificent Bedfordshire demesne which she had planned for him. He surrendered his property to King James I, who two years later granted it to the Scottish family of Bruce in return for their support of his claim to the English throne.

When John was summoned to the house with his tools the head of the family was Thomas Bruce, who had taken possession of the estate between 1623 and 1627, and in 1633 had been created Earl of Elgin. His son, Robert Bruce, destined to succeed his father and became the first Earl of Ailesbury in 1663, was a cultured and learned man whose collection of books and antiques added further richness to the decorative interior of Ampthill House.

John Bunyan, going upstairs to mend a metal hip-bath in a top storey bedroom, found it difficult to pass these treasures with only the hurried glance expected from a hired tinker. Because he could not stop to examine them, his fancy became busy with the

THE OLD PULPIT

from which Christopher Hall preached his sermon against Sunday sports is still in Elstow Church.

THE BELFRY DOOR OF ELSTOW STEEPLE

Marks still shown at the top of the doorway are said to have been made by the bell-rope which Bunyan pulled from outside the door.

"HOUSE BEAUTIFUL"

The ruins of Houghton House on Ampthill Heights, reputed to have been the original of "House Beautiful" in *The Pilgrim's Progress*.

"Records of the greatest Antiquity" which he knew that the books contained. As he mounted the stairs he pictured the old swords, polished shields, and ancient helmets in the Armoury, and the fine furniture, curiously and beautifully carved, which was hidden behind the closed doors with their costly handles.

Neither he nor the wealthy owners guessed that, less than a century and a half later, this handsome embodiment of Stuart civilization would lie, unroofed and dismantled, a heap of abandoned ruins on the hillside.

In 1728, the Bruce family sold their mansion to the fourth Duke of Bedford, who gave it to his heir, the Marquis of Tavistock, on his marriage in 1764. Three years afterwards, the young Marquis was killed while riding with the Redbourn Hunt. When his disconsolate widow died a year later, the embittered Duke took no further interest in the property.

For a short period it was occupied by a sporting peer, the Earl of Upper Ossory. He moved to Ampthill Park in the time of the fifth Duke, and Houghton House and gardens were left, for reasons never fully explained, to lapse into decay. The prey of owls and ivy, unpruned trees and encroaching weeds, the conspicuous vermilion walls would have fallen into total ruin if they had not been bought and handed over to the Ministry of Works.

When John Bunyan reached the top-floor back bedroom, he still found it difficult to concentrate on his job. This time it was not books or museum pieces that stole his attention, but the view lying due south of the chestnut avenue directly below.

"If I had an upper chamber like this to sleep in," he thought, "I should always lie with my window open, to get the first glimpse of the sun's rising."

From the lofty room he looked over open hill country, occasionally broken by isolated clumps of oak, beech, and fir. Immediately beyond the park, broad ribbons of ploughland stretched east and west between the dark woods. A grassy slope on which hens were feeding and horses grazing carried John's eyes to the far distance, where the soft blue of the chalk hills twelve miles away melted into the horizon. They were less than a thousand feet high, but they appeared to him as mountains; not the harsh, frightening peaks of the Welsh hills across the Dee, but delectable mountains, beautified with flowers, and vineyards, and fountains and springs.

Though he welcomed the work which took him to the great house where he could see the Chilterns, John depended mainly upon the householders of Bedford for opportunities to practise his trade. Often he paced the High Street from St. Peter's Church to the Great Bridge, advertising his presence in the traditional cry handed down by Dr. Woelkes, the contemporary organist of Chichester Cathedral:

Have you any worke for a tinker?
Have you any old bellowes to mend?

It was on one such visit to Bedford that a new encounter precipitated the second stage of John's conversion.

CHAPTER VI

THE YEARS OF CONFLICT

Prudence: "Do you not find sometimes, as if those things were vanquished, which at other times are your perplexity?"
Christian: "Yes, but that is seldom; but they are to me golden hours, in which such things happen to me."

JOHN BUNYAN: *The Pilgrim's Progress*, Part I.

ONE morning John Bunyan was passing through a mean Bedford street, when he was arrested by the conversation of three or four poor women sitting in a doorway enjoying the sunshine. They were discussing religious topics and he drew near hoping to take part, for he was now as ready to join in discourses on religion as the Talkative of his future invention.

But, to his dismay, their conversation was far above his head. Though he did not know it, these unpretentious women were among the twelve founder members of a Free Church recently started in the town. They spoke with a joy and conviction that put them beyond his spiritual reach, of the love of Jesus, the promises of God, and their new birth into a state of grace which was a sure defence against the temptations of Satan. Yet, most perturbing of all, they seemed to be dissatisfied with their own righteousness, and convinced that without God's power in their souls it would avail them nothing.

Shaken out of his escapist complacency, John stole away. He realized now that the outward conformity which he had practised was a mere pretence unrelated to true salvation. But, immersed in his lonely bewilderment, he was desperately anxious to be reassured, and his sore need for consolation drove him to seek, again and again, the company of these poor women.

They received him with kindness and sympathy; their tenderness towards his baffled tumultuous youth finally convinced him that their interpretation of the Scriptures was better than his, and compelled him to meditate on the unknown Kingdom of Heaven which he vaguely identified with the blue range of the Chilterns seen from Ampthill Heights.

In his hour of need, John found no help from his previous companions. He had once enjoyed the society of his Elstow friend Harry, but this young man's profane and promiscuous habits now suggested that he was best avoided. Meeting him one day in a lane, and remorsefully mindful of their recent friendship, John tentatively inquired after his health.

"Well enough!" Harry replied, following his answer with an outburst of obscene oaths.

John was genuinely shocked.

"But, Harry," he protested with the naive tactlessness of the newly converted, "why do you swear and curse thus? What will become of you, if you die in this condition?"

Harry regarded his former comrade in vice with angry contempt.

"What would the Devil do for company," he exclaimed furiously, "if it were not for such as I am?"

Crestfallen and abashed, John sought for guidance in the publications of a recently-formed antinomian sect known as the Ranters, but found neither comfort nor wisdom in their fanatical pantheism. Rapidly his respect for his own insight decreased.

"O Lord," he prayed in despair, "I am a fool, and not able to know the Truth from Error . . . Lord, I lay my Soul, in this matter, only at thy foot; let me not be deceived, I humbly beseech thee."

Further consternation came upon him when he discovered that the humble villager whom he had regarded as his one sound religious companion was himself falling under the Ranters' influence. They had persuaded him, as they now sought to persuade the lusty and vulnerable John, that they had attained to a state of perfection in which they could satisfy their carnal desires and yet remain free from sin.

No companionship seemed safe but that of his own young wife, who had been baffled and grieved by his restless preoccupation, but now rejoiced to see him spend so much time in reading the Scriptures and especially the Epistles of St. Paul.

"I began," he recorded, "to look into the Bible with new eyes, and read as I never did before."

His acquaintances in the Bedford Church had diverted his attention from the Old Testament to the New, but his reading was still childlike and literal. Before long, another obsession preyed upon his mind. Had he really any faith? he wondered. Without faith a man was sure to perish for ever; how could he tell whether he had it or not?

One day, as he walked from Elstow into Bedford, the idea came to him of testing his faith by trying to work a miracle. At that time, after a period of wet weather, there were many puddles on the much-trodden road. Suppose he told the puddles to be dry, and the dry places to become puddles? The idea occurred to him to go under the hedge and pray to God to give him the power to perform this miracle, but immediately the fear came that both prayer and miracle might prove a failure. That indeed would drive him to despair; and despair, as always, was the most dangerous of his spiritual enemies. Better, he decided, to postpone the experiment, than become a castaway, faithless and lost.

Soon after this episode, John had another of those waking visions which were then as surely the source of his suffering as they were later to become the basis of his immortality. He seemed to see the poor Bedford women, whose state of grace presented so tranquil a contrast to his own distracted vicissitudes, as though they dwelt in pleasant warmth upon the sunny side of a high mountain. In the light of that sunshine their homely town became as a land of glory, in which there was neither sorrow nor sighing for those former things were passed away.

But the glory was for them, not for him; he was far from the golden comfort of salvation, shivering in frost and snow on the hither side of a wall that ran round the mountain. Seeking to warm himself by their sun, he crept round the wall and at last discovered a little doorway, through which the passage was "very strait and narrow". Struggling into it head first, he managed after much wrestling to manœuvre his whole body through the small gap and to join his new friends on the sunny hillside.

For a time John's heart was uplifted by this vision, for it seemed to him easy to interpret. The mountain was surely the Church, and the sunshine symbolized the smile on that Face which had frowned upon him, a sinner, on Elstow Green. The narrow passage meant that only those who really intended to give up their sins could have access to God the Father, for it was the Way of Jesus Christ in which there was room only for Body and Soul, but not for Body and Soul and Sin. Yet he, John Bunyan, the young reprobate, did get through.

But the comfort of that reflection was soon banished by new and terrible doubts. What if it were too late for him to make his way through the gap? Suppose the Day of Grace were past and gone? How could he tell whether he was elected? If not, what purpose was there in fighting to be saved? Oh, that he had turned to God seven years ago!

Like a rudderless ship in a storm he seemed to be driven now this way, now that. Occasional messages of consolation flashed into his mind, and desperately searching through the Scriptures, he sought to identify them with the recorded words of God. At other times, on the long solitary walks between towns and villages demanded by his lonely calling, fits of despondency darkened his spirit until he was ready to sink where he stood. For a year of reading, searching, and introspective thought, these fathomless doubts and amorphous questionings continued.

"By these things," he wrote long afterwards, "I was driven to my wits end."

All the pent-up experiences of the past seven years seemed to flood his memory; recollections came back of his desultory reading, of his hours of shame as a soldier, of the religious "disputations" in Newport Pagnell Church, and the prayers and sermons by the Parliamentary chaplains to which he had thought, at the time, that he was paying no attention. How could he have listened so indifferently to those deeply disturbing doctrines, those merciless penetrating words?

Hitherto John had hardly realized that he lived in an age distinguished by great awakenings of the mind and spirit; of political excitement and religious zeal, intensified on all sides by persecution. Now he began to perceive the causes of these things, which were reflected in the ferment stirring within his own soul. But he saw them as in a glass darkly, a mirror distorted by the shadows of his limitations.

"To respect him as he deserves," wrote Southey in his biographical introduction to the 1830 edition of *The Pilgrim's Progress*, "to admire him as he ought to be admired, it is necessary that we should be informed not only of the coarseness and brutality of his youth, but of the extreme ignorance out of which he made his way and the stage of burning enthusiasm through which he passed, a passage not less terrible than that of his own Pilgrim in the Valley of the Shadow of Death."

John Bunyan was a peasant, the would-be follower of another peasant, his Master, Jesus Christ. But the Roman Empire of the first century A.D. gave a better education to the village carpenter than seventeenth-century England provided for the village tinker. The scientific revolution of that century affected only the aristocracy of intellect and learning, thereby increasing the gulf which stretched between the educated classes and the others. Those "others" were equally outcast from the specialized world of classical knowledge, in which the studies of Lipsius, Scaliger, and, later, Richard Bentley occupied the place of honour.

The young tinker, grappling with problems which baffled the learned Christian Fathers, had only the rudiments of education to help him, and no sense of perspective. "How shall he learn wisdom whose talk is of oxen?" asks the writer of *Ecclesiastes*.

To the end of his life John Bunyan's knowledge of society was mainly local, though his understanding of mankind became universal. His religious faith had been defined for him by theologians who believed in hell-fire and a personal Devil; the majority of his contemporaries regarded toleration with scorn, though they never rooted it from his innermost being.

They taught him to identify morality with one religious doctrine and the literal interpretation of the Scriptures; they represented "justice" as judgment and condemnation, followed by punishment. Like his teachers he remained blind to some of the greatest evils of his age, such as the slave-trade; he recognized inequalities, but perceived only dimly the case for social reform. He was equally unaware of the attempts to restrict and control war which had begun outside England three years before his birth, though he was to understand their significance before his death..

Undisciplined and undirected, the vehement forces of Nature welling up within those who spring from the soil are liable to turn inward and rend their possessor if they are allied with a strong, primitive imagination. John Bunyan shared the peculiarly compelling quality of that imagination with other inspired peasants such as Joan of Arc, who like himself heard voices, obeyed supernatural commands, and carried on conversations audible, as in a dream, to themselves but to no one else.

Today we recognize "voices" as a symptom of the condition too easily dismissed as "schizophrenia"; they are the echoes of subconscious thoughts, seeming so clear as to belong to the material rather than the abstract universe. Many dedicated souls share this schizophrenic quality; their inner preoccupations become so dominant that, in relation to consciousness, the abstract and the concrete exchange places.

Apart from the late-published account of his imprisonment, John Bunyan records the events of his life with a casual meagreness which has baffled and exasperated his biographers. Even the cataclysms of history, deeply though they affected him, appeared insignificant and unsubstantial; the little kingdom of his own soul imprisoned him until its spiritual force burst its bonds and made it the soul of the world.

In whatever epoch he had lived, John would have passed through a period of deep psychological conflict. From childhood he had been a divided personality, as the "terrible dreams" originating in a sense of guilt would make clear if the fact were not confirmed by some of the verses on childish anxieties in *A Book for Boys and Girls*. Conversion and its aftermath were necessary before the integration of his mind and spirit could be accomplished. For such twice-born persons, says William James in *The Varieties of Religious Experience,* the natural life must be lost before the spiritual can be found.

Struggles of this kind are intensified when their subject is part of an apocalyptic age, in which great good and great evil are alike made manifest. Yet without those years of subjective anguish, John Bunyan could never have wrought his pilgrim philosophy from the lessons of experience and the fruits of penitence, terrible in its pain yet glorious in the sense of release which acceptance brings.

After several months of lonely agitation, with hope and despair in perpetual sequence, John found that he could no longer endure the burden of his thoughts in solitude. Embarrassed yet relieved, he confessed his torments to the poor women whom he had pictured upon the sunny side of a high mountain.

"THE DELECTABLE MOUNTAINS"
A distant view of the Chilterns from "House Beautiful".

ST. JOHN'S CHURCH AND RECTORY, BEDFORD

Under the Cromwellian settlement the Independent Church, which later became Bunyan Meeting, occupied St. John's from 1653–1660. The Rectory was the "Interpreter's House" of Bunyan's Experience.

Large and powerful as he had now grown, his face was so pale and his expression so anxious that it stirred them to compassion. They told him of their Gospel Church and introduced him to their minister, John Gifford, who had himself been saved from a wicked life by divine Grace. But at first the only result of this new contact was a deeper conviction of sin.

"My soul," he lamented, "is as a clog on the leg of a Bird, to hinder me from flying. I grow worse and worse; now I am farther from conversion than ever I was before."

His Bedford friends, pitying his distress, spoke to him of the promises of God to those who truly repented of their sins, but now his conscience was too sore to be healed even by the words of the Gospel. There was no hope and no stability; he walked on a miry bog; in his own eyes—and surely, alas! in God's eyes too—he seemed more loathsome than a toad. How, he wondered from the depths of complete abstraction, was it possible for the old to be so concerned with the trivialities of life, the learned so disturbed by worldly losses, when all that mattered was the health of the soul!

Now indeed he entered into a darkness as solitary and intense as that of his own Valley of Shadows. He lived in a waking dream, in which his divided mind was haunted by texts, promising comfort at one moment, but threatening damnation at another.

A sermon by John Gifford on a theme from the Song of Songs, "Behold, thou art fair, my love", assured its hearers that Christ's love was not withheld from the tempted and afflicted soul; this promise filled him with so much hope that he could have told of God's mercy to the crows that sat upon the ploughed fields. But a few days later a new threat blotted out the welcome consolation, and the text "Simon, Simon, behold Satan hath desired to have you", sounded so loudly in his ears that he turned his head, thinking that someone behind his back was calling to him from a great distance.

Storms of blasphemous thoughts assaulted his mind, and refused to be banished by texts from St. Paul's Epistles; their noise echoed through his brain till he believed that he was possessed by the Devil, and was sometimes driven to shriek and cry. Whatever the sin against the Holy Ghost might be, he felt impelled to commit it, until he wished that he could change places with the dogs and horses who had no souls to perish in hell. The Tempter himself at times seemed to wear strange concrete shapes. Sometimes he was a bush, sometimes a bull, sometimes a besom; at others he was not seen but felt, an invisible hand which tugged at John's clothes from the empty air.

One day, while Mary was hanging up the washing in the garden, John sat wearily by the fire and watched their eighteen-months-old daughter, who was playing in her rough wooden cot. With her eyes already in her fingers, she explored the clumsy bars; for the hundredth time he wondered whether her blindness was a punishment for his sins. His love must atone to her for that catastrophe; because of it she was dearer to him than all the world. Never, never could he love her enough!

Suddenly, as he mused wretchedly on his guilt, some words of hope seemed to hover in the room.

"Forasmuch then as the children are partakers of flesh and blood, he also himself likewise took part of the same, that through death, he might destroy him that had the power of death; that is, the Devil; and deliver those who, through the fear of death, were all their life subject to bondage."

The glory of proferred deliverance came upon John with such a tumult of relief that he almost swooned as he sat. Soon afterwards he was tormented again by questionings familiar to all who struggle, in all ages, with the agony of unformulated thought. Was Jesus Man as well as God? Was God also Man? At last a text from the Revelation appeared to solve the problem, and he caught again at the fringes of his salvation. It seemed to him now like a written message from Heaven, fastened with golden seals which hung visibly in his sight.

John's violent alternations of hope and despair had blotted the wider world of England from his consciousness; he did not know that a greater than Mary, John Milton, was also condemned to total blindness. In 1649, when England became a Commonwealth, Milton had published another book with a classical title, *Eikonoklastes*, but John read only the Bible, with its alternating terrors and consolations.

He had never seen Richard Baxter's *The Saints' Everlasting Rest*, or Jeremy Taylor's *Holy Living and Dying*, published in the year of Mary's birth, though he would have appreciated both. But he did wish that he could read the experience of some "ancient godly man", from whose temptations he might learn wisdom.

Soon afterwards this desire was fulfilled. God guided him, it seemed, to a shop where, amidst a pile of old volumes, he found a copy of Martin Luther's Commentary upon the *Epistle of St. Paul to the Galatians*, "first collected and gathered word by word out of his preaching, and now out of Latine faithfully translated into English for the unlearned".

This book, a black-letter edition published at "The Blacke frears by Ludgate" under the imprint of Thomas Vautroullier in 1595, was so old that it was almost ready to fall apart. But John took it home and eagerly read the publisher's commendation of the author,

> "who being first a frear, in what blindenesse, superstition and darkenesse, in what dreames and dregges of Monkish idolatrie he was drowned, his history declareth, witness recordeth, and this booke also partly doth specifie . . . After he had thus continued a longe space, more pharisaicall and zealous in these monkish wayes then the common sorte of that order, at length it so pleased almightie God to beginne with this man first to touch his conscience with some remorse and feeling of sinne, his minde with fears and misdoutes, whereby he was driven to seeke further . . ."

Was not the experience of this "ancient godly man" almost John's own? Were the feelings of sin, the doubts and fears, perhaps the beginning of God's grace? If He could choose Martin Luther, the superstitious Papist, as his instrument, might He not also choose John Bunyan, the penitent sinner?

No wonder that he was led to read Luther's own preface, and then go on to the Commentary—"so plentiful in wordes", as Luther himself described it—which discoursed on St. Paul's Epistle, not only verse by verse, but sentence by sentence, for 542 pages. It seemed almost as though it were to him personally that Luther had addressed his concluding words:

> "Thus haue ye the exposicion of Paules Epistle to the Galathians. The Lord Jesus Christ, our justifier and Sauiour,

who gave unto me the grace and power to expound this Epistle, and to you likewise to heare it, preserve and stablish both you and me (which I most hartely desire,) that we daily growing more and more in the knowledge of his grace and faith unfayned, may be found unblameable and without fault in the daye of our redemption. To whom with the father and the holy Ghost be glory world without ende, Amen."

How clearly those words spoke to John's condition, "as if his Book had been written out of my heart"! He saw his own soul reflected in Luther's passions and doubts, his own wretchedness in the agonized wrestlings of the great theologian with unbelief and fear. Except for the Bible, this Commentary seemed to him to be better fitted for a wounded conscience than all the books he had ever read.

Yet even Luther did not release him from self-torment, for now the strangest of John's many temptations seized him in its grip. "And that was, to sell and part with this most blessed Christ, to exchange him for the things of this life, for any thing."

He did not stop to ask himself how a faith, a conviction, an idea, could be exchanged for some concrete benefit. In the midst of the most trivial actions, such as eating his food, picking up a pin, or chopping a stick, the words "Sell Christ for this, sell Christ for that; sell him, sell him!" echoed through his brain until he seemed, for days together, to be tortured on the rack.

One morning, as he lay in bed exhausted, the thought passed through his mind, "Let him go, if he will!" Believing that this time Satan really had won the battle, he sank, "as a Bird that is shot from the top of a tree, into great guilt, and fearful despair". Getting out of bed he staggered alone into the fields, and for two hours lay there like a man half-dead. In his tormented mind he began to identify himself with Esau, who sold his birthright for a morsel of meat, and afterwards "found no place for repentance, though he sought it carefully, with tears".

From this time onwards, for two years, John lived in continual "expectation of damnation", with only occasional moments of relief after searching the Bible for encouraging texts. Scriptural sentences acquired a curious animism; they leapt from the pages like embodied spirits, torturing him with their stings, bolting in upon him, rushing like wind through the window, perpetually reminding him of Esau's fall and the unpardonable sin. He was now in the final depths of despondency, the lowest circle of spiritual hell.

The creation of Giant Despair in *The Pilgrim's Progress* was foreshadowed in John's account of this crisis. In those early years despair, largely self-induced but masquerading as the Tempter, became his worst assailant; in imagination he saw all his wrongdoing relegated to some unique category of sin for which Christ had not died. The extremity of his conflict appeared in his detailed recollection of it many years afterwards, and in his loving tenderness towards the group of timid, feeble and despondent pilgrims who accompanied Christiana to the River.

During those crucial months of doubt, John came across another book which in his agonized frame of mind was as distressing as the discovery of Luther's *Commentary* had been providential. Finding every sentence as painful as salt rubbed into a fresh wound, he began to read the "dreadful story of that miserable mortal, Francis Spira".

This book, *A Relation of the Fearful Estate of Francis Spira in the Year* 1548, "Compiled by Nath. Bacon Esq." and published in 1649, described an extreme example of the religious tension which was afflicting John, and in this case brought its victim to a miserable end.

Spira had been a rascally Italian lawyer who was converted by the "wandering opinions" of Martin Luther, and began to discuss them at public meetings throughout Padua. This heretical enthusiasm naturally displeased the Papal Legate, who compelled Spira, after much conflict between his conscience and his worldly interests, to make a public recantation in Venice.

For the rest of his life Spira endured agonies of remorse; his spiritual conflict became so famous that it was carried on in public with his personal friends and official advisers, including bishops and physicians. The physician's verdict unexpectedly foreshadowed twentieth-century psychiatric knowledge of the intimate relationship between body and mind:

"They could not discerne that his body was afflicted with any danger or distemper originally from itself, by reason of the

> overruling of any humour; but that this Malady of his did arise from some griefe or passion of his minde, which being over-burthened, did so oppress the spirits, as they wanting free passage, stirred up many ill humours, whereof the body of man is full."

This unhappy victim of guilt finally wore out the patience of his would-be comforters, who "began to take their leaves of him" as his symptoms steadily became worse.

> "Then roaring out in the bitterness of his spirit, (he) said: 'It's a fearful thing to fall into the hands of the living God': the violence of his passion and action sutable, did amaze many of the beholders; insomuch as some of them said with a whispering voice that he was possessed."

After a frustrated attempt at suicide the agonized Spira eventually died, doubtless to the relief of his family, and certainly to that of the reader. His biographer closed with a final exhortation: "So mayest thou take good and no hurt, by the reading of this terrible Example."

Upon John Bunyan that "terrible Example" had precisely the effect that any modern psychologist would predict. If he had suspected that he was "possessed" before, he began to be sure of it now, and his body reacted in a fashion reminiscent of Francis Spira's to the torment of his mind. He was stricken with sudden tremblings which made him "shake and totter" for days together; his terror created so much internal "clogging and heat" that he felt as though his breast-bone would split asunder. His tumultuous thoughts began, "like masterless hell-hounds, to roar and bellow, and make an hideous noise within me".

At one period, to the alarm of his despairing young wife, he developed all the symptoms of tuberculosis, and paced up and down the house "in a most woful state", his sickness doubled by the extremity of his apprehensions. Like Spira's physicians he began, when beset by the Tempter, to realize the intimate relationship between mind and body.

"I find he is much for assaulting the Soul, when it begins to approach towards the grave," he wrote, "then is his Opportunity."

For weeks on end his distraught spirit seemed to him as "a broken Vessel, driven as with the Winds, and tossed sometimes head-long into despair". Gripped by primitive forces beyond his mental control, his thoughts were like chaff blown in a bitter gale or leaves whirled away on the rushing surface of a stream. For him the whole creation groaned and travailed together without respite or relief.

One day, when his work took him to Bedford, he sat down, worn out, on a settle in the street, and began yet again to meditate upon his dreadful state of sin. The sun seemed to grudge him light, and the very stones to be in league against him. In his agony he cried aloud: "How can God comfort such a wretch as I?" Almost immediately, "as an echo doth answer a voice", came audible words: "This sin is not unto death," and a flood of joy lightened his heart, "as if I had been raised out of the grave."

"This therefore," he wrote afterwards, "was a great easement to my mind; to wit, that my sin was pardonable, that it was not the sin unto death. None but those that know what my trouble (by their own experience) was, can tell what relief came to my Soul by this consideration: It was a release to me from my former bonds, and a shelter from the former storm: I seemed now to stand upon the same ground with other sinners, and to have as good right to the Word and Prayer as any of they."

Though the end of this terrible period was still far off, the growing consciousness of God's mercy, derived from his study of the New Testament, marked the slow on-coming of relief. For two and a half years altogether, his conflict continued; texts fought in his fevered brain like white angels with wicked hobgoblins.

Each new struggle took a metaphorical form; two Scriptural passages became so real that he could almost see their physical shape reflected from his brain upon the clouds. One was the old fear-inspiring sequence relating Esau's loss of his birthright; the other the words "My Grace is sufficient for thee", which "in a Meeting of God's people" broke in upon his mind with repetitive power.

His hopes now took the same material shape as his former fears; at this meeting which began the final reconciliation of his warring emotions, he seemed to see the face of Jesus looking down upon him from Heaven through the tiles, and directing the words of comfort into his heart. To the end of his life that divine countenance was to have for John a concrete reality which he shared with his own pilgrims, such as Mr. Fearing, whose one dread as he approached the River was that he should be drowned, "and so never see that Face with Comfort, that he had come so many miles to behold".

At last the dreadful conflict was almost over; there "remained only the hinder part of the Tempest, for the thunder was gone beyond me". Though his sore and battered conscience was still tender, John was able, by contrast with his mental suffering, to rejoice all the more in the grace and love of God; God who had so miraculously changed from the angry Judge of Sinai to the forgiving Saviour on Calvary.

No longer did his sins separate him from his fellows; now he could seek, as a friend and brother, the society of those to whom he had so often gone for help and sympathy. He would join the Bedford Church, and become a member of its humble but happy congregation.

"Now," he joyfully recorded, "did my Chains fall off my Legs indeed, I was loosed from my Afflictions and Irons, my Temptations also fled away; so that from that time those dreadful Scriptures of God left off to trouble me . . . Therefore I lived, for some time, very sweetly at peace with God through Christ; O me thought Christ! Christ! There was nothing but Christ that was before my Eyes . . . O, I saw my Gold was in my Trunk at home! in Christ my Lord and Saviour! Now Christ was all; all my Wisdom, all my Righteousness, all my Sanctification, and all my Redemption."

This period of John Bunyan's life has given unlimited opportunity to those writers who regard the world-wide appreciation of a great man or woman as a form of uncritical sentimentality. They have sought to be "different" by presenting him as a mental invalid or congenital defective.

But moral delinquency and spiritual tumult are not the same as mental aberration; nor is genius. An exceptional power to make the abstract real, which was the essence of John's permanent achievement but also the most painful feature of his spiritual struggle, is not a form of lunacy just because some lunatics possess it. Even his desperate conviction of human depravity, mirrored in his own sins, was a belief which he shared with many others.

In one of the essays published at the time of the Bunyan Tercentenary in 1928, Mr. R. Ellis Roberts showed that the idea of possession by original sin was not the fruit of Puritan theology, but an opinion, inherited from certain passages in the writings of St. Augustine, almost universally held in Western Europe by Catholic and Protestant alike.

John was not, therefore, merely the creature of his time; he was heir to a fashion of thought followed by most Christian theologians before his day. This fashion was emphasized when the Churches which seceded from Rome at the Reformation decided to adopt the rigid Old Testament values of Luther and Calvin, rather than the tolerant humanism of Erasmus.

In spite of the abnormal faculty for visualization which John Bunyan possessed, we are not entitled to regard him, in Dr. Caroline Spurgeon's words, as "a Puritan endowed with a psychopathic temperament sensitive to the point of disease", unless we turn our backs upon historical perspectives, insist upon endowing him with such additional knowledge and wisdom as humanity has acquired in the course of three centuries, and expect him to respond as we should respond in a like situation.

There is, however, no such thing as a like situation. It is possible to imagine the conflict between a naturally gay, kindly, robust personality, and the standards of his day which exalted condemnation and vengeance as virtues. Every good-natured official who believes himself morally compelled to carry out the cruelty or murder demanded by the modern totalitarian State in the name of patriotism, faces a similar conflict. But we cannot reconstruct, for ourselves, the particular limitations which obscured John's vision and warped his judgment.

Whether we regard a man as writer, or as human being, or as both, we are entitled to ask where he stands, first, in the light of eternity, and secondly, in relation to his own time. What we are not entitled to do is to judge him in the light of *our* time; to apply to his conflict contemporary values painfully evolved by means of new historical experience.

It is partly through their lack of this historical perspective that the critics who subject John Bunyan to the process now known as "debunking" appear to fail. But they also fail, and more gravely, in their pagan and materialistic assumption that a man is "conditioned" in advance by his physical and mental equipment, whether average or exceptional, and is thus deprived of that free will which is the chief weapon in his spiritual armoury.

Judged by the standards of any age, *Grace Abounding To the Chief of Sinners* remains one of the richest and strangest records of psychological phenomena ever presented to the spiritual practitioner and the mental scientist, though the story becomes less abnormal if we do not credit the young Bunyan with unlikely asceticism, and admit the probability of carnal sin. Its author was a man of natural genius. So far the origin of such genius has proved inexplicable, particularly by the learned. Its tumultuous growth invariably causes trouble, especially to the worthy.

The outstanding feature of John Bunyan's spiritual conflict lies in the fact that a semi-educated and distraught young man, with no help more expert than that of "holy Mr. Gifford" and his small group of provincial Christians, ultimately did triumph over his passionate obsessions and remain a conqueror. This in itself is a proof that his power to exercise his free will was never lost, as it is lost by the true psychopath. Though he was the victim of extreme and abnormal emotions, he was not wholly at their mercy.

Writing in 1666 as a completely normal man despite several years of prison, he was even able to admit the absurdity of the fears which had tortured him.

"These things," he affirmed, "may seem ridiculous to others, even as ridiculous as they were in themselves, but to me they were most tormenting cogitations."

How far they actually were ridiculous may appear less certain to an age—as revolutionary as John Bunyan's and far more calamitous—which has had to abandon some cherished illusions regarding human perfectibility.

"The same cause will always produce the same effect," wrote Sir William Temple in his *Observations on the United Provinces* in 1672. He described this law as "the fundamental postulate of science", but it is also the fundamental postulate of religion. This twentieth century is the first since John Bunyan's era in which death and imprisonment have been, in many countries, the cost of integrity, and men have learnt that the battle against evils which they proudly believed they had conquered for ever must be fought and won, in different forms, over and over again.

It is always in the moment of pride that the risk of reversal is greatest; the nineteenth "century of progress" is followed by the twentieth century of spiritual failure, with its outcome in universal disaster. John Bunyan's frantic belief in human wickedness is but one aspect of the bitter truth that we have learned in our time; the truth that the price of sin has to be paid, by the innocent only with their blood, but by the guilty with demoralization and spiritual death.

The Puritan was not mistaken in fearing sin and its consequences. Where he usually went wrong was in under-estimating the power of love to achieve sin's atonement.

"The cross," wrote John Bunyan in *The Heavenly Footman* with the deeper insight of his closing years, "is the standing way-mark by which all they that go to glory must pass by."

CHAPTER VII

COMMUNION OF "SAINTS"

"I can remember my Fears, and Doubts, and sad Months with comfort; they are as the head of Goliah in my Hand."
JOHN BUNYAN: Preface to *Grace Abounding.*

THROUGH his new sense of mystical union with a forgiving Jesus, peace had begun to enter the soul of John Bunyan. But it was still far from England, which was now at war with Holland, and from Ireland where Cromwell was confiscating land for English and Scottish immigrants after the Act of Settlement.

Least of all was there peace in London, where Inigo Jones lay dead and Milton mourned his blindness. The Regicides, grown conservative like most revolutionaries who find themselves in power, had begun their régime by attempting to silence John Lilburne and the Levellers. Anarchy, they knew, was the alternative to their despotic rule, which maintained order only through the disunity of their enemies.

The populace showed their dislike of the Government by making Lilburne the hero of the hour. On his return from banishment in 1653, his second trial and acquittal were attended by 6000 spectators, who voiced their partisan excitement in two lines of doggerel:

And what, shall then honest John Lilburne die?
Three score thousand will know the reason why.

In June the "Little" Parliament, an Assembly of Nominees, was summoned to succeed the corrupt and self-interested Rump. Posthumously nicknamed after one of their members, Praise-God Barebone, the Nominees placed their power in Cromwell's hands and resigned.

The following December, Cromwell became Protector under the Instrument of Government, which also decreed that those who had fought for the King were to be excluded from the next four Parliaments. England was divided into eleven military districts under Major-Generals, and the House of Commons set to work to complete the ecclesiastical reforms begun by the Long Parliament.

After dispatching Strafford to the scaffold and Laud to the Tower, this Parliament had set up two Committees to deal with the practical problems of Church government. The Committee of Scandalous and Malignant Ministers sequestered both the clergy who offended Puritan susceptibilities by their dogma and ritual, and those who "malignantly" opposed the Parliamentary Party. A second body, the Committee of Plundered Ministers, aimed at reinstating clergymen who had been dispossessed by Archbishop Laud.

In his *Sufferings of the Clergy*, published in 1714, Dr. John Walker recorded many cases of hardship which occurred when the "scandalous" were replaced by the "plundered". After the Root and Branch Bill the Bishops joined the sufferers; they were banished from the House of Lords and deprived of their sees.

The Government had then to decide what kind of State Church it wanted. An attempt at Presbyterian domination followed the disappearance of the Bishops; in 1643 and 1644 the people of England were ordered to swear to the Solemn League and Covenant, which was read aloud in parish churches and imposed on the soldiers of garrison towns. The movement reached its peak in January 1645, when the Lords and Commons abolished the Prayer Book, adopted the New Westminster Directory, and decreed that England as well as Scotland should become Presbyterian.

But the country whose juries had acquitted John Lilburne in the face of all the evidence was not prepared to have its form of worship decided by Act of Parliament. Though Anglicans and Independents might differ in everything else, they were alike in resisting Presbyterianism; the one group wanted no State Church but its own, while the other regarded the individual congregation as the source of authority.

In Bedfordshire the opposition to a State religion was led by William Dell, who had succeeded his sequestered predecessor, Dr. John Pocklington, as Rector of Yelden in 1642.

During the Bishop of Lincoln's Visitation at Ampthill in 1635,

Dr. Pocklington had preached, and subsequently published, a sermon entitled *Sunday No Sabbath*. This offended the Puritans so deeply that in 1640 an order issued by Parliament condemned the sermon to be burnt by the common hangman in London and at the two universities. Dell's appointment in Dr. Pocklington's place suggested an official determination to sweep the old orthodoxy out of Yelden parish, but, like other forms of external pressure, it succeeded only in thrusting the opposition underground.

Through his chaplaincy under General Fairfax in 1645, William Dell had been brought into close contact with the Commonwealth leaders. When Cromwell became Protector four years after Dell's Cambridge appointment as Master of Gonville and Caius, the State Church of the Commonwealth reflected Dell's belief that "all Churches are equal as well as all Christians, all being daughters of one mother, beams of one sun, branches of one vine".

This "equality" did not embrace Catholics and "heretics", but it included all the forms of Protestantism accepted by the three types of Puritan which had sprung from the Revolution. The first had desired only to modify the Established Church without uprooting it; the second had tried, and failed, to institute Presbyterian coercion. The third, which objected to all coercion, upheld the freedom of individuals to form congregations at will, and produced such groups as the Bedford Church.

Cromwell's recognition of these separate churches was a long step towards the full toleration that came a few months after John Bunyan's death. Thanks to his own strong convictions he could respect the views of others, however extreme; he was able to appreciate and even to laugh with George Fox. The freedom given by him to the Independents lasted just long enough to create the religious variety which England has cherished and never lost.

His Establishment set up no Church Courts, assemblies, or laws; it laid down no rules regarding baptism, Holy Communion, or other rites. Nevertheless it attained the unity which the Protector failed to achieve in politics. In presenting an incumbent to a living, the Ecclesiastical Commissioners considered only his character and ability. As evidence of this they required a certificate from some responsible person who knew him, guaranteeing his fitness for the post.

Under this elastic arrangement, adopted in England only

between 1653 and 1660, Nonconformists were sometimes put in charge of parish churches. That was how, when John Bunyan joined the Free Church founded by a group of Bedford citizens in 1650, it came to be in occupation of St. John's Parish Church, with its pastor, John Gifford, appointed by Bedford Corporation to act as Rector of the Church and Hospital.

In the seventeenth century Bedfordshire was included in the diocese of Lincoln, where it remained until 1836. It was then transferred to Ely, and subsequently to St. Albans.

Under Queen Elizabeth the Bedfordshire clergy, like others, had been powerful, for the laws commanded regular attendance at the parish church, and prescribed a fine of 1*s*. a Sunday for absence not caused by illness. The Statute known as "35 Eliz."—an early Conventicle Act under which John Bunyan was to be kept for twelve years in Bedford Gaol—also authorized the imprisonment of persons over sixteen who refused to go to church "without lawful cause" for a month or more.

The story of the clergy during the Commonwealth showed that both sides in the religious struggle had their martyrs, among whom, in Bedfordshire, was Dr. Giles Thorne. During their twenty years of power between two long periods of persecution, the Puritans were so far men of their century that they could not refrain from using prison, confiscation, and ejection as their own weapons.

Since only the highest human nature is capable, when deeply injured, of acceptance and forgiveness, it is not surprising that the Churchmen retaliated after 1660, though they had enjoyed a longer innings, and were usually more intolerant than their opponents. Under Cromwell many Churchmen of dubious allegiance were left in possession of their livings. They included Christopher Hall, the Vicar of Elstow, and William Lindall, with whom John Bunyan was to come into conflict at Harlington.

In Bedford itself the clergy were less fortunate. Giles Thorne, who made no attempt to placate the opposition, was said to be a victim of Sir Samuel Luke; he was released from Ely House, where he had been sent from the Fleet Prison, in August 1646, when the Presbyterians were losing influence in Parliament.

Giles paid dearly for maintaining against all comers that

"Confession to a priest was as ancient as Religion . . . yea, as ancient as God Himself". In March 1644, after thirty months' imprisonment, his petition for a month's leave to see his wife, who had been reported "sick, even unto death", was officially marked: "Noted. Read. Nothing Done."

After the Restoration Giles was to receive his reward, being made Archdeacon of Buckingham and a D.D. of Oxford, in addition to recovering his old position at St. Mary's. But two years after launching his petition, he was still writing with stalwart determination from prison: "If God suffer the enemies of the Church to prevail against her, yet be we not dismayed."

The contemporary Vicar of St. Paul's, John Bradshaw, was a Bedford churchman of Puritan sympathies and practice very different from Giles Thorne. When the Church authorities ordered him to keep within the Altar rails at the celebration of Holy Communion, he resisted and was supported by his leading parishioners, John Eston, John Grew, and Anthony Harrington. These three later seceded from Anglicanism, and became founders of the Bedford Free Church.

During the Commonwealth John Bradshaw disappeared without waiting to be sequestered, and was not restored until 1666. His Church meanwhile became the scene of extemporary services held by the Independents under Cromwell's Broad Church policy. One of John Bunyan's many debates with the Quakers occurred there in 1656.

Another Bedford clergyman, Philip Collier of St. Peter de Merton, had turned his Church into a refuge for local Anglicans before he died in 1643. The second bell in St. Peter's belfry still bears the date 1650, and the defiant inscription, "God save the King", engraved upside down.

At St. John's Church the Rector displaced by John Bunyan's friends was Theodore Crowley, who had held the living for twenty years. He had been presented to it by Bedford Corporation, where Puritan influence had become strong by the time of his sequestration in 1653. A contemporary Corporation Minute records the growth of Puritan practices:

> "At a Common Council held in the Guildhall Chamber by Robert Bell, Mayor, on Monday 15 day of March 1651, Mr.

Francis Bannister, Dr. of Physic, Mr. John Eston, the Elder, Mr. John Grew and Mr. John Hancock, Aldermen, appeared at this Council without their gownes, contrary to the ordinance made on that behalf, wherefore each of them hath forfeited according to the ordinance, two shillings."

After long persistence in breaking regulations by the founders of the Bedford Independents, fines were remitted and the wearing of gowns was abolished. In 1653, with the departure of Theodore Crowley, this group seized the opportunity to appoint their pastor, John Gifford, as an "intruder" at St. John's.

Among their supporters was Colonel John Okey, who now lived at Ridgmont, near Ampthill, as a Justice of the Peace. When the litigious Charles Williams of Bedford renewed his claim after the Restoration "to the religious house called St. John the Baptist", he complained that he had been ejected from lawful possession by Major-General Harrison, Colonel Okey, and others who had employed the property "to the maintenance of one Bunnion, a tincker, Burton a coachsmith, and one Gifford, all schismatics".

Owing to threatened litigation and other perplexities, life was seldom a rose-garden for "intruders". Four years after the Bedford Meeting took possession of St. John's, the Commonwealth Government passed an Act which insisted, with better intention than success, upon the "quiet enjoying of sequestered Parsonages and Vicaridges by the present Incumbent".

The Church occupied by the Independents stood at the end of a short flagged path leading out of St. John's Street on the south side of Bedford Bridge. Behind a high tower of light grey stone which faced the street, the long narrow nave hardly twenty feet wide extended eastwards, with one row of high-backed pews on either side of the single aisle. A red brick wall surrounded the ancient tombstones in the long grass of the churchyard, dividing it from the Rectory and medieval garden. Beyond the wall the open fields stretched north-east to Potters Street and Duck Mill on the banks of the Ouse.

At the time of the Reformation, the Hospital altered and extended in 1280 by Robert de Parys had already ceased to fulfil the purpose for which it had been founded at some unknown earlier date. A note in the Chantry Records reports: "Hospytalle is not used accordying to the fowndacyon as it is sayd for there is found never a poore person nor hath not been by the space of many years."

Even before the Hospital became the Rectory, St. John's had become the Church of a parish and the Master of the Hospital its Rector. This parish, entirely surrounded by the parish of St. Mary's, was a tiny area of twenty-nine acres. In 1546 its parishioners numbered only "87 houselinge people", and were to be no more than 254 by 1801. Their occupations, recorded from 1714 onwards, gave a fair sample of the trades and professions then followed by Bedford citizens. The lists included glovers, pipemakers, blacksmiths, labourers, a laceman, a clog-maker, an excise officer, a miller, a ropemaker, a hempdresser, a weaver, a bedesman, one militiaman, and three soldiers.

Through the centuries these successive parishioners moved up to the Communion table over grey stone slabs, bearing the names of a dozen Masters and Rectors who once ministered at St. John's. The Independents, during their seven years' occupation, also used the Elizabethan Communion cup, dated 1570 and inscribed "FOR THE PARISHE OF S. IOHN BAPTIST IN BEDFORD".

That cup still stands on the altar, but much else is changed. Nineteenth-century "restoration" has impaired the Church that John Bunyan knew, though the exterior is almost unaltered and the long corridor-like nave remains.

John Speed the map-maker, who sometimes used his imagination as well as his eyes, gave St. John's Hospital a large gateway, like a castle frontage, standing next to the churchyard and facing the street. It is difficult to see where this gateway could have been, for the side wall of the Tudor reception rooms, earlier than both Speed and Bunyan, runs parallel with the road close to the Church. The photograph of St. John's Church and Rectory, facing page 125, shows their position.

The doorways at the back of the Rectory, with their white paint and patterns of iron studs, face the churchyard behind a low box hedge. At the front, leaded and latticed window-panes look across the deep turf of the lawn in the medieval garden to the north of the red-brick house. During some stage of its history it acquired a pebble-dash finish, later than the lichen-decorated roof of crooked vermilion tiles.

North of the street wall, a modest entrance leads beneath a towering ilex past the reception rooms into the old garden. The present entrance-hall under a wooden gallery was the seventeenth-century dining-room; the room now used for meals is the ancient hospital refectory, with oaken beams and dark panelled walls, where John Gifford and John Bunyan talked together.

In the garden are trees said to be older than the Rectory itself; a spreading cedar, with light and dark green branches like the wings of a fantastic bird; two ilexes similar to the guardian at the entrance; and, in the long grass beyond the churchyard, a mulberry beneath which, says tradition, John Bunyan used to sit. On the lawn a recently imported maple adds the warmth of its autumn colours to their sombre dignity.

When I saw the house, it had been temporarily transformed into a Day Nursery by the local authority. Seventy-three small children, with their Matron and nurses, filled the ancient rooms with little chairs and tables, mugs, lockers, pictures and drawings. In the garden a large sandpit, dug at the foot of a hawthorn crimson with berries, proclaimed that life goes on.

The pious benefactor of the Hospital, Robert de Parys, would have approved, I felt, of their presence; so would John Bunyan, the industrious writer of rhymes for boys and girls. On the street wall of the Rectory, a tablet put up by the present Rector pays tribute to his memory:

The Rectory and ancient Hospital of
St. John the Baptist.
Founded *c.* 1180. The Buildings date from
the 13th century.

JOHN BUNYAN

Author of "Pilgrim's Progress" used to come
Here for Talks with Rector John Gifford.
In 1653 he joined the St. John's Congregation.
In 1657 he was ordained in St. John's
For preaching (in the villages).
This Place was the Interpreter's House of His Experience.

. . . . .

The group of Bedford Nonconformists which took possession of St. John's Church and Rectory in 1653 had started with twelve members, taking the twelve apostles as their model. Fortunately for posterity, since John Bunyan was to be identified with them for thirty-five years and to act as their pastor for seventeen, they began, six years after their foundation, to keep regular Minutes of their meetings in a Church Book.

This book contains one of the most remarkable records in English history of a Christian community which maintained its vigour through suffering, persecution, internal controversy and the development of its own peculiar ritual, until it became, and remains, part of the religious system of Britain. A large folio bound in limp vellum which is still preserved at the Bunyan Meeting in Bedford, the Church Book tells the story of Christianity in miniature.

Retrospectively introducing an historical summary to complete its later records, the narrative begins by describing the origin of the Meeting in terms which would not disgrace the Acts of the Apostles:

> "In this Towne of Bedford and the places adjacent, there hath of a long time bene persons godly, who in former times (even while they remained without all forme and order as to visible Church Communion according to ye Testament of Christ) were very zealous according to their light, not onely to edify themselves but also to propagate the Gospell and help it forward, both by purse and presence, keeping always a door open and a table furnished, and free for all such ministers and Christians who shewed their zeale for and love to the Gospell of Christ. Among these that reverend man, Mr. John Grew, was chief, also Mr. John Eston, sen., and brother Anthony Harrington, with others; Men that in those times were enabled of God to adventure farre in shewing their detestation of ye bishops and their superstitions."

After these Bedford citizens had consulted together under the leadership of the exceptional man who was to become their first pastor, and had set days apart to seek counsel of God, "at length twelve of the holy brethern and sisters began this holy worke, viz: Mr. John Grew and his wife, Mr. John Eston, the elder, Anthony Harrington and his wife, Mr. John Gifford, sister Coventon, sister Bosworth, sister Munnes, sister ffenne, and sister Norton, and sister Spencer; all antient and grave Christians well knowne to one another, sister Norton being the youngest. . . .

Now the principle upon which they thus entered into fellowship one with another, and upon which they did afterwards receive those that were added to their body and fellowship, was ffaith in Christ and Holiness of life, without respect to this or that circumstance or opinion in outward and circumstantiall things. By which meanes grace and faith was incouraged, Love and Amity maintained, disputings and occasions to janglings and unprofitable questions avoyded, and many that were weake in the faith confirmed in the blessing of eternall life."

This group came into existence when national religious standards were high. It continued to uphold those standards after cynicism and corruption had swept over English social and moral life. The community had its backsliders, who were dealt with severely, and its disputatious members, who were heard with patience, though a long record of correspondence with William Whitbread, one of the most substantial "saints" whose doubts and questionings became prolific during the worst period of persecution, showed that even this patience was liable to wear and tear.

But the life of the group, like a tiny candle, burned undimmed through fair weather and raging tempest. Its Minutes described the acceptance of new converts; the visiting of prisoners in the County Gaol; calls on members, especially delinquents whose offences are sometimes related in detail; the punishment of such wrong-doers by the "withdrawal" of the congregation or, at worst, the offender's expulsion; and, increasingly towards the Restoration, the seeking of guidance from God in national "troubles" which affected Nonconformists.

Although, from regard for secrecy and the safety of members, the records after the Restoration were sometimes omitted for months and even years on end, no Minute ever suggested the abandonment of this Independent congregation owing to persecution. The Bedford Meeting remains a permanent witness to the achievements of which a determined minority is capable. For this reason its story continues green while that of more imposing bodies has vanished into oblivion.

The men amongst the founders of the congregation enumerated in the Church Book were all persons of local influence. John Eston was three times Mayor of Bedford, the third occasion being the year in which the Church was formed. John Grew had been Mayor in 1646, and in 1650 became a Justice of the Peace. Anthony Harrington, a cooper, was a tradesman of good repute who had been prominent amongst local Churchmen.

As the Meeting slowly increased in size, new members came in from the surrounding villages. One, Robert Holdstock, an Elstow trader, joined after being impressed by the change which membership of the group created in John Bunyan. He was one of several Elstow villagers persuaded by John's conversion to listen to the preaching of John Gifford.

"Almost all the town at first at times," John Bunyan reported in *Grace Abounding,* "would go out to hear at the place where I found good."

Though the women founders of the Church had outnumbered the men, they soon ceased to be prominent and were mentioned in the Church Book only as delinquents or converts. The original group of women fulfilled their most significant function when they persuaded the distraught young tinker who had sought help from them to consult their minister, and thus guaranteed their own remembrance.

Through their mediation, John Bunyan met John Gifford and heard him preach. Later, talking with him in the panelled room where the diamond-shaped panes of the leaded windows looked out upon the churchyard, he entered into the Interpreter's House of his experience.

A more suitable Interpreter could hardly have been found, for John Gifford himself had emerged only recently from the painful process of conversion. Before that period no one could have guessed that he would become the pastor of an Independent congregation, for at the outbreak of the Civil War he was a major in the King's Army.

As a Kentish man he had been engaged in the ferocious battle of Maidstone, fought by the Royalists against the Parliamentary forces under Fairfax in a torrential storm. When storm and battle alike ended, leaving Fairfax the victor, John Gifford was one of 1400 Royalists who surrendered as prisoners. His courage and energy had made him a conspicuous candidate for punishment, and though most of the captives were released, he and eleven others were imprisoned in Maidstone Gaol to await the gallows.

The night before the sentence was due to be carried out, his sister, coming to visit him, found all the prison guards in a drunken sleep, and helped him to escape. For three days, until the search for him was over, he lay concealed in the bottom of a ditch; then, after a period of disguise in London, he hid from his enemies in the homes of eminent Royalist friends. Finally he came to Bedford, where Francis Bannister, the town physician, was growing decrepit, and began to practise medicine.

At this time his experiences had not affected his philosophy; "he abode," runs the biographical description in the Church Book,

> "still very vile and debauched in life, being a great drinker, gamester, swearer, etc. But in his gaming, so it was that he usually came off by the losse, which would sometimes put him into some dumpish and discontented fitts and resolutions to leave ye practise: but these resolutions were but like the chaines on the man mentioned in the gospell which would not hold when the fit to be vile was upon him, wherefore he went on and broke them still."

One night, after losing an exceptionally large sum, Gifford went home in a rage and "thought many desperate thoughts against God". Perhaps it was divine retaliation for this unjust allocation of responsibility which caused him, for some reason unexplained, to look into a theological work by a Scholar of Brasenose College, Oxford, named Bolton. This book was probably the author's *Last and Learned Worke of the Foure Last Things: Death, Judgment, Hell, and Heaven,* published by George Miller of Blackfriars in 1633.

> "Something therein took hold upon him and brought him into a great sense of shame, wherein he continued for y^e^

space of a moneth or above. But at last God did so plentifully discover to him by His word the forgiveness of his sins for the sake of Christ, that (as he hath by severall of the brethren been heard to say) all his life after, which was about ye space of five yeares, he lost not the light of God's countenance."

Being an older and more experienced man than John Bunyan, John Gifford in this spiritual crisis deliberately cultivated the friendship of local men and women known to him to be Christians. To begin with, remembering his wild life and his antipathy to religious devotees which had been particularly vented on Anthony Harrington, Gifford's fellow townspeople doubted the reality of his conversion. But he persisted, and they finally invited him to preach.

His first sermon was successful in converting a local woman, Sister Cooper, whom his new friends respected. Gradually they came to accept him, and it was he, seeking to bring them into closer communion, who "attempted to gather into Gospell fellowship the saintes and brethren in and about the towne". The Church had been formed, and John Gifford elected as its pastor, only a short time before John Bunyan sought his place of repentance, "carefully, with tears".

At first it was difficult even for Gifford to make much impression upon the swirling perplexities of John's spiritual agony. As they talked that first day in the ancient refectory, old Andrew Dennys, in cap and ruff, looked down with shrewd, calculating eyes from his portrait on the wall. The heavy brows and long nose brought back to John the day in his childhood when he had seen the elderly Rector leaning on his staff outside St. John's Church.

John Gifford persuaded the agitated tinker to sit quietly in his room and listen while others came for spiritual advice. Afterwards, in summer, they paced up and down together in the shade of the cedar or sat beneath the mulberry in the Rectory garden, while John Bunyan learned to decant into words the trouble that lay upon his soul.

The new Rector had not been a physician in vain. Through his spiritual therapy the younger John's God of Wrath gradually gave place to a God of Reconciliation, and his terrible fears were transformed into faith, hope and confidence. The broad and

THE RECTORY GARDEN

Here John Bunyan walked and talked with "holy Mr. Gifford".

DUCK MILL BAPTISING PLACE, BEDFORD

The bend of the Ouse near the corner of Duck Mill Lane, where Bunyan was re-baptised by John Gifford, probably in secret at night.

tolerant principle upon which John Gifford had formed his "Church of Christ" inspired all his teaching; "he made it his business," John Bunyan recorded, "to deliver the people of God from all those false and unsound tests, that by nature we are prone to," and urged them to take no truth upon trust until God had convinced them of its reality.

A year or so later, when the thunder of the tempest had passed from his soul and his tender conscience was recovering from its anguish, John felt that the time had arrived when he could honestly become part of the Bedford fellowship. He asked John Gifford to accept him, and though the Rector never insisted upon baptism as a preliminary to membership, requested him to conduct the ceremony as a symbol of that acceptance.

Adult baptism by immersion was customarily performed at night, with watchers in all directions; the risk of a breach of the peace which would have arisen from a public daytime ceremony involved not only the convert, but the minister who officiated and the attending witnesses. The baptizing-place used by the Bedford Meeting was an inlet of the Ouse beneath an elm-tree, near the corner of Duck Mill Lane. This long by-path leading between orchards and market gardens from the High Street to the banks of the river still exists almost unchanged, a strange survival from the country at the centre of the modern town.

One quiet night when the population was asleep and only starlight challenged the darkness, a small party from the Bedford Meeting crept silently along the lane to the sheltered inlet. When John Bunyan first met John Gifford he had not realized that the pattern of his future was already decided, but the quiet solemnity of his midnight baptism did make him feel that a divine power, profound, mysterious, and never again to be denied, had at last taken charge of his tempestuous life.

CHAPTER VIII

BUNYAN'S BEDFORD

"It had always a sufficiency of provisions within its walls; it had the best, most wholesome, and excellent law that then was extant in the world. There was not a rascal, rogue, or traiterous person then within its walls: they were all true men, and fast joined together; and this, you know, is a great matter."

JOHN BUNYAN: *The Holy War.*

IN April 1654, when blind Mary was nearly four years old, John's second daughter, Elizabeth, was born. To the relief of her apprehensive parents she was a healthy child, without blemish or defect. At that time they still lived in the roadside Elstow cottage with the lean-to forge, so Mary took Elizabeth to be baptized and registered in the Abbey Church.

A year later John decided to move with his family to Bedford, and be close to the Meeting which was already the centre of his life and work. Strange temptations sometimes assaulted him still; once, at the Lord's Supper, a fierce impulse to blaspheme had seized him, and a wish that some evil might befall his fellow communicants. Struggling Sunday after Sunday with these "wicked and fearful thoughts", he came to believe at last that Christ's Body had been broken for his sins and His Blood shed for his transgressions.

John's new dwelling was in the parish of St. Cuthbert's, the smallest of the five Bedford parishes; under Queen Elizabeth it had held only ten families. According to the Hearth Tax Roll of 1673–4, there were no more than forty-seven when the Bunyans lived there, though Bedford now contained 446 householders.

To the small town cottage with its one hearth, John and Mary moved their few possessions—the feather-bed, the rough square table, the wicker chairs, the pewter platters, and the cushion on which, in her scanty spare time, Mary made bone-lace with carved wooden bobbins weighted by beads.

This modest house had a bedroom with a gabled roof above the only doorway, which opened straight on to the street, and two small living-rooms with double windows on either side of it. The smaller room on the right came to be known as Bunyan's Parlour; the upper bar of the grate was a steelyard, inscribed with the initials J.B. On the left of the doorway a larger living-room was used for the family. At the back, John's miniature study looked east over the garden and the green meadows stretching towards Newnham. In the garden an outhouse provided a useful workshop.

The street in which the Bunyans lived was then on the very edge of the built-up area, for the mansion and gardens of the Peck family occupied the east side of Bedford. Except for the few cottages with thatched roofs and high chimneys close to St. Cuthbert's Church, the road itself formed the boundary of an open field. It was the common street of the parish to which Speed's map of Bedford gives no name, though it was known later as St. Cuthbert's Street.

The Bunyans' cottage, on the east side, faced the Church at the southern end. Standing behind a rough wall in a green square overhung by trees, the white-painted, low-roofed structure, its pocket turret crowned by a weather-vane, resembled a village church which was startled to find that it had strayed into a town. This little country building could claim a long history, reaching back into the Bedford of the Danes and Saxons. Tradition held that Offa, King of Mercia, had founded the Church, and after his death was brought to Bedford and buried in a small chapel beside the Ouse.

At the time that John Bunyan left Elstow, the name Bedanford, mentioned in the Anglo-Saxon Chronicle, had continued almost unchanged for ten centuries. The borough itself was still small and unimportant, for it lay in a geographical backwater between the great North Road and Watling Street, the chief highways leading north and south. Its own roads, formed from the heavy Bedfordshire clay, remained primitive, muddy, and ill-kept.

In the seventeenth century the inhabitants of England were thinly and evenly distributed over the whole country; the flight to the towns had not yet begun. Those who lived in them were carefully chosen; the Statute of Apprentices ensured that each craftsman had a technical education, and the laws against wastrels prevented an influx of beggars. The country, not the town, took care of the surplus population; membership of a borough was a privilege, and its freedom was seldom bestowed upon "aliens" from other towns and villages. The only exceptions were occasional refugees from abroad, such as the Huguenots, whom England received with sympathy after Louis XIV revoked the Edict of Nantes in 1685.

Like many small boroughs of its size and type, Bedford had a long and proud tradition of civic freedom. Its earliest existing Charter, granted by Henry II, confirmed still earlier Charters which entrusted the management of the town to freely elected Mayors, Aldermen and bailiffs. The ingenious Charles II was the first monarch to interfere, in Bedford as elsewhere, with these immemorial rights. When John Bunyan moved into the borough, the Burgesses were still the ruling class from which local officials were chosen; sixty-one names had appeared on the Burgess Roll of 1625.

Speed's map of Bedford in 1610 shows a magnified village built in the shape of a double cross, with St. Paul's Church at its centre. In its more complex twentieth-century form, this pattern is still visible. The five parishes familiar to John Bunyan suggest that the little town had once been more important. In 1349 it was severely smitten by the Black Death, which left its economic effects behind long after the plague itself had been almost forgotten.

Beyond the small built-up area lay the open country of woods, farms and meadows, easily accessible to the poorer population for walking, fishing, and sports. On Speed's map the single rows of houses are backed by cornfields and orchards right into the centre of the town. Except for these few streets, the borough was an agricultural territory cultivated, like the Bedfordshire countryside, on the Anglo-Saxon strip system. Nearly a century after John Bunyan's death, when the enclosure of the Borough of Bedford began in 1779, seven-eighths of its area still lay in intermingled strips.

To the north a large uninhabited stretch of country divided the villages of Goldington on the north-east and Clapham on the north-west. Today 5000 acres of this undulating countryside beyond Foster Hill is crossed only by foot-paths, and remains almost unchanged from the green slopes that the Bunyans knew.

The streets themselves were gay, varied and insanitary. Infant mortality and disease checked any substantial increase in the small population, which washed little and cheerfully subscribed to primitive standards of public decency. Town ditches known as "Kennels", intersecting the borough and serving as open drains, provided the only system of sanitation.

The oldest of these, the "King's Ditch", had been mentioned in ancient records as early as 571 and was attributed to the legendary Offa. Originally a defence work guarding the southern half of the town against the Danes, its use for drainage purposes was incidental.

This watercourse still exists south of Bedford Bridge, where it once enclosed the parishes of St. Mary's and St. John's in a large uneven triangle with the Ouse as its base. It crossed the main road south of St. John's Church, and was spanned by a narrow bridge which John Bunyan used on his journeys from Elstow.

Four other channels, the large Saffronditch rising in Clapham Hill, the Goose Ditch, the Green Ditch, and the Sanne Ditch, converged before they reached the Ouse. With their burden of rags, bones, domestic slops, and tanners', brewers', and chandlers' refuse, they ran as one noisome stream into the river near the Grammar School. This building, now used as the Town Hall, had been founded under Queen Elizabeth, when Bedford's Dick Whittington, Sir William Harper, was Lord Mayor of London.

The heavy effluvia from the "Kennels" in summer came back to John's mind, an obnoxious memory, when he piloted Christiana and her children through the Valley of the Shadow.

> "Yet they were not got through the Valley; so they went on still, and behold great stinks and loathsome smells, to the great annoyance of them. Then said Mercy to Christiana, there is not such pleasant being here as at the gate, or at the Interpreters, or at the House where we lay last.
>
> O but, said one of the Boys, it is not so bad to go through here, as it is to abide here always, and for ought I know, one reason why we must go this way to the house prepared for us, is, that our home might be made the sweeter to us.
>
> Well said, Samuel, quoth the Guide, thou hast now spoken

like a man. Why, if ever I get out here again, said the Boy, I think I shall prize light and good way better than ever I did in all my life."

John Bunyan, whose appreciation of light, air, fragrant flowers and open windows was as far in advance of his time as his views on baptism, had been fortunate in finding a cottage on the side of the High Street farthest from the Saffronditch. But in spite of their noxious smells and population of fleas, the Bedford streets had their compensations. From the corner of the Bridge where the sign at the top of the steps outside the Old Swan Inn showed a large white swan against a dark background, the half-timbered houses with their gabled dormer windows and over-hanging storeys climbed the High Street in a colourful sequence of carved frontages and painted signboards.

Each house had its own sign, in the shape of a Blue Boar, Black Swan, or Red Lion. One swung above the doorway of John Fenn, hatter and deacon of the Bedford Meeting, who sold John Bunyan his steeple hat and hose; another decorated the shop of Thomas Pare, where Mary purchased her groceries "over against ye Pillorie". Their town had not only its pillory as a warning to evil-doers, but its gallows beyond the Grey Friars Precinct on the road to Bromham, extending from Bendhouse Lane.

Soon, now, the time was coming when John in prison would recall the executions that he had witnessed there, and fear lest he, if summoned to climb that ladder to eternity, "should either with quaking or other symptoms of fainting, give occasion to the Enemy to reproach the Way of God and his People, for their Timorousness. . . . Methought I was ashamed to die with a pale Face, and tottering Knees, for such a Cause as this".

In 1655 John still had five years in which to learn, with a pictorial precision that never faded, the features of the small town where the rest of his life was to be spent. According to William Camden at the end of the previous century, Bedford was so completely divided by the Ouse "that it might be looked upon as two towns, if the two parts were not joined by a fair Stone Bridge, whereon are two Gates to stop the Passage as Occasion shall require".

Whenever he crossed this bridge on the way from Elstow before he lived in the borough, John never failed to glance eastwards at the rough nettle-grown field, with a line of ruined walls—described as "Ould Ruines" in Speed's map—stretching along the north side of the river bank. Here, he knew, had stood the Norman castle built in the twelfth century. Part of its foundations lay beneath the great mound, its sides covered with bushes and its summit a bowling green, which was known as Castle Hill. Three centuries later the mound with its crown of smooth rich turf was still to be there, though the players of bowls would have vanished.

The Castle had once been protected on the north, east, and west by a strong rampart with an inner parapet, and a deep encircling fosse joining the river on the south side. In the days of its glory, when it dominated the town, it had been seized from its owner, William de Beauchamp, by Fulke de Breauté, a soldier of fortune who had become the leader of King John's foreign mercenaries and a terror to Bedford citizens.

After Fulke had incurred the wrath of John's successor, Henry III, in 1224 by capturing one of the King's itinerant justices, Henry Braybroke, and imprisoning him in the Castle, Henry ordered the stronghold to be demolished. Fulke fled; Sir William was restored, and permitted to build himself a house with the Castle materials though he was not allowed to fortify it.

Besides that story of ancient maraudings and tumults, there was much else to attract an itinerant tinker from outside the town. The beautiful Priory of the Grey Friars, for instance, stood at its north-west corner, and Cauldwell Abbey spread over the fields on the south bank of the Ouse opposite Trumpington Mead.

The three water-mills in the neighbourhood had a picturesque and comforting homeliness; Duck Mill stood close to the island almost opposite the Castle mound, and the horse-mill known as Trinitye Mill, lying still further east on the north bank, had once been driven by the Castle moat. Along the same bank John could walk to the Mill of Newnham Priory, a mile and a half nearer to the river's mouth. The town house of its Prior was the old building known as the Prioratus, close to Silver Street and the County Gaol.

But none of these links with the past had the same fascination for John as the half sinister, half romantic ruins of the Castle itself. As he walked over the Bridge back to Elstow at twilight it was easy to imagine a giant hiding in the dark bushes on Castle Hill, waiting to lure unsuspecting travellers along the footpath through the nettles and throw them into the "dungeon" or tunnel attributed to the avenging soldiers of Henry III.

The Bedford Burgesses were very proud of their "fair Stone Bridge"; it was always described as "the Great Bridge" in the Corporation Minutes. An inscription on the present Bridge, built in 1813, truthfully tells the traveller that its origin goes back to remote antiquity. The statement that it was built when Bedford Castle was demolished seems to be more questionable; the Bridge may have been made from the Castle materials, but was probably erected a hundred years after the siege.

On either side of the Bridge, two markets were held regularly; the corn market on the north bank drew villagers into the town every Saturday from the surrounding country. It still draws them to the open square in front of St. Paul's, though instead of corn they now buy fruit, vegetables, and substantial underwear from the stalls and booths. On Tuesday a different market for "all living Cattel" brought buyers to the south side. Besides the regular markets, seven annual fairs were held in the town.

Every night at ten o'clock, the Great Bridge was closed to traffic until five next morning. Its upkeep, and the lighting of adjacent areas for stray travellers endangered by pot-holes and ditches, caused perpetual headaches to conscientious Burgesses. On 10 October, 1656, a year after the Bunyans moved to Bedford, a strict and precise injunction appeared in the Corporation Act Book:

> "Ordayned: That on S. Luke's Day next comyng until Candlemas following and so yearlie for ever, lights shall be sett forth in the High Streete of this town all along on both sides of the River of Ouse from the house called the Peacock in St. Peter's parish to the Bridge in St. John's Parish on the way to Ampthill. And they shall be sett up at the Shutting in of the Evening and be continued unto eight o'clock following. Each occupier of Shops and other Edifices next the Streete shall each of them according to the turne of the side, set out a Candellight of the Bigness at least of sixteen in the pound."

Note.—The illustration opposite should be John Speed's Map of Bedford, *not* Bedfordshire.

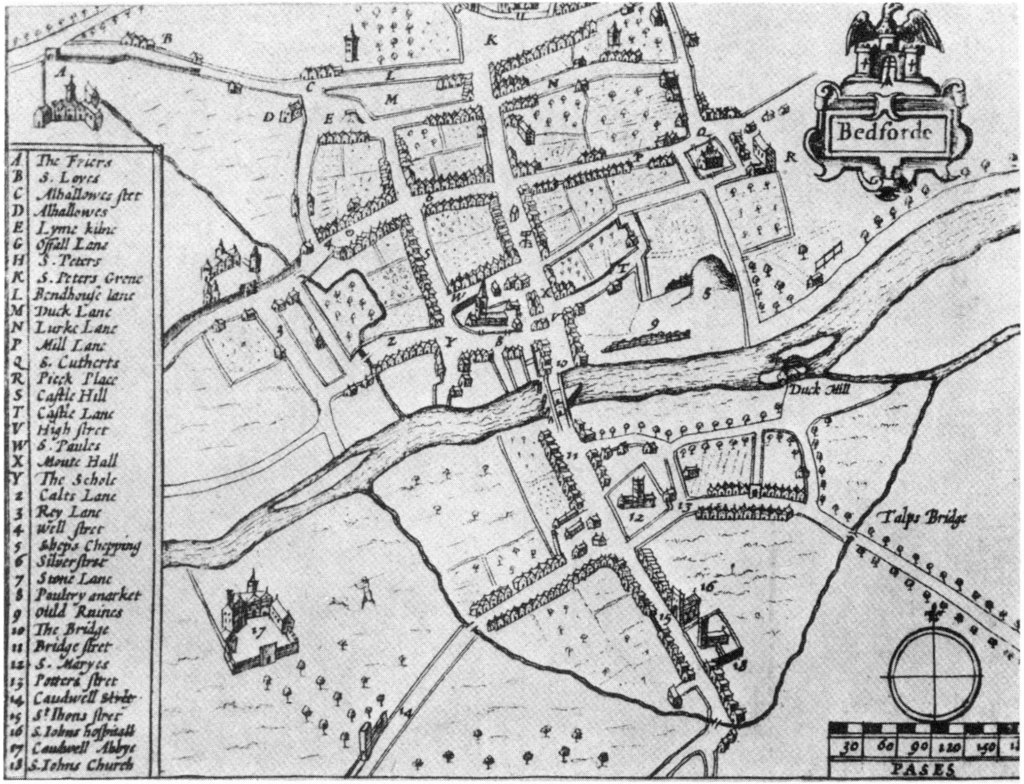

JOHN SPEED'S MAP OF BEDFORDSHIRE, 1610

OLD BEDFORD

The reproduction of a painting based on old prints.

The phrase "for ever" applied three hundred years ago to this primitive system of street-lighting leads to interesting speculations on the type of illumination likely to be used in 2256. Will unheard-of glories rivalling sunny daylight be permanently available to local authorities—or will mankind have reverted to the farthing dip?

John Bunyan and his family were hardly settled in their St. Cuthbert's Street cottage, when a bitter blow fell upon him and the Bedford Meeting. In September 1655, after acting as John's Interpreter for only two years, John Gifford died.

Seven years earlier he had come into Bedford, as it were from the void, to bear witness to the vitality of the cause against which he had fought in the Civil War. Now he vanished into the void again, to become part of the dust in St. John's churchyard contributed by those that have no memorial. He left behind him only his wife and three daughters, born during his sojourn in Bedford, and a letter enjoining tolerance and wisdom which was his legacy to the Church that he had founded.

In this letter, written on his death-bed and witnessed by two members of his congregation, he reminded his followers of the broad principles which united them in love and preserved their Church from minor dissensions. Many times, in the period before them, they were to return to those principles as to a hiding-place from the tempest.

> "Concerning separation from the Church, about Baptisme, laying on of hands, Anoynting with Oyls, Psalmes, or any externalls; I charge every one of you respectively, as you will give an account of it to our Lord Jesus Christ who shall judge both quick and dead at his coming, that none of you be found guilty of this great evill."

Those, he continued, who had thus been intolerant owing to misplaced zeal, "have erred from the Lawe of the Love of Christ, and have made a rent from ye true church which is but one".

Urging his friends to choose his successor carefully and to love each other as Christ Jesus had loved them, he ended with an injunction which echoed like a prophecy in the years ahead: "Stand fast; the Lord is at hand."

For John Bunyan and his fellow-worshippers, the business of standing fast was shortly to become a full-time occupation. But their immediate problem, which was to prove difficult, concerned the appointment of a successor to John Gifford. The living remained vacant for several months owing to a dispute between Bedford Council, which desired to nominate a certain Mr. Hayes of Papworth, and the Church, which wanted a young man, fragile but much beloved by its members, named John Burton. Eventually the problem was referred to Cromwell himself, who decided in Burton's favour.

John Burton was appointed pastor on 16 January, 1656. Four months later, on 24 May, the keeping of detailed and regular entries in the Church Book began.

At the top of Folio 15, under a mention of the first gathering of the Church, these words have been added in a later hand:

> "N.B. Mr. Bunyan began to preach some time in the year 1656. But was not ordained Pastor till 21st of October 1671.* He entered into the joy of his Lord 31st of August 1688. So that He was a preacher of the Gospel 32 years—& Pastor of this Church 17 years."

John Bunyan, now the father of a third child—this time a son, also named John—had already made rapid progress in the congregation which he had joined with so deep a sense of unworthiness. He had been a member for about two years, when a request by his fellow-members to say a word at one of their gatherings led to the discovery of a gift for preaching which surprised both himself and them. Soon he was invited to accompany his brethren on expeditions into the country, where the words that he added to their homilies showed that his eloquence could be relied on.

In 1657, when he had been preaching for about a year and had begun to take village services on his own responsibility, John became involved in disputes with some members of the Society of Friends.

* Actually 21 December.

Controversy, both political and religious, was then in the air. Earlier in the year, an unsuccessful attempt on Cromwell's life had started a movement in the House of Commons to make him King. In Bedfordshire a strong party opposed to this change was led by William Dell and John Donne, a young Puritan who on leaving Cambridge in 1653 had become Rector of Pertenhall, two miles from Keysoe in the north of the county.

They and others drew up a document known as "The Humble and Serious Testimony", a petition signed by hundreds of their followers against Cromwell's assumption of the Crown. The Civil War, they declared, had been fought to recover civil and religious rights and liberties, and a Commonwealth was better able to withstand the Stuarts than any individual.

By the orders of Cromwell's Secretary Thurloe, all those who signed "The Humble and Serious Testimony" were arrested. When the Mayor of Bedford, Robert Fitzhugh, asked for their release, he submitted evidence showing that the local left-wing preference for a republic exceeded the right-wing desire for a monarchy. Cromwell may have been influenced by this evidence in returning his answer, which to Bedfordshire's satisfaction refused the Kingship, and instead accepted an amendment of the Constitution by the Humble Petition and Advice.

The series of disputes between John Bunyan and the Quakers, which led to the publication of his first two books, had started some time before the Second Protectorate began on 26 June, 1657. George Fox, the weaver's son with whom Quakerism originated, had a more pugnacious character than John; his persistent craving for truth and spiritual perfection brought him a series of religious experiences very different from John's prolonged struggle with temptation.

After many wanderings in search of inspiration and much catechising of "Professors of Puritanism", George Fox evolved the doctrine of an inner light arising from the presence of Christ in the heart of a believer. The idea that this in-dwelling Christ could cleanse the soul of sin led to some popular confusion between the Quakers and the Ranters, from whose methods of justifying their unconventional behaviour John had fled in alarm.

In *Grace Abounding*, misled by the mysticism of Quaker theology, he persisted ten years afterwards in condemning "the

Errors of the Quakers" and the "vile and abominable things fomented by them". Their fervour sometimes outran both law and sanity; they attracted such saintly fanatics as James Naylor, who in October 1655 had ridden into Bristol strangely imagining himself to be the Messiah entering Jerusalem. He was punished by being flogged through the Bristol streets with a ruthlessness which remains a black indictment against English Puritanism.

Today, in a perspective denied to John Bunyan, we can see those extremists as part of the mystics' protest against the arid theology of that age, and their extravagances as evidence of the mental and spiritual ferment amongst the common people which had hitherto been suppressed by successive orthodoxies. There was no essential difference between John Bunyan and George Fox; Fox's belief in an inner light merely carried to its logical conclusion the Puritan witness against formal religion in the name of which John went to prison. Both alike taught the poor and humble to use their minds and apply their imagination in the service of God.

But "it may be doubted whether the century affords a single instance of the reconciliation of two divided religious bodies", writes Professor G. N. Clark in *The Seventeenth Century*. Sometimes there was a considerable intolerance inside the Churches themselves; the Jansenist controversy within the Roman Catholic community still lives in the *Lettres Provinciales* of Blaise Pascal, published in the year that the Bedford Church began to keep its Minutes.

In 1654 a county magistrate and Member of the Little Parliament, John Crook, had been converted to Quakerism, and thenceforth turned his estate, Beckring's Park, between Ampthill and Woburn, into a local stronghold of the Society of Friends. From that time onwards individual Friends made their way to Bedford and, as their manner was, interrupted the meetings of other denominations in order to bear their witness and denounce the preacher. They proclaimed the influence of example, the sinfulness of war, and the spiritual value of non-violent resistance to evil.

John Bunyan, personally challenged on several occasions, regarded the Quaker doctrines as tantamount to contempt for the written word of God. The Quakers, in turn, criticized his emphasis on external revelation and the historic facts of the Christian faith.

MODERN BEDFORD

Showing the Bridge over the Ouse, St. Paul's Church, and the Swan Hotel. On the extreme left the Food Office occupies the site of the Chapel of Herne.

STEVINGTON CROSS

This ancient Gothic monument is said to be the scene of Bunyan's allusion to the Cross where Christian lost his burden.

One clash between John and the Friends occurred in the High Street at the Market Cross, a small pent-house between Mill Lane and Silver Street where the farmers' wives sold butter and eggs on Saturdays. Another followed some remarks made by John at the village of Pavenham in April, and a third turned into an open argument, joined in by both John Bunyan and John Burton, at St. Paul's Church on 23 May, 1656.

I reflected on these disputes after I had witnessed another between the disciples of a modern "John Bunyan", and his open-air audience. One fine Saturday evening in mid-September, when the bright half-circle of the harvest moon climbed a sky tender with starlight, I walked down the High Street to Bedford market-place and there had a remarkable experience. It was none the less remarkable because the Rector of St. John's had already prepared me for it.

In the centre of the modern square where three centuries ago John Bunyan preached before the Moot Hall, a group of young men and women had set up a rostrum. Beneath it was their banner, inscribed with the words "National Young Life Campaign".

On the rostrum a series of youthful speakers, five boys and a girl, stood up in succession and told a large crowd of good-humoured sceptics how they had "found Jesus". The girl's story was a modern version of *Grace Abounding*; she had been a great sinner, she said, and really knew what sin meant. She took to going to church, but that only made her feel worse; she tried confession, and felt worse still. Finally she chanced to attend a meeting at which the simple fact of "coming to Jesus" was explained to her, and had changed her life as soon as she accepted Him.

The young orators were all fluent and obviously accustomed to public speaking, but in their own fashion they were inarticulate. They could not explain what they really meant by "accepting Jesus", and were easily floored by clever questions. One tall unbeliever in the audience demanded an explanation of God's motives in permitting pain; his courtesy survived the fact that none of the speakers was qualified to give him either a philosophical or a theological answer.

Yet it seemed clear that each had passed through a real spiritual experience, which had brought peace to him or her. All were prepared for insults; a paper pellet flung at one speaker from the edge of the crowd caused not a second's hesitation in the humble yet confident flow of his oratory, punctuated by the admonition "Listen, folks!" at regular intervals.

At last their leader took the rostrum, a farmer's labourer, tall, handsome, dynamic. This time I felt startled indeed; in the lamplight the young man's hair was flaxen, not red, but his eyes were the eyes of the Bunyan Statue on St. Peter's Green. Unconsciously he also adopted the posture of the statue, which stands "as if it pleaded with men".

On his right the sculptured figure of John Howard, the prison reformer, in eighteenth-century coat and hat, looked with benevolent dignity upon the High Street. Above his head the spire of St. Paul's soared into the velvet sky, spread like a canopy over the trees in the square. From the half-cleared stalls left by the weekly market, a smell of fish and rotting fruit mingled with the warm human odour of the crowd. To the south the moon, now reflected in the placid Ouse, hung like a Chinese lantern over Bedford Bridge.

As I listened to the handsome labourer explaining in his Bedfordshire accent how man alone of all creation had rebelled against God, and brought judgment on himself by sins for which only Christ could atone, I understood why the Rector of St. John's had called him "a modern Bunyan". So might the young John Bunyan have looked as he started out, at twenty-eight, to preach with similar verve and inspiration in the Bedfordshire villages after his conversion. So must he have appeared in 1656 when he brought so much sincerity and animation to his theological disputes—directed against, of all people, the Quakers.

At another Bedford controversy in that year 1656, a woman Friend, Anne Blackley, entered into the discussion with a characteristic reprimand; from the audience she urged John Bunyan to "throw away the Scriptures". But John was ready with a prompt reply.

"No!" he answered, "for then the devil would be too hard for me!"

His absorption in the questions raised by these recurrent

arguments led him into his first attempt at authorship; it is perhaps the Friends to whom English literature owes John Bunyan the "man of letters". But this early experiment, like its author throughout his life, paid no attention to literary canons.

"Written rapidly and in a heat", under the title "*Some Gospel Truths Opened, by that unworthy servant of Christ, John Bunnyan of Bedford*", it protested in 216 pages against Quaker "spiritualization" of the living, literal Christ, who died, was crucified, and rose again. John Burton, the pastor of the Bedford Church whose mission was to be so brief, contributed an Introduction explaining that the tinker-author was "not chosen out of an earthly but out of the heavenly university, the Church of Christ".

This pamphlet roused the wrath of Edward Burrough, a fervent young Quaker who was destined to die for his faith in Newgate Prison six years later. He replied to John's effort with another, *The True Faith of the Gospel of Peace*, in which his criticism of the "professed minister in Bedfordshire" hardly reflected the meeker aspects of Quaker testimony.

John was roused to reply in *A Vindication of Gospel Truths Opened*, published like its predecessor by both a London publisher, John Wright, and Matthias Cowley of Newport Pagnell. In this new booklet he linked the Quakers with the Ranters of his sore recollection, and Burrough with the retinue of worldlings "who are as mad against me as thyself".

The crude intolerance of this controversy lost nothing by the youth of the antagonists. Though John had passed through deep waters of experience and now supported a wife and three children, he was still only twenty-seven, while Burrough was barely twenty-three when he began to attack John in print. His second reply fulminated against "John Bunion's foule dirty lyes and slanders", but at this point John abandoned the slanging match himself.

By nature he was neither provocative nor malicious, and a new work, of exposition rather than argument, was taking shape in his mind. He meant it to interpret the story of Dives and Lazarus, under the title *A Few Sighs From Hell*, and this time he would ask his friend John Gibbs of Newport Pagnell to write the Preface.

When the book was published in 1658, John Bunyan's own

foreword, "The Author to the Reader", explained the lesson of humility that he had learned from his disputes with Edward Burrough and the Quakers:

> "I must tell thee, the world rages, they stamp and shake their heads, and fain they would be doing: the Lord help me to take all that they shall do with patience, and when they smite the one cheek, to turn the other to them, that I may do as Christ hath bidden me; for then the Spirit of God, and of glory shall rest upon me. Farewel."

He added a postscript, pathetic in its revelation of the periodic failures of confidence from which he still suffered.

> "I am thine, if you be not ashamed to own me, because of my low and contemptible descent in the world. John Bunyan."

Though the subject and treatment of this book shows John as still shadowed by the terror of his conversion, he had already left behind the Old Testament concept of retaliation. Two years later, facing magistrates and judges, he was to practise what he now preached. Before that period of persecution—which however bitter carries its own stimulus—he was again to be acquainted with personal grief.

On 3 September, 1658, just after John's publication of *A Few Sighs From Hell,* Oliver Cromwell had died. Whatever his political miscalculations, he had secured the continuation in English life of the Quakers and other Nonconformist sects who, but for him, might have been crushed by the bigots of organized religion. He closed his honest and unflinching life with a plea for divine forgiveness for himself and his enemies.

> "Thou hast made me, though very unworthy, a mean instrument to do Thy people some good and Thee service: and many of them have set too high a value upon me, though others wish and would be glad of my death. Pardon such as desire to trample upon the dust of a poor worm, for they are Thy people too; and pardon the folly of this short prayer, even for Jesus Christ's sake, and give us a good night, if it be Thy pleasure. Amen."

A great storm ushered Cromwell to his tomb, as though Heaven itself recognized that a Titan had vanished from the earth. Storms of another kind would soon blow upon those who had espoused his cause in Church and State, but death, which carried away the mighty, came also with sombre impartiality to visit the humble.

By the end of that year another son, Thomas, had been born to John Bunyan and his wife. Soon afterwards Mary died, a frail young woman prematurely exhausted after ten years of marriage, though her child-bearing had been moderate by the ruthless standards of her day.

Before he was thirty John was left alone with four young children, and the shadow of prison already beginning to creep from the grave where England's stern ruler lay dead.

CHAPTER IX

THE SHADOW OF THE CROSS

"Thus far I did come loaden with my sin,
Nor could ought ease the grief that I was in,
Till I came hither: What a Place is this!
Must here be the beginning of my Bliss?
Must here the Burden fall from off my Back?
Must here the strings that bound it to me crack?
Bless'd Cross! bless'd Sepulchre! bless'd rather be
The man that there was put to shame for me."
JOHN BUNYAN: *The Pilgrim's Progress*, Part I.

MARY'S death was a crippling blow to John Bunyan, for ever since his early companionship with Margaret, women had meant more to him than to most men of his epoch.

In the second part of *The Pilgrim's Progress*, he was later to express both the general attitude of his day, and the individual response aroused in him by the women whom he had known. They were, of course, weaker vessels who had to be helped along the roadway of life by such champions as Mr. Greatheart, but the voluminous feminine draperies of the age and the habitual condition of the roads gave this view a basis of commonsense rather than prejudice. England had recently prospered under a strong-minded queen; John's contemporaries looked back to her with the same nostalgic regret for better days as the twentieth century feels towards Queen Victoria.

John put a more personal estimate into the mouth of Gaius, the innkeeper with whom Christiana and her children stayed on their way from the Valley of Shadows to a reformed Vanity Fair. After saying that he is going to speak "on the behalf of Women", Gaius recalls that God's Son is "made of a woman", and continues:

"I will say again, that when the Saviour was come, Women rejoyced in him, before either Man or Angel. I read not that ever any man did give unto Christ so much as one Groat, but the Women followed him, and ministered to him of their Substance. 'Twas a Woman that washed his Feet with Tears, and a Woman that anointed his Body to the Burial: They were Women that wept when he was going to the Cross; and Women that followed him from the Cross, and that sat by his Sepulcher when he was buried: They were Women that were first with him at his Resurrection Morn, and Women that brought Tidings first to his Disciples, that he was risen from the Dead: Women therefore are highly favoured, and shew by these things that they are sharers with us in the Grace of Life."

This passage suggests that John was exceptionally fortunate in both his wives; there is a significant contrast between the stability of his domestic relationships and the desolate chaos of Milton's.

For the devoted loyalty of his second wife, Elizabeth, we shall soon find abundant evidence. The gentler Mary, as *Grace Abounding* shows, rode out with him his spiritual tempest; her patience and pity have led some biographers to identify her with Mercy in Part II of *The Pilgrim's Progress*.

Their identification of Elizabeth with Christiana seems less convincing. Like Christiana, Elizabeth was the stronger personality, but she would never have allowed her Christian to set out for the Celestial City alone.

It was Elizabeth who came to John's rescue now. With the help of women friends in the Bedford Church he managed after Mary's death to take care of his family, all under ten, but that did not fill her vacant place at table or her empty chair by the fire. He began to understand better the haste with which his father had twice re-married. His work, too, was increasing; at this time of personal trouble, more and more calls came to him to preach in the neighbouring villages.

He believed that Mary's friend Elizabeth, for all her reticence, had long sincerely loved him, and though she was so young, her courage and sense of responsibility made her seem older. She would be a mother to his children, he knew, if he made her his wife. It seemed a great deal to ask, but after much thought and prayer, he did ask it.

A year after Mary died, they were married. The empty chair was filled now, though his memory of Mary remained so clear that sometimes she and Elizabeth seemed to sit together at his table.

At last he could leave his family without misgivings and go forth on his long preaching expeditions.

When his brethren first asked him to preach, the request had found him shy and diffident; from a sense of his own inadequacy he had sought to excuse himself. But when, under pressure, his gift to his astonishment was revealed, he found that he not only felt grateful to God for bestowing upon him the mercy of eloquence, but was secretly anxious to use his powers of speech. A study of St. Paul's First Epistle to the Corinthians finally persuaded him that the possession of a great gift carried also the obligation to use it.

In spite of his consciousness of exceptional ability, he started on the work of unsupervised preaching with "great fear and trembling", but the immediate response showed him that his boldness was justified. Even in the thinly populated areas to which he was sent, the people came in hundreds to hear him.

His sermons were lucid, virile, humorous, direct: his knowledge of the Bible was already intimate, and he used the Scriptures as though they were part of himself. He became the type of preacher whose vigour and inspiration are a speaking rebuke to professional conventionality. Though his right to preach was frequently questioned because he was known to be a tinker, his eloquence made its own reply.

For the first year or two he spent his time in expounding the doctrine of original sin, for his sense of his guilt still lay heavily upon him. However remarkable his gift might be, he was only a sinner addressing sinners.

"I preached what I felt, what I smartingly did feel," he recorded in *Grace Abounding*; "even that under which my poor Soul did groan and tremble to astonishment. Indeed I have been as one sent to them from the dead; I went myself in Chains to preach to them in Chains, and carried that fire in my own Conscience, that I persuaded them to beware of."

Before long John was undergoing experiences familiar to all public speakers; he was often ashamed before he spoke and painfully distressed afterwards, but his sense of unworthiness disappeared as soon as his sermon began.

"I have gone full of guilt and terror even to the Pulpit-door," he admitted, "and there it hath been taken off, and I have been at Liberty in my mind until I have done my work."

Sometimes he found that a chance word had more effect than his carefully prepared theme; at others he was discouraged by overwhelming apprehensions, "fearing that I should not be able to speak a word at all to edification; nay, that I should not be able to speak sense unto the people; at which times I should have such a strange faintness and strengthlessness seize upon my body, that my legs have scarce been able to carry me".

Occasionally, even now, the old temptation to blaspheme returned; at such times he felt "so straitned in my speech, as to utterance before the People, that I have been as if I had not known or remembered what I have been about, or, as if my head had been in a bag all the time of the Exercise".

Notwithstanding these weaknesses, freely admitted with a mingled humour and humility which only endeared him the more to his congregations, the demand for his sermons became so great that he encountered a new and unexpected temptation "to pride and liftings up of Heart", all of which "were easily blown up at the applause and commendation of every unadvised Christian".

"I saw therefore," he concluded realistically, "that he that hath Gifts, had need be let into a sight of the nature of them, to wit, that they come short of making of him to be in a truly saved condition, lest he rest in them, and so fall short of the grace of God."

Amongst the places which John first visited was Stevington, one of Bedfordshire's loveliest villages on the outcrop of limestone running north-west from Bromham Bridge to Sharnbrook. Here the Ouse, after a great bend between Clapham and Bromham, meanders placidly through water-meadows and cornfields dominated by the ridge of high land on which the stone-built village stands.

During the Middle Ages pilgrims came here in their thousands to visit the Holy Well and the spring still trickling from the great rock which makes a platform for the Church. The double-splayed windows of the building, once used by the Saxon archers, look across the river from a square tower, transformed by the lichen which covers it from the original greyish-green of the stone to the colour of pale rust. In late summer the dark firs and yews in the churchyard contrast sharply with the warm gold of the cornlands beyond the Ouse.

In the sanctuary of the Church stood a straight-backed medieval chair of solid oak, where John sometimes sat and rested after the five-mile walk from Bedford. But it was not in the Church that he preached, for Stevington had an Independent group formed in 1655 which was closely linked with the Bedford Meeting. Their own records describe their origin:

> "Some of the faithful did gather together at Stevington, in the County of Bedford, for to walk in the commandments and ordinances of the Lord with their beloved brother and teacher, Stephen Hawthorn their overseer."

Stephen Hawthorn, who lived three miles further west in Turvey, was to be minister of Stevington Independent Church until the distant year 1705, when to his extreme old age even the Revolution of 1688, which ended thirty years of peril and persecution, was already a memory. In winter the village group which he founded as a young man met in each other's homes or walked to St. John's Church in Bedford.

In 1656 the Bedford Church Book for "the 26th of the 4th moneth" (26 June)* recorded the permission given to Stevington Church for these visits:

> "It was concluded likewise that the members of the Church of Christ in and about Steventon may breake bread with us and we with them as the Lord shall give opportunity."

Sometimes in summer the small community of worshippers met out-of-doors in The Holmes wood on the banks of the Ouse, half a mile from the village; its density, like its encircling hawthorns and brambles, was to serve them well in the days to come. Here, in a rushy inlet of the river well screened by thorns and elders, they had established their private baptizing-place. Further uphill, in a large natural clearing under a roof of beeches, the services were held. The preacher stood against a smooth tree-trunk and his hearers sat before him on the dry ground, where the fallen leaves of centuries lay brown and thick as a deep pile carpet.

* In seventeenth-century England (and until 1752) the old style calendar was still in use, by which the year began on 25 March, and March was reckoned as the first month.

When John preached in this wood he walked to it from Stevington village by a footpath which led downhill beneath damp dock-like weeds past the Holy Well. The footpath took him on through the fields above the Ouse, and joined The Holmes wood on the other side of a marshy triangle thickly covered with shrubs. Between this narrow path and the lane leading uphill from Stevington village stretched a sunlit pattern of green and golden fields, like a painting by the future Vincent van Gogh. On the other side of the Ouse, beyond the field adjoining The Holmes wood known as Dancing Meadow, a jigsaw puzzle of unenclosed strips in a dozen shades of jade, brown and pale yellow climbed to Oakley Hill on the horizon.

As John waited for his congregation, two mallards with gleaming necks of emerald velvet rose suddenly from the reeds which surrounded the baptizing-place. When they had flown away, the afternoon silence of the wood seemed hardly broken by the soft chirping of smaller birds, and the gentle splash of fish leaping from the river just visible through the screen of leaves. He was still not fully accustomed to the idea that he, a sinner weighed down by his burden of guilt, could give help and counsel to others. Yet the summer air seemed to be filled with whispers of hope, of promise.

When the service was over he climbed a grassy path leading from Dancing Meadow to the lane, and walked back to the village cross-roads between hawthorn hedges glowing golden in the level evening light. At the centre of the village stood the slender Gothic column of grey stone, raised on steps, which was known as Stevington Cross. Pausing here for a moment to look downhill towards the Church and the Holy Well, John suddenly experienced an extraordinary feeling of exhilaration.

It seemed to him that he had at last begun to expiate his riotous, irresponsible life, and now received the assurance of forgiveness from an inner Voice, not so much heard as felt, which spoke to him as he reached the old monument between the cross-roads. So strong was the sense of relief that it appeared to take a physical form, as though a heavy burden which he had been carrying had fallen from his shoulders.

He could almost imagine that he saw it rolling away, down, down, down along the incline leading to the Church, until it disappeared into the opening of the rock where the Holy Well still poured its waters over the weed-covered stones. At that moment the source of the water seemed to his pictorial imagination to be the Sepulchre of Christ: the Lord Christ whose burial-place had received the burden of his sins.

The feeling of wonder and thankfulness was so overwhelming that, hardly realizing what he did, he began to weep. Standing below the Cross with the healing tears pouring down his cheeks, he lost all consciousness of the quiet village. In that moment of final reconciliation with the God whom he had once rejected, he thought that three angels descended and stood beside him. They saluted him and brought their gifts, of peace, and forgiveness, and a new garment of righteousness.

John never forgot his walk home from Stevington, with the long shadows of the elms on the meadows taking strange shapes which resembled outstretched Hands, and the cornfields, red-gold beneath the sunset, shining like the streets of a heavenly City. From that moment the character of his preaching changed: "for still," he wrote, "I preached what I saw and felt."

Hitherto, during the two years of his work in the villages, he had been chiefly conscious of the burden of sin, and had felt constrained to warn his congregation of their fearful state. But now he had a new experience, a new consciousness, to put before his hearers; he could tell them that, through the atonement of Christ, their just punishment could be lifted, their sins washed away by the Blood shed in compassion.

"Now therefore," he thankfully recorded, "I did much labour to hold forth Jesus Christ in all his Offices, Relations, and Benefits unto the World. . . . After this, God led me into something of the Mystery of the Union of Christ; wherefore that I discovered and shewed to them also."

This transformation in John's thinking was the basis of his fourth book, *The Doctrine of the Law and Grace Unfolded*, published in 1659 by "M. Wright, at the sign of the King's Head in the Old Bailey", and again by his friend Matthias Cowley, of Newport Pagnell. In this book, as later in *Grace Abounding*, he told the story of his early struggles, and then how he had seen "through grace that it was the blood shed on Mount Calvary that did save and redeem sinners as clearly and as really with the eyes of my soul as ever methought I had seen a penny loaf bought with a penny".

But though the realization of forgiveness was now to sustain him throughout his pilgrimage, he never lost sight of his continuing need for grace. In the epistle which he wrote as an Introduction to *The Law and Grace Unfolded*, he begged his readers to remember that necessity.

"Pray for me to our God, with much earnestness, fervency, and frequently, in all your knockings at our Father's door, because I do stand very much in need thereof."

Between his first call to preach and the publication of *The Law and Grace Unfolded*, John visited many villages besides Stevington. To those within walking distance of Bedford he travelled on foot, but on horseback he often crossed the county borders of Cambridge, Hertford, Buckingham and Huntingdon.

One of the villages to which he went with most satisfaction was Ridgmont, the home of the Bedford Meeting's patron, Colonel John Okey, on the highroad from Ampthill to Woburn. Riding uphill for the last five miles, he passed thickets of silver birch uncommon in Bedfordshire until, with Ridgmont village, he reached the summit of the Greensand Ridge.

Here he preached in the small square-towered church, chrome-grey against a huddle of tall elms, which stood at the end of a muddy lane half a mile from the village street. This lane took him across a stretch of high, open country between oaks and firs, with wide views of the wooded countryside. John Okey's farmyard, a prosperous place well-equipped with barns and straw-stacks, pushed close to the churchyard where the grey tombstones stood like ghosts beneath the elders.

Sometimes on his way home John visited the handful of brethren who lived in the nearby Greensand villages of Lidlington and Millbrook. He preferred to ride down Lidlington Hill rather than up, for it was very long and steep, winding between the massive trees which crept across the slopes of the Ampthill range.

Past Millbrook the way led through a deep gorge; at sunset a sound like a waterfall came from the blackbirds, starlings, blue tits and nuthatches roosting on the boughs of the dense oaks and firs, which already brought night to the country road. On either side of it spread the deep morass that formed the bottom of the valley, a perpetual threat to waggons travelling over the rough track which slipped away beneath their wheels. In wet weather the powerful brook that turned the mill three-quarters of a mile to the north transformed the marshy ground into a chain of ponds.

High above the gorge, on a huge natural platform even more dramatic than the rock at Stevington, stood the old red church of squared ironstone; its low embattled tower, dangerously close to the western escarpment, had been built 300 years before John was born. To the south lay the pleasant valley of the River Flit, but on a clear day, looking north-east towards Huntingdon and Lincoln, it was possible to see the Wash from the highest point.

Immediately north of the churchyard the tops of the firs and oaks concealed Millbrook Gorge. In that sinister yet romantic forest country many strange legends had grown up. One related how fairy gold was buried on Moneypot Hill south-west of the village; on moonlit nights the villagers sought the treasure in silence, for fear of disturbing the guardian fairies. It was said, too, that a century ago a great knight in armour, luminous in the mist like an infernal apparition, used to travel on horseback along the road to Millbrook from Ampthill.

Alone in the churchyard one stormy evening, John looked down upon the dark summits of the tossing trees. He thought of the demon knight charging through the lampless valley, and felt suddenly lonely and afraid. But almost at once, as though he had prayed for courage and been answered, his mind seized upon the words of the twenty-third Psalm.

"Yea, though I walk through the valley of the shadow of death, I will fear no evil: for thou art with me; thy rod and thy staff comfort me."

His sense of solitude vanished; he remembered that the man who has given himself to the service of God is never alone. Going down into the deep gorge he unfastened his tethered horse, and rode home, comforted, through the gathering twilight.

One February day in 1658 John encountered, for the first of many occasions, trouble with the law. This time his destination was Eaton Socon, a large village on the banks of the Ouse close to the Huntingdon border. Its beautiful Church of St. Mary the Virgin, begun in the twelfth century, was fated to be destroyed by fire in 1930, and within two years to arise gloriously, a medieval poem wrought by modern imagination.

At Eaton, John had promised to address not only a gathering of local brethren but some friends from Hail Weston, a Huntingdonshire village north-west of St. Neots which ten years later, in the midst of daily perils, was to form its own congregation. To his right, as he rode from Bedford along the road to St. Neots, John passed the rounded hump of Risinghoe Castle, which guarded the meandering Ouse. Further along the river, the grey tower of Great Barford Church, with its short leaded spire, looked at him across the level meadows. For all its massiveness it appeared light, almost unsubstantial, like a dream church gilded by the pale sunshine of early spring.

He rode on through Roxton and into the great northern road, ultimately leading to York and Edinburgh, which linked the hamlet of Wyboston with Eaton Socon. Beyond Wyboston the remains of Eaton Castle, once inhabited by a younger branch of the De Beauchamp family, became visible in a field across the Ouse. Its high mound still surrounded by a moat reminded him of the castle at Bedford.

As he came into the village, with its timbered cottages built round the triangular green, there seemed already to be a smell of spring in the air. Starlings chattered noisily on the ash trees above the thatched and gabled cottages at the bottom of Peppercorn Lane. The grass on the green looked young and bright; even the firs in the churchyard showed some emerald spikes on their smooth dark boughs.

But this time the feeling of promise was deceptive, for the meeting had hardly begun when the village constable arrived, and arrested John for illegal preaching. Charging him to appear at the next Assizes, the constable broke up the unofficial gathering and the brethren, surprised and perturbed, went home.

In those closing days of the Commonwealth there was not yet any large-scale persecution, though the history of the Quakers shows that more occurred than the Protector would have allowed if he could have prevented it. But many Presbyterian ministers in charge of parishes could not endure the intervention of unordained preachers; as John himself noted, "when I went first to preach the word abroad, the doctors and priests of the country did open wide against me".

On 20 December, 1657, two months before John's journey

to Eaton, the Rev. Thomas Becke had been appointed to the parish church of St. Mary the Virgin by the House of Lords. Like all their appointees he was a strong Presbyterian, incensed by lay preaching. He had probably instigated the indictment against the "illiterate tinker", though under the laws as they were then interpreted the legality of his attempt to suppress John was dubious. Since nothing further came of it, his concern was probably less to punish the intruder than to keep competition out of his parish.

When John reported the news of his arrest, his brethren in the Bedford Church were troubled. On "the 25th of the 12th moneth" (25 February) their Book recorded a request for divine guidance on several difficult matters:

> "It is also agreed that the 3rd day of the next moneth be set apart to seeke God in the behalf of our bro. Wheeler who hath bene long ill in body, whereby his ministery hath bene hindered, and also about ye Church affairs, and the affaires of the Nation, and for our bro. Whitbread, who hath been long ill: and also for counsaile what to doe with respect to the indictment against bro. Bunyan at ye Assizes for preaching at Eaton."

Though the threat to brother Bunyan was disturbing, it proved to be less menacing than the affairs of the nation. The second Protectorate Parliament which met on 20 January, 1658, had been dissolved on 4 February, since the House of Commons would do nothing but debate the Constitution. Meanwhile the Army was roused to mutiny and, through the secret activities of the Duke of Ormond in Drury Lane, men were enlisted to serve in the cause of the exiled Charles.

Between February and July the Government seized, tried, and executed the chief plotters, while some contemporary murmurings accused the Baptists of increasing the spirit of unrest. At Eaton, John may have been indicted by men who honestly believed that his preaching tended to stir up sedition.

Meanwhile he was free once more to exercise his gift, and during 1659 paid several visits to villages near Cambridge. Before one of his sermons at Melbourn, a Cambridge scholar joined the crowd in

"THE SEPULCHRE"

To this Holy Well at the bottom of the hill leading up to Stevington Cross, thousands of pilgrims came in the Middle Ages. The well springs from the rock beneath Stevington Church.

STEVINGTON BAPTISING-PLACE

An inlet of the Ouse in The Holmes Wood, near Stevington, where secret baptisms were held.

the churchyard "to hear the tinker prate", and staying, became converted. Another university don, meeting John on a country road near the city, inquired how he dared to preach, not having the original Scriptures.

"Have you the originals, the actual copies written by the prophets and apostles?" John inquired.

"No," was the reply, "but I have what I know to be true copies."

"And I," said John, going on his way, "believe the English Bible to be a true copy also."

On a May morning he visited Toft, a hamlet west of Cambridge, which climbed the brow of a hill four miles south-east of Caxton village and six from the cross-roads farther north. A friend, Daniel Angier, had invited him to hold a service in his tithe-barn at the centre of the village green. Beside it a clump of elms, bright with young leaves, shaded a mossy pool.

At the end of John's sermon another learned man, Thomas Smith, the Cambridge Professor of Arabic, told him that he lacked charity in describing his congregation as unbelievers. An altercation ensued, in which Daniel Angier joined; it ended, on Thomas Smith's part, with the usual denial of a tinker's right to preach. John argued that the Bedford Church had sent him, but the Professor insisted that a gathering of laymen could not confer upon a tinker an authority which they did not possess themselves.

When the argument was over John rode home, turning west at Caxton cross-roads through St. Neots and thence south-west to Bedford. Close by the cross-roads stood a black gibbet on a grassy mound, the tarred corpse which hung from it hardly swinging in the mild air. It was another grim warning that John would remember when the prison doors closed upon him.

Seven months later, on Christmas Day, 1659, John Bunyan set out early upon an unusual mission; he had been invited to preach the Christmas sermon in Yelden Church by his friend the Rector, William Dell.

As his horse's hoofs rang on the frozen road he thought tenderly of his children, left to spend Christmas with their young stepmother, Elizabeth. Already they loved her, and would be safe in her care; his anxieties, like those of the Bedford Meeting itself, were now less domestic than national.

In London the struggle for control between Army and Parliament had produced confusion nearing anarchy. Richard Cromwell, known as "Tumbledown Dick", had resigned; a rising in Cheshire demanding the return of Charles had been put down by Colonel Lambert. In October the Colonel had turned out the Rump Parliament, which had been recalled by the Army a few months earlier.

Nobody knew what would happen next. It seemed certain only that many things, long familiar, were coming to an end, and that reactionary interests and standards, twenty years buried, would soon enjoy a vigorous resurrection.

Five miles from Yelden, John stopped to carry a Christmas greeting to the brethren at Keysoe, another north Bedfordshire village where an Independent group had been in contact with the Bedford Meeting since 1652. For over twelve months John's Puritan contemporary, John Donne, the Rector of Pertenhall, had been preaching to this group.

As he galloped away, John looked back at Keysoe Church; poised on the hill-top some distance from the village, its fifteenth-century perpendicular spire resembled a tall pale flower against a dark background of trees.

The yew at the churchyard gate was said, like the spire, to be two hundred years old, and a stile at the head of a sloping path gave a view of the wooded meadows known as Bury Fields, where an ancient Danish earthwork had stood. There, earlier that year, John had again been arrested for illicit preaching. He had been set free once more; but Keysoe, like Eaton Socon, was a warning of things to come.

John galloped into Yelden past the ruins of another Bedfordshire castle, mentioned in Domesday Book but already derelict by 1361. Its forgotten story had ended before the fourteenth-century builders erected the church of light grey stone on the hither side of the small, flat-bottomed valley.

This castle had been one of the strongest Norman fortresses in the county, constructed not only for defence but as the seat of a lord who would rule the countryside with a ruthless hand. On that bleak December day the great green hump looked gloomy and sinister; the ghosts of the victims who had awaited death there seemed to hover above the frozen water of the half-buried moat. To John the place was the tomb of a bygone age of feudal barbarity, now replaced by the Puritan enlightenment of William Dell.

Through the valley ran the narrow stream of the River Till, hardly bigger than Cardington Brook and thickly choked with reeds. John crossed it and climbed the small hill to the church, its candle-extinguisher summit looking south-west over a grey wall darkly screened by firs and yews. Beyond the church lay wild, open country, like a stretch of moorland. Three centuries later this bleak common towards the Northamptonshire border would still be known as "Yelden open field".

At the church porch with its thirteenth-century door of grey nail-studded wood, the Rector greeted John Bunyan gravely; he realized the risk that he had taken in asking the tinker to preach on this conspicuous day. Together they watched the village congregation filtering through the grassy churchyard, with sidelong glances of hostile curiosity. Behind the worshippers, as they climbed the slope, stretched wide, windy fields dotted with leafless elms. Above the horizon streaks of orange light, pale harbingers of snow, gleamed from the lowering winter sky.

When the service began and William Dell uttered his extemporary prayers, John, standing opposite to him, glanced round the small austere church. Like the Abbey Church at Elstow it had stone pillars and arches; beneath the oaken beams of the roof its plain diamond-leaded windows showed glimpses of red tiles and the bare boughs of trees. Close to the pulpit a strange recumbent figure in a recess held a heart between his praying hands. On the floor to the right of the altar a brass memorial recorded that "Christopher Strickland, Gent", a good benefactor to the parish, had died at the age of eighty in the year of John's birth.

When the time came for his sermon, John mounted the narrow oaken stairs of the fifteen-century pulpit. Before he spoke, his knees quivered with apprehension, for he wanted to please his distinguished sponsor. The address, as often happened when he felt nervous beforehand, was one of his best, but it did not appear to grip his congregation. Restless and unresponsive, they observed him critically from their high-backed wooden pews; the Christmas spirit of good-will was conspicuously lacking.

At the end of the service, John accompanied William Dell to the Rectory to take Christmas dinner with him and his family. A long, low house of yellowish grey stone with a red gabled roof, it was built at the end of a muddy lane opposite the church. From the slight hollow in which it stood, the front windows looked towards three giant beeches over an open meadow.

There, for the first time, John Bunyan met his friend's wife and children; his son William, who was to marry Elizabeth Wingate, of Harlington, in 1672, and his small daughters, Anna and Mercy. They were better behaved than John's own noisy, affectionate family, and seemed a little intimidated by the donnish figure of their father.

After dinner the two men sat alone over the table, discussing the local anti-Puritans and the state of the nation. The present anarchy could not continue, said Dell; unless some unexpected event united the country, those who were planning to restore the monarchy would have their way.

Each of them fell silent, picturing what such a change might mean. William Dell, the elder by twenty years and a scholar of long experience, realized the probable outcome better than John Bunyan. In his writings this original and controversial man had outlined the beginnings of a University Extension movement; he believed that academic culture should be made available to the inhabitants of all large towns. Now, in his fifties, he faced the arbitrary ending of those hopes and ideals which had directed his life.

William Dell had not long to wait for the outcome of his invitation to John. On 20 June, 1660, a number of charges brought against him by his discontented parishioners were summed up in a petition to the House of Lords:

> "He has reported that the King and his followers were like the devil and his angels, and has approved of the murder of the king and the taking away of the House of Lords; he has for twelve years past neglected the due administration of the Sacraments, in consequence of which many children are unbaptized; he has ceased to sing any psalms or read any chapters in the Holy Bible on the Lord's Day in the congregation; he has cut down most of the timber trees growing on the

STEVINGTON BAPTIST MEETING

On the site of "Meeting Farm". The inscription on the tablet reads: "Erected 1720. Church Founded 1655. Repaired 1835. Renovated 1891."

STEVINGTON WINDMILL

The windmill belongs to the eighteenth century, but the beautiful countryside surrounding it is typical of the Bedfordshire that Bunyan knew.

parsonage . . . he hath declared in the public congregation that he had rather hear a plain countryman speak in the church, that came from the plough, than the best orthodox minister that was in the county; upon Christmas Day last one Bunyan, a tinker, was countenanced and suffered to speak in the pulpit to the congregation, and no orthodox minister did officiate in the church that day. Since the restoration of the secluded members of Parliament he hath declared that the power was now in the hands of the wicked, and that the land was like to be over flowed again with Popery; he hath put forth several seditious books, and before the horrid murder of the late King he declared publicly in the congregation that the King was no king to him, Christ was his King; Venice and Holland were without a king, and why might not we be without; and that he did not approve of earthly kings."

In spite of the return of Charles II two months earlier, this miscellaneous collection of indictments was dismissed by the House of Lords on 25 July, 1660. But William Dell's days as Rector of Yelden were numbered, and he knew it.

Twenty-four hours after John Bunyan's sermon at Yelden, the Rump Parliament was again set up. The populace cheered its hundred-odd Members, but this minority of politicians did not represent the nation. Bedfordshire, amongst other counties, had no Member. Sir Beauchamp St. John, Sir Roger Burgoyne, and Sir Oliver Luke were all outside; Sir Samuel Luke, as a Presbyterian, had been excluded by the test of 1648.

Early in 1660, a public meeting of "Gentlemen Freeholders and Inhabitants of the county of Bedford" sent up a vigorous protest regarding the daily invasion of their civil and religious rights and liberties in "this common day of calamity". Four days after John's Yelden visit, the Bedford Church had set a day apart for prayer "upon the account of the distractions of the nation".

As the New Year thus stormily came in, the community at St. John's had also its domestic troubles. Not the least of these was the increasing ill-health of their pastor, John Burton. On 29 March they agreed, "considering our bro. Burton's weakness", to invite Brothers Wheeler, Donne, Gibbs and Breeden to help him in succession with his Sunday duties.

Two years earlier, John Gibbs had introduced John Bunyan's book, *A Few Sighs from Hell.*

> "Concerning the Authour (whatsoever the censures and reports of many are) I have this to say, that I verily believe God hath counted him faithful, and put him into the Ministery: and though his outward condition and former employment was mean, and his humane learning small, yet is he one that hath acquaintance with God, and taught by his Spirit, and hath been used in his hand to do souls good."

Having thus apologized for his colleague who lacked "humane learning", Gibbs continued more vigorously:

> "He is not like your drones, that will suck the sweet, but do no work. For he hath laid forth himself to the utmost of his strength . . . and I fear this is one reason why the Archers have shot so soarly at him."

This "lean lone Pagnell saint" was now in a position to give more active help to John and his companions than the writing of literary prefaces. About the time that John Bunyan and William Dell were discussing the uncertain future, he had been ejected from his living at Newport for refusing to admit the whole parish to communion. Those to whom he denied the Sacrament had included a notorious but influential drunkard, who retaliated by procuring Gibbs's dismissal.

The young minister, still only in his early thirties, contemplated the formation of an Independent Church in Newport, but meanwhile was willing to help the Bedford Meeting and his friend John Bunyan. He had left the Vicarage for a modest cottage in Newport High Street, rented only at 4*d*. Behind it, at the end of a long yard, stood a barn where the Independents now held their services. Its secluded position was to prove convenient in the coming days of persecution.

That time, so long dreaded, was now at hand, precipitated by General Monk's march from Scotland to end the anarchy in London.

Two months after the Bedford Church had invited John Gibbs to help John Burton, Charles II was restored to the throne.

Summoned from Holland by the Convention Parliament which Monk had set up, Charles issued the Declaration of Breda, promising liberty to "tender consciences" and an amnesty for all except those excluded by Parliament. His return was especially welcome to the landed gentry, politically and financially oppressed by Puritan rulers whose greatest error had been to deny all non-Puritans a share in the Government.

The swarthy, dark-haired, thick-lipped man of thirty who stepped ashore on 25 May, 1660, declared, on receiving an English Bible from the Mayor of Dover, that "it was the thing that he loved above all things in the world". Enchanting the delirious crowds between the coast and London by his tact and wit, this Royal new broom swept into his capital on 29 May.

Three days after the King's proclamation, William Dell resigned the Mastership of Gonville and Caius, and retired to Yelden to await events. Simultaneously John Okey fled from his Ridgmont farm to live for two years under an assumed name at Hanau in Germany; he was one of the eleven who had sat in judgment on Charles I and were now called upon to pay the full price.

Before the end of that year, the surviving Episcopal clergy returned like migratory birds to the livings from which they had been driven. Back in triumph at St. Mary's, Bedford, was Dr. Giles Thorne; back also to St. John's came the aged Theodore Crowley, and his assistant, Robert Guidot. At a meeting of the Bedford Church in late August, the Minutes not only recorded that "the Lord hath taken to himself our teacher, bro. Burton", but enumerated the practical steps required by another calamity.

> "We desire our bro. Harrington, bro. Coventon, bro. John ffenne to take care to informe themselves of a convenient place for our meeting so soone as they can (we being now deprived of our former place) and reporte it to ye Church."

The members of the stricken community did not know that for twelve years they would be driven perilously into fields and woods, private attics and guarded barns, before they found an abiding home. Even without that knowledge, the prospect before them was dark enough.

England had entered upon a new age; the full tide of reaction against Puritan sobriety was swinging into fashion the licentious dramas beloved by the gay, extravagant Court. Not even the Edwardian reaction against Victorian respectability would bring so great a change in so short a time.

Yet we, with our twentieth-century knowledge of unlimited intolerance, cannot withhold honour from the men of the Restoration. We owe it even to Edward Hyde, who returned with Charles and soon applied the full rigours of the Clarendon Code to "tender consciences".

Though they exacted from the Regicides their lives for a life, Charles II and Clarendon did not extinguish their political opponents in suffocation chambers, or herd them into concentration camps. They dug up the bodies of Cromwell, Bradshaw and Ireton, hanged them at Tyburn before the people, and buried them at sunset in the anonymous dust of a future Connaught Square; but they dealt more leniently with the living.

Cromwell's son, Richard, was permitted to survive in the amiable seclusion of a country gentleman. Cromwell's Latin Secretary, John Milton, whose pen was worth more to the Parliamentarians than Goebbels's broadcasts to the Nazis, was pensioned off, a blind recluse, to write his religious dramas unmolested. Even Cromwell's chaplain, William Dell, remained in his living until the Act of Uniformity.

The work of the Restoration was not lethal but social, for under it Puritanism disintegrated into classes and sects. The upper classes, with Catholic exceptions, tended to become Anglican; the middle and poorer classes identified themselves with various forms of Dissent.

In spite of Parliament and of Cromwell, in spite of the spiritual zeal put into their faith by the Bible readers of innumerable cottage homes, the hereditary social order had triumphed over the ideal of a pious democracy. Henceforth its pattern, associating privilege and affluence with the State religion, was to be imposed for centuries upon England's history.

CHAPTER X

CONSCIENCE ON TRIAL

"Therefore thought I, what God says is best indeed, is best, though all men in the World are against it. Seeing then that God prefers his Religion, seeing God prefers a tender Conscience, seeing they that make themselves Fools for the Kingdom of Heaven are wisest . . . Shame depart, thou art an Enemy to my Salvation."

JOHN BUNYAN: *The Pilgrim's Progress*, Part I.

ON 12 November, 1660, John Bunyan went by invitation to hold a service at Lower Samsell, near Harlington, thirteen miles south of Bedford and two-thirds of the way to Luton.

John's long walk took him through Ampthill and Flitwick to Westoning with its fourteenth-century church, where a rare lead spire sprang from the battlemented tower. Here he turned left into an uphill lane, and then sharply to the right along a rough track leading more steeply to the farm where he was to preach. It stood, surrounded by a moat with a drawbridge, in a large field thickly encircled by elms.

On the south-east side the trees became thinner; through a wide gap he could see the Barton Hills, reddish-brown in the pale autumn sunlight. These steep hills were a dramatic outcrop of the Chilterns; unlike the wooded undulating slopes of the Greensand Ridge, their chalk foundation caused them to assume the colours of the surrounding country. As John ascended the slope, a cold wind sharply reminded him of the high altitude of the isolated farm.

Though the place was remote, he knew it well. Near the house grew a large hawthorn, later to be known as "Bunyan's thorn", under which he had preached in the summer. Today the service was to be held indoors, but when he entered the room where a few friends had already gathered, the customary cheerful welcome was lacking. Instead there were whispers and nods, and a strange feeling of apprehension.

Finally the owner of the farm took John aside. There was a warrant out, he told him, for his arrest, and meanwhile a strong watch was being kept on the house—"as if," John ironically

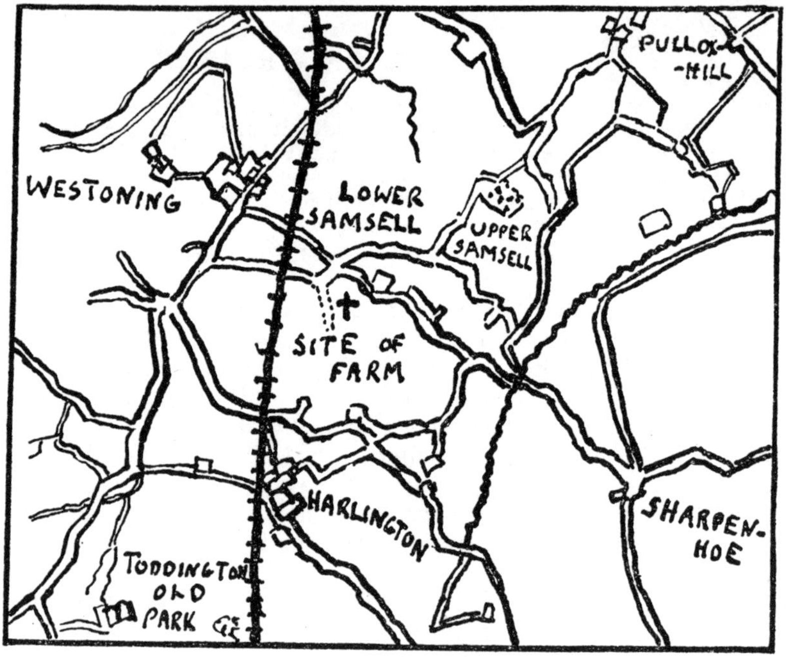

Diagram of the site at Lower Samsell, which is difficult to find. The left turn uphill from Westoning now goes under a railway bridge; a little distance beyond this bridge is the sharp short turn to the right. The lane into which this turning leads quickly becomes rough and grassy, as a lane would which once led to a farm and is now unused. This grassy track carries on slightly to the left up a hill beneath occasional elms until it ends at a large unenclosed meadow thick with weeds. To the left of the track just before it ends is a ploughed field still thinly ringed with elms. The furrows largely disguise the remains of the farm which once stood there, but some deep dips in the ploughland not far from the verge of rough unhedged grass still show the outlines of the moat that surrounded it.

The sketch is roughly copied from the Survey Map (scale approximately one inch to the mile), with acknowledgments to the exact copy of an older map in *John Bunyan*, by Dr. John Brown.

recorded later, "we that was to meet together in that place did intend to do some fearful business, to the destruction of the country".

He did not know, as the local Justice of the Peace, Francis Wingate, knew, that in London the peculiar sect which called itself the Fifth Monarchy Men had become suddenly active after a long period of quiescence. It was Francis Wingate's business to guard against sedition; who knew but that these so-called religious meetings in barns and farms might not be a cloak for the hatching of plots or the collection of arms?

John's friend the farmer was frankly alarmed; he had a law-abiding disposition, and knew the character and attitude of the local authorities better than his visitor. There was still time, said he, to call off the meeting.

"If they take you," he urged, more concerned for John than for himself, "they will have you before the Justice, and then send you to prison. The constable will not be here for an hour; if you leave before he comes, nothing will happen."

To reassure him, John replied immediately.

"By no means; I will not stir, neither will I have the meeting dismissed for this. Come, be of good cheer, let us not be daunted, our cause is good; we need not be ashamed of it. To preach God's word is so good a work, we shall be well rewarded if we suffer for that."

Then, wishing to consider his position more carefully, he excused himself and went out into the field. He knew that the crisis which he and William Dell had foreseen a year ago was now upon him. Walking up and down beneath the elms, his head bent and his hands clasped behind him, he recalled the national changes which, even before the repressive legislation which rumour continually prophesied, were precipitating reaction.

Earlier that year the Convention Parliament still sitting at Westminster had passed an Act of Indemnity and Oblivion, which granted pardon to all political offenders except the Regicides. These "offenders" were not quite sure how far that pardon was watertight, but they had continued their meetings. Throughout the year John had travelled regularly to Kensworth, near Luton, to preach to the three hundred members who gathered from that wide area at the Dallow Farm.

Their doubts were well justified, for during the Parliamentary recess the county magistrates at the Bedfordshire Quarter Sessions had issued an order "for the publick reading of the Liturgy of the Church of England". The following Sunday the minister at Leighton Buzzard, William Annand, preached two sermons which he afterwards published as *A Short Discourse to prove the Legality, Decency and Expediency of Set Forms of Prayer.*

On 17 October a new Bishop, Robert Sanderson, had been appointed to the see of Lincoln, vacant for sixteen years, to guide a diocese being reconditioned to accept the Prayer Book. The new order was changing, giving place to the old.

Contemplating the unmistakable trend of events, John recalled his own work during the previous five years. Whatever private failures of confidence had preceded his sermons, he had been, he knew, a vigorous preacher, giving strength and courage to others.

If now, confronted by danger, he ran away, what effect would this have upon the weak and the newly converted? God had chosen him to be a leader of forlorn hopes; if he, being the first to meet with opposition, gave ground, what would happen to the whole body of believers?

At that moment the sight of the farmer's family playing in the yard reminded him of Elizabeth and the children. An iron hand seemed to grip his vitals, for Elizabeth was pregnant; their baby was expected soon after Christmas. Then, resolutely, he pushed the thought even of her away. Dear as they all were, dependent on him as they would be for years, he must not allow their existence to influence him. The problem he had to settle was even more profound than family claims; he must not permit himself anxieties that might tempt him to compromise. "He that loveth father or mother more than Me is not worthy of Me."

His mind made up, John went into the house. Whatever happened now, he would face it out.

"I was resolved," he wrote, "to see the utmost of what they could say or do unto me: for blessed be the Lord, I knew of no evil that I had said or done."

His congregation was now assembled. By private roads and secret footpaths from Westoning, Flitwick, Pulloxhill, and Harlington, they had stolen like uneasy phantoms to the farm,

"BUNYAN'S BARN" AT TOFT

Four miles from Cambridge. According to local tradition this building stands on the site of Daniel Angier's barn where Bunyan preached, and may include part of its material.

"THE VALLEY OF THE SHADOW"
Millbrook Gorge, near Ampthill, from Millbrook Churchyard.

subconsciously forewarned of danger, yet uncertain where the servants of the new régime would strike.

Without delay John began the meeting, but he had hardly spoken before the watchful constable came in with his warrant. The policeman looked a little abashed when he found no weapon more threatening to the State than that sword of the spirit, the English Bible. But he had to obey his orders, so he seized John and arrested him.

His agitated hearers sprang from their chairs, but John quieted them. They should not, he insisted, be discouraged by his fate; it was a mercy to suffer on so good an account.

"We might have been apprehended as thieves or murderers or for other wickedness," he said, "but blessed be God, it is not so. We suffer as Christians for well doing, and had better be the persecuted than the persecutors."

But the persecutors, in the shape of the constable and a servant sent by Francis Wingate, were not prepared to hear any more eloquence. They hurried John away, and, as the magistrate would not be at home till tomorrow, left him at the house of a friend, who undertook to bring him to the policeman in the morning.

"Otherwise," he concluded, "the constable must have charged a watch with me, or have secured me some other ways, my crime was so great."

The next morning, 13 November, the constable took John through the damp fields between Samsell and Harlington to appear before Francis Wingate, whose status as a typical country gentleman had become, in Stuart England, a profession in itself.

From him and his kind the Privy Council expected the provision of employment, the relief of want, and the local operation of the Elizabethan Poor Law. The best of them successfully held the balance between despotic monarchs and republican propagandists; all of them, good, bad and indifferent, were not only J.P.s, but judges and police magistrates. They maintained a form of rough justice which often inflicted punishment on the innocent and unfortunate while allowing the guilty to get away.

Escape was not difficult, since police areas were small. As the farmer at Samsell knew, a criminal was safe as soon as he had left the district where his crime was committed.

The Nonconformists soon learned to make use of these loopholes in the law by holding their conventicles near county boundaries. In Northey Farm House, near Bogeat by Wellingborough, they met at the junction of Bedfordshire, Buckinghamshire and Northamptonshire, and were able at short notice to flee from their own county into another. John Bunyan remembered this elementary form of self-preservation when he described the escape of Christian and Hopeful from Giant Despair on to the King's Highway, where they "were safe, because they were out of his Jurisdiction".

Under this system few criminals were caught, and little trustworthy evidence was collected. Since most of it came from uninvestigated hearsay it was applied in a totally unscientific fashion, resulting in the death of such men as Raleigh and the execution of guiltless old women as witches. Those idealists who, like John Bunyan, allowed themselves to be taken for conscience's sake, tended to pay vicariously for all the thieves and wastrels who escaped unpunished.

Harlington House, where he was now going, stood at the northwest corner of Harlington cross-roads, a few minutes' walk from the church with its great nave, built by the monks of Dunstable. The gabled manor, though small, was ancient; the oldest part, occupied by a family named Belverge in 1396, had been transferred through marriage to a Wingate from Sharpenhoe.

The front of the house faced the church and vicarage; from its tiled roof five small dormer windows looked over a low stone wall, broken by two dominating pillars on either side of a wooden gate. Through this top-heavy gateway John passed with the constable, and was taken along the dark, oak-panelled hall to a small "Justice's room" at the back to await the magistrate's pleasure.

Through the window John could see a wide, well-kept lawn, smooth as emerald velvet, and beyond it a finely-wrought iron gate leading into a walled garden. The long flower-bed running through this garden was now empty, but two months earlier its sunflowers, dahlias, asters and marigolds had shouted with colour like an exuberant chorus. Recently Charles II had spent a night in the house and walked in the garden; the china bowl, decorated with blue dragons, from which he had breakfasted was later to be cherished as an heirloom by the family.

After waiting for ten minutes, John and the constable were summoned to the "great parlour", a panelled room with double full-length windows opening on to the garden, and a large cross-beam, centred in a carved Tudor rose, supporting the low ceiling. Here, behind a desk of polished oak, sat Francis Wingate.

The young man who now stood to John Bunyan in the relation of magistrate to malefactor had also been born in the autumn of 1628. For four hundred years his ancestors had ranked as the leading family in the Streatley and Harlington parishes. Soon after the outbreak of the Civil War his father's death had made him a ward of the Crown, and his stepmother took him to the King's headquarters at Oxford.

In February 1642, they returned to Harlington, where he lived in relative peace during the Protectorate. But in 1651, when he was twenty-three, he complained that his Harlington property had been wrongly sequestered for the delinquency of Lord Wentworth, Lord of the Manor at Harlington, who had other property in Toddington two miles away.

Whether this memory of injustice rankled, or whether he was really concerned lest Fifth Monarchy propaganda had penetrated to Bedfordshire, Francis Wingate had been within his legal rights in arresting John under the Conventicle Act of 1593. This Act provided that any person who went to any place of worship, other than the parish church, with more than five persons outside his family should be imprisoned for three months "without trial or mainprise". He had then publicly to do penance, and promise never to repeat the offence, if he wished to avoid the choice between exile and execution.

The magistrate was, nevertheless, in a hurry to provide Nonconformity with its most conspicuous martyr. Though the Elizabethan statute had been four times re-enacted and made permanent since 1624, it had largely fallen into disuse, and the Act of Uniformity was still eighteen months ahead.

Francis Wingate brusquely motioned John to stand aside while he questioned the constable. He was now a few weeks past his thirty-second birthday, just as John was a few days past his. But though he was still young, he was already the father of nine children. A tenth, the second of numerous daughters, had died in 1652. His second son, now a baby of two months old and christened Charles after the royal visitor, was doomed like two of his successors to join her in childhood.

This family, destined to reach a total of fourteen and produced almost annually, was then typical of well-to-do country households, though the death-rate amongst the upper classes easily exceeded that of the poorest families today. The eldest daughter, Lettice, now nearly fifteen, had been born in January 1646, fifteen months after her father's marriage to Lettice Pierce, the eighteen-year-old daughter of the late Vicar of Hitchin who had died in 1636. Francis himself had been only sixteen years and one month old at the time of the wedding on 11 October, 1644.

The physically precocious young aristocrat, who never made any apparent effort to restrain his natural impulses, now appeared as judge of his contemporary the tinker, whose passions were certainly as compelling as his and who lived in the confined space of a small cottage where self-discipline is never easy. But John's four children were spaced as a modern father might space them; the intervals between them suggest some realization on his part that women would never be able to develop their minds and souls as well as their bodies unless the inexorable cycle of child-bearing was controlled.

His admired predecessor, Martin Luther, had expressed the opinion that if a woman bore children till she died from bearing, it did not matter, for she was there to do it. But only a century after Luther, John Bunyan was to record in *Grace Abounding* his compassion for his wife in travail which led him to "tempt God".

> "Upon a time my Wife was great with Child, and before her full time was come, her pangs as of a Woman in Travel, were fierce and strong upon her, even as if she would immediately have fallen in labour, and been delivered of an untimely Birth: Now at this very time it was, that I had been so strongly tempted to question the Being of God; wherefore, as my Wife lay crying by me, I said, but with all secresie imaginable, even thinking in my heart, *Lord, if thou wilt now remove this sad affliction from my Wife, and cause that she be troubled no more*

> *therewith this Night,* (and now were her pangs just upon her) *then I shall know that thou canst discern the most secret thoughts of the Heart.*
>
> I had no sooner said it in my heart, but her pangs were taken from her, and she was cast into a deep sleep, and so continued till Morning; at this I greatly marvelled, not knowing what to think; but after I had been awake a good while, and heard her cry no more, I fell to sleep also."

In marital sympathy, as in doctrinal tolerance, John was ahead of his time. "Mercy," he makes Prudence say in Part II of *The Pilgrim's Progress,* "in our days is little set by, any further than as to its Name: the Practice, which is set forth by thy Conditions, there are but few that can abide."

It was hardly mercy that John was to receive now, though we have, for what it is worth, the word of William Foster, Francis Wingate's brother-in-law, that "my brother is very loath to send you to prison". When he learned from the constable that no weapons had been discovered at John's meeting, but only a few people met together to preach and hear the Scriptures, Francis was embarrassed by his own precipitate action, and hardly knew how to proceed. He had no alternative but to put some questions.

"What were you doing at the meeting?" he asked. "Why are you not content to follow your calling? It is against the law for such as you to do as you did."

Determined now to bear his witness, John made no attempt to conciliate him.

"The intent of my coming thither," he said, "was to instruct and counsel people to forsake their sins, and close in with Christ, lest they miserably perish. I can do both these things without confusion—that is, to follow my calling, and to preach the word."

This theological language jarred on the worldly young magistrate, who immediately lost his temper.

"I will break the neck of your meetings!" he cried furiously.

"It may be so," John answered serenely, fortified by the tranquillity of those whose minds are made up.

Francis Wingate then demanded sureties, which were promptly provided, and warned John and his sponsors that if he preached before appearing at the Quarter Sessions, their bonds would be forfeited. Immediately John released his friends from their undertaking, for he would not promise to refrain from speaking the word of God.

This pronouncement ended the interview, and the magistrate retired to draw up the writ committing John to Bedford Gaol.

While John waited for the document which would make him an example to his brethren, another member of the family came in. This was Dr. William Lindall, destined to be for ever branded by the despised tinker with a contemptuous phrase—"an old enemy to the truth". He had previously been curate to Dr. Stephen Pierce, the father of the elder Lettice Wingate, and after marrying his widow had succeeded him at Hitchin.

In 1665 Dr. Lindall, now step-father to Francis Wingate's wife, was to be instituted Vicar of Harlington. At that time the young man whom he now came to taunt and revile would still be lying in Bedford Gaol, as little aware as Dr. Lindall himself of the Christian revenge that time was to take on the arrogant Vicar in the tinker's name. So strange are history's reversals that in 1929 a Bishop of St. Albans was to dedicate in Harlington Church one of the first Anglican memorials to John Bunyan in the so-called "Bunyan country". This window shows Evangelist urging Christian to flee from the wrath to come.

Though John endeavoured to protect himself by saying that he was there to speak with the Justice, not the Doctor, the scornful cleric could not refrain from improving the occasion. He condemned John for "meddling" with that for which he had no warrant; how could it be lawful for him to preach? When John replied in St. Peter's words, "As every man hath received the gift, even so let him minister the same," his visitor fell back on a derisive reference to Alexander the coppersmith who disturbed the Apostles ("aiming 'tis like at me, because I was a Tinker").

The determined patience which John had imposed on his natural vehemence was beginning to wear thin under strain, and he answered the Vicar sharply.

"I also have read of very many priests and pharisees, that had their hands in the blood of our Lord Jesus Christ."

"Ay," retorted Dr. Lindall, "and you are one of those scribes and pharisees. With a pretence you make long prayers to devour widow's houses!"

John was now thoroughly roused, and the altercation might have reached a crescendo had not a phrase from the Scriptures flashed into his mind: "Answer not a fool according to his folly." From that moment until the writ was drawn up, he made his replies as brief as he could.

He was starting on his way to Bedford with the constable, when two friends stopped him and offered to intercede with Francis Wingate for his release. Though he was growing weary from the prolonged uncertainty and delay, John waited with the constable while his friends entered into a lengthy discussion with the magistrate. Eventually they returned in triumph; if John would only go back and say "certain words" to Mr. Wingate, he would be released. Because of their persuasions he returned to the house, but doubted his chance of being set free without committing some dishonourable action.

"If the words are such that may be said with a good conscience, I will say them," he affirmed. "Otherwise I will not."

By this time the long day was wearing to its end, and when John reached Harlington House again, night had already come. Returning to the same room and expecting to see the magistrate, he was surprised when a door opened and in the candlelight he recognized a figure hitherto familiar to him only at a distance. This was William Foster of Bedford, Doctor of Laws, a Justice of the Peace and the legal champion of orthodox religion.

Though he did not realize it John had encountered quite a family party, for William Foster was the widower of Francis Wingate's sister Amy, who had died the previous year. The magistrate, satisfied that the meeting at Lower Samsell had no political significance and reluctant to convict John under a statute which had long been a dead letter, had evidently asked his learned brother-in-law to win the misguided fanatic's confidence and persuade him to give the simple promise that would set him free.

William Foster started on this mission with exaggerated goodwill.

"Who is there?" he cried genially. "John Bunyan?"

He spoke, John related, "with such seeming affection, as if he would have leaped in my neck and kissed me".

But this simulated cordiality was guaranteed to fail from the start. Like all peasants John had a natural suspicion of effusiveness, to which five years of preaching against opposition had added the realism of professional experience.

Referring to "this instant November, 1660", he described the scene immediately after it occurred. But some time later, perhaps with the knowledge in his mind of William Foster's adaptable careerism and perpetual harrying of Nonconformists, he laconically added, in a footnote subsequently published in the first edition of *A Relation of the Imprisonment of Mr. John Bunyan,* the words "a right Judas". Foster could hardly have appeared in this light during the brief interview at Harlington, but the text, "Their tongues are smoother than oil", did occur to John, followed by the injunction, "Beware of men". He therefore became even more wary of Dr. Foster's carefully marshalled arguments than he had been of Dr. Lindall's taunts.

John Bunyan, explained Dr. Foster, had merely to promise that he would not call the people together, and he could go home. After all, he was a craftsman, not a preacher; and in any case such meetings were against the law. To take the Scriptures literally was to resemble a Papist; since John did not know the original Greek he could hardly be expected to understand what he was talking about, and the foolish, ignorant people who listened to him understood even less. Surely, then, he could promise not to call the people together any more?

None of this made the smallest impression; for every legal argument that the Doctor advanced, John had a theological or moral answer. The man of law and the man of inspiration proceeded on parallel lines which, as every schoolchild knows, never meet.

At length Dr. Foster gave up the attempt, and a number of Francis Wingate's servants tried to persuade John to forego the folly of landing himself in gaol. These efforts only led to a long dissertation by John on the precise meaning of "calling the people together". Finally Francis Wingate and William Foster combined tried again. Their united ineffectiveness caused Foster to advise his brother-in-law to send John to prison. He added in exasperation that John would also do well if he presented all those on whose behalf he went to meetings.

The long controversy ended, and John stepped out of Harlington House with the constable into the cold November night. He was so triumphantly aware, for all his mental weariness, that it was he and not his interrogators who felt at peace, that he was tempted to tell them so. Throughout the interview he had clung with determined tenacity to one simple idea: the belief that God's children had the right to worship Him in their own way and to meet in order to do so.

Neither threats, taunts, nor legal subtleties had prevailed against that profound conviction. It seemed clear, however, that such men as Francis Wingate and William Foster would never understand it. So, after all, John held his tongue, "and blessed be the Lord, went away to prison with God's comfort in my poor soul".

The County Gaol to which John was now taken stood at the northern corner of Silver Street and the High Street, opposite the road then known as Mill Lane.

It had two floors, the ground floor with two day-rooms and several sleeping cells being used for felons. On the first floor, reserved for debtors, who usually numbered between five and ten, were four lodging-rooms and a common day-room, used also as a chapel. These rooms had no fireplaces, and the prisoners, who slept on straw, often suffered from gaol fever as well as from cold.

The prison owned neither an infirmary nor any kind of bath. Below the ground floor were two underground dungeons, one reached by eleven descending steps being in total darkness. The other had a narrow window on street level, and was usually occupied by six or more felons. The prisoners took their exercise in a small common courtyard. Two or three iron grilles, through which they held out bags for alms on Sunday mornings, looked on to Silver Street.

The Rev. C. F. Farrar, author of *Old Bedford*, believed that this County Gaol was reserved for men, and that, until a penitentiary was built in 1800, women prisoners went to a "Bridewell" near Cauldwell Street. But the prison lists for 1665 and 1672 show that a Quaker, Tabitha Rush, was apparently in the County Gaol with John Rush, her husband.

The prisons of that day were not mainly intended for criminals, who were usually flogged or hanged; they were houses of detention for political prisoners, debtors, and accused persons awaiting trial. Since vindicative punishment took other forms and the idea of a prison as a reformatory was still three centuries ahead, these gaols become collecting-centres for victims of misfortune rather than sinners.

If a number of condemned criminals did have their sentences commuted to imprisonment, the prison became overcrowded and the normal occupants suffered from starvation and disease. They were also victims of "graft", since the magistrates farmed out much of their responsibility to jailors who not only exacted the legal fees, but made fortunes for themselves out of any prisoners with cash to spare. Poverty-stricken captives, who could not afford to pay for privileges, were left to rot their neglected lives away for years on end.

Into this place of shadows John Bunyan came on 14 November, 1660. When the massive oaken door, fastened with iron bolts and barred across the open centre, shut him into a cell only eight and half feet high, he did not dream that it was closing upon his freedom until 9 May, 1672. He knew only that he was prepared for whatever his enemies might do to him.

The respect now felt for him by his friends was shown in their readiness to act as sureties—in modern terms, to go bail for him —though they knew that so long as the law violated his conscience, he would never conform. Immediately the news of his imprisonment reached his fellow-members of the Bedford Church, they tried to find a distinguished sponsor who would guarantee his freedom until the Quarter Sessions, when his case would be heard.

They approached the Elstow magistrate, a young man named Crompton, who knew John and at first agreed to help him. But later he demurred because he was puzzled by the writ, which stated only that John had attended conventicles in the county, "to the great disparagement of the government of the church of England". Arrests for preaching were still almost unknown, and the young J.P., thinking that some political offence might be concealed by the accusation, feared to commit himself.

When John's jailor gave him this news, he was uplifted rather than intimidated by Mr. Crompton's refusal. Before going to see him he had prayed to be set at liberty if he could do more good that way, "but if not, his will be done; for I was not altogether without hopes but that my imprisonment might be an awakening to the Saints in the county, therefore I could not tell well which to chuse".

His imprisonment had, however, brought consternation to someone more vulnerable than the members of the Bedford Church. Elizabeth Bunyan, so near to her first confinement, was suddenly seized with the pains of premature labour, and for over a week struggled in agony while John, hardly more than a stone's-throw away but unable to help her, waited anxiously for news. Neighbours and friends who came in to report on her condition looked graver as each day went by, and blind Mary, now almost eleven and able to find her way safely through familiar Mill Lane and across the High Street to the gaol, continually shook her head in reply to his urgent question, "Is the baby born yet?"

Desperately he prayed for Elizabeth and their child. Often he thought guiltily that he had worn out one wife by his spiritual tempests; was his conscience now to be responsible for the death of another? He hardly knew who eventually brought him the tidings that he awaited.

"It's over, John—but the baby's dead."

"But Elizabeth . . . ?"

"Very weak, but I think she will recover. She said you were not to be anxious for her."

Elizabeth was hardly on her feet again and able to visit him, bringing soup in an earthen jug with a wide mouth and a zigzag pattern running from neck to base, when Robert Sanderson, the newly-appointed Bishop of Lincoln, made a journey to Bedford. Reading in his cell, John heard the sudden commotion which heralded the public entry of the seventy-three-year-old Bishop into the town. Following the shouting populace came the trained bands, which symbolized the traditional alliance between Army and Church by firing a "handsome volley" with their muskets as they marched past the gaol.

The second week of January 1661 was the time appointed for the Christmas Quarter Sessions. Since Bedford lacked the splendour of an Assize Court, the Sessions were held in an ancient semi-ecclesiastical building on the banks of the Ouse known as the Chapel of Herne, or "the chapel in the corner", meaning the south-west corner of St. Paul's churchyard.

Built in Gothic style of stone with a tiled roof, this primitive court-house had a bricked-up church-like window between two buttresses on the north, with an entrance below. Because it was used by the adjacent Grammar School, it was sometimes known as "the School-house Chapel". At its north-west corner a tall wrought-iron gate divided the courtyard from the river-bank.

From John's standpoint the time of his appearance at the Sessions was unfortunate, for a few days earlier the Fifth Monarchy insurrection which Francis Wingate apparently feared had occurred in London.

The Fifth Monarchists, ancestors of the modern millenarians and much influenced by the writings of John Lilburne, had originally supported Cromwell's government in the belief that it was a preparation for the "fifth monarchy". This monarchy, succeeding the monarchies of the Assyrians, Persians, Greeks, and Romans, was to be a period in which Christ would reign on earth with his saints for a thousand years. Those who looked for it aimed at abolishing all existing laws and institutions, and substituting a simpler code based on the law of Moses.

Under the Commonwealth the Fifth Monarchists were disappointed by the non-fulfilment of their hopes, and began to abuse Cromwell. The arrest of their preaching leaders, Christopher Feake, John Rogers, and others, suppressed them for a time, but the Restoration renewed their revolutionary ardour. On 6 January, 1661, a band of them headed by a cooper named Thomas Venner attempted to get possession of London. Many were killed or taken prisoner, and on 19 and 20 January, Venner and ten others were executed.

Between the rising and the executions, John Bunyan's examination took place at Bedford. It was hardly a favourable moment for the trial of a religious rebel whose motives, in the prevailing atmosphere, would inevitably be given a political colour. There was no evidence to prove that John had any connection with the Fifth Monarchy Men, but he and his companions had been in touch with their friends and publishers. In a subsequent interview with John in prison, the Bedford Clerk of the Peace, Paul Cobb, was to speak significantly of those that "make religion their pretence only".

Not only were suspicions of collaboration increased; about the time of John's appearance the law against conventicles was being strengthened as an immediate consequence of Venner's insurrection, which had provided a not unwelcome excuse. On 10 January a proclamation was made prohibiting "all unlawful and seditious meetings and conventicles under pretence of religious worship". All classes of Dissenters were anxious to prove that they had not been accomplices of the rebels, but as the Baptists and Quakers, who were expressly mentioned in the proclamation, could not conscientiously acknowledge the King's ecclesiastical supremacy, many of them were thrown into prison and kept there until the Coronation.

Even if the trend of national events had been more reassuring, their effect would not have been improved by the personalities on the Bench. Of the five county magistrates awaiting John Bunyan, one, Sir Henry Chester of Lidlington, was Francis Wingate's uncle, and another, George Blundell of Cardington Manor, had been a "delinquent" whose Bedfordshire estates were sequestered in 1655. But even they, with old scores to pay off against Puritanism, were less formidable than the Chairman of the Sessions, John Kelynge, who was due for knighthood on 21 January.

Sir John, a Member of the Inner Temple, had been called to the Bar in February 1632, and for some years had practised with his father, also a barrister, on the side of the Crown in the Forest Courts. In 1642, at the Spring Quarter Sessions in Hertfordshire, he had tried to persuade the Grand Jury to present some persons found drilling in consequence of the Militia Ordinance. For this he was summoned to the Bar of the House of Commons, arrested, and kept in prison until the Restoration.

Kelynge appears to have been generally unpopular, but writers who become expansive on the subject of John Bunyan's twelve years' imprisonment sometimes forget to mention that the Chairman before whom he appeared had just endured eighteen. Even a saint would have been tempted to retaliate, and Kelynge was no saint. Called to the degree of Sergeant-at-law on 4 July, 1660, he had been one of the counsel for the Crown at the trial of the Regicides. His bearing on the Bench was invariably haughty and brutal, especially after he was made Chief Justice in November 1665, and he did not scruple to browbeat, fine, and even imprison a jury whose response to the evidence did not follow his wishes.

The rebellious tinker was now called before John Kelynge and his colleagues, and listened to the Bill of Indictment which declared "that John Bunyan, labourer . . . hath devilishly and perniciously abstained from coming to church to hear divine service, and is a common upholder of several unlawful meetings and conventicles, to the great disturbance and distraction of the good subjects of this Kingdom".

This pompous pronouncement put the small gathering at Lower Samsell right into the picture of the national struggle for freedom of worship. From that standpoint, John did not find it discouraging. When the Clerk of the Sessions asked him, "What say you to this?" he was ready with his reply.

"I am a common frequenter of the Church of God," he said. "I am also, by grace, a member with them people, over whom Christ is the head."

This grammatical inaccuracy on the part of a preaching tinker was exactly what Justice Kelynge expected.

"But do you come to church?" he asked testily. "You know what I mean, to the parish church, to hear divine service?"

"No," answered John, "I do not."

"And why not?"

"Because I do not find it commanded in the word of God."

"Well, didn't He say we were commanded to pray?"

"Yes, Sir, but not by the Common Prayer Book."

"How, then?"

"With the spirit," affirmed John. "As the Apostle saith, 'I will pray with the spirit with understanding'."

"But," argued the Justice, "he said we might pray with the spirit with understanding, and with the Common Prayer Book also."

A long discussion now ensued between John and the magistrates on the nature of prayer and the status of the Prayer Book, which would sound like Greek to a twentieth-century police court accustomed to question refractory car-drivers and the anti-social owners of delinquent dogs. John soon became so eloquent on a subject long familiar to him, that one of the magistrates grew alarmed lest he might get the better of the argument.

"He will do harm," he insisted. "Let him speak no further."

"No, no, never fear him," responded Justice Kelynge, "we are better established than so; he can do no harm. We know," he continued, "the Common Prayer Book hath been ever since the Apostles' time, and is lawful to be used in the church."

The uneducated tinker felt a half-amused pride in being a better theologian than the learned Judge who had produced this astonishing piece of historical information.

"Sir," he said, "shew me the place in the epistles where the Common Prayer Book is written, or one text of Scripture, that commands me to read it, and I will use it. But yet, notwithstanding," he added tolerantly, "they that have a mind to use it, they have their liberty; that is, I would not keep them from it, but for our parts we can pray to God without it. Blessed be his name!"

At this point one of the justices decided that it would be better to change the discussion, and accused John of adopting Beelzebub for his god. John refused to be provoked, and once more invoked a blessing on the holy Name. Justice Kelynge, well-qualified to exchange posts with those modern wartime editors who specialize in the selection of disparaging names for Christian virtues, told him that this was "pedler's French", and ordered him to "leave off his canting".

The examination then turned on the more practical question of John's authority to preach, and again he defended his position by reference to a higher Authority than the State.

" 'As every man hath received the gift'," he quoted, " 'even so let him minister the same unto another, as good stewards of the manifold grace of God'."

"Let me a little open that Scripture to you," said Sir John derisively. " 'As every man hath received the gift'; that is, as every man hath received a trade, so let him follow it. If any man have received a gift of tinkering, as thou hast done, let him follow his tinkering. And so other men their trades, and the divine his calling."

But John was too long accustomed to have his occupation flung in his face, like a rotten egg or a mouldy apple, to be disturbed by ridicule.

"Nay, Sir," he said with dignity, "but it is most clear, that the Apostle speaks here of preaching the word." He continued to enlarge on the point, but the Bench had heard as much of his oratory as they were prepared to endure.

"We cannot wait upon you any longer," the Chairman said sharply. Ominously he added, "Then you confess the indictment, do you not?"

John faced him, resolute but startled. "Now, and not till now," he recorded, "I saw I was indicted." Until that moment, he had not realized that he was steadily incriminating himself by his eloquence.

He had, in fact, puzzled the Bench by making long speeches, instead of pleading Guilty or Not Guilty. The chance to bear conspicuous witness to his convictions had seemed to him a means of strengthening "the Saints in the county", but to the legal experts he appeared to be deliberately producing a deadlock. Without a formal plea, the trial could neither proceed nor reach a conclusion.

When such a failure to plead occurred under a felony, the penalty was extremely severe. The law ordained that the offender should be stretched on his back and have heavy weights of stone or iron piled upon him till he pleaded or died. Not three years earlier a Cavalier had actually been submitted to this torture; the by-standers could not endure it, and some of his friends jumped on him to end his agony.

John's offence, however, was not a crime, but a mere statutory misdemeanour, for which punishment by agonizing torture was totally disproportionate, and could never have been enforced. One of the more attractive qualities of English citizens who are neither idealists nor fanatics, but ordinary decent human beings, is their quiet disregard of laws which do not command their respect. The Elizabethan Conventicle Act had fallen into disuse largely because contemporary police officers were unwilling to arrest or convict.

Sir John Kelynge desired to suppress the loquacious rebel who answered him back at such length, but he was not prepared to do it illegally. He therefore reverted to a suggestion made by Henry Bracton, the thirteenth-century jurist and Chancellor of Exeter Cathedral, that if a prisoner insisted upon substituting long explanations for the simple plea required, his arguments should be treated as tantamount to a confession, or plea of guilt.

Without having warned John of this possible interpretation of the law, Kelynge by the character of his question elicited from him exactly the form of words that he wanted.

"I confess," John said slowly, "we have had many meetings together, both to pray to God, and to exhort one another, and there we had the sweet comforting presence of the Lord among us for our encouragement. Blessed therefore be his name! I do not confess I am guilty otherwise."

"Then," thundered Kelynge, "hear your judgment. You must be had back again to prison, and there lie for three months following; and at three months' end, if you do not submit to go to church to hear divine service, and leave your preaching, you must be banished the realm. And if, after such a day as shall be appointed you to be gone, you shall be found in this realm, or be found to come over again without special license from the King, you must stretch by the neck for it, I tell you plainly."

After instructing the Clerk of the Court to enter what John had said as a confession of the indictment, he beckoned to the jailor.

"Take him away!"

The jailor seized John's arm, but John shook him off. Drawing himself up to his impressive height, he confronted the magistrates. His eyes blazed with anger; wrought up to a high pitch of emotional excitement, he felt at that moment no fear of consequences either for himself or for others.

"I am at a point with you," he exclaimed. "If I was out of prison today, I would preach the Gospel again tomorrow, by the help of God!"

This time the jailor caught him more roughly and pulled him away. For a second or two, rage flared up in the hearts of his judges; then an uneasy silence fell upon the court.

CHAPTER XI

THE MIDSUMMER ASSIZES

"The law hath provided two ways of obeying: The one to do that which I in my conscience do believe that I am bound to do, actively; and where I cannot obey actively, there I am willing to lie down, and to suffer what they shall do unto me."
JOHN BUNYAN: *A Relation of the Imprisonment of Mr. John Bunyan.*

HIS examination at the Quarter Sessions was to remain in John Bunyan's mind as the prototype of all such semi-political, semi-religious trials. Sixteen years later he was still able to describe not only the court-house, but the Judges, jury and witnesses, and to confer upon Sir John Kelynge an inglorious immortality as Lord Hategood in Vanity Fair.

For the next three months John remained shut up in Bedford Gaol with debtors, vagabonds, and occasional criminals. He was not, however, the only political prisoner, for John Rush of Kempston Hardwick, an outstanding Quaker and a friend of John Crook, was brought in immediately after himself.

John Bunyan had now plenty of time to meditate upon his uncertain future. He was still wondering what was going to happen to him when, on 3 April, he was visited in gaol by Paul Cobb, the Clerk of the Peace, who summoned him from his cell into a private chamber.

This official, destined to be conspicuous in the story of Bedford Corporation for the next twenty-five years, explained to John that he had been sent by the magistrates to admonish him and demand his submission to the Church of England. He also made quite clear to him what the alternatives to submission would be, "even to be sent away out of the nation, or else worse than that". The magistrates, he added, intended to prosecute the law against John, if he did not submit.

John thereupon called in question the purpose of the law under which he was imprisoned; surely it was intended for those who used religion as a cloak for wickedness, and not for worshippers of God, whose object was to do as much good as they could?

"Everyone will say the same," commented Cobb realistically. "You see the late insurrection at London, under what glorious pretences they went, and yet indeed they intended no less than the ruin of the kingdom and commonwealth."

John attested his loyalty in eloquent phrases, which Cobb interrupted by saying that he did not profess to be a man able to dispute. He merely wanted to persuade John to exhort his neighbour privately, and to hear the word of God publicly; it was only calling the people together into private conventicles, with their obvious political risks, that the law forbade.

Again, as in John's earlier controversy with William Foster, the disputants continued on parallel lines. The one was concerned, like Mr. Legality who dwelt in the Village of Morality, to uphold the law as it actually stood; the other sought to prove that the commands of God, given either in the Scriptures or through personal inspiration reinforced by conscience, were superior to the laws of men.

"Sir," John insisted, "Wicliffe saith, that he which leaveth off preaching and hearing of the word of God for fear of excommunication of men, he is already excommunicated of God, and shall in the day of judgment be counted a traitor to Christ."

Paul Cobb attempted a new method of persuasion.

"Would you be willing," he asked, "that two indifferent persons shall determine the case, and will you stand by their judgment?"

But John had little confidence in the proposed method of arbitration.

"Are they infallible?" he inquired.

"Well, no—not exactly infallible."

"Then it is possible my judgment may be as good as theirs. But yet I will pass by either, and in this matter be judged by the Scriptures; I am sure that is infallible, and cannot err."

"But," objected Paul Cobb with reason, "who shall be judge between you, for you take the Scriptures one way, and they another?"

John explained that it was always possible to arrive at the truth by comparing a number of Biblical passages. They then went on to discuss the laws of the State and the ethics of submission to governments. Again the prisoner firmly told his visitor that he regarded himself as bound by conscience to walk according to the law of righteousness whether there was a king or not, and if this course contravened the law of the land, to bear the penalty with patience. He desired, he added, to live quietly in his country, and, to prove the political harmlessness of his doctrine, would willingly submit to anyone the notes of his sermons.

Supported by the jailor, Paul Cobb returned like a recurring decimal to his original point.

"Well, neighbour Bunyan," he said patiently, "indeed I would wish you seriously to consider of these things, between this and the quarter-sessions, and to submit yourself. You may do much good if you continue still in the land: but alas, what benefit will it be to your friends, if you should be sent away beyond the seas into Spain, or Constantinople, or some other remote part of the world?"

John, to whom Spain and Constantinople appeared as remote as they did to Paul and as likely to be included amongst the King's possessions, found no fault with this geographical description; he merely said that he desired in all godliness and honesty to behave himself in the nation. But when Cobb insisted that the powers-that-be were ordained of God, and if the King declared against private conventicles the prohibition was indirectly God's command, John replied that both Christ and St. Paul had suffered under authority, yet were surely not to be condemned as sinning against God in rejecting earthly commands.

"Sir," he concluded, finding simple and final words for his determination to endure to the end rather than repudiate his convictions, "the law hath provided two ways of obeying: The one to do that which I in my conscience do believe that I am bound to do, actively; and where I cannot obey actively, there I am willing to lie down, and to suffer what they shall do unto me."

Paul Cobb sat still and looked at him. There was obviously no way of moving this irrational fanatic; he had done his best, and was obliged to accept defeat. He rose to leave, but his baffled expression moved John to an emotion strangely akin to pity.

"Sir," he said gently, "I must thank you for your civil and meek discoursing with me."

On that quiet note they parted. Afterwards, recording his memories of this episode, John could still look back upon their interview without exasperation or pain. In all sincerity he concluded his recollections with a devout wish:

"O! that we might meet in Heaven!"

The legal aspects of John's misdemeanour were clearer to Paul Cobb than they appear to have been to some Bunyan biographers. On 10 December, 1670, nearly ten years after John's conviction at the Quarter Sessions, Paul sent an account of it to Roger Kenyon, Clerk of the Peace for Lancashire, apparently as a guide to procedure in similar cases.

"This important document," wrote Mr. W. T. Whitley, in *Bunyan's Imprisonments: A Legal Study*, "lay unnoticed among the Kenyon family papers until 1894, when it was transcribed and printed for the Historical Manuscripts Commission. Even then the transcriber and editor failed to notice either the legal or the literary and historical interest of the letter; even Bunyan's name remained unrecognized, and owing to a confusion of 'o' with the antique form of 'e', was printed as 'Benyon'."

Paul Cobb wrote as follows to instruct his colleague:

> "One Bonyon was indicted upon the Statute of 35 Elizabeth for being at a Conventicle. He was in prison, and was brought into Court and the indictment read to him; and because he refused to plead to it, the Court ordered me to record his confession, and he hath lain in prison upon that conviction, ever since Christmas Sessions, 12 Chas. II. And my Lord Chief Justice Keelinge was then upon the Bench, and gave the rule, and had the like, a year ago, against others. Bonyon hath petitioned all the Judges of Assize, as they came the Circuit, but could never be released. And truly, I think it but reasonable that if any one do appear, and afterwards will not plead, but that you should take judgment by *nihil dicit*, or confession."

John was not, therefore, as some of his indignant admirers declare, kept in prison in defiance of Habeas Corpus, since this writ was never applied for on his behalf. By contemporary standards he had received a fair trial, and was sentenced to exactly what the existing regulations prescribed—imprisonment until he conformed. He remained in prison because he broke, and deliberately continued to break, repressive laws which violated his conscience.

Behind those laws there was, of course, a philosophy. Archbishop Laud and his colleagues had reasoned that England was a Christian country, and that to be a Christian country meant sharing in Christian public worship. This sharing involved one common worship, established and uniform, in which all should take part.

John's examiners, it is true, catechized him intemperately, but most of them had old scores to wipe off, and were exasperated by his determined eloquence on matters which seemed to them irrelevant. From Francis Wingate, self-indulgent and impatient, but politically apprehensive with good reason and genuinely anxious after recovering his temper to prevent John from penalizing himself, to Paul Cobb, who patiently explained the consequences of an attitude which seemed to him mere wrong-headed obstinacy, the Bedfordshire authorities behaved well.

They treated John with that peculiar British reasonableness which is both the admiration and the despair of other nations. They were as reasonable with him as police-constables with stone-throwing suffragettes, and wartime Tribunal Judges with discursive conscientious objectors. They merely shared the self-interested inability of all established authority to understand the sacrificial nature of militant idealism.

Years, even centuries, usually elapse before the function of troublesome but selfless fanatics is seen to lie in changing the laws, and established authority with them.

Paul Cobb had been sent in his full official capacity to warn John in Bedford Gaol of the possibilities before him if he did not conform to the law. At the same time he required him to appear at the next Quarter Sessions, but before this routine procedure could occur, it was interrupted by the King's Coronation on 23 April, 1661—a function that ended in a "portentous thunderstorm".

The way in which this event altered his position was clearly described by John himself in *A Relation of the Imprisonment of Mr. John Bunyan.*

> "Now at the coronation of Kings, there is usually a releasement of divers prisoners, by virtue of his coronation; in which privilege also I should have had my share; but that they took

me for a convicted person, and therefore, unless I sued out a pardon, (as they called it) I could have no benefit thereby, notwithstanding, yet forasmuch as the coronation proclamation did give liberty from the day the King was crowned, to that day twelvemonth to sue them out: Therefore, though they would not let me out of prison, as they let out thousands, yet they could not meddle with me, as touching the execution of their sentence; because of the liberty offered for the suing out of pardons. Whereupon I continued in prison till the next assizes, which are called Midsummer assizes, being then kept in August, 1661."

Between the Coronation and the Assizes many events, both national and international, emphasized the recent reversal of policy. On 8 May a new General Election returned to Westminster the Cavalier Parliament, alternatively known as the Pensionary Parliament owing to the bribes received by its Members, and the Long Parliament of the Restoration.

For eighteen years this Parliament was to endure. Its Members when young emphasized the new cleavage of party and class, and when older gradually evolved into the national factions to be known as Whigs and Tories. From Bedfordshire went four Members to whom the description "Tory" aptly applied; Lord Bruce and Sir John Winch represented the county, while Sir John Kelynge and Richard Taylor were elected for the borough. Kelynge then lived at Southill Park, Bedfordshire, now the home of the Whitbread family, famous as brewers. His portrait still hangs in the house.

Some changes of power on the Continent coincided with England's swing to the right. On 9 March Jules Mazarin, France's second successive great minister, had died at Vincennes. His death left Louis XIV, now twenty-three, in control of the foreign policy which was to bring him and England's half-French, newly-crowned monarch, eight years his senior, into close and sinister contact.

Louis's accession to personal power soon showed itself in the increasing repression of the Huguenots, who since the time of Henry of Navarre had enjoyed, through the Edict of Nantes, a measure of toleration denied to Protestants in other Catholic countries, and far exceeding that given to English Nonconformists. Richelieu had withdrawn their privilege of maintaining self-governing communities in several parts of France, but left unimpaired their liberty of worship. To Louis this liberty was abhorrent, and he began a policy which was soon to link the French Huguenots with the English Puritans as victims of the wave of reaction now sweeping Europe.

At present it was reaction at home, not abroad, which concerned John Bunyan. Bravely as he had stood up to Sir John Kelynge and Paul Cobb for principles incomprehensible to legal authorities, there were periods of loneliness and fear when his courage failed.

During his first months in prison he was haunted continually by the memory of the gibbets, with their tarred decomposing corpses, which he had passed so often on the way to Bromham and at Caxton crossroads. After Paul Cobb's admonitions, which had made abundantly clear his probable fate if he continued obdurate, he often pictured himself mounting the gallows, and wondered how he would encounter death.

For weeks the fear troubled him that, by trembling or fainting on the ladder, he would give reason to his enemies to despise the people of God for their cowardice. He was ashamed to die "with a pale Face, and tottering knees" for the cause of religious freedom, and therefore constantly imagined himself on the ladder with the rope round his neck. If only he could get used to the idea before his time came, he might then be able to speak some final sentences to the multitude which would come, he believed, to see him die. Were but one soul to be converted by those last words, he would not have died in vain.

But continued apprehension was wearing down his resistance, and the confidence born from the vision of a courageous death soon vanished before another anxiety which tore his heart more cruelly than any fear for himself. When he confronted his judges at the Quarter Sessions he had been able, in the exaltation of the moment, to forget his family, but now the thought of their fate if he were hanged bitterly recurred to challenge his resolution.

"I found myself a man, and compassed with Infirmities," he wrote later of these emotions, poignantly remembered in a still distant tranquillity. "The parting with my Wife and poor Children hath often been to me in this place, as the pulling the

HARLINGTON HOUSE

The house of the magistrate, Francis Wingate, who had Bunyan arrested. From an old print kindly lent by the present occupant, Mrs. G. M. Tabor.

THE CHAPEL OF HERNE, BEDFORD

Here Bunyan was examined by the Justices at Quarter Sessions in January 1661. From an old print dated 1783.

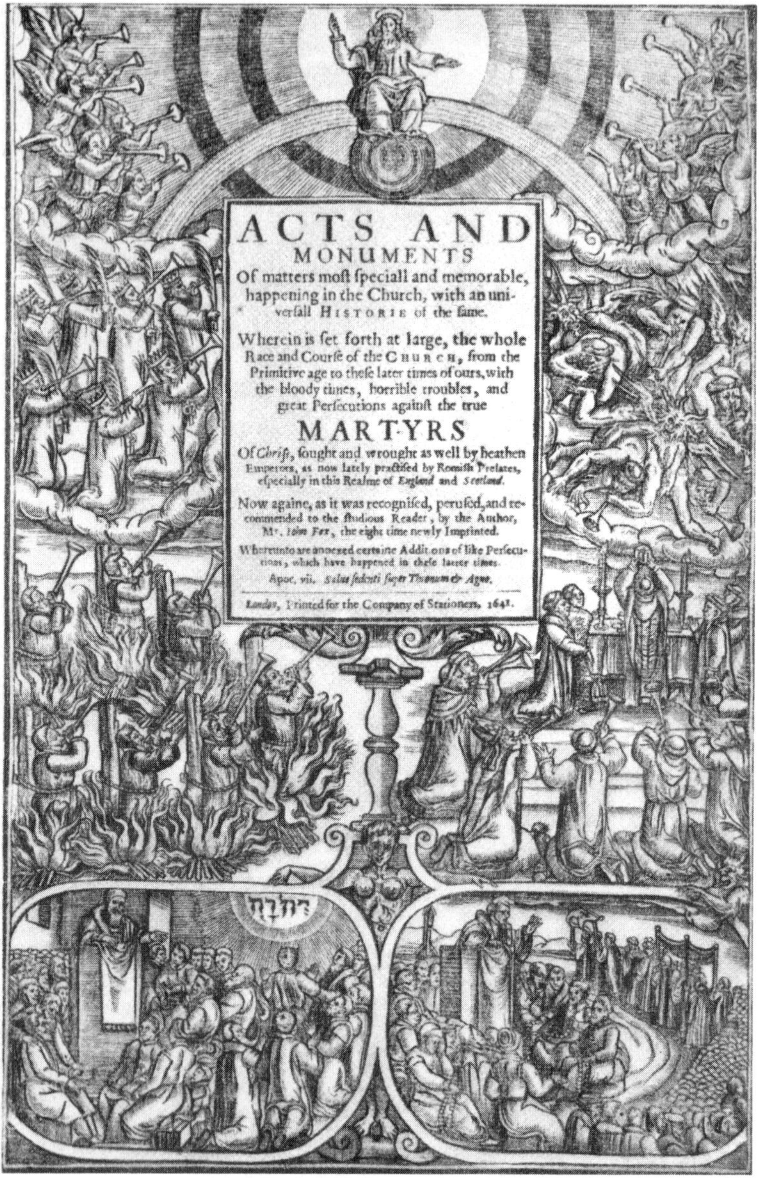

FOXE'S BOOK OF MARTYRS

The black letter edition of 1641, said to be the only book besides the Bible which Bunyan had in gaol. A copy of this edition is in the John Bunyan Library, Bedford.

Flesh from my Bones; and that not only because I am somewhat too too fond of these great Mercies, but also because I should have often brought to my mind the many hardships, miseries and wants that my poor Family was like to meet with, should I be taken from them, especially my poor blind Child, who lay nearer my heart then all I had besides; O the thoughts of the hardship I thought my blind one might go under, would break my heart to pieces."

In spite of his struggle to evolve a philosophy of life and death, he could not put his fears for blind Mary aside.

"Poor Child!" he thought, "what sorrow art thou like to have for thy Portion in this World? Thou must be beaten, must beg, suffer hunger, cold, nakedness, and a thousand Calamities, though I cannot now endure the Wind should blow upon thee."

But though it wounded him to the quick to leave them, he believed that he had no alternative but to "venture them all with God". He was as a man who was pulling down his house on the head of his wife and children, and yet he must do it; he must do it!

He had now, however, another year before the worst could happen; the abjuration proceedings which would result in his banishment were postponed until 23 April, 1662. They were actually never to be pursued; much evidence exists in the histories of other prisoners that exile, for such an offence as his, was coming to be regarded by public opinion as a punishment disproportionate to the crime. But this he did not know; and he resolved to neglect no possible means that might lawfully secure his release.

As John Bunyan recorded, the King did not order the gaol doors to be opened automatically at his Coronation; certain prisoners, including those in John's category, were invited to apply for pardon. Since he was uncertain of the procedure, Elizabeth agreed to undertake the intimidating journey to London to interview a peer, Lord Barkwood, from whom they had been advised that they might obtain help.

Leaving the children with neighbours for two or three days, she made the fifty-mile journey and delivered a petition for John's release to Lord Barkwood at the House of Lords. He did not give her, as they had secretly hoped he might, the £30 needed to sue out a pardon. But he consulted other members of the House, who told her that John could only be released by the Judges at the next local Assizes, and advised her to approach them.

At these Assizes the Judges on circuit did not appear solely for the purpose of trying criminals; they were held responsible to the Government for the conduct of magistrates, whose activities they investigated. The Assizes, therefore, became an informal meeting of the county for every conceivable purpose. The Judges inquired into the administration of the shire, lectured the company assembled to hear cases, and explained national policy and social needs to persons whose outlook was bounded by local interests.

In Bedford the Judges and magistrates met at the Guildhall Chamber or "Market Place", south of the County Gaol on the same side of the High Street. This Jacobean building, now demoted to the purposes of a fish-shop, was used as an Exchange, a meeting-place of the Merchant Burgesses, and a rendezvous for "deals", in addition to its chief function as a Shire Hall. On the first floor was a spacious salon, forming part of a series of wainscotted chambers, with two bow windows looking over the road.

From this dignified room the Judges emerged in ermine and scarlet, and climbed, with the Sheriff and Chaplain, into the official coach behind coachmen wearing powdered wigs and trumpeters tootling on emblazoned trumpets. The coach took them past the butcher-rows and fish-rows in St. Paul's Square to divine service in St. Paul's Church. After listening to prayers and a sermon, they moved on to the Chapel of Herne. Between Sessions and Assizes this scene of John Bunyan's examination was let as a storeroom, and had to be cleared each time the Judges and magistrates required it.

The prospects of a sympathetic reception for John's petition were both good and bad. One of the two Judges of Assize, Sir Thomas Twisden, was a hard man of conventional outlook, likely to be swayed by the prejudices of the magistrates by whom John had been examined. But another more famous Judge, Sir Matthew Hale, happened to be coming to Bedford on circuit that summer. In administering the Conventicle Acts he "showed a certain tenderness towards Dissenters", and did his best to mitigate the severity of the law.

Sir Matthew, born in 1609, was on the whole sympathetic to the Royalists, but he had been brought up by a Puritan guardian.

He sat for Gloucestershire in the Convention Parliament which met in April 1660, and took an active part in the Restoration. A month after Charles's arrival in London he had been called to the degree of Sergeant-at-law, and was included in the commission for the trial of the Regicides.

The following year, at Bury St. Edmunds Assizes, Sir Matthew Hale was to be concerned with Sir John Kelynge in a case where they appeared to exchange rôles. At this celebrated witch trial on 10 March, 1662, two old women were indicted for witchcraft on the ground that they had caused some children to be seized with fainting fits, to vomit nails and pins, and to see mysterious ducks, mice, and flies invisible to others.

At the trial, Sir Thomas Browne, the Norwich author of *Religio Medici* and *Urn-burial,* gave evidence for the prosecution, but Serjeant Kelynge, the haughty lawyer, openly expressed his dissatisfaction with the case, and after performing, at Hale's request, some simple experiments on the children supposed to be bewitched, declared his belief that "the whole transaction of this business was a mere imposture". Sir Matthew, who probably disliked his overbearing colleague, "made no doubt at all" of the existence of witches when he directed the jury; he abstained from commenting on the evidence, and the two women were convicted and executed.

Elderly women accused of witchcraft were perhaps Sir Matthew Hale's blind spot. The Puritan divine, Richard Baxter, who in his later years lived near Sir Matthew at Acton and discussed with him such questions as the nature of the spirit and the rational basis for a belief in the soul's immortality, spoke with eloquent warmth of this distinguished lawyer who was to succeed Kelynge as Chief Justice:

> "He was a man of no quick utterance, but often hesitant; but spoke with great reason. He was most precisely just; insomuch as I believe he would have lost all that he had in the world rather than do an unjust act."

To this well-intentioned man, fundamentally humane if sometimes inconsistent, Elizabeth Bunyan now presented John's petition. His pale, gentle face and deep eyes beneath dark brows gave her confidence. He received it from her "very mildly"; he would do his best for them, he said, though he feared that would be little.

To make sure that his case would not be overlooked, John had made three copies of the petition, and the following day Elizabeth intercepted Sir Thomas Twisden as he drove through St. Paul's Square in his white stock and fur-edged cape. He was seven years older than Sir Matthew Hale, and she felt intimidated by his loose, fleshy cheeks, bulbous nose, and down-turned mouth between loose locks of straight hair streaked with grey.

Summoning all her courage, she threw a second copy of the petition into his coach. This made him very angry and he "snapt her up", insisting that John was a convicted person who could not be released unless he would promise to stop preaching.

Determined to be heard, the persistent girl made a second expedition to the Chapel of Herne, and presented the third copy of the petition to Judge Hale as he sat on the Bench. He seemed inclined to give her audience, but Sir Henry Chester, one of John's examiners at the Quarter Sessions, intervened and dissuaded him.

"My Lord," he said, "this man was a hot-spirited fellow, who was convicted in this court!"

The Judge then waved Elizabeth aside, and she fell back, crest-fallen and close to tears, into the crowded body of the Court. But the High Sheriff, who happened that year to be a kindly man, Edmund Wylde of Houghton Conquest, had observed her failure. Feeling sorry for her, he encouraged her to try yet again. There would be an opportunity, he said, when the Assizes were over, and the two Judges met various justices and country gentry in the Swan Chamber to discuss the business of the shire.

The Swan Chamber was the upper room of the Swan Inn; its tall, oblong-paned windows, which faced both the Ouse and the High Street, were built out on piers over the courtyard. A narrow strip of bank, broken by a flight of steps, divided the inn from the river. In the eighteenth century it was to be pulled down and rebuilt, incorporating a staircase from Houghton House, farther back from the water as the Swan Hotel.

To this upper chamber, crowded with the important and the self-important, Elizabeth Bunyan, her face flushed and her heart sinking, now went to make her last endeavour. Somehow she penetrated the noisy, indifferent throng of men, and for a third time stood before Sir Matthew Hale.

She wore her hair brushed into a knot at the back of her head, unadorned by ringlets such as the Cavaliers' ladies wore; her grey dress was untrimmed except for a plain white collar and cuffs, though to supplement her family's meagre resources she had become an assiduous lace-maker. She was only a young peasant woman, without means, education or influence, yet incalculable chance made her a minor beacon of history, destined to survive in public esteem all the busy gentlemen who regarded her as less than the dust.

"My Lord," she began, trembling, "I make bold to come once again to your Lordship to know what may be done with my husband."

This time the just Sir Matthew was a little exasperated.

"Woman," he said, "I told thee before I could do thee no good, because they have taken that for a conviction which thy husband spoke at the sessions. Unless there be something done to undo that, I can do thee no good."

Elizabeth began to plead that John had never confessed the indictment and was, therefore, kept unlawfully in prison, but a magistrate standing by contradicted her. She started again.

"My Lord, it is false. He only said that he had been at several meetings, both where there was preaching the word, and prayer, and that they had God's presence among them."

This time Judge Twisden himself intervened, annoyed by the awkward interruption.

"Do you think we can do what we list?" he exclaimed angrily. "Your husband is a breaker of the peace and is convicted by the law."

Sir Matthew sent for the Statute Book, and Elizabeth persisted.

"My Lord, he was not lawfully convicted!"

When Sir Henry Chester, also close to the Judge, again denied this, she repeated: "It is false. It was but a word of discourse that they took for a conviction."

"But it is recorded, woman, it is recorded!" cried Justice Chester irritably, as though this fact guaranteed the truth of the indictment. He tried to check Elizabeth with further arguments, but she had now gained more confidence. Turning to Sir Matthew, she described her visit to Lord Barkwood in London and the advice that he gave her.

"And now," she concluded, "I come to you to see if anything may be done in this business, and you give me neither releasement nor relief."

This bold pronouncement was followed by an embarrassed silence, in which Sir Henry Chester continued to mutter that John was a pestilent fellow, there was not such another in the country, he had been convicted and it was recorded. Finally Judge Twisden inquired: "Will your husband leave off preaching? If he will do so, then send for him."

"My Lord," said Elizabeth, her deep unity with John compelling her to resist the proffered compromise, "he dares not leave preaching, as long as he can speak."

Judge Twisden turned to Sir Matthew Hale with an angry gesture.

"See here," he exclaimed, "what should we talk any more about such a fellow! Must he do what he lists? He is a breaker of the peace!"

Again Elizabeth insisted that John only desired to live peaceably and to follow his calling in order to maintain his family.

"My Lord," she added, "I have four small children, that cannot help themselves, of whom one is blind. We have nothing to live upon but the charity of good people."

"Hast thou four children?" asked Sir Matthew, moved by her predicament. "Thou art but a young woman to have four children."

"I am but mother-in-law to them, having not been married to him yet full two years," she explained. Intuitively perceiving pity in his heart, she decided to go further.

"Indeed," she continued, "I was with child when my husband was first apprehended. But being young and unaccustomed to such things, and being smayed at the news, I fell into labour and so continued for eight days. Then I was delivered, but my child died."

"Alas, poor woman!" exclaimed the Judge sympathetically, for this sad story genuinely distressed him.

But Judge Twisden now decided that the appeal being made to his benevolent colleague was altogether too moving.

"You make poverty your cloak!" he told Elizabeth roughly. "I understand your husband was better maintained by running up and down a-preaching than by following his calling."

"What is his calling?" Judge Hale inquired.

"A tinker, my Lord!" answered several voices.

"Yes," said Elizabeth bravely, "and because he is a tinker and a poor man, therefore he is despised and cannot have justice!"

Sir Matthew turned to her and gently tried to explain that, according to the law as it had been interpreted, John's conviction was just.

"I tell thee, woman," he said, "seeing that they have taken what thy husband spake, for a conviction, thou must either apply thyself to the King, or sue out his pardon, or get a writ of error."

The last of these expedients was new to Elizabeth; it implied that Sir John Kelynge's ruling, identifying discursive eloquence with a confession of guilt, was arbitrary and could be challenged. If, by means of a "writ of error" his judgment could be reconsidered by another court in much the same way as a modern Court of Appeal reconsiders verdicts, it might be condemned as bad law and the decision reversed.

John recorded Judge Hale's advice, but his subsequent history shows that neither he nor Elizabeth ever understood its significance.

Sir Henry Chester, however, grasped the point immediately, and was much incensed at this implied criticism of a judgment in which he had taken his share.

"My Lord!" he blustered, "this man will then preach and do what he lists!"

"He preacheth nothing but the word of God," said Elizabeth firmly.

But Judge Twisden, too, had become enraged.

"He preach the word of God!" he exclaimed, leaning towards her so angrily that she thought he was going to strike her. "He runneth up and down, and doth harm!"

"No, my Lord, it's not so," Elizabeth persisted. "God hath owned him and done much good by him."

"God!" cried the outraged Twisden. "His doctrine is the doctrine of the Devil!"

But Elizabeth, being now beyond hope and therefore immune

to fear, did not intend this disparagement of John to be the final word.

"My Lord," she said with dignity, "when the righteous Judge shall appear, it will be known that his doctrine is not the doctrine of the Devil."

Judge Twisden turned his back on her.

"My Lord," he urged his colleague, "do not mind her, but send her away."

Sir Matthew Hale had no alternative. It was his duty to administer the law as it stood, however unfair he thought it, and however much he disliked Kelynge's recent identification of eloquent explanations with guilt. Quietly and clearly he repeated his advice, again enraging Justice Chester by his new reference to a writ of error.

Elizabeth, still believing John and herself to be the victims of illegal treatment rather than of repressive but indubitable legislation, begged them to send for John himself; he could explain things so much better than she could. But she was gently dismissed, and realizing that she could not prevail, she made her way to the door through the murmuring crowd. When she entered the Chamber she had been tense with fear, but now she broke into tears.

"It was not so much because they were so hard-hearted against me, and against you," she explained afterwards to John in prison, "but to think what a sad account such poor creatures will have to give at the coming of the Lord, when they shall there answer for all things whatsoever they have done in the body."

Just as she left the Swan Chamber the Statute Book arrived, but she never knew what the Judges said when they had examined it, nor did she hear from them again. So she went back, without any child of her own to comfort her, to take care of John's children in the cottage in St. Cuthbert's Street, and to endure without complaint the woman's share of the burden imposed by oppressive laws.

John himself, a conscientious objector against State-imposed orthodoxy, remained in Bedford Gaol.

Should he have been such a conscientious objector?

A hundred and fifty years after John Bunyan's death, men of

CAXTON GIBBET

At Caxton cross-roads between Cambridge and St. Neots. An exact copy of the original, said to have been sold to American soldiers.

BUNYAN'S HOUSE IN BEDFORD

A painting made from an old print by Mr. A. Breanski, showing the cottage in St. Cuthbert's Street where the Bunyans lived for about thirty years.

letters began to debate that question. They continued to debate it almost up to the outbreak of the Second World War.

> "John Bunyan" [wrote Robert Southey in 1830] "did not ask himself how far the case of those Martyrs whose example he was prepared to follow resembled the situation in which he was placed. Such a question, had he been cool enough to entertain it, might have shown him that they had no other alternative than idolatry or the stake: but that he was neither called upon to renounce anything that he did believe, nor to profess anything that he did not. . . . He was only required not to go about the country holding conventicles."

Nearly a hundred years later, in a *Bookman* Tercentenary article which deliberately set out to "debunk" John Bunyan, the poet Alfred Noyes used the same argument, though more vehemently. Disregarding the abundant evidence in John's own writings of his tolerance towards those who differed from him on such matters as baptism and the Prayer Book, he maintained that John was a perverse obsessionist who preferred his own opinions to the welfare of his wife and family.

> "He was imprisoned for stamping with his cloven hoof on the opinions of others. His personal vanity claimed a divine personal right to lay down the law for others, on matters of which he was utterly ignorant. . . . Rather than abstain from clamorous public assertion of his own personal authority on subjects of which he knew almost as much as Newton's dog could grasp of the differential calculus, he abandoned his wife and children. Again and again he was offered freedom if he would abstain, not from his personal opinions, but from his public attacks upon the religious views of any sect but his own."

According to this argument the conscientious objectors of the Second World War, who received exemption from military service when they convinced the Judges at legal tribunals that their conscience forbade them to kill, could have been dismissed if they were unable to explain the medieval Doctrine of "the Just War".

Five years before that Second War, Robert Bridges, who had the self-conscious craftsman's distaste for the "indiscriminate vulgarity" of the instinctive artist, adopted a similar standpoint when writing of John Bunyan in his collected Essay Papers, published in 1934.

> "Having the choice between silence with imprisonment and silence with freedom, his conscience forced him to prefer the material fetters, and leave his family to the charity of his friends."

These comments do not suggest that poet Southey, poet Noyes, or poet Bridges understood the problem of conscience in any profound sense, or ever had to meet its challenge in their personal experience. Had they done so they would have known—as those who still live in the midst of a struggle against world-wide totalitarianism know—that the alternative before John Bunyan was not as they describe it.

It is false to say that his imprisonment was self-inflicted because he would not accept the proffered terms of freedom. With liberty of worship at the core of his belief, he could not have accepted them. His duty as a Christian was to save not merely his own soul, but the souls of his brethren. Silence with freedom would have violated his conscience, since it would have involved the deliberate choice of silence. For silence imposed on him by the law, he was not responsible. No honest man deeply moved by conviction could, in his circumstances, have chosen personal liberty, whatever the cost of refusing it might be for himself or for others.

By Southey's word "only", the whole issue of spiritual integrity is raised. John Bunyan and his fellow-Independents were fighting for the right of a Christian to decide, without interference from the State or its Established Church, the character of his relationship to God. If that relationship seemed to his conscience, through which he believed God spoke, to be best fulfilled by the holding of conventicles, then he could not abjure conventicles without renouncing a conviction which was essential to his faith.

Today it is possible to see John Bunyan's conflict with the State in twentieth-century terms, for it has occurred throughout recent history in many different forms. Two voices have sounded for years through the court-rooms of Europe, and the first is a voice as old as Bunyan's own.

"Give me the liberty to know, to utter, and to argue freely according to conscience, above all liberties!"

But sometimes the voice of the presiding official drowns the immortal challenge of Milton.

"You have only to say you will join the Party and I will not send you to a concentration camp."

For nearly two decades, millions of Europeans have taken that official step—for the sake of their wives, their families, their art, their jobs. Only the few have refused to take it, risking their children's lives with their own, but preferring, like John Bunyan, to "venture them all with God".

Yet, strange as Southey, Noyes, and Bridges might find it, it is the few whom we admire today, and not the many who erected that little word "only" between themselves and death. The Quaker, the Christian Socialist, the anti-Marxist Catholic, the member of the Confessional Church, will not shelter behind it, so he goes to the concentration camp—a troublesome fellow, only fit for the gas-chamber—in the same way as John Bunyan went to Bedford Gaol,

His choice may not be yours; you may honestly believe that some form of compromise is always best, and you are as much entitled to express your opinion as Southey, Noyes, and Bridges were to ventilate theirs. But you cannot force your view upon John Bunyan, or George Lansbury, or Clement von Galen, or Martin Niemöller. With the dedicated soul, whether he belongs to the seventeenth century or the twentieth, it is God, as always, who has the last word.

CHAPTER XII

HOME TO PRISON

"So being again delivered up to the Gaolers hands, I was had home to Prison, and there have lain now compleat twelve years, waiting to see what God will suffer these men to do with me."

JOHN BUNYAN: *Grace Abounding.*

CONSCIENCE is a white angel; but even angels have their temptations, and the temptation of this one is spiritual pride.

The first reaction to persecution is heroic and aggressive.

"You can't get me down; I have conquered. I am the master of my fate, the captain of my soul!"

In our day that brave, aggressive voice has often been heard, just as it was heard among the Dissenters of the seventeenth century. It sounded through all the Resistance Movements of Europe and Asia, and came not least from the exponents of non-violence, who are sometimes quite belligerent.

It is only with time that the loud note of defiance changes to the quieter accents of the still, small voice. The proud challenge "I will not fear!" is deepened by love until the very words alter.

"I will suffer what men shall do unto me"—yes, and I will suffer without anger, without bitterness, without judgment. "Father, forgive them, for they know not what they do."

Only gradually, during his twelve years in prison, did John Bunyan move from the one position to the other, slowly exchanging the hot temper of the rebel for the composed acceptance of the saint. The man who cried at the Quarter Sessions in January 1661, "I am at a point with you, for if I was out of prison today, I would preach the Gospel again tomorrow!" was able to write in 1672 during a controversy on baptism: "Divisions are to churches like wars in countries; where war is, the ground lieth waste and untilled, none takes care of it. It is love that edifieth, but division pulleth down."

Outside the walls of Bedford Gaol during the twelve years of John's imprisonment, the apostles of Puritanism were expounding by their own lives the prophetic quality of Milton's sonnets.

In secret woods and dells and attics, in the noisome holds of the crowded little ships which carried them across the Atlantic to settlements now stretching from the borders of French-occupied Canada to the coast of South Carolina, the Nonconformists under Charles II posted "o're Land and Ocean without rest". In English prisons and on English scaffolds, they became the "slaughter'd Saints" whose bones the inward eye of the blind poet had seen "scatter'd on the Alpine mountains cold".

But nothing proved more conclusively than the development of John Bunyan's mind and spirit in prison that "They also serve who only stand and waite".

To begin with, standing and waiting did not accord with John's temper at all. Between the King's coronation in April 1661 and the Spring Assizes in March 1662, he spent part of his year of grace on fruitless efforts to obtain release.

At that time considerable freedom was allowed him by his jailor; he continued with his "wonted course" of preaching and visiting, and, as Southey recorded, "he was often out in the night, and it is said that many of the Baptist congregations in Bedfordshire owe their origin to his midnight preaching". He even went up to London to consult his friends there on the best line to pursue.

Sir Matthew Hale had advised Elizabeth that a writ of error would be the cheapest procedure, but John was only an obscure mechanic unlikely to find champions among lawyers looking for legal reputations. In any case he had never understood the Judge's advice, and therefore did nothing. The Christmas Quarter Sessions, at which he expected to be "roundly dealt with", went by without incident because his twelve months' respite was still unfinished.

Meanwhile his visits to London and the continued alarm caused by Fifth Monarchists made the prison authorities so angry that John's jailor almost lost his job; "they charged me also," John wrote indignantly, "that I went thither to plot and rouse division and make insurrection, which, God knows, was a slander; whereupon my liberty was more straightened than it was before; so that I must not look out of the door".

Determined to be called before the court by one means or another, he next persuaded the jailor to put his name down on the list of criminals awaiting trial at the March Assizes, and through friends approached the High Sheriff and the Judge, who promised that he should be called. But when the Assizes came on, the Justices and the Clerk of the Peace removed his name; Paul Cobb especially was angry, pointing out that John was not a prisoner awaiting trial, but one who had been tried and convicted.

The ruling under which Sir John Kelynge had convicted him could only be challenged by legal argument at Westminster, where also an alternative procedure, the application for a writ of Habeas Corpus, would have to be dealt with. If, therefore, argued the Clerk, John was allowed to go before the Judge and was released, the jailor would be liable for John's fees and could be penalized for drawing up "false Kalenders". He had doubly offended by representing John's crime to be "worse in itself than it was by far".

This abortive effort evidently convinced John that the law's complications were too idiotic and irrational to be worth recording, for here his own story of his imprisonment ended with an abrupt "Farewell". Actually, the ruling laid down by Kelynge was soon endorsed at the trial of that influential Quaker, John Crook.

On 25 June, 1662, Crook appeared at the Old Bailey with two other Friends, Isaac Gray and John Bolton, for refusing to take the Oath of Allegiance. After his long experience as a Justice of the Peace under the Protectorate, he defended himself brilliantly.

In this famous trial he led on Chief Justice Foster to lay down a rule that the Oath should not be tendered repeatedly, and that even once would suffice; then he submitted evidence that he had taken it years before. But the Judge held him to the point that he was charged with not taking it now, and required him to plead Guilty or Not Guilty; he also ruled that the only alternative to pleading was a "Praemunire". This meant that he would be out of the King's protection, with his property forfeited and himself subject to life imprisonment.

John Crook, living on his estate between Ampthill and Woburn, had long been an important figure in Bedfordshire; both the trial and Chief Justice Foster's ruling soon became familiar to Paul Cobb. His official attitude in the case of John Bunyan was now reinforced by the knowledge that if John moved for his writ of error he might obtain it, but the upshot would be imprisonment for life, with only the possibilities of death and exile removed.

These niceties of the law were Greek to John, but the failure of his efforts had made it clear that he would not easily get out of prison. Dismal as the place was, he was at least receiving the treatment given to debtors rather than felons, and could be visited by Elizabeth and the children. It was for them, not himself, that he was still concerned, though the uncertainty of his fate oppressed him.

His friend John Holden, a Bedford brazier, was now helping them, and Elizabeth's lace-making brought in a pittance, but these combined efforts were not enough to support a family of five. John therefore taught himself to make long-tagged thread-laces, and sold many hundreds gross of these to add to their tiny income.

His opportunities of preaching and visiting were now at an end. For seven years his name was to vanish from the records of the Bedford Meeting.

In April 1662, John's year of grace ended. The further penalties to which he was liable were not imposed, but their possibility filled him with constant dread.

Season after season he continued, as Paul Cobb later reported in his letter to Roger Kenyon of Lancashire, to send in petitions to the Judges at the periodic Assizes. But these could not be effective as the law then stood. He had been convicted and was in prison; at any time he could make formal submission and come out. Since he declined to do this, the law insisted that he must remain in prison until he conformed.

Meanwhile, the oppressiveness of the laws themselves steadily increased. The new Parliament, which had met on 8 May, 1661, proceeded within the next five years to stamp an Anglican pattern on English society by means of the four great penal laws known as the Clarendon Code.

Legislation of this type was to be wiped for ever from the English Statute Book by the Toleration Act of 1689, but it lasted just long enough to restrict the social sphere of Puritanism to the middle and poorer classes, and to divide the religious life of England into Church and Dissent.

The first measure to be passed was the Corporation Act of December 1661, which restricted membership of municipal bodies to those who would receive the Communion according to the rites of the Church of England, and take an oath that armed resistance to the King was unlawful.

By the Act of Uniformity, which Sir John Kelynge helped to draw up, this oath was imposed on all clergymen and teachers, and the use of the Revised Prayer Book, together with ordination by an Anglican bishop, was made compulsory for all ministers of religion.

Even in a reactionary House such a drastic measure was unpopular; at each stage it was opposed, and eventually passed the Commons only by 186 votes to 180. Further opposition held it up in the Lords, which did not accept it until 8 May, 1662.

Thousands throughout the country hoped that the narrow Commons majority and the Lords' opposition would cause the King to withhold his assent, but he finally gave it on 19 May, and the measure became law. Its immediate results were to sever the Church of England from all connection with other Protestant bodies, and to drive from their benefices two thousand clergymen who could not conscientiously accept its conditions.

Although Charles had given his assent, he accepted Clarendon's law-making without enthusiasm. The preoccupation of posterity with his amorous adventures has caused his intellectual qualities to be underestimated; in 1662 he was more interested in the incorporation of the Royal Society, and in such books as Robert Boyle's newly-published *The Sceptical Chymist*, than in religious persecution.

He had, in addition, strong Catholic preferences of his own, and hoped to make life easier for the English Recusants by tolerating Nonconformists. On 26 December, 1662, he sent out a Declaration of general Religious Toleration from Whitehall, and the following year tried unsuccessfully to persuade Parliament to mitigate the Act of Uniformity. Instead, on 18 June, Sir John Kelynge was raised to the Bench.

About this time, an incident in Buckingham illustrated the severity of the long-lived Elizabethan Conventicle Act under which John Bunyan had been imprisoned. Ten men and two women taken at Baptist worship in Aylesbury were brought up at Quarter Sessions to "abjure the realm". They refused and, quite legally under the Statute, had their property confiscated and were sentenced to death.

The son of one of them, Thomas Monck, "King's Messenger" for the district, at once rode to London and told Clarendon, who passed on the information to Charles. The King was astonished that such a sentence could be possible, and at once reprieved the offenders. It had become clear that neither he nor his people would tolerate the wholesale execution of conventiclers. But as thousands were now listening with sympathy to sermons by ejected Nonconformist ministers, Clarendon and Archbishop Sheldon wanted a new measure making penalties as severe as public opinion would accept.

In the spring of 1663, Clarendon thwarted Charles's Declaration of Indulgence by persuading the Lords to abandon a Bill based upon it. After surviving an attempt to impeach him the following July, he carried through in May 1664 a new temporary Conventicle Act, forbidding all religious meetings but those of the Anglican Church.

This Act, which was to hold good for three years, provided for an alternative series of punishments, ranging from a fine of £5 or three months' imprisonment, to a fine of £100 or seven years' transportation. It also embodied in its fifth section Kelynge's method of dealing with a prisoner who refused to plead:

> "If such offender shall refuse to plead the general issue, or to confess the indictment . . . such offender shall be transported beyond the seas to any of His Majesty's foreign plantations (Virginia and New England only excepted) there to remain for seven years."

This clause raised a new legal point: Could John Bunyan,

convicted under the Elizabethan Act, now be transported under the Act of Charles II? It was still possible for the Bishop or some other over-zealous person to serve John with a citation under the earlier Act; the constant apprehension which he suffered was comparable with that of twentieth-century political prisoners in Nazi or Allied hands.

"They did sentence me to perpetual banishment because I refused to conform," he reported in *Grace Abounding*, and in his *Prison Meditations* sought divine consolation for the ever-present threat:

When they do talk of banishment,
Of death, or such-like things,
Then to me God sends heart's content,
That like a fountain springs.

In October 1665 the Five Mile Act supplied the fourth pillar to Clarendon's edifice of Anglican repression. This measure, passed at Oxford owing to the plague in London, was directed like the Act of Uniformity against the Nonconformist ministers rather than their congregations. Under a penalty of £40, it forbade them to teach in schools or to live within five miles of a corporate town. Hundreds of preachers and teachers were deprived of their work, and banished to obscure places where they could not earn a living.

A month after the passing of the Five Mile Act, Sir John Kelynge succeeded Lord Chief Justice Hyde, Clarendon's cousin, as Chief Justice of the King's Bench. If John Bunyan now applied for a Habeas Corpus or a writ of error, his chances of success were likely to be nil.

This new legislation, like the trial of Christian and Faithful at Vanity Fair, resulted, particularly amongst the Quakers, in a numerical increase of those against whom it was directed. During two decades the affection for Puritan forms of worship had grown so deep that thousands of men and women were prepared to risk heavy penalties rather than give them up. A few emigrated but the majority stayed, believing that sooner or later the pendulum would swing again.

In many parts of the country, of which Bedfordshire was one, local authorities were reluctant to enforce the full rigours of the law. John Donne and Thomas Haynes, for instance, were sentenced to banishment before 1668, but in 1672 they were still in Bedford Gaol to take advantage of the King's Declaration of Indulgence.

The poor and humble who so passionately read their Bibles and said their prayers, the Dissenting merchants and shopkeepers whose damaged businesses became a favourite argument for toleration, were no longer moved, as before the Civil War, mainly by theological differences with their persecutors. It was the human consequences of those incompatible opinions which now stirred them, together with loyalty to long-established religious practices.

The Dissenters of the Restoration risked their freedom and possessions for simplicity of worship, extempore prayer, direct interpretation of the Scriptures, and the right to choose their ministers outside the ranks of men episcopally ordained. Their readiness to suffer for their convictions distressed even their critics. Samuel Pepys saw victims of the Clarendon Code on their way to a terrible exile, and wrote in his Diary:

> "They go like lambs without any resistance. I would to God that they would conform or be more wise and not be catched."

In Bedfordshire, after the Act of Uniformity, John Donne and William Dell were ejected from their livings at Pertenhall and Yelden. With eleven other local clergy they departed on 24 August, 1662, the "Black Bartholomew" of the English Church.

John Donne moved to Keysoe and became the first pastor of the Independent group, summoning them regularly for worship by night to the depths of Keysoe Wood. William Dell, his worst expectations confirmed, retired glumly to Samsell, in the parish of Westoning, near the spot where John Bunyan had been arrested.

He had now nothing left but his memories—memories of the great days of the Civil War, when the soldiers had climbed the trees to hear him preach before Cromwell's tent at Oxford, and he had been conscious of "a very sensible presence of God". Now he was growing old, and could never hope to know such glory again; Cromwell was dead, and a new régime, which had no use for such preachers as himself and his friend John Bunyan, dominated the land.

Reaction in Bedford itself centred round the official person of Dr. William Foster, Francis Wingate's brother-in-law, who was now Commissary of the Archdeacon's Court. In 1661 Dr. Foster, with four of John Bunyan's judges, Kelynge, Chester, Beecher, and Blundell, had been admitted to the Town Guild as a Burgess by Bedford Corporation. He cherished political ambitions; aligning himself with order and uniformity against the sects which he regarded as anarchical and chaotic, he believed that orthodoxy would triumph and subsequently reward him.

Of William Foster, as of Saul of Tarsus, might well have been recorded the desire "that if he found any of this way, whether they were men or women, he might bring them bound to Jerusalem". A year after the new Conventicle Act, an order issued by the Bedford Quarter Sessions reflected this determination.

> "It is ordered by this Court that the watches and wards in every particular parish Towne and hamlett within the said County be duely sett kept and observed And that the watches doe consist of halfe as many more as they usually have formerly bin of and the sd number not to be changed . . . And it is further ordered that all Conventicles and unlawful meetings and assemblies be carefully enquired into And that all dilligence be used by the watch and ward to prevent and discover them."

Unfortunately for the Nonconformists, Dr. Foster was not destined to experience a modern variant of the Pauline conversion on a Bedfordshire road. He had his reward when the most articulate of his unpretentious victims wrote him down as "a right Judas", for this label subsequently obliterated the professional attainments of a long life, and seems likely to be attached to him for all time.

Within Bedford Gaol, reaction had already produced its tragedy under the eyes of John Bunyan. He who had so often encountered death among those nearest to him now witnessed its removal of an opponent who was yet, in his contribution to their joint purpose, a colleague.

In May 1659 a Quaker named Alexander Parker had written to George Fox of a speaking tour undertaken in Bedfordshire with John Crook and his friend John Rush of Kempston Hardwick:

> "On the 2 day Jo. Crook, Joh. Rush and I was att a meeting where never any was before and had a good meeting, severall yt. never heard before were made to confesse to ye Truth; onely one woman of Bunian his society opposed but was manifested to most: Yesterday Jo. Crook and I had a meeting att another Towne where never any before had been where many people were and many of Bunyans people and one of them made great opposition but did soe manifest his folly that most people cryed ag^t^. him."

Two months after the said "Bunian" had been taken to Bedford Gaol, John Rush was brought there for refusing to pay tithes to "priest Wells of Wilkhampstead". Another Quaker came in about the same time, Thomas Green, the author of *A Few Plainwords to the Inhabitants of England,* which was partly written in "the Common Goale in Bedford the 11th of the 2nd month 1661" (11 April).

Mutual misfortune is a greater reconciler, particularly when the differences between men are superficial rather than profound. Inevitably, among the debtors and felons, John gravitated into the company of these two Friends; intent upon their own readings and writings, they shared with him the glimmer of light which came through the barred windows. Beneath them he was now at work on his fifth book, a volume of verse subsequently called *Profitable Meditations.*

For all his resolute endurance, the cold, darkness and damp affected the elderly middle-class Quaker more drastically than the vigorous young peasant. Slowly John Rush's life ebbed away until, lying unconscious upon a heap of straw in his corner of their cell, he died on 11 January, 1662.

John Bunyan had hardly recovered from witnessing this death, when a comrade from the Bedford Meeting brought him grave news of their old friend and benefactor, Colonel John Okey of Ridgmont. After spending two years as a refugee in Hanau, John Okey had been arrested during a visit to Delft in

Holland through the intervention of another Judas, Sir George Downing, the English Ambassador.

Downing owed his career to Okey, who had given him his first post as a chaplain in his own dragoon regiment. Even Samuel Pepys, that consistent man-about-the-court, tells us that "all the world takes notice of him for a most ungrateful villain for all his pains". The present Downing Street is dubiously indebted to this careerist for its name.

As one of the fugitive Regicides, John Okey had no hope of reprieve. To the dissenting congregations associated with him in the City of London, he left a short pamphlet written "at his dying hour". It included the religious sentiments expressed by him in the Tower and at Tyburn, and the text of his prayer at the scaffold, where he publicly forgave Downing and others who had been responsible for his arrest. His last speech to the crowds who came to see him die on 19 April, 1662, contained a challenge to the English people which was subsequently reported to John Bunyan in prison:

> "This nation . . . hath been a Nation that hath professed the Gospel, which indeed hath flourished here more than in any other Kingdom, and so it hath had more glory and honour than other nations; and I desire it may continue, that you may have Peace within your Palaces and Plenty within your dwellings."

John Rush and Thomas Green were not the only Nonconformists in prison with John Bunyan during these earlier years. Sometimes, especially after the new Conventicle Act, so many were brought into gaol that living conditions became harassing for the more permanent occupants. One of John's earliest biographers, a friend who published *The Life and Death of Mr. John Bunyan* in 1700, visited him in prison and described the consequences of a recent raid:

> "There was above three-score dissenters besides himself there, taken but a little before at a religious meeting at Kaistoe, in the county of Bedford; besides two eminent

dissenting ministers, to wit Mr. Wheeler and Mr. Dun . . . by which means the prison was much crouded."

This company of co-religionists made writing difficult, but gave John an opportunity to practise his gift of preaching. His friend continued:

> "In the midst of the hurry which so many new comers occasioned, I have heard Mr. Bunyan both preach and pray with that mighty Spirit of Faith and Plerophory of Divine Assistance, that has made me stand and wonder."

The debtors who had been accustomed to use the gaol day-room on the first floor regarded with surprise and interest the new purpose to which it was put. "Here they could sing without fear of being overheard, no informers prowling round and the world shut out."

John was already accustomed to write down his sermons for the purpose of expanding them into books, and it was one of these prison addresses which grew into *The Holy City*, published in 1665. "Upon a certain first day," he related,

> "I being together with my brethren in our prison chamber, they expected that according to our custom, something should be spoken out of the word for our mutual edification; but at that time I felt myself, it being my turn to speak, so empty, spiritless, and barren, that I thought I should not have been able to speak among them so much as five words of truth with life and evidence."

This sense of weariness came, as so often, before a moment of vision; suddenly there appeared to him "something of that jaspar in whose light you there find this holy city is said to come or descend". Renewed by that light he preached his sermon, and drew from the experience as much inspiration as his hearers. "We did all eat and were well-refreshed."

It was in 1664 that "Mr. Dun" of "Kaistoe" joined John in prison. He had called his friends into Keysoe Wood once too often; late at night he had been caught by the police and marched with his congregation into Bedford Gaol. There, like John, he was to remain for many years; the Calendar of Prisoners shows him still present in 1668 and 1669. A young man of undaunted spirit, he was another Dissenter who lacked the advantage of sturdy peasant stock. Although he was spared the "transportacion" to which he was sentenced, he did not long survive his years in prison. By 1677, his successor at the Keysoe Meeting had come and gone.

In 1665 another conventicle surprised at Blunham carried into gaol several prisoners whose names were familiar in the story of Bedfordshire Nonconformity. Amongst them was John Wright, the saddler in whose house the worshippers had met, and a grocer, George Farr. Modest but determined men from the dissenting groups came and went—Simon Haynes, Thomas Haynes, Edward Sandon, William Wigmore, and John's close associate in the Bedford Meeting, Samuel Fenn. In 1665 John Rush, son of John's dead companion, with Tabitha, his wife, entered the gaol. There might be little light and no warmth in prison, but there was friendship, congenial and sincere.

Among John's prison companions was one who had been gaoled for a felony committed in a tavern at Leighton Buzzard. John Bubb had joined a brawl in which a man named Edwards received an injury from his pipe and died a month later. Bubb was condemned to death and taken, in 1666, to Bedford Gaol. His petition against his sentence was supported by a doctor from Eversholt and by Dorothy Sparks, a well-established "gentlewoman surgeon" from Woburn. But nothing happened, and he remained in prison.

A year later he sent a petition to the King, complaining that "he hath suffered as much misery as soe dismall a place could be capable to inflict, and soe is likely to perish without His Majesty's further compassion and mercy towards him". Another petition, to Sir William Morton, one of the Judges at Bedford Assizes, prayed to be released from gaol, "where he hath long remained in a calamitous condicon". After a third petition, this time acknowledging that his sentence was just, Budd was finally reprieved.

John Bunyan did not share this attitude of self-pity, for he, at least, had no "calamitous condition" to contend with in himself. He was not a felon but the prisoner of conscience, and as such he was ready to endure his fate without repining. But if only he could know the length of his confinement, the limits of his punishment! Sometimes even the scaffold seemed so near that he was moved, in the closing sentences of his seventh book, *Christian Behaviour*, published in 1663, to send his comrades a message of farewell:

> "Thus have I, in few words, written to you before I die, a word to provoke you to faith and holiness, because I desire that you might have the life that is laid up for all them that believe in the Lord Jesus, and love one another, when I am deceased."

Apart from this unresolved anxiety, he suffered most, as a countryman, from losing the rural sights and sounds that he loved. Worse than the damp and darkness was the enforced inactivity after years of tramping from job to job, and from meeting to meeting, along the level country roads brilliant at dawn or softened by shadows as the sun went down. Sometimes in spring, when he was quite alone, he wept as he pictured the catkins hanging from the boughs of the willows beside the Ouse, and the buzzards wheeling in pairs above Dunstable Downs.

The members of the Bedford Meeting did their best to console him by frequent visits and small gifts of food to add variety to his prison diet. But they could not help him with his main problem of obtaining release, for most of them, after the passage of the new Conventicle Act, were themselves perpetually on the run. In the spring of 1664 they had even, for safety's sake, given up keeping their Minutes. For four and a half years the Church Book was locked away, leaving the acts of the small community unrecorded while its members went in and out of prison or faced ruin through accumulated fines.

Soon after John's arrest, as he had foreseen at Lower Samsell, some of the weaker brethren began to fall away under the stress of persecution. A Minute in the Church Book, dated 28 August, 1661, recorded a summons to John, who was then enjoying his early period of relative freedom, to visit two of the backsliders.

> "Our meetings (viz. of this sort) having bene for some time neglected through the increase of trouble, the 28th of

the 6th month 1661, the Church through mercy againe met: agreed, That whereas certaine of our friends have not onely withdrawne themselves, but also otherwaies failed, some of our ffriends be sent to admonish themselves of the same, viz: Our brother Samuel ffenne to Sister Pecock of Okely, and sister Phebe Gibbs; our brother Bunyan to brother Robert Nelson and Sister Manly."

A note added to the record of a meeting on 15 April, 1662, stated that "About this time the persecution raged very fiercely". A new pastor had not yet been chosen by the Meeting, and the members invited brothers Donne, Wheeler, Gibbs and Holcroft "to spend their paines with us once in three weekes by turnes". The search for a pastor continued; an entry early in December 1663, related that, as the Church's hope of obtaining John Wheeler had been disappointed owing to the reluctance of his Cranfield congregation to part with him, a joint pastorship had been arranged.

"The Church (notwithstanding their sore persecutions now come upon them) having spent many dayes in prayer with fasting, to seeke a right way of the Lord in this matter; did jointly make choice of brother Samuell ffenne (now lately delivered out of prison) and brother John Whiteman for their pastors and elders."

During the opening weeks of 1664, it became evident that some stalwart spirits were strengthened rather than weakened by persecution. The indecent scramble of the few who invariably dissociate themselves from a minority movement in time of peril was balanced—"God appearing in His glory to build up His Zion"—by fifteen new members. The entry recording this triumphant increase was the last before the Church's long period of silence, for in May came the new Conventicle Act with its challenge to courage and resourcefulness.

That challenge was accepted; for the next few years the members of the Bedford Church met, usually at night, in private houses, farmhouse kitchens, attics, barns, open fields and secluded woods, while "informers" climbed trees and beat through copses in the hope of reward. When the Five Mile Act brought a new crescendo of troubles, the Meeting at Stevington, now grown to fifty members, offered refuge to hunted Nonconformists, as its own Minutes recorded:

> "Stevington being five miles from Bedford, in a sequestered vale, allowed many tried Christians to retire to it under the Five Mile Act in order to worship God according to their consciences."

Now, as never before, were used The Holmes wood beside Dancing Meadow, and the reedy inlet of the Ouse whence the newly baptized ran shivering up the midnight fields to the shelter of Meeting Farm. On rainy evenings the women came with their men to hear the preaching of John Allen and Stephen Hawthorn; one entry in the Stevington Book testifies to their usefulness:

> "The females screened their minister's head from the damps of the night with their aprons."

You can find that hidden meeting-place today if you follow Bunyan's footsteps along the path from the Holy Well through the fields above the Ouse to The Holmes wood, though you must resolve in advance to be deterred neither by bulls, brambles, nor five-barred gates. At the entrance to the wood a moss-grown path, obviously old, leads through nettles and briars to a small natural clearing. A sentry posted at this point would have a clear view of intruders taking the path from the church, unscreened by trees for quarter of a mile.

On a dark afternoon in late autumn, the dense wood is oddly frightening; the mossy, bramble-impeded paths, in places almost impenetrable, seem to be hugging the secret of their past. But there is reassurance in the small grey chapel, with leaded windows and a red-tiled roof, which stands on the site of "Meeting Farm". If you see it first, as I did, in September sunshine, you can look from the garden of the Manse behind it at the green meadows and golden cornfields that John Bunyan knew, leading downhill to the silent wood on the banks of the Ouse.

. . . . .

Though the Bedford Church could do little for John, he had his own resources; it was his reading and writing which best helped him to endure without complaint the long tedious years.

Some notable works of literature, destined to survive their day, were published by others soon after he went to prison. The first part of Samuel Butler's *Hudibras*, which appeared in 1663, was followed by the second part a year later. Also in 1663 came *Wild Gallant*, the first drama of Dryden, born three years after John in Northamptonshire, but a London resident since 1657.

Hudibras might well have moved John to the reminiscent mirth characteristic of ex-soldiers who find their once awe-inspiring commanders irreverently derided. Nevertheless, he read neither Butler nor Dryden. His prison library included only two books, one being his Bible with its silver corners and clasps. The other, John Foxe's *Book of Martyrs*, had been published in 1641; it was the last of the black-letter three-volume folios, with double columns of print and a dramatic pictorial jacket showing scenes of torture and triumph.

To make sure that no other prisoner would appropriate this treasure, he printed his name, JOHN BUNYAN, in large capitals at the foot of each title-page, and on the third added the date, "1662".

Ever since its first publication in 1563 this unique collection of documents, presented in graphic detail with a forcible simplicity, had been read in Puritan households as authentic Church history. It certainly provided an armoury of arguments for Protestants against Catholics. The Puritan clergy so often based their sermons on the stories of the martyrs that in 1638 Archbishop Laud had refused to issue a license for a new edition.

This refusal, of course, only added to the book's value in the eyes of its devotees, and at his trial Laud was charged with having ordered it to be withdrawn from some parish churches. Though the gigantic compilation was neither scrupulous nor scholarly, it bore useful witness to the temper of the age, and its influence on John Bunyan's life and work was second only to that of the Bible.

His edition began with a long series of Introductions. Amidst a "Kalender of Martyrs", and Epistles to Jesus Christ and Queen Elizabeth, it contained "A Protestation to the Whole Church of

England". This appeal ended with a prayer which often brought comfort to John in his moments of discouragement:

> "The God of peace, who hath power both of Land and Sea, reach first his merciful hand to help them up that sink, to keep up them that stand, to still these windes and surging Seas of discord and contention among us, that we professing one Christ, may in one unity of doctrine gather our selves into one Ark of the true Church together, where we continuing stedfast in faith, may at the last luckily be conducted to the joyfull Port of our desired landing place, by his heavenly grace."

The Book of Martyrs did more than bring John comfort; it supplied him with a series of heroic examples, beginning with the ten Persecutions of the Primitive Church, which made his own sufferings seem indeed a light affliction, lasting but for a moment. After his imagination had been stimulated by the German woodcuts which accompanied the text, he could study the story of Thomas Haukes, who at the time of his death fulfilled a promise to his friends by raising his scorched arms to heaven after his speech was gone. Or he could read the passionate letter written from prison by the Italian martyr, Pomponius Algerius of Padua:

> "I have found a nest of honey and honey-comb in the entrails of a lion . . . Behold, He that was once far from me, now is present with me . . . He that feareth not to be burnt in the fire, how will he fear the heat of the weather? Or what careth he for the pinching frost, who burneth with the love of the Lord?"

But the story to which John turned most often was the graphic and gruesome account of the martyrdom of John Huss. He came to know it so well that it seemed almost to be part of his own history; the grim sentences which rang in his head gave a pattern to his determination to face death in advance:

> "In the meane season the hangmen stripped him of his garments, and turning his hands behinde his backe, tied him

> fast unto the stake with ropes that were made wet. . . . Then was his necke tied with a chaine unto the stake, the which chaine when he beheld, smiling he said, that he would willingly receive the same chaine for Jesus Christs sake, who, he knew, was bound with a farre worse chaine. Under his feet they set two fagots, admixing straw withall, and so likewise from the feet up to the chin he was inclosed in round about with wood. . . .
>
> Then was the fire kindled, and John Hus began to sing with a loud voice, Jesus Christ the sonne of the living God have mercy upon me. And when he began to say the same the third time, the wind drove the flame so upon his face, that it choked him. Yet notwithstanding he moved a while after, by the space that a man might almost say three times the Lords prayer. When all the wood was burned and consumed, the upper part of the body was left hanging in the chaine, the which they threw down stake and all, and making a new fire, burned it, the head being cut first in small gobbets, that it might the sooner be consumed into ashes. The heart, which was found among the bowels, being well beaten with staves and clubs, was at last pricked upon a sharpe sticke, and rosted at a fire apart untill it was consumed. Then with diligence gathering the ashes together, they cast them into the river of Rhene, that the least remnant of the ashes of that man should not be left upon the earth."

The purpose of this ghoulish industry was doubtless to make sure that Huss's body would be missing at the Resurrection.

Upon such mental diet—1033 huge pages of it, in addition to the extensive introductory material—was John Bunyan nourished in prison. Charles Kingsley, in one of his letters, suggested that the cruel death inflicted upon Faithful at Vanity Fair originated in the European atrocities of the Thirty Years' War. I doubt if John was ever so Europe-conscious, though one cannot discount the effects of unconscious influence. He looked, I think, no further for his models than this prison companion, whose eloquent martyrs also suggested the farewell utterances of the Pilgrims before crossing the River.

. . . . .

During the first half of his period in Bedford Gaol, the hours which John spent on reading were surpassed by the time occupied in writing. In those six years he wrote no fewer than nine of the books which represented religion to thousands of the persecuted poor.

His first prison book, *Profitable Meditations*, contained 186 stanzas of small literary merit. They are memorable only because, in an imaginary discussion between Satan and a tempted soul, occurs the probable origin of the dialogue between Apollyon and Christian in *The Pilgrim's Progress*.

More interesting was the book's publisher, Francis Smith of the Elephant and Castle, who produced its seven successors but was obliged, owing to his own political troubles, to allow John's first important book, *Grace Abounding*, to go to a twenty-two year old publisher, George Larkin. Francis Smith, who must have been a godsend to writers on controversial topics, obtained licenses for their books when he could. If the licenses were refused, he obligingly laid the blame on the authorities who unreasonably propelled him into irregular publication.

It was hardly astonishing that at the time of Venner's insurrection his house was ransacked though he was ill in bed. His books were constantly seized under warrant, and he himself often landed in prison. John Bunyan was by no means the only author of books unacceptable to Roger L'Estrange, the Press Censor, though he was to graduate to a position immune from official repression before he died.

His next book, *Praying in the Spirit*, contained the substance of a prison sermon, in which he had pleaded for spontaneity in prayer. In places it foreshadowed those characters in *The Pilgrim's Progress*—Mr. Legality, Mr. Formalist, Mr. Hypocrisy—of whom John felt that "the letter killeth". To him, formal and creative praying were mutually exclusive; tolerant as he was, he had no intuition that a day would come when a combination of written and extempore prayer would be used by such progressive clergymen as the late Canon H. R. L. Sheppard and his successors at St. Martin-in-the-Fields.

Christian Behaviour, a treatise on a true life arising from a sure faith, was published in the same year, 1662. Written in evident fear of pending execution, it contained the farewell passage to his friends in the Bedford Church. It also anticipated the scene in Part II of *The Pilgrim's Progress* in which the Interpreter shows Christiana the flowers in his garden; "where the Gardiner has set them, there they stand, and quarrel not with one another".

Seeing through his narrow prison window only the walls of the house opposite and the dusty street, John thought of the hedge of wild roses blooming round the cottage at Harrowden where his father still lived. Half grieved and half-gladdened by the memory, he picked up his pen, and wrote:

> "Christians are like the several flowers in a garden, that have upon each of them the dew of heaven, which, being shaken with the wind, they let fall their dew at each other's roots, whereby they are jointly nourished, and become nourishers of each other."

Sometimes, as year followed year and his periodic petitions failed, the months seemed to John to speed away, taking the prime of his life with them. At other times the hours appeared to stand still, and his imprisonment became a perpetual Purgatory, world without end. In such periods of gloom he turned to map-making and versifying, for pious doggerel, largely inspired by the metrical efforts of John Foxe in his account of the martyrs under Mary, flowed out of his mind like water from a spring.

Between the appearance of *Christian Behaviour* in 1663 and the publication of *Grace Abounding* in 1666, John published as a broadside a "copper-cut" map showing "the order and causes of Salvation and Damnation", and three books of verse, *Serious Meditations on the Four Last Things* in 1200 lines, *Ebal and Gerizim* in 800, and *Prison Meditations* in 76 stanzas.

Occasionally the spate of verse reached, by accident, the level of poetry. The hymn of Mr. Valiant-for-Truth, "Who would true Valour see" (usually misquoted today as "He who would valiant be"), and the song of the Shepherd Boy, "He that is down, needs fear no fall", were maturer verses in *The Pilgrim's Progress* which borrowed their style from the Elizabethans. *Prison Meditations*, at a lower level, contained an assertion of John's faith in reply to encouragement given by a friend:

For though men keep my outward man
Within their bolts and bars,
Yet, by the faith of Christ, I can
Mount higher than the stars.

Two volumes of prose, *The Holy City* or *The New Jerusalem*, and *The Resurrection of the Dead, and Eternal Judgment*, occupied the year 1664. The first of these sprang from the sudden vision, like that of the other John on Patmos who saw a new heaven and a new earth, which came to him in prison when he had felt too weary to speak. In his *Preface* he gave a truthful description, recognizable as authentic by any writer, of the process by which the sermon had turned into the book:

> "The more I cast mine eye upon it the more I saw lie in it. Wherefore setting myself to a more narrow search, through frequent prayer to God, what first with doing and then with undoing, and after that with doing again, I thus did finish it."

It was his first resplendent dream of the Celestial City, and a proclamation of faith which also included the prophecy of a universal church, in spirit far ahead of his time:

> "In the end it shall not be as it is now, a Popish doctrine, a Quaker's doctrine, a Prelatical doctrine, and the Presbyter, Independent, and Anabaptist, thus distinguished, and thus confounded and destroying. Then the city is of pure gold, as showing how invincible and unconquerable is the spirit of the people of God."

The spiritual development which made John capable of this vision fitted him to spend the year 1665 in writing *Grace Abounding to the Chief of Sinners*, one of the great religious books of the world. It belongs to the same class of spiritual self-revelation as Augustine's *Confessions*, Thomas à Kempis's *Imitation of Christ*, and the *Pensées* of Pascal; but because its author was a poor man, a peasant and a prisoner, it speaks more directly than the others to the humble bewildered sufferers who seek in their millions the road to divine redemption from the catastrophes of this world.

In his own autobiography, *The Summing-Up*, Somerset Maugham describes the process by which such agonies of the soul as John Bunyan experienced reach the state of conscious mental discipline which comes with their transcription on to paper.

> "The disadvantages and dangers of the author's calling are offset by an advantage so great as to make all its difficulties, disappointments, and maybe hardships, unimportant. It gives him spiritual freedom. To him life is a tragedy and by his gift of creation he enjoys the catharsis, the purging of pity and terror, which Aristotle tells us is the object of art. For his sins and his follies, the unhappiness that befalls him, his unrequited love, his physical defects, illness, privation, his hopes abandoned, his griefs, humiliations, everything is transformed by his power into material and by writing he can overcome it. Everything is grist to his mill, from the glimpse of a face in the street to a war that convulses the civilized world, from the scent of a rose to the death of a friend. Nothing befalls him that he cannot transmute into a stanza, a song or a story, and having done this be rid of it. The artist is the only free man."

In this sense, *Grace Abounding* represented John Bunyan's final freeing of himself from spiritual torment, by putting it all down. He was not always grammatical and he never thought of himself as an artist, but he had the natural writer's privilege of being perpetually articulate. When he finished the story of his conversion and was writing the Preface, he realized that he could now remember his fears and doubts and sad months with comfort; "they are as the head of Goliah in my hand".

Of course he could. He had decanted all that misery into words. To this full release the enforced monotony of prison had contributed, giving him time to think and freedom from that sense of responsibility which would otherwise have sent him, a perpetually itinerant evangelist, travelling through the countryside in search of souls to save.

It has been said that *The Pilgrim's Progress* could not have been written unless *Grace Abounding*, its "raw material", had preceded it; and this is true. That open confession left John free to absorb his spiritual experiences and by an inner process of transformation to recreate them, as a flower grows from the seed sown in the earth. Of no one has it been said more truly than of him, that "that which thou sowest is not quickened, except it die". He had to die to sin before he could be raised to the power of achievement. *Grace Abounding* was both the completion of that process of death, and the birth of a new individual.

But if John could not have written *The Pilgrim's Progress* without first writing *Grace Abounding*, it is equally true that he could not have written *Grace Abounding* if he had not grown in prison from the hot immaturity of the young preacher to the full stature of adulthood. The fever of his convictions was assuaged as his mind deepened and enlarged, surrendering itself to the profounder truths of religious experience. An inward peace and even happiness triumphed increasingly over external hardship as he read his Bible and Book of Martyrs, content to find himself one of so great a cloud of witnesses.

> "I never had in all my life" [he wrote] "so great an in-let into the Word of God as now: them Scriptures that I saw nothing in before, are made in this place and state to shine upon me; Jesus Christ also was never more real and apparent than now; here I have seen him and felt him indeed. . . . I would not have been without this Tryal, for much; I am comforted every time I think of it, and I hope I shall bless God for ever for the teaching I have had by it."

This paragraph showed that John had now achieved that measure of acceptance which is the first stage in the creative endurance of injury and wrong. Few, perhaps, attain it, but they come from all ages and many nations.

In an article in *The Observer* for 28 November, 1948, entitled "Faced with Blindness", its author, Robert Silvey, writes of his reconciliation with misfortune:

> "Acceptance is not passive submission. It is a positive act of embracing reality. One cannot dogmatize about how this attitude can be achieved; one can only describe one's own experience. I knew that for me there was only one way, and that was to come to terms with my situation once and for all."

This process of coming to terms with his situation—and with himself and his God—forms the spiritual history of John Bunyan's years in gaol. Across three centuries the imprisoned author of *The Pilgrim's Progress* speaks, in his *Grace Abounding*, to the condition of the man faced with blindness. John had first seen his way to that means of consolation when he read, in the cheerless spring which followed his abortive struggles for release, the opening chapter of the Second Book of Corinthians, and found a passage which brought some light into the gloom:

"But we had the sentence of death in ourselves, that we should not trust in ourselves, but in God which raiseth the dead."

In gratitude he recorded the change of attitude which those words gradually created in his soul.

> "By this Scripture I was made to see that if ever I would suffer rightly, I must first pass a sentence of death upon every thing that can properly be called a thing of this life, even to reckon my self, my Wife, my Children, my Health, my Enjoyments and all, as dead to me, and my self as dead to them."

The first step, he resolved, was to learn to live without hope, and face the worst that might come. If he made up his mind only to prison, then the whip or the pillory might be inflicted on him unawares. If he prepared himself for no more than these, then he would be unfit for banishment; if he regarded banishment as the worst possible fate, death itself might take him by surprise.

"I see the best way to go thorow sufferings," he continued for the guidance of "the weak and tempted people of God" faced with the same awful uncertainty,

> "is to trust in God through Christ, as touching the World to come; and as touching this World, to count the Grave my House, to make my Bed in Darkness, to say to Corruption, Thou art my Father, and to the Worm, Thou art my Mother and Sister; that is, to familiarize these things to me."

To accept; to "familiarize these things" so that nothing further could hold any terror because it was all part of the experience which brought a man to full maturity—that was the way in which John Bunyan, through the Lord of his life, became in truth the captain of his soul.

By the "popular reader" as distinct from the conscious student, *The Pilgrim's Progress* has been far better known than *Grace Abounding*, largely owing to an over-prolonged belief that fiction alone provides the type of absorbing literature in which a man or woman can find interest and relaxation.

This period of dominance by fiction is, I believe, already past; the growing popularity of truthful records suggests that, after a few more years of education by the circulating libraries, autobiography and biography will share its appeal.

At least we are already witnessing the end of the superficial assumption that autobiography is the product of superlative egotism, rather than the most direct and, after poetry, the most effective way of conveying spiritual and emotional experiences to the reader.

> "I could have enlarged much in this my Discourse of my Temptations and Troubles for Sin" [wrote John Bunyan in the Preface to *Grace Abounding*]; "I could also have stepped into a Stile much higher than this . . . but I dare not: God did not play in tempting of me; neither did I play, when I sunk as into a bottomless Pit, when the Pangs of Hell caught hold upon me; wherefore I may not play in relating of them, but be plain and simple, and lay down the thing as it was."

The popularity of *The Pilgrim's Progress* seems now unlikely, in spite of the "debunkers", ever to be shaken, but the time may well be near when *Grace Abounding* will stand beside it, a twin pillar of creative religion and unconscious literature. It must be taken in small doses if its cumulative effect is to be obtained, but how absorbing those doses are in their joint appeal to courage and pity!

The autobiography is the raw material of the allegory, but it is more than that; it penetrates deeply into the suffering and exultation of the soul in its search for God, conveying first the bewildered blindness of that seeking, and then the gradual attainment of direction with the slow and painful infiltration of light. At last anguish changes to joy, fear to hope, conflict to harmony.

By most literary authorities, *Grace Abounding* has been treated as cruder and more elementary than the Pilgrim story. It is, perhaps, more elementary in the sense that the different elements of the narrative are more easily recognized and disentangled. But it is also more elemental; its emotions wear a catastrophic colour. It is wilder and darker (even, in places, than the fight with Apollyon in the Valley of the Shadow), so that the high lights when they come seem more brilliant, and the catharsis of reconciliation with God heals deeper wounds.

It is easy to understand the enthusiasm for *The Pilgrim's Progress* in Victorian England, which was both comfortable and evangelical. Life, at any rate for the book-reading classes, was a safe and usually prosperous affair; they preferred their emotional experiences and spiritual struggles to be presented indirectly.

Today, in a starker, intenser age, we have had to confront them directly, and can thereby better appreciate the direct experience of John Bunyan. Though he came to it by a different path he trod before us the long road from the Slough of Despond to the gates of the City, shining beyond the shadow of our self-inflicted night.

CHAPTER XIII

MY BED IN DARKNESS

"I have not hitherto been so sordid as to stand to a doctrine right or wrong, much less when so weighty an argument as above eleven years imprisonment is continually dogging of me to weigh and pause, and pause again, the grounds and foundation of those principles, for which I thus have suffered; but having . . . examined them and found them good, I cannot, I DARE NOT, now revolt or deny the same on pain of eternal damnation. . . . If nothing will do unless I make of my conscience a continual butchery and slaughter-shop . . . I have determined, the Almighty God being my help and shield, yet to suffer, if frail life might continue so long, even till the moss shall grow on mine eyebrows, rather than thus to violate my faith and principles."

JOHN BUNYAN: *A Confession of my Faith: And a Reason for my Practice* (1672).

JOHN BUNYAN was not always in the state of spiritual exaltation which produced *Grace Abounding*; no one could spend twelve years keyed up to such a pitch of reminiscent emotion. There were many Sunday evenings of quiet relaxation when he was able to indulge his love of bell-ringing without qualms of conscience, by listening to the chimes of St. Paul's Church summoning the evening worshippers to the Square beside the Bridge.

When the chimes had ceased and he sat dreaming in the twilight, he would remember with longing the music of the harps, flutes, and pipes which he had heard during his thirty-five years; the drums and trumpets at Newport Pagnell; the lutes and virginals to which, pausing in his kettle-mending, he had listened as they echoed from the elegant reception-rooms at Ampthill House.

One day they were to live for him all over again in the bells that rang for joy in the Celestial City, in the soft music which accompanied the dying moments of the old Puritan in *The Life and Death of Mr. Badman*, and in the drums beating throughout the sieges and battles of *The Holy War*. But now, with a sudden desire for the lost consolation which God, he thought, would not begrudge him in this dismal place, he decided to make for himself a musical instrument which would also enable him to practise his too long neglected craftsmanship as a mechanic.

Long ago, when he was still at Elstow, he had fashioned a fiddle of thin iron plates on his brazier's anvil, making it of the same pattern as a full-sized Italian violin, and inscribing on it his name, "JOHN BUNYAN, HELSTOW", by zig-zagging with a graving tool. Now he spent many secret hours in shaping a flute from the rail of his prison stool. He hollowed the wood very carefully, and used his candle-flame to burn the small note-holes into the barrel.

To his joy, the flute when finished made faint musical notes, like the reed-piping of a river god. In the evenings, after the jailor had made his rounds, he played on it, hurriedly replacing it in the socket of the stool when the man, surprised by the sound, returned to look for its source. Finding nothing, the jailor appeared uneasy; he regarded John with resentful awe, as though he suspected him of possessing the power to summon angels to his cell.

"When I get out of here, if I ever do, I'll give the flute to the boys," thought John, never dreaming that nearly three centuries later both fiddle and flute would be rediscovered and, like his anvil, reverently preserved by his admirers as "relics" of his life.

As the months of his imprisonment lengthened into years, he came to count more and more upon the visits of Elizabeth and the children. Whenever she was busy with cooking or lace-making, they were now all old enough to come and see him by themselves.

Mary, already in her 'teens, would soon be a woman, and young Elizabeth showed signs of becoming tall like himself. John and Thomas were growing into sturdy little boys; they had been only four and two years old when he was arrested, but already they were getting too big to play with their alphabetical bricks which he had made for them after the design invented by Sir Hugh Pratt in the reign of Elizabeth. They still used the new materials for toys—modelling clay, and bright strips of paper to make baskets—which he had brought back from London on his last visit, now so long ago.

The Moravian teacher called Komensky, or Comenius, had set the fashion for these constructive toys. When he was still able to snatch afternoons out of prison, John had sat at the heavy oak table in the cottage and helped to make baskets too. He never tired of his children, though their inevitable poverty and shabbiness weighed heavily on his mind.

"I love to play the child with them, and to learn something by so doing," he wrote in a manuscript, *The Saints Priviledge*, which he left unpublished at his death. He added in his *Book for Boys and Girls*:

> Nor do I blush, although I think some may
> Call me baby, 'cause I with them play.

As an Introduction to these "Divine Emblems", he composed a short lesson in reading. He wrote out half a dozen different alphabets, giving lists of vowels and consonants, and taught children to spell their own Christian names by dividing them into syllables.

In his scholarly but solemn Introduction to this charming collection of moral lessons in spontaneous verse by a man who obviously loved the very young, Dr. John Brown wrote, "It is somewhat difficult for us to imagine Bunyan doing this." But surely the little reading lesson is exactly the kind of exercise that a conscientious father of six would produce repeatedly for his own children, and then suddenly think of publishing.

John brought up his family with the strictness of the Puritan who regarded religious discipline as the first essential of a well-ordered life, but, whatever case may be made by detractors who belittle the compulsions of conscience and declare that he "deserted" his wife and family, his own writings prove that he was a devoted husband and a kindly, perceptive father.

In *The Heavenly Footman*, a description of the man who runs to Heaven, which he left in manuscript at the time of his death, John found that his enduring love of loyal, hard-working Elizabeth prevented him from offering unmitigated admiration to Lot, whose single-minded escape from Sodom he was trying to hold up as an example to the reader.

> "When Lot and his wife was running from cursed Sodom to the mountains, to save their lives, it is said, that his wife looking back from behind him, and she became a pillar of salt;

and yet you see that neither her practice, nor the judgment of God that fell upon her for the same, would cause Lot to look behind him."

Meditatively he added a sentence quite out of keeping with the ruthless Puritan judgments of his day, "I have sometimes wondered at Lot in this particular."

Long before the self-centred inhumanity of Lot produced this protest, John had written, in his early book *Christian Behaviour*, a paragraph urging parents not to reprove their children much or often, but to be "Pertinent to them with all gravity"—that is, to explain reproofs or prohibitions so clearly that the children perceive the reasons which inspire them. This advice, so closely in line with modern child-psychology, was to be re-emphasized and enlarged in *The Life and Death of Mr. Badman*, published in 1680.

Here Mr. Wiseman, who is John's converted self sitting in judgment on his unconverted behaviour, explains to Mr. Attentive that "the children of Godly Parents are the children of many Prayers: they are prayed for before and Prayed for after they are born, and the Prayer of a godly Father and godly Mother doth much".

In an earlier passage, Mr. Wiseman has already declared to his companion that love and leniency in parents are always best, even if the child resembles Mr. Badman and does not respond.

> "I tell you, that if Parents carry it lovingly towards their Children, mixing their Mercies with loving Rebukes, and their loving Rebukes with Fatherly and Motherly Compassions, they are more likely to save their Children, than by being churlish and severe toward them: but if they do not save them, if their mercy doth them no good, yet it will greatly ease them at the day of death, to consider; I have done by love as much as I could, to save and deliver my child from Hell."

Unfortunately the fatherly reactions of Bedford Corporation towards its erring municipal children were less civilized than John's canons of parental conduct, and he was often disturbed in his reading and writing by the public chastisements which occurred just outside the walls of the gaol.

John Smith, for instance, was punished for drunkenness and assault on the bitter morning of 7 January, 1666, being flogged at the cart tail from the Moot Hall to the Market Cross by the Bedall of Beggars. His howls as the lash descended on his bare shoulders had hardly died away when William Perks was put in the pillory just below the window of the Guildhall Chamber, and pelted with rotten eggs, tannery refuse, horse dung, dead cats and cabbage stalks, for hawking "sanded" sugar.

If only, thought John when these noisy consequences of local wrong-doing assaulted his ears, he could go home even for a short time, and exercise his influence on his growing family! He could then make sure that the children in whom he felt so much pride would never stray, like John Smith and William Perks, from the strait and narrow path of righteousness.

The day now approached when John's prayer would be briefly fulfilled, for the nation was passing through a period of calamity, and harassed jailors had no time to spend in watching trustworthy prisoners.

It all began, people said, with the comet that appeared in December 1664; that comet seen by Samuel Pepys on Christmas Eve, "which now . . . appears not with a tail, but only is larger and duller than any other star, and is come to rise betimes and to make a great arch". Comets, it was well known, always heralded disasters, though some declared that the French and the Papists were responsible for the troubles which now caused the fickle public to look back nostalgically to the "good government" of Oliver Cromwell.

Wherever the responsibility actually lay, the Great Plague of London certainly began just when the comet appeared. The following year England, after capturing New Amsterdam from the Dutch and later rechristening the city New York, found herself again at war with Holland. Before the War was over, the Dutch had sailed right into the Medway and burned British ships. God must indeed have been angry before he permitted such an insult to "His Englishmen"; it could never have happened under the Great Protector!

The Plague was the last of many periodic visitations which

had terrified England ever since the Black Death. It was not, perhaps, much worse than the outbreak which carried off 30,000 people at the time of James the First's accession, but it seemed worse because in sixty years the standards of health and hygiene had risen despite "kennels" and "ditches".

Thanks to the new impetus of science, centred in the Royal Society, and to the patronage of scientists by Charles II, the idea of law as the force moulding the universe was gradually penetrating downwards from the intellectual hierarchy. Even some of the theologians were prepared to acknowledge that a God who manifested Himself through inexorable law was a more powerful Deity than one who set His own laws aside to work miracles.

This new vision already illuminated the minds of thoughtful men and women, though the source of the light which banished the dark corners from their understanding was still only half realized. Causes, they saw, had their effects, and effects their causes; squalor and neglect, not witches, produced disease. Slowly the persecution of witches, a dark blot on the growing enlightenment of England, diminished and died away.

Upon a people thus becoming genuinely civilized, the plague, ushered in by the comet, fell like the scourge of an outraged Jehovah. Before the year 1665 was half over, the cry "Bring out your dead!" sounded through London, and the laden death-cart trundled noisily along the deserted streets. Samuel Pepys, after walking towards Moorfields with a morbid desire to see the corpses being carried away, recorded the blight which had descended on men's minds as well as their bodies.

> "But, Lord! how everybody's looks, and discourse in the street, is of death and nothing else; and few people going up and down, that the town is like a place distressed and forsaken."

In the second week of September he found "the Angel Tavern at the lower end of Tower Hill, shut up; and more than that, the alehouse at the Tower Stairs; and more than that, that the person was then dying of the plague when I was last there, a little while ago, at night". On the 20th of the same month, the number of deaths for the City of London reached "the biggest Bill yet";

the Lord Mayor's weekly returns showed that, of 8297 deceased persons, 7165 had died of the plague.

The hideous rumours which filtered down from the capital smote Bedford's population with dread. Like the inhabitants of other small towns under the first two Stuarts, they had lived in constant fear of the plague. Haunted by the surviving tradition of the Black Death, which in 1348-9 had carried off one-third of their burgessdom and commonalty, the people spoke in whispers of houses then left vacant and unlocked as they were said to be in London today, with the remnants of the last meal left rotting on the table because all the occupants were dead.

Some of Bedfordshire's isolated churches, such as Chellington, grimly reminded the country-dwellers of that earlier time when entire populations of villages perished, and a new village grew up far from the church and the mouldering plague-stricken cottages beside it. Town and country-dwellers alike now kept an unhappy eye upon the activities of the grave-diggers in the fields and churchyards where the dead were carried.

To the north of Bedford lay an area ominously known as Pest House Close, alternatively called "Bury Field". Already this abomination of desolation was ridged and corrugated with death-pits from previous outbreaks of pestilence, but the local victims of the Great Plague were not carried there till 1666. Owing, perhaps, to the cold early autumn of 1665, the disease did not spread to Bedfordshire and Buckinghamshire until some time after it reached its height in London. It exacted its toll from the country towns during a long spell of warm weather the following summer, and out of Bedford's small population took forty lives from the area north of the river which surrounded the gaol.

But Bedford's visitation was far exceeded by the blow which fell upon Newport Pagnell, where the last three days of July 1666 accounted for another death-roll of forty persons. In the former garrison town, 697 bodies were buried that year in comparison with 37 the year before. Among the victims of the plague was John's old friend the bookseller, Matthias Cowley.

During the same year, though not through the plague, John lost another associate of his unregenerate past. The Rev. Christopher Hall, whose sermon against Sunday sports had begun the process of his conversion, died in 1666 and was buried at Elstow.

The tragedies of the Great Plague were still being mourned by the survivors when, between 2 and 7 September, 1666, stories of the Great Fire of London followed it to Bedford. The Fire carried away old St. Paul's, of which the Gothic spire, once the tallest in Europe, had been burnt in another fire a century earlier; and eighty-eight other churches. It destroyed most of the City between the Temple and the Tower, but left almost untouched the squalid "Liberties" where the Plague had found the greater proportion of its victims.

Samuel Pepys, who managed to get up to the top of Barking steeple after the fire there had been quenched, witnessed, on 5 September,

> "the saddest sight of desolation that I ever saw; everywhere great fires, oil-cellars, and brimstone, and other things burning. I became afraid to stay there long, and therefore down again as fast as I could, the fire being spread as far as I could see; and to Sir W. Pen's, and there ate a piece of cold meat, having eaten nothing since Sunday, but the remains of Sunday's dinner."

John Bunyan, absorbed in the remembered tumults which had taken shape in *Grace Abounding*, characteristically mentioned neither the Plague nor the Fire in his writings, but they both affected him none the less. *Grace Abounding*, published in 1666 by George Larkin in London, became one of the scarcest of his books; the British Museum Library acquired its sole copy of the first edition only in 1883.

The reason for the almost total disappearance of the first printing is explained by a book entitled *Scriptures Self-Evidence*, published in 1667, and quoted in *The Bookman* during 1888. In this work the author tells the reader that

> "the late dreadfull Fire . . . proved extremely prejudicial and destructive to most Companies of the City, yet none of them received so grand losses and dammages by the devouring Conflagration as the Company of Stationers, most of whose Habitations, Store-houses, Shops, together with all their Stocks, Books, bound and unbound (by reason of their

combustableness, and difficulty to remove them) were not only consumed in a moment, but their ashes and scorched leaves . . . were scattered in sundry places above 16 miles from the City."

He might indeed have been writing prophetically of the second Great Fire of London which followed the incendiary raid of 29 December, 1940—the year in which the late Dr. Frank Mott Harrison compiled the typewritten "Record of Recent Research" where this quotation appears. The writers who lost entire editions of their works on that lurid night when millions of books perished, can at least take comfort from the thought that they share the fate of John Bunyan and his *Grace Abounding*.

If the Plague and the Fire cost John one old friendship and many new books, they nevertheless operated indirectly for his benefit. The number of deaths and invalids due to the Plague, combined with the rumours of plotting Papists and marauding Dutch inspired by the Fire, caused, if not a panic, at least a measure of pandemonium in Bedford for several months of 1666. The prison staff was depleted; supervision slackened; and John was allowed out of gaol for a short period of irregular freedom such as he had been permitted in 1661.

Returning to his little house in St. Cuthbert's parish, sleeping in a feather-bed instead of lying on grubby straw scattered over the floor of his cell, sitting in a comfortable wooden chair before the log fire on cold autumn evenings, John felt at first like a ghost coming back after long years to the scenes of its earthly existence. He was still only thirty-seven, but he seemed to himself to have grown, in experience, into the father or grandfather of the young man who had defied his judges in 1661.

Now, at last, he and Elizabeth could create together the child for which they had longed ever since the loss of her first-born had followed his arrest. In her arms he could forget, for a little while, the long prison nights of loneliness and frustration.

Eighteen months after John's return to prison, when their baby Sarah was a year old, the lively diarist of the Plague and the Fire rode into Bedford. Samuel Pepys was then a handsome young man with dark eyebrows above eyes which slightly protruded, a long nose, full lips, and an abundance of brown hair, well brushed and tended, falling to his shoulders.

That bright day of 8 June, when the sun seemed to shine even into the gaol, contrasted pleasantly with the two spring seasons which John had endured since his weeks of freedom. In comparison with the warmth of his home, he had found especially hard to bear the intense cold of March and April 1667, when great frosts had turned their drinking water to ice, and bitter winds, rising to ferocity at the Equinox, had swept across the Fens to buffet the walls of the old County Prison.

By the time that Pepys cantered gaily up the High Street, those acute discomforts had departed even from the prisoners. The elegant Samuel had no thoughts to spare for these forgotten men. He would have been horrified to learn that posterity, which was so ruthlessly to decipher his private diary, would link his name with one of them by that strange process which winnows the wheat of a century from its chaff, and causes incongruous companions to meet in Valhalla.

The previous year, the thirty-four-year-old diarist had recorded the inquiries of a Parliamentary committee into the unorthodox behaviour of Lord Chief Justice Kelynge, who had fined and imprisoned a jury for acquitting a number of accused persons brought before him under the Conventicle Act of 1664.

> "I hear that they do prosecute the business against my Lord Chief Justice Keeling with great severity . . . and a great crowd of people to stare upon him. . . . They have voted my Lord Chief Justice Keeling's proceedings illegal; but that, out of particular respect to him, and the mediation of a great many they have resolved to proceed no further against him."

On 8 June, 1668, Pepys was in a mood for simple enjoyments. His father's house, "Pepys' Farm", where he had spent the previous night, lay between Buckden and Brampton. From here the next stage of his journey demanded no exertion.

"Pleasant country to Bedford, where, while they stay, I rode through the town; and a good country-town; and there, drinking, 1s."

He travelled on to Buckingham, and spent the night at Newport Pagnell.

> "A good pleasant country-town, but few people in it. A very fair, and like a Cathedral, Church . . . the town, and so most of this country, well watered. Lay here well, and rose next day by four o'clock; few people in the town; and so away."

Evidently the scene of John's military service had not yet recovered from the aftermath of the Plague. New men and women, unlike conscripted soldiers, are not made in a day.

That same year, Archbishop Sheldon called for a general return of the number of conventicles being held throughout England, and of the persons attending them. This inquiry followed the fall of Clarendon amid the political excitement caused by the Plague and the Fire, and the lapse of the Conventicle Act which the House of Lords had failed to renew after its expiry on 2 March, 1668. Sheldon, like Clarendon, was determined not to tolerate conventicles, and sought evidence which would enable him, when the return had been made, to persuade Parliament to reintroduce the Act.

The new Cabal Ministry, of Clifford, Ashley, Buckingham, Arlington, and Lauderdale, had begun to discuss proposals for "Comprehension". There was not one sound Anglican amongst them, and the King, who was to disclose to Clifford and Arlington in January 1669 his private adherence to Roman Catholicism, encouraged their debates. The Archbishop did not intend them to succeed, and in Bedfordshire he had an equally determined supporter in Dr. William Foster.

The Visitation Record of the Archdeacon of Bedford during the years 1668–9 uncovered the strength of Nonconformity in Bedfordshire villages. While the number of "Anabaptists" in Bedford itself was entered as "about 30", the small village of Stevington owned no fewer than 50. At Keysoe, a place of equivalent size, the "Independents with y[e] Quakers" totalled 100. The Stevington Nonconformists were labelled "Ordinary", but the Bedford and Keysoe Independents found themselves described as being of the "Meanest Sort" and "Meanest Quality".

The number of Bedfordshire Nonconformists amounted altogether to about 1000, a remarkable number for a sparsely populated county after eight years of persecution. The Quakers, who never quailed before it, were returned as numbering 390, the Baptists as 277, and the Independents as 220.

Dr. William Foster did not intend these low-grade citizens, with their sordid collection of gaol-birds, to create anarchy in his well-ordered community. At the Visitations of the Archdeacon between 6 May, 1668, and 8 October, 1669, he held eight Courts, four at Bedford and four at Ampthill. Though some of the cases related to church necessities—"Stevington Chancell" we read, "is almost downe"—the majority, as his own records showed, were those of Dissenters who came before him to be fined, excommunicated, or imprisoned for staying away from church, attending conventicles, teaching school without licence, and a variety of other offences springing from Nonconformist convictions.

One case was that of John White, the under-jailor at Bedford, whose refusal to pay the church rate suggests that he had responded to the influence of John Bunyan and his fellow-prisoners. Another offender, Josias Ruffhead the cord-winder, was presented "for refusing to come to Church at the time of dyvyne service for about one month last". Josias's refusals were to persist until, in 1672, he was in a position to sell to the members of the Bedford Church an orchard containing a barn on the site of which the present Bunyan Meeting in Mill Street stands.

During the two years in which the lapse of the Conventicle Act meant relative freedom for the Independent community, more than fourteen hundred cases, chiefly from small villages, came before William Foster. The Quakers were the most persistent offenders, but numerous Baptists, Independents, and occasional Presbyterians were sentenced by that inexorable upholder of the law.

Again and again they included the respected names of the Bedford Church members, and in their ranks were a few "gentlemen", yeomen and farmers. But the great majority came from the throng of poor and humble citizens—weavers, warreners, husbandmen, gardeners, labourers—who throughout history have suffered most severely from persecution, social injustice, and war, and have fought most stoutly for freedom, equality, and peace.

William Foster's real opportunity arrived when the Cavalier Parliament, which had received numerous complaints regarding the increase of conventicles and wooden "tabernacles" during the period of quiescence, passed a new "Permanent" Conventicle Act which reached the Statute Book on 10 May, 1670.

Under this Act the definition of conventicles became more comprehensive; an "Illegal Conventicle" was described as any meeting for worship other than Anglican which, if held in a house, "should have present thereat" more than four persons outside the family, or, if held in a field or wood, more than four persons altogether. On the other hand the penalties were milder, rising from a 5*s*. fine for a first offender at a meeting, to £40 for a preacher after the first offence, and £20 for a householder who allowed a conventicle to be held on his premises.

Such penalties were more likely to be enforced than the extreme punishments of exile and execution, especially as baits were offered to "informers" in the shape of one-third of the fine. Another third went to parishes, and the remainder to the King.

Justices of the Peace and constables were empowered to break doors open and Lieutenants of counties to disperse assemblies, if necessary with troops. The reluctance of the ordinary Englishman to enforce even such relatively moderate legislation was recognized in Clause 11, which imposed heavy fines on justices and constables who failed to act. This measure, though it fell into disuse after the Toleration Act, actually remained on the Statute Book until 1813, and thus achieved "permanence" of a kind.

On the "8th Day of the 3rd Month" (8 May, 1670) the Bedford Church, which had started keeping Minutes again on 9 September, 1668, recorded a meeting at which "brother Samuell ffenne and brother Bunyan" (whose jailors had again been complacent during the period of relaxation) were appointed "farther to discourse with Sister Landy and to relate to them in what frame they find her". But Sister Landy's frame of mind was never disclosed, for after this Minute the Church reverted to a further ten months of silence. The explanation lay with Dr. William Foster.

On the Sunday, 15 May, which followed the new Conventicle

Act of 10 May, a large group of Bedford Dissenters, who had not yet fully grasped this fresh danger, were surprised at the house of John Fenn, the hatter. On a warrant from William Foster, two informers, Francis Feckman and Robert West, with a Bedford constable, Edward Sims, discovered a meeting at which Nehemiah Cox, a cordwainer, was the preacher, and twenty-eight worshippers, including Samuel Fenn, John Fenn, Mary Tilney, and Josias Ruffhead, had assembled to hear him.

The conventiclers were taken to William Foster's house, a substantial dwelling with "nine hearths" in Well Street, and fined according to their supposed ability to pay. The preacher, Cox, was sent to prison, after being "committed by William Foster J. for speaking seditious words to wit that the Church of England (as now established) is antichristian". Later, "brought into court he asserted it". A Churchwarden of St. Paul's, named Thomas Battison, was meanwhile appointed to collect the authorities' large haul in fines.

Early in the morning of 20 May, John Bunyan was roused from his writing by a commotion in the High Street outside the County Gaol. It was the kind of commotion which is peculiarly characteristic of the British people, and will continue to be characteristic so long as this race endures.

In the volume entitled *British Rebels and Reformers*, in the *Britain in Pictures* series, the author, Dr. Harry Roberts, quoted a distinguished Christian minister who said that "all our liberties are due to men who, when their conscience has compelled them, have broken the laws of the land".

To break the law at the dictation of conscience usually requires some measure of personal heroism, such as a John Bunyan possesses, or a William Cobbett, or an Emmeline Pankhurst. But almost as effective is a mass resistance to the law on a local or national scale. Like John Bunyan, the common man and woman of Britain tends to regard the law as "a hass", and not once or twice in our island story this resistance has taken the form of ridicule. When Thomas Battison set out to collect his fines, the men and women of Bedford proceeded to apply it.

Thomas began at the malt-house of one John Bardolf, but the percipient John had forestalled this invasion and sold his malt. Was it, in the circumstances, legal to break into the malt-house?

While Thomas and the other officers were debating this question in the open yard, the commotion arose which had disturbed John Bunyan.

A contemporary pamphlet, anonymous for obvious reasons, described its cause. Under the title of *A True and Impartial Narrative of some Illegal and Arbitrary Proceedings by Certain Justices of the Peace and others, against several innocent and peacable Nonconformists in and near the Town of Bedford upon pretence of putting in execution the late Act against Conventicles*, it can now be read in the Bodleian Library at Oxford.

> "A great number of all sorts of persons were gathered about them, expressing (by turns) their indignation against him for attempting this against Bardolf, whom the whole Town knew to be a just and harmless man; and the common sort of people covertly fixing a Calves tayl to Battison's back, and deriding him with shouts and hollows, he departed without taking any distress there."

Somewhat abashed, the unfortunate Thomas next called at the house of the grocer, Edward Coventon, whom the Bedford Church had reported in their Minutes of 16 November, 1669, as "through mercy hopefully recovering from his backsliding". Evidently by now Edward had recovered completely, for he refused to pay his 5*s*. fine. Thomas thereupon confiscated a brass kettle and gave a boy 6*d*. to take it away to an inn-yard;

> "but when the youth had carried the kettle to the Inn-gate (being hooted at all the way by the common spectators), the Innkeeper would not suffer the Kettle to be brought into his yard, and so his man set it out in the middle of the Street."

The men and women of Bedford who derided "old Battison" on that May morning of 1670 were in more than a genetic sense the direct ancestors of the generation which in 1940 laughed "Cooper's Snoopers" out of their brief and undignified existence, and five years later compelled the withdrawal of the order forbidding soldiers to "fraternize" with their fellow humans in Germany. For a time, of course, the authorities won a temporary victory, as authorities with the power and the arms invariably do. The pamphlet went on to describe the manner of it.

> "The next day, which was the market-day, the Justices understanding how Battison was discouraged in his work, commanded the officers to break open the doors and levy the distresses. Immediately old Battison, with a file of soldiers and the constables, in the middle of Market-time, advanced again to the malt-house of John Bardolfe (scituate in an Inn-yard in the middle of the Market-place) and breaks open the doors and distreyned fourteen Quarters of Malt."

After John Bunyan had listened to this further campaign in the one-sided Battle of Bedford, his comrades proceeded next day, which was Sunday, to meet at John Fenn's house as before. They were again seized on another warrant from William Foster, and the fines were doubled. Throughout the following week "old Battison", with his running accompaniment of soldiers, constables, and jeering mob, proceeded to collect the fines.

He and his associates took three cart-loads of wood, used for his work, from Thomas Cooper the heel-maker; his best coat from Daniel Rich, the tanner; his household goods and all the materials of his trade from Thomas Arthur, a locally famous pipe-maker; and from Mary Tilney, a well-to-do widow who had been fined £20, all the goods of any value that she possessed and even the sheets from her bed. "To make her exemplary in suffering for that offence Mr. Foster himself . . . will see the fine effectually levied upon her Goods."

As this process of distraint continued, the townspeople who had first ridiculed the officers of the law now decided to boycott them instead.

> "Mr. Foster, the Justice, appears early in the streets, with old Battison and the two Apparitors, a file of soaldiers and some constables, to see the fines levied upon the Meeters' Goods; charging to his assistance such persons as he sees, and sending for others to their houses, but got few or none besides his first company; most of the Tradespeople, Journey-men, Labourers, and Servants having either left the Town or

hid themselves to avoid his call. The Town was so thin of people, that it looked more like a Country Village than a Corporation; and the shops being generally shut down, it seemed like a place visited with the Pest, where usually is written upon the Door, Lord have mercy upon us!"

The pamphlet quoted has a further interest for twentieth-century readers owing to its inclusion, at this early date, of a statement of the policy made famous by Mahatma Gandhi, Aldous Huxley, and the anti-Nazi Norwegians, under the name of "non-violent resistance".

"Councels for public good are the Province of our Superiours; ready Obedience or peacable Sufferings are the lot of Private Men. There is no intention to meet Violence by Violence; it is the intention of their Enemies to hurry them into a disturbance of the Publick Peace. But all Endeavours of that kind will be in vain, and the hopes of some about it wholly frustrate. It is nothing Else but the Authority of God in their Consciences which imposes a necessity upon them to practise those things in their Christian Profession for which they are made obnoxious to so great Sufferings, and gives them a supportment under them. The disturbance of the Publick Peace would be at once to renounce the Principle of their Actings and to deprive themselves of the Comfort of their Sufferings."

In spite of their immediate defeat, the townspeople who preferred derision and passive resistance to reciprocal violence won a long-range victory. They helped to inspire the determination by which a freedom-loving people ultimately overcomes oppression; they created the atmosphere of contempt for spies which caused John Bunyan's stories of ill-fated informers in *The Life and Death of Mr. Badman* to find so many sympathetic readers. In their implacable thousands throughout the towns and villages of England, they built up the body of opinion by means of which, through the Revolution of 1688 and the Bill of Rights, they changed the laws of the land.

. . . . .

When John went back to his dark cell after the short respite at home, he had determined to write a book evaluating the principles for which he had spent so many years in prison. Perhaps, if he could sufficiently vindicate those principles, he might convince his opponents that he really was not a menace to the State, and thereby secure his liberty.

As usual, he gave his book a title which expounded the subject-matter, and called it *A Confession of my Faith: And a Reason for my Practice; or with who, and who not, I can hold Church-Fellowship, or the Communion of Saints.* In it he set down his belief in those main doctrines of Scripture which for him were the road to eternal life, and explained the terms on which he could accept fellowship with other believers.

> "I believe that when he comes, his saints shall have a reward of grace, for all their work and labour of Love which they shewed to his name in the world. . . . I believe that Election is free and permanent, being founded in Grace and the unchangeable will of God. . . . By the word Communion I mean fellowship in the things of the Kingdom of Christ, or that which is commonly called Church Communion, the Communion of Saints. . . . I am for holding communion thus, because Love, which above all things we are commanded to put on, is of much more worth than to break about Baptism. It is Love, not Baptism, that discovereth us to the world to be Christs Disciples."

He was thus writing

> of the way
> And race of Saints in this our Gospel Day,

when one evening he fell into a doze, and had an extraordinary dream. Its details were so vivid that, even after he was fully awake, they appeared more real than the grimy prison walls and his unwashed companions.

It seemed to him that he had seen a man clothed in rags, with a book in his hand and a great burden on his back, setting out under the compulsion of prophetic terror to leave his doomed town, which resembled Bedford, but also suggested the lanes and fields of Elstow. Obviously he was starting on a journey, but where was he going, and why?

In his dream John followed the travels of this haunting figure across Bedfordshire's swamp-ridden plains and along its familiar highways, through its brick-and-timber villages, and beside the flower-covered summer banks of the Ouse. And yet—was it really his own well-known countryside that the traveller was tramping through? A light such as he had never seen even at noon seemed at times to shine upon those villages, glowing from the walls of the houses, and outlining the edges of the roofs with gold.

Could this actually be the River Ouse, which flowed through a meadow, curiously beautified with lilies, that was green all the year long? Were these blue mountains, so rich in fruits and flowers and vineyards, really only the remembered ridge of the Chilterns seen from the top storey of Ampthill House?

The scene suddenly changed. Leaning drowsily over his pages beside the guttering candle in the deep winter darkness, John saw his dream-companion walking up a gentle incline from a valley where he could hear the trickle of water. As the traveller climbed, weighed down by his clumsy burden, to the top of the hill, he seemed to be approaching a stone-built village that John felt sure he knew.

In a moment the man had passed between the walls of some houses, and stood before a slender grey monument set in the midst of the village cross-roads. Now, starting in his semi-consciousness, John recognized the place of his dream; it was Stevington Cross. At that moment a rose-red glory of sunset anointed the Gothic stone, and in its light John saw the great burden fall from the traveller's shoulders and roll down the hill.

In his dream the man leaped into the air for joy, and then, overcome by the revulsion of his relief, stood weeping silently beside the Cross. At last he turned to go home and, seeing his face for the first time, John realized that the traveller was himself.

The dream took hold of his imagination, and would not be shaken off. Whenever he took up his pen to continue *A Confession of my Faith*, he would find himself pursuing his phantom self along the level Bedfordshire roads. New paths constantly awaited that tireless traveller; new comrades helped him; new obstacles barred his route. Hour after hour John lay, half sleeping and half waking, upon the pile of straw in the dark corner of his cell, until the hours lengthened into days, and the days into weeks.

At last he began to set down his dream. He had no need to invent scenes, characters, or conversations; they were there before he required them, crowding upon his mind so fast that it was a difficult feat to net them in words before they escaped. They were like the sparks from coals of fire, which suddenly multiplied in a gleaming shoal, and as suddenly were gone.

John was writing rapidly one day when, with rueful guilt, he remembered that *A Confession of my Faith* was still unfinished. It never would be finished, he perceived, unless he put this strange preoccupation aside for the time being. With great reluctance he laid the sheets together on a stool in the corner, right away from the rest of his work.

He resolved only to go back to them when he had nothing more important to do, such as teaching the prisoners, or transcribing letters for the Bedford congregation, or finishing his *Confession*. Firmly taking himself in hand he completed it, putting down the final section on baptism and the terms of communion, and leaving only the Address to the Reader to be added.

Eventually he did add it—and realized with a shock that five years had gone by since he began this treatise. It was now the end of 1671, and he who had turned out two or three books nearly every year when he was first in prison, had nothing to show for this long stretch of time but one serious work and innumerable pages of frivolous narrative!

"I have not hitherto been so sordid as to stand to a doctrine right or wrong" [he wrote remorsefully], "much less when so weighty an argument as above eleven years' imprisonment is continually dogging of me to weigh and pause. . . ."

Far beyond his prison, another writer who was still only a name to him had been preoccupied too. Between 1667 and 1672 John Milton, whose youthful masques and lyrics had created a literary fashion which associated deep religious feeling with imaginative poetry, now produced those great works to which his spiritual, political and literary life had all contributed.

Paradise Lost, published in 1667, coincided with the death of

Jeremy Taylor and the birth of Jonathan Swift. In 1671, the year after Dryden became Poet Laureate at the age of thirty-nine and Benedict de Spinoza produced his *Tractatus Theologico-Politicus* in Amsterdam, came *Paradise Regained* and *Samson Agonistes*. But though John Bunyan's prolonged allegory, *The Holy War*, was to show some evidence of Milton's influence, his capacity for literary appreciation as such bore no relation to his own imaginative power.

The book which most moved him during the second half of his long imprisonment was *The Design of Christianity*, published by Edward Fowler, Rector of Northill, Bedfordshire, in 1671. It stirred him so much, when he read it at the beginning of 1672, that he abandoned his pilgrim-traveller on the slopes of the hills which he had called the Delectable Mountains, and began to compose an answer to the Rector's arguments.

Edward Fowler, later Bishop of Gloucester, had been one of the ejected clergy who refused in 1662 to accept the conditions imposed by the Act of Uniformity, but who later conformed. He is said to have inspired the addition of Mr. Worldly Wiseman to the second edition of *The Pilgrim's Progress*. His book rekindled the Bunyan impulse towards controversy owing to John's conviction that changes of principle which coincide with personal interests are questionable feats of spiritual gymnastics.

In six weeks he wrote, as his fifteenth book, a long reply to Fowler, entitled *A Defence of the Doctrine of Justification by Faith in Christ Jesus*. In this he protested that Fowler's book was alien "to the Evangelistic spirit of the Articles of the Church of England and therefore to the Gospel itself".

The Rector, with the probable help of his curate, published an indignant response to the impudent tinker, *Dirt Wip't Off*, in which he made full use of the fallacy known to Logic as the *argumentum ad hominem*. Provocative as John's criticisms might be, they were not answered by references to his "Gross Ignorance, erroneousness and most Unchristian and Wicked Spirit", or by calling him "as rank and Ranting an Antinomian as ever foul'd paper".

Edward Fowler's reply was not published until September 1672. By that time John was out of prison, and indifferent to him and his book.

In September 1668, after Charles II's first Conventicle Act had lapsed, the Bedford Church had begun not only to keep Minutes again, but to collect and reorganize its members scattered by persecution. Some had lapsed but the majority had remained steadfast, though one or two were driven—like the aged Anthony Harrington in 1669—away from their homes "to avoyde being taken with a writ *De Excom. capiend.*" after excommunication by the Bishop for failure to attend the parish church.

Yet others had developed complicated spiritual scruples, which tended to vary with the severity of the persecution. One of these was the most socially distinguished member of the Church, William Whitbread, whose family successors are still Lords of the Manor at Elstow.

At the same meeting, on 14 December, 1669, that the Church agreed to "cut off" one of the worst backsliders, Humphrey Merrill, it was also decided that "an admonition be prepared to be sent to brother William Whitbread, for withdrawing from the Church and ordinances of God". The members, who were obviously reluctant to boycott this conspicuous disciple, continued, in a long series of letters, to remonstrate with their eminent brother "ffor your so long forsaking the Assemblies of this Congregation".

At length, after a unique exhibition of patience continuing until 9 October, 1670, and occupying almost the entire Folio 29 of the Church Book, Brother Whitbread was received back into communion, "he making a gracious acknowledgment of his sorrow and repentance for all those miscarriages of which he had been admonished".

Owing to the tendency of John's jailors to swim with the political tide and relax their supervision when persecution lessened, he was able, after the lapse of the Conventicle Act in 1668, to give his brethren considerable help in their task of reorganization. On 30 November of that year, the Church selected him to reprove brothers Nelson, Merrill, and Coventon. He was again admonishing recalcitrant brethren on 14 October and 16 December, 1669, and on 21 January, 1670, was one of the seven who testified to the delinquency of Humphrey Merrill. He also took part in writing some of the letters* sent to encourage Church

* Preserved in the text of the Church Book, where they can still be seen.

members "wanted" by the police and absent from home in order to avoid arrest.

These members included "our beloved Sister Katharine Hustwhat", John Wilson, later the first pastor of the Independent Church at Hitchin, and "our brother Harrington". The letter to Anthony Harrington, though signed by three other members besides John, contains at least one paragraph which testifies that the actual composition was his.

> "You, brother Harrington, have lived to see the slippery and unstable nature that is in earthly things; wherefore we beseech you to expect no more therefrom, then the word of God hath promised, which is as much in little as in much thereof, if not more in many respects. While Israell sate by the flesh-pots in Egypt they had no manna from heaven, they dranke not the water out of the Rock. We hope it is because God loveth you that he hath driven you from your incumbrances, that you may have occasion before you dye to solace yourself with your God and the Lord Jesus Christ. We meane that you may doe it with more leisure and lesse distraction than when ye lowing of the oxen hath continuall sound in your eares."

During this period of reconstruction, the hand of death fell with impassive neutrality upon both John's friends and his enemies. On 5 November, 1669, his old colleague William Dell, dour and disillusioned to the last, died and was buried in unconsecrated ground. He chose the spot himself, a small copse on his own estate at "Samshill in the parish of Westoning". There his bones lie, now part of the same red-brown earth that composes the ploughland where the farm in which John was arrested once stood.

In August 1670 the man who had been associated with them both, John's erstwhile commander, Sir Samuel Luke, died at Cople still embittered by the mockeries of Butler's satire. Nine months later, on 9 May, 1671, Lord Chief Justice Kelynge followed him to the grave, and was thereby spared the knowledge that, exactly twelve months afterwards, the preacher whom his ruling had kept in prison for a dozen years would be free to preach again.

On 23 June, 1671, another famous Bedfordshire figure who shared the Judge's opinions departed; the aged Giles Thorne, Archdeacon of Buckingham, who had endured so many vicissitudes, died and was buried in the Chancel of St. Mary's. The following autumn the Bedford Meeting assembled at Haynes to consider the choice of a new pastor.

One of the better-justified complaints of the elusive Brother Whitbread had concerned the dual control of the Bedford Church by Samuel Fenn and John Whiteman after the death of John Burton. In his apology to the members, William Whitbread explained that "to dismember myself I never intended, as having bene persuaded from Scripture grounds of the consonancy of the Congregationall way with the rule. I waited to see if any doore might be opened for redresse by the choyce of a fit Pastor and the mercy of a spirit of government among us, which since the death of our Pastor hath been greatly wanting".

It was the personality of that "fit Pastor" which the Church, a fortnight after its reconciliation with Brother Whitbread, now met to discuss. They decided to meet again a week later at John Fenn's house to "consider and debate" regarding "the gifts of the Church, and their disposall in an orderly way. . . . The Church was also minded to seeke God about the choice of brother Bunyan to the office of an Elder, that their way in that respect may be cleared up to them."

After twelve years in prison, John's status had changed beyond recognition from that of the impulsive young preacher who toured the villages and had written three or four controversial booklets. During that prolonged and tedious confinement, he had produced no fewer than eleven books, including the powerful *Grace Abounding* with its vivid picture of a converted sinner. His preaching, enhanced by adversity, had grown in vigour; the integrity of his convictions had survived both assault and persuasion; and his character had acquired that strong tranquillity which only creative suffering and accepted experience can bring.

He was now allowed so much liberty that the choice of him as pastor had become a practical proposition. When the "permanent" Conventicle Act was passed Archbishop Sheldon had sent out a whip to the Bishops to see that its provisions were enforced, but after the theft of the Regalia and Great Seal in May 1671,

Charles became convinced that his crown and even his life were in danger.

Toleration for Nonconformists had always been, for him, a convenient counterblast to his own secret Catholicism. From the late summer of 1671 it became clear that he was contemplating "indulgence", and now, instead of opposition by the formidable Clarendon, he had the support of Ashley, the strongest member of the Cabal, who was soon to become Earl of Shaftesbury.

The change of atmosphere was fully appreciated by the Nonconformist community. On 21 December, 1671, after prolonged meetings and meditations, the Bedford Church, "with joynt consent (signifyed by solemne lifting up of their hands)", appointed John Bunyan to be their pastor.

"And he accepting thereof, gave up himself to serve Christ and his Church in that charge; and received of the Elders the right hand of fellowship."

His release from prison was now only a matter of weeks. On 15 March, 1672, Charles II issued his most famous Declaration of Indulgence, pointing out that it was "evident by the sad experience of twelve yeares that there is very little fruit of all these forceable Courses", and suspending by royal prerogative the penal laws against Recusants and Nonconformists. The prison doors opened, and thousands of England's finest citizens at last received a period of respite from their long endurance.

On 29 March, owing to private intervention reinforced by Quaker pressure, letters were sent out requiring the county sheriffs to return the names of all the Quakers in prison. These were produced on 8 May, and sorted into four classes. Inquiries were set on foot to make sure that no private person would be wronged by anyone's release, and an order was given to prepare a pardon freeing "all those persons called Quakers, now in prison for any offence Committed, relating only to his Matie and not to the prejudice of any other person". The number scheduled was 471.

That same day, John Bunyan and five of his fellow prisoners, John Fenn, John Donne, Thomas Haynes, Simon Haynes, and George Farr, put in a petition to the King in Council, professing to be imprisoned for "being at Conventicles and Nonconformity". This petition was referred to the Bedfordshire County Sheriff, Thomas

Bromsall of Blunham, who acted promptly in certifying the truth of the petition only three days later. The names were therefore accepted, and added to the Quaker Pardon, dated 13 September, 1672, which is now in London at Friends' House, Euston Road.

Long before this official date, John Bunyan's unofficial "leaves" from prison had lengthened into actual release. On 9 May, 1672, the day after his petition, he was licensed as a teacher under the Declaration of Indulgence, and had won a temporary victory in the long struggle to establish his right "to call the people together".

For the last time in twelve years he rolled his few shabby garments into a bundle, put his Bible and Book of Martyrs under his arm with the bulky manuscript story of his dream between them, and stepped through the prison door into the mild spring sunshine. The air was sweet with the scent of hawthorn as he passed the gardens in Mill Lane; from the orchards to the north came the full, rich whistle of a blackbird calling to its mate.

Turning the corner by St. Cuthbert's Church he opened the door of his house, but almost before he touched the handle Elizabeth was on the threshold to greet him. Now pregnant for the third time with their youngest child, she caressed the face and hair of the grave middle-aged husband into whom time and endurance had transformed her young hot-headed lover.

Putting down the bundle and the books John drew her close to him, and went into his cottage, a free man.

CHAPTER XIV

PERILOUS FREEDOM

"A Christian can never be overcome, unless he shall yield of himself."

JOHN BUNYAN: *The Pilgrim's Progress,* Part II.

THE mature prisoner who came out of Bedford Gaol in May 1672 did not even physically resemble the young man who had entered the prison in November 1660.

His face, framed in long auburn hair, had then been ruddy in tone, and healthily bronzed from perpetual riding and tramping in the open air. His eyes, lively as a blue candle-flame, held a latent hint of gaiety even when he was praying or preaching.

Twelve years afterwards, though he was still no more than forty-three, grey threads appeared in the bronze hair, cut short like that of his fellow prisoners. The puffiness of his flesh reflected the interminable hours spent in darkness; the deep lines beneath his eyes emphasized their grave reflectiveness, half visionary and half reminiscent.

Already something of the stern temper which Charles Doe noted during his final years had come into his countenance. He had that air of authority which men and women acquire who have been through deep waters of experience and come out victorious. His eyes had looked upon visions of heaven, but on earth they had seen death, squalor, and vice. If he lived for another thirty years, like his father, he would never forget the fetid stench of the rat-infested dungeon beneath the gaol; the raucous quarrels of detained felons; the vicious practices of long-term prisoners cut off from normal living; the dirt and the lice; the cruelty and corruption of some of his jailors.

His prolonged ordeal was over at last, though he had returned home to find, as one contemporary biographer records, that "his temporal affairs were gone to wreck, and he had as to them to begin again as if he had newly come into the world". None the less it was, as usual, his public mission which occupied his mind.

As the newly-appointed pastor of the Bedford Church, he had been given seven of their most reliable members, John Fenn, Oliver Scott, Luke Astwood, Thomas Cooper, Edward Dent, Edward Isaac, and Nehemiah Cox, to work with him as deacons in the surrounding villages. But the "people of God", as the returns from the Archdeacon's Visitation of 1668–9 had shown, were now widely scattered throughout Bedfordshire and the adjacent counties. Many more teachers were needed for this large "diocese" than the Bedford Church could supply.

When John applied, in May 1672, for his own license to preach, he therefore requested licenses for twenty-five other teachers, and for thirty buildings as meeting-places. The King's Declaration of Indulgence had provided for this necessity in specific terms:

> "That there may be no pretence for any of Our Subjects to continue their illegall Meetings and Conventicles, Wee doe Declare, that wee shall from time to time allow a sufficient number of Places, as they shall bee desired, in all parts of this Our Kingdome, for the use of such as doe not conforme to the Church of England, to meete and assemble in, in Order to theri Publick Worship and Devotion; which Places shall be open and free to all Persons."

Many of John's old friends and colleagues were included in this request for licenses. He asked for the help of John Donne, whose remaining time on earth was to be so short; of Stephen Hawthorn, "for his own house in Turvy"; of John Allen, "for the house of the Widow Reade in Steventon", and of John Gibbs, "for William Smyth's barn and his own house in Newport Pagnell". On behalf of one of his deacons, Edward Isaac, he requested permission to teach in "the house of Gilbert Ashley in Godlington",* thus naming the man who five years later, on 16 April, 1677, was to marry his second daughter Elizabeth.

The activities of these newly-licensed preachers, and hundreds like them throughout England, were gloomily noted at this time

* i.e. Goldington.

by the aristocratic writer of memoirs, John Evelyn. "Papists," he complained, "and swarms of sectaries now boldly showing themselves in their public meetings."

Like other Nonconformist congregations, the Bedford Church also required a place to meet. Ever since their loss of St. John's Church just after the Restoration they had been driven from pillar to post, seeking to evade the assiduity of William Foster and his supporting battalion of informers in woods, fields, farm-house kitchens, and private homes.

For some time Josias Ruffhead, the cordwinder who had been "presented" at the Archdeacon's Court for refusing to go to church, had kept his eye upon an orchard in Mill Lane which contained a barn. It stood next to John Eston's garden on a strip of land, adjoining Castle Lane, which was lower than the street on the north side, and was said to have once been part of the moat round Bedford Castle.

The orchard and barn belonged to Justice Crompton of Elstow, who twelve years earlier had declined to go bail for John Bunyan, but had now no objection to selling him and his colleagues a plot of land. Josias Ruffhead duly acquired the orchard and John's application for licenses included the barn, which was thereupon permitted "to be a place for the use of such as doe not conforme to the Church of England who are of the Perswasion commonly called Congregationall". This comprehensive word, which had also been used in the preaching license given to John himself, included all those who regarded the individual congregation as the highest authority, under God, for decisions upon doctrinal and moral questions.

When these necessary formalities had been completed, the orchard and barn were conveyed by indenture from "Josias Ruffhead to John Bunyan, of the Towne of Bedford, Brasier", and to five of his colleagues, in return for a sum of £50. It was conveniently situated for John, being only a few steps from his house in St. Cuthbert's Street.

The present Bunyan Meeting at the south-east corner of Mill Street stands on the site of this orchard, though a flight of steps now leads up to it instead of down, as steps once led down into the Old Meeting with its three gabled ridges which in 1707 replaced the barn. On the east side of the Meeting House, the sunken Garden of Remembrance and Memorial Sundial are probably on the same level as the original orchard.

The members of the Bedford Church gave their spare time to clearing and furnishing the barn, and when John preached there on the opening day, the large building could not contain all those who wished to attend. So they stood outside in the orchard, crowding close to the door while the pigeons from Josias Ruffhead's dove-house circled gracefully overhead.

The date of the indenture by which the barn and orchard passed to John Bunyan and his colleagues was 20 August, 1672. Only the previous afternoon, a phenomenal storm had passed over Bedford. It is described in a quarto pamphlet (the newspapers of the seventeenth century) now in the British Museum.

After violent thunder and lightning, accompanied by rain, travellers on the road reported a "great combustion in the air", as though the clouds were fighting with one another, and at a distance the town appeared to be on fire. The gates of the Swan Inn were thrown off their hinges into the street, and smashed in pieces after being whirled round like a football. Haystacks were blown away and "are not yet to be found"; elms were torn up by their roots, and one great tree was carried from beyond the Ouse over St. Paul's steeple "as if it had been a bundle of feathers".

These melodramatic performances on the part of Nature were duly recorded by Anthony Mithnal the Mayor, John Gardener the Recorder, Thomas Christie the Attorney, and four others who included John Rush, Waggoner and a member of the Bedford Church.

This violent tempest only reflected the stormy events in which the nation had become involved through the second Secret Treaty of Dover in 1670 between Charles II and Louis XIV. The treaty agreed that Charles was to help Louis against the Dutch in return for an immediate payment of £150,000, to be increased by further large sums so long as the war continued. A sea-fight had followed in Southwold Bay, in which the Dutch fleet more than held its own against the English and French.

After this event the Dutch, implacable in war, cut their dykes against the invaders, as they were to cut them again in 1944.

While cities drowned and citizens rioted, Jan de Witt, grand pensionary and virtual ruler of Holland, was murdered with his brother by a mob at The Hague. A saviour and Stadtholder was summoned in the person of young William of Orange, who seventeen years later, as England's king, was to accept a measure granting that religious freedom for the sake of which John Bunyan had just spent twelve years in gaol.

While William was engaged in saving the liberties of one country before turning his attention to another, John took advantage of the freedom now permitted him to visit Leicester. He preached there on Sunday, 6 October, at a house close to St. Nicholas Church, after showing to "Mr. Maior Mr. Overing Mr. Freeman and Mr. Browne" his license dated 9 May, 1672, "to teach as a congregationall person". When these officials had chronicled his visit in the Borough Records, John walked about the pleasant country town, observing the Roman Forum and Jewry Wall beside St. Nicholas Church, and the great gateways of the Newarke, a fourteenth-century addition to the Castle. He was to remember them clearly ten years later when he was describing the fortifications of Mansoul in *The Holy War*.

John returned from Leicester just in time for the birth of his son Joseph, the youngest of his six children. On 16 November, Elizabeth took him to be christened in St. Cuthbert's Church. The old font in which the baby was baptized would still stand there three centuries later, less controversial in its indubitable survival than some denominational reactions to John's equitable attitude towards the baptismal ceremony and the apparent orthodoxy of both his wives, neither of whom joined the Bedford Meeting.

Some members of the Nonconformist community have endeavoured to prove that the "Joseph Bunyan" baptized on 16 November, 1672, was not John's son but his grandson, the child of his elder boy John. But unless the younger John came between Mary and Elizabeth (in which event he would have been registered at Elstow) he could not have been born before 1655.

Seventeen, despite Francis Wingate, was even in those days an early age to become a father. It seems more probable that the elder John, with his habitual forbearance, allowed his wives to decide for themselves how their children should be baptized.

At the time of Joseph's christening, John Bunyan happened to be engaged in a controversy on baptism itself. Towards the end of his book *A Confession of my Faith,* he had dealt briefly with the terms on which Christians should be admitted to communion. In this, more open-minded than some of his successors, he deplored undue attention to questions of ritual, "taking off Christians from the more weighty things of God, and to make them quarrel and have heart-burnings one against another".

For the tolerance thus expressed he was now violently attacked by three leaders of the more rigid type of London Baptist, William Kiffin and his two colleagues, Paul and d'Anvers. He replied to them in 1673 in his sixteenth book, *Differences in Judgment about Water Baptism no Bar to Communion,* in which the title itself embodied his preference for putting first things first.

In his attitude to baptism, and to other forms of ritual, John had been influenced by the broad principles of two men whom he deeply respected, John Gifford and William Dell. When writing his farewell letter to his colleagues, John Bunyan's first Interpreter had clearly warned them to avoid "separation from the Church, about Baptisme, laying on of hands, Anoynting with Oyls, Psalmes, or any externalls", and to concentrate on fundamental truths. William Dell, dynamic and revolutionary, had believed in dispensing with baptism altogether, leaving the soul to be redeemed by the power of the Spirit and the cleansing fire of righteousness.

Such counsel had caused the members of the Bedford Church to enter into fellowship on the principle of "ffaith in Christ and Holiness of life, without respect to this or that circumstance or opinion in outward and circumstantiall things". Only twice was baptism mentioned in the Church Book between 1650 and 1690. John's own "believer's baptism", which he had felt compelled to accept for himself though he never imposed such ceremonies on others, was not even recorded.

At no time did he become a strong denominationalist; for him the grace of God was wide enough to embrace all Christians in one common fellowship. He lived through the political and religious factions of his day without showing any bias except for liberty of worship in itself—a fact which explains the appeal of

Grace Abounding and *The Pilgrim's Progress* to all sections of the Christian Church.

> "I dare not say" [he wrote], " 'No matter whether water-baptism be practised or not'. But it is not a stone in the foundation of a church. . . . The saint is a saint before, and may walk with God, and be faithful with the saints, and to his own light also, although he never be baptized. . . . I am for communion with saints because they are saints . . . shew me the man that is a visible believer . . . and although he differ with me about baptism, the doors of the church stand open for him."

During 1674, the year in which death the leveller removed both Milton and Clarendon from the scene upon which each had exercised so decisive an influence, John published a further rejoinder to Paul and D'anvers in *Peaceable Principles and True*. But before this book appeared, the affairs of the nation and their possible effect upon his Church again demanded his attention.

In February 1673, the King had attempted to introduce a Bill for Indulgence, but the Commons told him that he could not suspend penal statutes in "matters ecclesiastical" except by Act of Parliament. Even some of the Dissenters and their friends in the House suspected the Declaration to be a cloak for Papacy, and Charles realized that he had misunderstood Protestant psychology, which feared Catholicism more than it loved what would now be described as "phoney" freedom.

This new trial of strength between King and Parliament ended in Charles withdrawing the Declaration of Indulgence in March 1673 and breaking the seal to it with his own hands. He had little choice, for he stood virtually alone; even his continental colleague, Louis XIV, was temporarily engaged in a quarrel with Pope Innocent XI.

A Bill "for ease of Protestant Dissenters" passed the Lower House, but was stopped by the Bishops in the House of Lords. Before the prorogation of Parliament on 29 March, the two Houses had compelled Charles to accept the Test Act, which was expressly aimed at the Roman Catholics but imposed fresh disabilities on the

Nonconformists. It obliged all those holding office under the Crown to take the Sacrament according to the Anglican rite, and to make a declaration against transubstantiation.

From 3 February, 1673, no new licenses were issued for preachers or meeting-places, and the Bedford Church, like other Nonconformist communities, became uncertain where it stood. Had the old licenses became valueless under the cancelled Declaration, or were the holders retrospectively protected? John's Pardon, it seemed, was impregnable; he could not be imprisoned again on the 1661 conviction under his old enemy, 35 Eliz. But how was he placed in relation to the "permanent" Conventicle Act of 1670?

Once more freedom had become perilous, with the application of the laws uncertain, and informers anxious to make hay under this new outburst of sun. Greedy for a fresh harvest of fines, they threatened constables and magistrates with maximum penalties unless they renewed their old policy of scooping cash and goods from attenders at conventicles.

In October 1674 the King, equally dubious about the Nonconformists' position and his own, consulted the Bishops. The outcome of their advice was hardly surprising; on 3 February, 1675, Charles issued a proclamation ordering the execution of the penal laws, disclaiming that conventicles were tolerated, and even asserting that "His Licenses were long Recalled".

It was doubtless owing to the uncertainty of the national policy that the Bedford Church kept 14 June, 1673, as "a day of humiliation and praire upon several weighty accounts". But as usual the Church, resembling in this respect those idealistic bodies which are nowadays known as "voluntary organizations", found that the day-by-day problems and misdemeanours of its members tended to impair its vision of the larger destinies of mankind.

The women in particular seemed to cause trouble during this uncomfortable period. On 18 October, 1673, the Church decided to cast out "the wife of our brother Witt, for railing and other wicked practices". During 1674 Sister Landy was admonished, and finally "withdrawn from", for not only playing cards herself, but teaching her children this scandalous accomplishment. Sister

Elizabeth Maxey was also reproved for some lively altercations with her parents, and "our sister Elizabeth Burntwood" strongly rebuked for "her immodest company keeping with carnal and light young fellows at Elstow".

The men, too, were far from perfect. Nehemiah Cox, though a deacon, expressed repentance at a meeting of the congregation in Cotton End for using provocative words tending to divide the people, and John Bunyan was obliged to employ his gift for vivid language in recording the shortcomings of his flock. There was the occasion, for instance, when John Rush—not the Quaker from Bedford Gaol but the waggoner who witnessed the storm—was "cast out" for being not merely drunk, but drunk

> "after a very beastly and filthy manner, that is above the ordenery rate of drunkerds, for he could not be carried home from the Swan to his own house without the help of no less than three persons who, when they had brought him home, could not present him as one alive to his familie he was so dead drunke."

From the time of his release, John had been overwhelmed with work. His Church was now far larger than any normal parish; its membership was drawn not only from Bedfordshire with its many villages, but from adjacent counties such as Cambridgeshire and Hertfordshire. As the "Bishop" of this large area, constantly in demand for his dynamic preaching, he had little time to write, or even to keep the Church Minutes up to date. If ever a man needed a good secretary it was he, and judging by the different hands in the Church Book, the community did its best to supply his needs.

Throughout his Ministry, the records are scanty; his handwriting when it occurs is vigorous and untidy, his entries are often blotted and defaced with erasures, suggesting that he was always in a hurry. Occasionally he left a page blank, to be filled up in spare time which never came.

As though the anxieties caused by a change of national policy were not a sufficient addition to this exacting routine, John now became involved in a new problem quite different from any that he had faced before.

From January 1670 the Bedford Church had occasionally held its meetings fifteen miles away at Gamlingay, a large village straggling along the side of a low hill on the Cambridgeshire borders, with the counties of Huntingdon and Bedford touching it on the north and west. Until 1600 Gamlingay had been an important market town, but on a dark and cloudy night of that year, all its thatched buildings and the market-square were destroyed by fire. Before the surviving population could complete the building of their new village, with its wide streets in the form of a cross, their trade and market had moved to Potton, and the fortunes of Gamlingay declined.

It was nevertheless an up-to-date, modern-looking place, with a cruciform church built of small stones as neat as bricks, and a row of ten new almshouses, with tiled roofs and diamond-paned windows, put up along the main street by Sir John Jacob in 1665. During the reign of Charles I Sir John had lived at Woodbury Hall, and lent the King money which was never repaid.

When John Bunyan came out of prison and began riding east from Bedford to take services at Gamlingay, the meetings were sometimes held at a barn in Mill Street behind the parish church, and sometimes at the house of Luke Astwood, whose licence to preach had been amongst those applied for in 1672. A strange legend persists in the village that John once rode there on a donkey.

The barn was destined to be destroyed in the Gamlingay "Mill Street fire" in 1897, but ceased to be used for its original purpose after a chapel was built in 1710. The large modern meeting-house which replaced the chapel (described as "Old Meeting Baptist Church") stands on the top of the low hill looking over a wide expanse of flat Cambridgeshire fields. It is built of red brick, with the characteristic iron staircase at the back leading outside the building to an upper chamber. An extensive graveyard surrounds it, containing many old graves and a large yew.

At one of the Gamlingay meetings, in November 1672, a young girl named Agnes Beaumont was received into the Bedford Church after the usual careful inquiries had been made. John Bunyan himself entered her name in the Act Book—"Agniss Behemont".

Agnes, then barely twenty, came from the Bedfordshire village of Edworth, midway between Gamlingay and Hitchin. At this lost little place, half a mile from the Roman Road leading to Biggleswade four miles distant, she lived with her widowed father, John Beaumont, in a farm standing beside a rough path at the corner of a large sloping field. The farm, though not the adjacent barn, is there still, some distance from the main hamlet, and difficult to find.

The tiny dwelling, disproportionately high like an outsize dolls' house, was built of pale terra-cotta bricks, the upper ones being half-chiselled in a simple pattern. On summer evenings the hazels behind the house flung their shadow-pattern across the red-tiled roof to the base of the tall brick chimneys, and rooks cawed somnolently in the elms surrounding the tussocky field. A moat protected the farm with its small cluster of out-buildings; beyond it the flat meadow-lands, interrupted only by spinneys planted to break the wind, stretched north to the Cambridgeshire boundary.

Once, on 3 October, 1673, the Bedford congregation met in Edworth itself, at the house of George Pridden. By this time Agnes had become an ardent member of the Meeting with the support of her brother and his wife. Though they did not actually belong to John Bunyan's Church, they were Puritans who had been presented by the Edworth churchwardens at an Archdeacon's Court held by William Foster in 1669 for refusing to take the sacrament at the parish church.

Originally John Beaumont senior had shared their views, but a malicious neighbour poisoned his mind against both the Bedford Church and John Bunyan himself. It was, therefore, with great difficulty that Agnes obtained his permission to go to Gamlingay for a meeting that she was anxious to attend in February 1674.

Her problem now was how to get there. Mud and thawing snow made a seven-mile walk impossible along the deeply-rutted country roads, and her brother was to carry his wife, pillion-wise, on the only available horse. At first it was arranged that Agnes should be carried behind John Wilson, who was travelling from Hitchin where he was to be appointed pastor in May. But when the time came to start, John Wilson failed to appear. Instead it was, unexpectedly, John Bunyan himself who rode past.

Her own version of this episode, *The Narrative of the Persecution of Agnes Beaumont in 1674*, reveals Agnes as a natural if illiterate and ungrammatical story-teller. It also suggests that she was an emotional convert whose attitude towards John had passed from admiration into a feeling which girls of her age would now describe as a "crush". If this callow adoration existed, it evidently met with no response from him.

> "At last vnExpected came Mr. Bunyan, and cald at my Brothers as he went to the meeting; but the sight of him caused sorrow and Ioy, in me; I was glad to see him but I was afraid he would not Cary mee to the meeting behind him; and how to Aske him I did not know, for feare he should deny mee. Soe I gott my Brother to ask him.
>
> Soe my Brother said to him, 'I must desire you to Cary my Sister today behind you.'
>
> And he Answered my Brother very roughly, and said, 'Noe, not I, I will not Cary her'. These was Cutting words to me indeed, wch made mee weepe bitterly.
>
> My Brother s^{d} to him Againe, 'If you doe not Cary her, you will breake her heart.'
>
> And he replyed wth the same words Againe, that he would not cary me, that he would not Cary mee. And he said to me, 'If I should cary you, yor father would be greivous Angry wth me.' Said I, 'If you please to carry me, I will venture that.' Soe wth a great many intreaties, at last my Brother did prevaile with him, and I did git up behind him. But oh, how glad was I that I was goeing."

John had been right about Agnes's father; as soon as he realized that she was riding behind the detested pastor, he hurried to a place on the road called "Close End" to try to pull her off the horse. But he arrived too late; the travellers had already passed the spot.

The road from Edworth to Gamlingay ran between wide, open fields, their covering of half-melted snow unbroken except for the occasional spinneys. Now and again individual oaks and elms, tall sentinels with bare boughs, marked the direction of the half-submerged lane. A study in black, white, and grey, the desolate scene stretched to the far horizon.

AGNES BEAUMONT'S FARM

The lonely farmhouse near Edworth, where Agnes Beaumont lived with her father, has survived until today.

WAINWOOD DELL

The large natural amphitheatre hidden in the woods at Preston, near Hitchin, where Bunyan held secret preaching services attended by hundreds of people.

Throughout the seven-mile ride, John remained glumly silent; he was uncomfortably aware of the palpitating devotion which glowed in the young girl sitting behind him. She could easily have been his daughter; she was, in fact, three years younger than blind Mary. He knew, as she did not, that men in their peculiar way are worse gossips than women, and the thought of the private guffaws of his less respectful acquaintances did not increase his enthusiasm for riding with Agnes into Gamlingay. But even he could never have foreseen what subsequently occurred.

Throughout the meeting, he was conscious of her rapt eyes on his face. She was an attractive young woman, and he, in spite of his deliberate gruffness, a man in the prime of life. He found the experience disconcerting, and made up his mind that on no account would he take her home. When the meeting was over he told her that he had to return to Bedford by another route, and left her to be dropped some distance from her house by a woman neighbour, "the wayes being soe durty and deepe".

Unprepared for the walk, Agnes went home "plosshing through the durt over shoes, haveing noe pattings on", only to find the door of the farm bolted against her. Her furious father refused to open it unless she promised to give up attending the Bedford Church meetings, so, with wet feet and no covering, she spent the frosty night in the barn. The sense of exaltation inspired by the meeting continued through the hours of solitary darkness.

Like John himself, during his period of conversion at the same age, the young girl was haunted by Scriptural phrases, and, also like him, she attached a prophetic significance to the ones that she happened to think of. In spite of the cold and discomfort, she was conscious throughout the night of "ravishing vissitts" from God. Her father was less favoured; in the morning he still refused to admit her, and she stayed at her brother's house till the following Sunday. Then, the victim of a conflict almost as agonizing as John's, she was moved by compunction for her father, left alone to look after himself. At last she gave way to his wishes, and returned home.

The night after she went back, she dreamed that one of their apple-trees had been blown down in a storm, and that she tried to lift it in vain. Afterwards the dream seemed to her prophetic, for the next night, in the sleeping chamber "where my ffather and I lay" in their two separate beds, John Beaumont was seized with a fatal illness and died before morning.

In those days of spies, uncertainties, and political tensions, rumours and scandals quickly spread. Hearsay evidence was implicitly believed, and remained unchecked by scientific analysis or legal machinery. Seventeenth-century informers, could they have foreseen our modern totalitarian empires, would have had little to learn from them in tale-bearing, scandal-mongering, intrigues, and betrayals.

As John had foreseen, he and Agnes had been recognized as they rode through Gamlingay; the clergyman, named Lane, who had observed them was now engaged in spreading a disreputable story through Baldock Market. John Beaumont's death after a period of strained relations between him and his daughter, which were widely known while their recent reconciliation was not, added fuel to the racing flame of scandal. "Mr. Farry," a lawyer named Farrow whose suit Agnes had recently rejected, was only too delighted to fan it to white heat.

He started a further rumour that she had poisoned her father. After this report, as Agnes recorded, came another.

> "That was, Mr. Bunyan was a Widower, and he gave me Counsel to poyson my Father so that he might have me to be his Wife, and this we agreed upon as we rid along to Gongy. And truly this did sometime make me merry, as other things did make me sad, and not only after it was said, *we were married*, but they were mistaken for he had a good Wife before. . . . It also troubled me to think that in case I suffered, another as innocent as myself must suffer too, but the Lord knew our innocency in this affaire, both in thought, and worde, and deede."

These titillating and dramatic tales caused commotion in Edworth parish. The funeral was deferred, the coroner called, and a jury summoned. With genial informality the coroner and his "Jewry" had dinner with Agnes's brother, and addressed her as "sweetheart", before starting the proceedings which might have ended in her sentence to death by burning (the punishment for parricide).

Eventually Agnes's innocence was proved and her malicious accusers confounded. Rough though the medical knowledge of that day might be, it was sufficient to ascertain, even without "opening" her father, that he had died from natural causes. Courageously, after his funeral, Agnes visited "the market-place" to quell further rumours with her presence. She lived to marry two husbands, the second, Mr. Story, being "a person of considerable substance and great seriousness", and to survive John Bunyan by more than thirty years.

After her death at Highgate in 1720 at the age of sixty-eight, she was buried by her request in the graveyard of the Tilehouse Street Chapel at Hitchin. The minister, John Needham, who conducted her funeral, preached a sermon from 2 Corinthians, iv, 17: "For our light affliction, which is but for a moment, worketh for us a far more exceeding and eternal weight of glory." In 1812 the young people of Tilehouse Street subscribed for a tablet, still to be seen on the back wall of the chapel facing the graveyard, to commemorate her story.

With rueful vigour John Bunyan commemorated it too, adding some famous and characteristic passages to subsequent editions of *Grace Abounding*:

> "When Satan perceived that his thus tempting and assaulting of me would not answer his design . . . then he tryed another way, which was, to stir up the minds of the ignorant, and malicious, to load me with slanders and reproaches; now therefore I may say, That what the Devil could devise, and his instruments invent, was whirled up and down the Country against me, thinking, as I said, that by that means they should make my Ministry to be abandoned.
>
> It began therefore to be rumored up and down among the People, that I was a Witch, a Jesuit, a High-way-man and the like.
>
> To all which, I shall only say, God knows that I am innocent. . . . But that which was reported with the boldest confidence, was, that I had my Misses, my Whores, my Bastards, yea, two Wives at once, and the like. . . .
>
> Shall I entreat them to hold their Tongues? no, not I, were it not for that these things make them ripe for damnation that

are the Authors and Abettors, I would say unto them; Report it! because 'twill increase my Glory.

Therefore I bind these lies and slanders to me as an ornament, it belongs to my Christian Profession, to be vilified, slandered, reproached, and reviled; and since all this is nothing else, as my God and my Conscience do bear me witness: I rejoyce in reproaches for Christs sake."

In addition to his visits to the Cambridgeshire borders John often now rode into Hertfordshire, where at least there were no emotional complications. From May 1674 onwards, he had the powerful support at Hitchin of John Wilson, who twenty years later was to contribute a preface to the earliest folio edition of his works. He came to know intimately the small, open town, with its main street leading up and down hill to the surrounding country and nearby villages.

At one of these, called Bendish, stood a barn which had been a malthouse, thatched and very low. This barn was a suitable place for meetings which had now again to be secret, for the building ran in two directions, with a large, square, movable pulpit standing in the angles. The pulpit formed part of a high pew in which ministers could sit out of sight of informers, and gave easy access to a way of escape into an adjacent lane. Three centuries later, in September 1948, this pulpit was to be installed next to the modern pulpit at Breachwood Green Baptist Church, near Hitchin, where it had long been stored in the vestry.

Two miles nearer Hitchin was the village of Preston, where some loyal friends of John's, the five Foster brothers, lived at Hunsdon House, a country mansion later to be known as Preston Castle. Close to its gateway, along the road to Hitchin, stretched the massed trees of Wain Wood, deep ochre in autumn against a background of dark firs. From the road a narrow grassy track led for quarter-of-a-mile to a clearing in which a gamekeeper's cottage stood. Built of weathered timber and deep vermilion bricks which were to survive for three hundred years, its walls glowed rose-red when the sun illumined them through the branches of the stalwart beech-tree standing near by.

John often spent an hour at this cottage before addressing a meeting in the wood. On the cold, dark evenings which the congregation selected for safety, he sat beside the leaping log fire in the Tudor fireplace with its inglenook and tiny wall cupboard where he kept his Bible. Once, when their meeting broke up in a hurry, he hid in the enormous chimney which stretched up to the roof.

The meeting-place in the wood lay further along the riding-road which led past the cottage; it was a huge amphitheatre with a dew-pond at the bottom, known as Wainwood Dell. It appeared to be natural but was probably an ancient excavation, for flints were sometimes found beside the dew-pond. Amid the thick undergrowth, majestic trees—oak, beech, and ash—towered from the sides and bottom of the hollow, gaily-patterned with primroses and anemones in spring.

To Wainwood Dell, in the depths of the night, worshippers would steal from the surrounding countryside, creeping in darkness along the grassy track and past the cottage until the thick leaf-screen of the trees hid the subdued light of their lanterns. In their hundreds they gathered so silently that the harsh, reiterated call of a disturbed jay seemed almost to deafen them, and the soft drumming of a woodpecker on a tree-trunk was louder than the gentle swish of the grass beneath their feet.

When the sentries were posted and the congregation seated on their coats along the sloping sides of the dell, John would enter as quietly as they, and standing beside the dew-pond in the deep hollow, speak to his people of salvation and the grace of God.

Sometimes he rode south-east from Hitchin to Kensworth, where in 1675 the Nonconformist Church numbered three hundred and eighty members. Occasionally he preached to them in a secret apartment hidden beneath the roof of Dallow Farm. Nineteen of these members, who lived in Luton, formed in that year a separate community, to be known later as the Park Street Church.

At other times John went due south, to a hamlet mid-way between Sandridge and Cromer Hyde, near Hatfield, known as Coleman Green. He was welcome there in a cottage which formed a convenient stopping-place on his journeys to London, and sometimes preached in its large garden. Its ancient massive chimney, long over-grown with ivy, still stands there, a rural monument on which an inscribed tablet records his visits.

It was difficult now for John to find much time for writing, but he managed during 1674 to produce one of his many sermons as a book. It appeared in 1675, under the title *Light for Them That Sit in Darkness*, or "A Discourse of Jesus Christ", with the indefatigable Francis Smith again as publisher.

Before this new volume reached its public he received yet another shock, of which the results were to be more lasting than the trouble due to Agnes Beaumont.

After the official withdrawal, on 3 February, 1675, of the licences granted to the Nonconformists in 1672, both Church and State, with the monarchy now firmly under their control, proceeded to enforce the harsh laws designed for the extirpation of Dissent.

Backed as it was by the squires, and equipped with a better-trained army than the earlier Stuarts could command, this régime appeared to be unshakable. The intrigues of the King with Louis XIV and the Catholics remained hidden and no one could foresee the panic created by Titus Oates, whose invented Popish Plot was to be as effective in shaking crowns and thrones as any discovery of the real one.

In Bedford the Nonconformists were as soon made aware of the withdrawal of the licenses as they had been of the renewed Conventicle Act in 1670. Before March was far advanced, John received a secret warning that a Warrant was out for his arrest.

Signed by thirteen county magistrates and dated 4 March, 1675, this Warrant authorized the constables of Bedford to arrest "John Bunnyon of your saide towne", and bring him before any county justice for preaching repeatedly at a conventicle during the previous month. Amongst the thirteen signatories, and undoubtedly their prime mover, was John's arch-opponent, William Foster, who seemed as much in a hurry to arrange for his arrest as he had been five years earlier to surprise and fine the large conventicle at John Fenn's house.

One name which might have been there was missing. A month and four days after the issue of the Warrant, William Foster's brother-in-law, Francis Wingate, died at Harlington. When the document was drawn up he had already, perhaps, passed too near to that state in which all things shall be made known, to care any longer to pursue the tinker whose pen was to inscribe his name upon a page of history.

From the time of the friendly warning, for more than eighteen months, John remained on the run. The penalty enjoined by the Conventicle Act of 1670 was not prison but a fine, which if levied on a teacher amounted to £20 for the first offence and £40 thereafter. If he refused to pay, the law provided that the fine could be levied on his goods and chattels; only if these failed to bring in the required amount would he be put in prison.

Neither on his own account, nor on that of Elizabeth and their still dependent younger children, could John afford to pay £40 or to lose all his possessions. A warrant of seizure or distraint had to be served personally on the culprit, whose goods could not be confiscated in his absence; there was therefore no alternative but to leave Bedford for the homes of those loyal friends in other areas with whom he could remain outside the jurisdiction of the Bedfordshire county magistrates. To John Gibbs in Newport Pagnell, John Wilson at Hitchin, Luke Astwood at Gamlingay, and many others, he now looked for the help which in time of trouble was never withheld.

Three months after his departure, on 27 June, the bells of St. Paul's were rung in Bedford to celebrate the consecration of a new Bishop of Lincoln, Thomas Barlow. In London six days earlier the foundation-stone of another St. Paul's had been laid, the new Cathedral designed to rise from the ashes of the Great Fire by the genius of Christopher Wren.

In the homes of his friends John managed to write three more books, in addition to preaching to their congregations. The first, in the form of a Catechism, he called *Instructions for the Ignorant*. He added a Preface, addressed to his distant congregation, by "your affectionate brother and companion in the Kingdom and patience of Jesus Christ".

Though his little book, he wrote, was meant for the public benefit, he "being driven from you in presence, not in affection", could do no less than present it to them owing to the "special bonds which the Lord hath laid upon me to you-ward". Significantly he signed himself "yours to serve by my ministry when I can to your edification and consolation, John Bunyan".

The next publication, his twenty-first book, was entitled

Saved By Grace. In it he discoursed once more of Salvation, describing the City, the Kingdom, and the everlasting habitations where the redeemed would walk in the light of God's glory. Remembering how sadly his life before his conversion had compared even with the uncomfortable present, he consoled himself for his lost home and family by grateful reflections on the mercy of Christ.

> "O blessed Son of God! Here is grace indeed! . . . Grace to make angels wonder, grace to make sinners happy, grace to astonish devils. And what will become of them that trample under foot this son of God?"

But while he was engaged on yet another book, an expanded sermon entitled *The Strait Gate or the Great Difficulty of going to Heaven,* those whom he regarded as the tramplers were busy again. William Foster, the legalist and formalist, did not intend to be outwitted by an ignorant, wrong-headed and misguided man who nevertheless, through his tongue, pen, pastoral authority, and London contacts, exercised great influence to the disturbance of law and order. John Bunyan had foiled his initiative under the Conventicle Acts, but there was an older procedure by which the Commissary could capture his elusive prey.

Two or three years earlier, John had been presented by the Vicar and Churchwardens of St. Cuthbert's for refusing to come to Church and receive the sacrament, and was subsequently excommunicated by Dr. Fuller, Thomas Barlow's predecessor at Lincoln. William Foster himself recorded that this sentence had been passed at an earlier date upon "John Bunnion, Tinckar", Nehemiah Cox, Cordwinder, and Thomas Arthur, Pipemaker, in a volume giving details of the proceedings at the Easter and Michaelmas Visitations of the Archdeaconary of Bedford in 1674, which he and the Deputy Registrar, William Johnson, had transmitted to the Bishop.

John had been summoned to appear before the Archdeacon at his Court, but like the majority of Dissenters he did not present himself. The censure of the Church of England upon him and his kind had become a matter of routine, and he received his sentence by default.

He was of course aware that, when an offender was obstinate and ecclesiastical patience exhausted, State action might be sought on behalf of the Church Court by way of a *significavit* or "signification of excommunication". This application was sent into Chancery by the Bishop in order that the writ known as "*de excommunicato capiendo*" might be served against the delinquent. From the operations of such a writ, Anthony Harrington had been in hiding when John wrote to him on behalf of the Bedford Church in 1669.

Though John realized the possibility of arrest it did not greatly trouble him, for he knew Nonconformists who had been presented as standing excommunicate year after year without further proceedings being taken against them. The process was a chronic nuisance, like highway robbery or outbreaks of the plague. He did not allow for the fact that his friends who were familiar with the operations of the Conventicle Acts had less knowledge of ecclesiastical procedure, and would fail to warn him of this new danger.

Eighteen months after the issue of the abortive Warrant in March 1675, John was taken into custody by the Sheriff under the older legal machinery, and found himself once more in Bedford Gaol.

CHAPTER XV

THE TRACK OF A DREAM

"Who would true Valour see,
Let him come hither;
One here will Constant be,
Come Wind, come Weather.
There's no Discouragement,
Shall make him once Relent,
His first avow'd Intent,
To be a Pilgrim.

"Who so beset him round,
With dismal Stories,
Do but themselves Confound;
His Strength the more is.
No Lyon can him fright,
He'l with a Gyant Fight,
But he will have a right,
To be a Pilgrim.

"Hobgoblin, nor foul Fiend,
Can daunt his Spirit:
He knows, he at the end,
Shall Life Inherit.
Then Fancies fly away,
He'l fear not what men say,
He'l labour Night and Day,
To be a Pilgrim."

JOHN BUNYAN: *The Pilgrim's Progress*, Part II.

SHORTLY before John was taken back to his old home the County Gaol, he had finished his twenty-second book, *The Strait Gate*. This treatise was based upon the thirteenth chapter of St. Luke, verse 24, "Strive to enter in at the strait gate: for many, I say unto you, will seek to enter in, and shall not be able."

Just as *Saved by Grace* had described the raptures of the blessed, so this book completed the picture by dwelling upon the other half of the story. In it John showed how not only "the Rude and Profane, but many great Professors will come short of that

Kingdom". The book was directed against the false profession of Christian life put forward by those "that make Christ's word and his name, and his ways, a stalking-horse to their own worldly advantage".

The completion of this work left John without a current treatise to mitigate the anxiety of his new imprisonment, which he had tried so strenuously to avoid. In the enforced leisure of the gaol, his mind turned to the strange dream which had come to him in that very place, and to the allegorical narrative arising from it which he had left incomplete on his release in 1672.

He had always intended to finish that absorbing story, already entitled "*The Pilgrim's Progress from This World to That which is to Come*", but the important pastoral duties which awaited him immediately he was free again for the work of evangelism had left little time for frivolous writing. He had turned to the manuscript only during his rare hours of leisure, half conscience-stricken and half amused by the number of pages written about he "knew not what" purely for his own gratification.

The story, though still incomplete, was already longer than *Grace Abounding*, his only other work of comparable size. But that had been a serious book, in which the technique was determined by the facts.

"God did not play in convincing of me," he had written then, "wherefore I may not play in my relating of these experiences, but be plain and simple, and lay down the thing as it was."

The Pilgrim's Progress was quite different. It was a mere by-product of his strenuous existence, a fairy-tale suited only to the "vacant seasons" of relaxation that so seldom came. In it he felt entitled to use those metaphorical descriptions which the prophet Hosea had called "Similitudes".

If someone had told him that *Grace Abounding* was the record of his life and *The Pilgrim's Progress* its interpretation, John would not wholly have understood. He had merely come to believe that the original dream must have sprung from his concentration, during 1665 and 1666, upon his past experiences. Having decanted into *Grace Abounding* the sad months which he could now remember with comfort, he was able to regard himself objectively, as an allegorical figure symbolic of all sinners.

In writing a story round that figure, his half-realized purpose had been to seek and to save those that were lost, as he had once been lost himself. He was not yet quite sure what to do with the narrative, but he was beginning to hope that, somehow or other, this lighter method of treatment might reach a few souls who would not be susceptible to his message if directly approached.

Looking now through the crumpled sheets of manuscript, he recalled the thought-processes which had contributed to the beginning of his parable. Its central idea sprang directly from the age itself, with its imaginative concentration upon the familiar theme of life as a pilgrimage. If he had forgotten the allegorical tales, masques, and trials upon which his youthful imagination had fed, he would have been reminded of them by the letter of the Italian martyr, Pomponius Algerius, which Foxe had quoted:

> "In this world there is no mansion firm to me, and therefore I will travel up to the New Jerusalem, which is in Heaven, and which offereth itself to me, without paying any fine or income. Behold, I have entered already on my journey, where my house standeth for me prepared, and where I shall have riches, kinsfolks, delights, honours, never failing."

To start with, the ingredients of his story had played hide-and-seek in his mind, first seized, and immediately lost again. Then they had crowded upon him all together in a company of unsorted ideas without coherence or pattern, finally coming so thick and fast that he felt he would never work swiftly enough to get them down before they vanished. Thus far the book had written itself; his difficulty had been to catch up with the scenes and characters racing through his brain.

He never realized how different was this informal method of composition from the assiduous labours of the great writer and scholar beside whose work future literary historians were to place his own, rating each as a superlative expression of their epoch.

> "We are not afraid" [wrote Lord Macaulay in 1830] "to say that, though there were many clever men in England during the latter half of the seventeenth century, there were only two great creative minds. One of those minds produced the *Paradise Lost*, the other *The Pilgrim's Progress*."

Nothing would have surprised John Bunyan more than that impending comparison of his intriguing allegory with *Paradise Lost*, "freighted with the spoils of all the ages".

The only spoils that John could command for his Pilgrim were those of his own experience, externally so limited, yet boundless in its heights and depths of human understanding. Whenever he wanted an emotion he seemed to have known it, whether it was joy or sorrow, love or hate, hope or fear, delirious happiness or suicidal despair. Whenever he needed an individual type to embody that emotion he could find it amongst his acquaintances, who ranged all the way from the faithful friends of his own communion to the "false professors" enumerated at the end of *The Strait Gate*.

Whenever, too, he required a scene as background that scene was there, supplied by the hitherto unrealized riches of his familiar countryside. Did he want a river? He could choose from the Ivel, the Flit, the Ouzel, the Till, in addition to the Ouse itself, with its green pastures and still waters which always brought back to his mind the lovely cadences of the Twenty-third Psalm.

Did he need a castle? He had only to picture the huge grass-covered mounds at Bedford and Yelden; the silhouette of Cainhoe Castle above the Flit near the village of Clophill; the hump of Risinghoe Castle towering abrupt and solitary from the level meadows beside the Ouse at Castle Mills, four miles from Bedford between Goldington and Great Barford.

For his mountains and valleys he need look no further than the russet Barton Hills or the azure southern Downs; than Millbrook Gorge or the highway from Sharpenhoe to Streatley. For his "way . . . straight as a rule can make it" he had examples older than the memory of man in the Roman Road which linked Biggleswade and Baldock, or in Watling Street running from London through Dunstable to Fenny Stratford. Here the surface was dry only in summer; here highwaymen lay in wait for travellers in spinney and heath, like the robbers who fell upon Little-Faith; here tired pedestrians slept by the roadside, and dead criminals swung from gibbets.

Along such a road John's pilgrims walked in their rough country shoes through the woods, fields, and villages of his native

Midlands, folded within the green slopes of their gentle hills. It was true that dragons, giants and hobgoblins did not actually haunt these highways, but for them John had only to go to the chap-books and romances which had absorbed him in childhood.

Had not these monsters been the opponents of his heroes, Bevis of Southampton, George on horseback, Guy of Warwick, and the rest of the Seven Champions of Christendom, who had fought with fiends like Apollyon, and giants such as Despair and his future brethren, Slay-good and Maul? Their stories came back to him with the didactic verses of Francis Quarles's *Emblems Divine and Moral*, and the polemical allegories which he had seen so long ago in the bookshop of his dead friend, Matthias Cowley.

Mingled with these memories were the ever-present phrases of his permanent companion the Bible, which after his years in prison he now knew as a husband knows the features of his wife and a mother the bodies of her children. He was still an assiduous student of Foxe and his unlimited source-book of martyrdoms, farewell speeches, and metrical variations, but the Bible had become as an indwelling spirit with a message for every occasion.

Its words were the words of human knowledge and human need, and he was writing for men and women who knew it almost as well as he did. They could follow his loftiest theological flights because they derived the imaginative strength of their own lives from its intimate study.

Long after he and his contemporaries were dead, its beautiful familiar language would shine through *The Pilgrim's Progress* like a bright lamp in a translucent bowl. To later readers accustomed to translate their thoughts into different symbols, the poetry of the Scriptures, echoing through John Bunyan's words, would speak of the permanent values which unite in one pilgrimage all the generations of men.

If John Bunyan had seen giants and angels only with the eye of his imagination, his mortal eyes had often watched the "Countrey Birds" which were to sing hymns for Christiana outside the House Beautiful. How many evenings had he not lain awake, listening to them chirp, whistle and twitter in the wild rose-bushes which surrounded the cottage at Harrowden?

During 1676 John had thought very often of that cottage and his childhood, for in February his old father, Thomas Bunyan, the tinker of Elstow, died there and was buried on the seventh day of the month. In his Will dated 22 January, 1675,* he left from his scanty savings one shilling each to his sons John and Thomas and his daughters Mary and Elizabeth. The rest of his goods he gave to his third wife Anne, John's stepmother, who survived him for only four years; and his soul he bequeathed, in a fashion showing the fundamental sympathy between him and his eldest son,

> "into the hands of Almighty God my Maker, hoping that throug the meritorious death and passion of Jesus Christ my only Saviour and Redeemer to receive pardon for my sins".

From the time that the traveller of his dream had turned at the Cross and shown his face, John had realized that he and his pilgrim were one. Had he not already written, in *Grace Abounding*, of the burden carried by that sinful man whom he now saw as clothed in rags?

> "Thus did I wind, and twine, and shrink under the burthen that was upon me; which burthen also did so oppress me, that I could neither stand, nor go, nor lie either at rest or quiet."

The City of Destruction represented his own unconverted state, and its background was surely Elstow, where he had so often walked "solitarily in the Fields" until the words of the Gospels, symbolized by the person of Evangelist, had shown him the way to Salvation. Evangelist had come to him across that "very wide field" over which his mother, long ago, had carried him to his christening.

She had taken him through the wicket-gate, beneath the "shining light" of the lantern that hung above it. That gate had been "very strait and narrow", for it was only a smaller door within the postern-gate at the west end of Elstow Church.

The way there had been physically perilous for his mother, just as it was to prove spiritually perilous for his struggling soul; it had led her past the Slough of Despond, where Cardington Brook overflowed in winter into the reeded pool beside the pathway

*i.e. 1675–6.

through the fields. She had negotiated it safely, helped by his father, but her son the Pilgrim had fallen into it, heedless of the stepping-stones, and had begun to sink in the mire.

Who was Help, the man that had pulled him out? Surely he was Martin Luther, the writer of that *Commentary* upon St. Paul's Epistle to the Galatians which in his sad days John had found "most fit for a wounded Conscience?"

It was not until the second and third editions of his book that he was finally to introduce those composite characters, Mr. Worldly Wiseman and Mr. By-ends, but while he was making his first draft, the idea of a literary revenge upon the "false professors" whom he had known came into his mind.

They included Edward Fowler of Northill, and perhaps even Christopher Hall, who had loved his benefice better than his principles. But their prototype was the leading antagonist of all Bedford Dissenters, William Foster. John, who regarded himself as Foster's prisoner, zestfully recorded in the language of Mr. Worldly Wiseman the comments on his own ignorance made by Foster at Harlington:

> "It is happened unto thee as to other weak men, who medling with things too high for them, do suddenly fall into thy distractions."

With delight John added his final touch of ironical description: "He looked like a Gentleman, and talked much to me."

Worldly Wiseman, according to the notes that John had made, would advise Christian, the Pilgrim, to seek counsel from Mr. Legality, of the Village of Morality. John could think of several Mr. Legalities; they tended to frequent police-courts and prisons. The one in his mind bore at least a family likeness to the well-intentioned Clerk of the Peace, Paul Cobb, who had found a tender conscience such a puzzling phenomenon.

Immediately he put into the mouth of Evangelist some words that he often wished he had said to the Clerk: "Ye cannot be justified by the works of the Law; for by the deeds of the Law no man living can be rid of his Burden."

His dream, in the inconsequential fashion of dreams, had suddenly left Elstow for the neighbourhood of Risinghoe Castle,

BUNYAN OLD MEETING

From an old print. Built in 1707 on the site of Josias Ruffhead's barn, which was Bunyan's church after his release from prison in 1672.

THE BUNYAN MEETING HOUSE, BEDFORD

On the site of the Old Meeting. The sundial in the Garden of Remembrance is a Tercentenary Memorial erected in 1928.

which had always seemed to John to resemble Mount Sinai. But now he was back at the wicket-gate beneath the shadow of Elstow steeple, that Castle of Beelzebub with its tempting bells whence the Devil shot arrows at unwary travellers. Good-will, from the Bedford Meeting, let him in through the gate before the arrows could fall, and, thanks to his help, John found himself, as Christian, at the House of the Interpreter.

He knew that House, of course. In his dreams for the past twenty years he had returned again and again to the Old Rectory to discuss the mysteries of God with John Gifford, just as each of us returns to his or her Interpreter with the appreciation born of growing wisdom. Sometimes that remarkable man had talked to him plainly, but he had also spoken in parables, using a dusty room, a burning fire, or a stately palace like Elstow Place, to illustrate his theme.

Above them as they talked had hung the picture of old Andrew Dennys, but though it was still in its former place, the subject had changed. It now represented "a very grave Person", and this, wrote John, "was the fashion of it, It had Eyes lifted up to Heaven, the best of Books in his hand, the Law of Truth was written upon its lips, the World was behind his Back; it stood as if it pleaded with Men".

In his dream he looked more closely at the portrait, and its face seemed to be the face of Christ, his Lord.

As he left the Interpreter's House John remembered "holy Mr. Gifford" with gratitude, and before continuing the story inscribed some verses to his honour.

> Here I have seen things rare and profitable,
> Things pleasant, dreadful, things to make me stable
> In what I have begun to take in hand:
> Then let me think on them, and understand
> Wherefore they shew'd me were, and let me be
> Thankful, O good Interpreter, to thee.

It was inevitable that the knowledge and faith he had learnt from the Interpreter should carry the Pilgrim straight to the Cross, where the consciousness of atonement had come to him so many years ago and he had again found himself when first he dreamed his dream. Remembering how the young preacher had wept before the monument at Stevington, he felt tears pricking his eyeballs as he described those moments which lay for him at the heart of religious experience:

> "He ran thus till he came at a Place somewhat ascending; and upon that place stood a Cross, and a little below in the bottom, a Sepulchre. So I saw in my Dream, that just as Christian came up with the Cross, his Burden loosed from off his Shoulders, and fell from off his Back, and began to tumble; and so continued to do, till it came to the mouth of the Sepulchre, where it fell in, and I saw it no more.
>
> Then was Christian glad and lightsome, and said with a merry heart, He hath given me Rest, by his Sorrow; and Life, by his Death. Then he stood still a while, to look and wonder; for it was very surprizing to him, that the sight of the Cross should thus ease him of his Burden. He looked therefore, and looked again, even till the springs that were in his Head sent the Waters down his Cheeks. Now as he stood looking and weeping, behold three shining ones came to him. . . ."

The shining ones seemed suddenly real, illuminating his cell with that golden light which had fallen upon the Cross from a sunset radiance too bright for mortal eyes. Time vanished in the glory of their presence, and another day had come when he found himself again turning the pages of his manuscript. He had left the valley below Stevington Church, where he had found Simple, Sloth and Presumption fast asleep near the Holy Well, and Formalist and Hypocrisie had come tumbling over the wall. Now he was in a different part of the country, looking towards Hill Difficulty, "at the bottom of which was a Spring".

Here, with the heights of the Greensand Ridge above him, he saw "the way which is called Danger" that led unwary travellers to the left of the true path into a thick wood. Opposite, on the right, a similar side-road turned into the field called Destruction, which in his dream was filled with the dark mountains that had terrified him as a young soldier waiting in Chester to go to Ireland.

Midway up the hill, a pleasant Arbor tempted unwary Christian to sleep; it was part of the garden of Ampthill House, that "very stately Palace . . . the name of which was Beautiful".

Yet, strangely enough, the Palace was inhabited by four nuns from Elstow Abbey, who made him welcome when he had braved the lions, and gave him a bed "in a large upper Chamber, whose Window opened towards the Sun-rising".

He recognized that Chamber called Peace; had he not humbly practised his trade there? On the way up to it he had enviously observed those "Records of the greatest Antiquity", containing "the pedigree of the Lord of the hill", which Discretion, Prudence, Piety and Charity now showed to Christian. But still better he knew the prospect from its windows.

As long as he could remember, John had seen hills to the south whenever he lifted up his eyes. From the Harrowden cottage on the level fields and the open village street at Elstow, they had been the dark-blue slopes of the Greensand Ridge. But from the top storey of Ampthill House he had looked on the loftier Chilterns, rising like Delectable Mountains above the dark oaks and firs of Ampthill woods.

Immediately below the Palace windows lay Ampthill town, and beyond it Flitwick Moor and the Vale of the Flit, where it was "an hard matter to go down into the Valley of Humiliation". Here, in the shape of Apollyon, Christian met the formidable Satan of John's turbulent years, and John bade his final farewell to that dark period in his closing description of the battle.

> "In this combat no man can imagine, unless he had seen and heard, as I did, what yelling and hideous roaring Apollyon made all the time of the fight, he spake like a Dragon: and on the other side, what sighs and groans burst from Christians heart. I never saw him all the while give so much as one pleasant look, till he perceived he had wounded Apollyon with his two edg'd Sword, then indeed he did smile, and look upward; but 'twas the dreadfullest sight that ever I saw."

At the end of this valley lay another, which John brought for his purpose from the farther side of the Greensand Ridge.

A similar valley had been known to St. Andrew, one of the Seven Champions, as the Vale of Walking Spirits. John called it the Valley of the Shadow of Death, after the Twenty-third Psalm, though to the local villagers it was only Millbrook Gorge.

Here danced the Hobgoblins, Satyrs and Dragons of the Pit, howling and spreading confusion before the Pilgrim struggling through pitch darkness to keep his footing between the "very deep ditch" on the right hand, and the "very dangerous Quagg" on the left.

Here too was the wicked one who "whisperingly suggested many grievous blasphemies to him, which he verily thought had proceeded from his own mind". Thus sanely John recognized the character of his past psychological troubles, and compassionately bestowed upon Christian the consolation which he, in his own Valley of Shadows, had sought in vain. During the terrible months before he knew John Gifford he had been quite alone, but Christian, like himself on the stormy evening in Millbrook churchyard, heard a comrade's voice uttering words of comfort through the darkness.

"Though I walk through the Valley of the shadow of Death, I will fear none ill, for thou art with me."

John thought he recognized that voice, but before Christian could catch up with its owner, he had to pass the Cave of Giants Pope and Pagan at the end of the Valley.

"I have learnt since," continued John,

> "that Pagan has been dead many a day, and as for the other, though he be yet alive, he is by reason of age . . . grown so crazy and stiff in his joynts, that he can now do little more than sit in his Caves mouth, grinning at Pilgrims as they go by."

This paragraph, the only expression of denominational prejudice that John permitted himself throughout *The Pilgrim's Progress*, was true enough at the time that he wrote it, though the old fear of "Giant Pope" was to be revived almost immediately by Titus Oates. The far-reaching claims of the Papacy were now archaic; Catholic as well as Protestant had been freed from them by the Reformation. Its influence rested, as it rests today, upon persuasion rather than power. With its authority had gone the medieval dream of human unity, half political, half ecclesiastical, never again to be revived in a form which commanded world-wide allegiance until the brief hour of the doomed League of Nations.

Giant Pagan was less dead than John supposed, but even his prophetic gifts could hardly have been expected to foresee the day when, over large sections of the earth, religion would be regarded as "the opium of the people", and the followers of Marx and Lenin would become the subtle enemies of his work and values. He would have been still more surprised to learn that Catholics would one day read his writings with joy, and twentieth-century critics discern a relationship between his allegory and the medieval Catholic conception of the Pilgrimage of the Soul.

At the end of the valley, Christian caught up with Faithful. In his dream John had watched how "they went very lovingly on together; and had sweet discourse of all things that had hapned to them in their Pilgrimage".

Who was Faithful? Like other interpreters of life in fiction, John could never quite decide. Looking back upon his own story, and remembering those friends with whom he had pursued so many adventures and shared so many risks, he experimented with new forms of literary invention which were to become familiar to his followers in the field of the English novel.

His native artistry instinctively rejected the wholesale appropriation of a character from life. He recalled John Gibbs, and John Burton, and Stephen Hawthorn of Stevington, and William Dell. Most clearly he remembered young John Donne of Pertenhall, who had already passed on before him; John Donne with whom he had so often held "sweet discourse" during their years together in prison.

Despite their differences—and William Dell, with his controversial scholarly mind and uncompromising speech, was especially distinguished from the others—they shared the readiness to be faithful unto death. One and all had their part in Faithful, and in drawing him John was depicting them.

When he started to think of the enemies of the Lord who obstructed Christian on his journey, it became more tempting—as he was to find in creating Mr. Worldly Wiseman and Mr. By-ends—to take models direct from life. Talkative, of course, was not unique; there were plenty of Talkatives among Bedford tradesmen and the occupants of Bedfordshire pulpits. Dr. Lindall of Harlington, that "old enemy to the truth", was one of them, and he himself, in the complacent months before his conversion, had been another. It was Talkative whom Christian and Faithful encountered now on their way to Vanity Fair; "a tall man, and something more comely at a distance than at hand".

In Vanity Fair John found himself on ground all too familiar; had not those vanities and that meretricious merchandise been part of his earliest memories? He would have thought Elstow Fair the biggest ever known if he had not once happened to go to Cambridge at the time of Stourbridge Fair, the oldest in England which went back to Carausius, Roman Emperor in Britain from A.D. 287 to 293.

This fair, subsequently judged by Defoe, now a youth of eighteen, to be the greatest in medieval Europe, was annually proclaimed by the Vice-Chancellor of Cambridge University and opened in great state by the Mayor and other members of the City Corporation. It was abolished only in July 1934 by Home Office decree, having become a forlorn affair of whelk stalls, cheapjacks, and swing boats. Its decay had begun after the Renaissance but it was still famous in the seventeenth century.

As soon as the corn had been cleared from the fields on the banks of the River Cam, the merchants of many trades—goldsmiths, hatters, milliners, haberdashers, mercers, braziers, drapers, and toy-men—began to set up their booths ready for the official opening on 24 August. In the centre of the main square rose a great maypole, surrounded by taverns, coffee-houses, music-halls, conjuring-booths, wild animals, dwarfs, giants, monsters, and rope-dancers.

A number of special fairs were set out each on its own pitch; these included the Leather Fair, the Horse Fair, the Hop Fair, and the Wool Fair, where wool manufacturers did remunerative business. The Oyster Fair and the eating houses on Fish Hill carried on an enormous trade for weeks in Colchester oysters and fresh herrings. Throughout the Fair a Court of Justice with its "great one"—the Mayor of Cambridge or his deputy—sat to settle disputes and keep the peace.

Such disputes were part of the common gossip which then made up the bulk of the news. John Bunyan had never read the adventures of Ben Jonson's two Puritans, in which one satirically known as "Zeal of the Land Busy" was put in the stocks for upsetting a basket of gingerbread. But he had seen swindlers in the stocks at Elstow Fair; and Puritans, whether named Zeal or Faithful, were liable to encounter similar mischances amid the worldlings taking their pleasures at fairs. Like George Fox who preached against the "deceitful merchandise" at Lancaster Market, they were themselves sometimes a source of provocation.

John had a cage all ready for Christian and Faithful in Vanity Fair. It resembled the village cage or "lock-up" standing against the church wall at Wootton, and was shaped like that similar small prison which later generations would call an air-raid shelter and enter voluntarily. There was also a Court-house at the Fair, with a family likeness to the Chapel of Herne; and a Judge called Hategood who favoured Sir John Kelynge, though Francis Wingate and Sir Thomas Twisden had contributed some of his qualities.

Lord Hategood was prophetic as well as reminiscent. Later generations were to find in him a forecast of Judge Jeffries conducting the trials of Alice Lisle, who was to die cruelly during the "Bloody Assize" of 1685 for sheltering fugitives after Monmouth's rebellion, and of ageing Richard Baxter, who in the same year complained in print of his colleagues' persecutions and was denounced by the Judge as "an old rogue, a hypocritical knave".

No one knew better than John Bunyan how to satirize contemporary trials, those legalistic mummeries which so often were merely "the predicament that precedes death". He had read of them during his youth in the old anti-Catholic pamphlet of 1547 called *The Examination of the Mass*, and in *The Isle of Man*, published in 1627 by the Puritan divine Richard Bernard of Batcombe, which described "the Legal Proceedings in Manshire against Sin".

The current processes of English "justice" had thus been familiar to him before he was himself trapped into a "confession" of guilt. His memories of that experience were keen as he made Lord Hategood pass his verdict on Faithful—"For the Treason he hath confessed, he deserveth to die the death"—and then sentence him to the fate of John Huss, though he had only argued with the Judge and expressed uncomplimentary opinions about Vanity Fair.

Faithful's creator would have been dumbfounded to learn that the enlightened men and women born three hundred years later than himself would witness, in totalitarian States, similar parodies of justice. The accusers of his day had not achieved that quintessence of devilment which deprives the prisoner of his true personality; hence he was able to give to Faithful's self-defence a quality of drama unattainable in bogus "confessions".

Macaulay referred to Judge Jeffries—in whom, as in Lord Hategood, "all the vices sat"—as a long-vanished phenomenon. Today we recognize Hategood again in the person of Gauleiter and Commissar, and realize once more the relationship of the particular to the universal.

After Vanity Fair, Christian's journey to the Celestial City was to be straightforward except for the alarming episode in Doubting Castle and the humiliating intervention of the Flatterer. When he went astray his troubles would be due to his own pride and stupidity, for by now John Bunyan understood himself too well to paint Christian as the perfect embodiment of religious aspiration.

In a few months he would be fifty years old, and knew that Mr. Would-be Goodman had his own special temptations, far subtler and less easily recognized than the unresisted temptations of Mr. Badman. He was liable to over-confidence, self-righteousness, spiritual pride, and to easy deception by plausible rogues; he was even capable, at times, of being vain, discursive, and worldly. He had also become susceptible to a contrary type of temptation, in those bitter moods of sudden despondency which come with the consciousness that youth's golden vision of achievement will never be fully realized, and are the bane of middle age.

John had to make sure that Christian, now more than half-way through his journey, did not fall victim to suicidal despair. So from the ashes of Faithful, who "died to bear Testimony to the Truth", he created for Christian a young man called Hopeful to be his new companion.

Hopeful was definitely a member of the rising generation. In drawing his portrait John remembered his own two sons, John, who was destined to be a member of Bedford Meeting for forty-five years, and Thomas, now just under twenty. He thought too of the younger members of his congregation; and again of John Donne, who had always been so hopeful in prison, though his strength, and not John Bunyan's, had failed through its hardships. Together they all fused into one symbolic picture of youth, to take the place of the friend whom he and Christian had lost.

It was at this point that John, in his third edition, introduced Mr. By-ends and his calculating acquaintances. He also caused him to describe his rich relatives, first cousins to the Wingates of Harlington, though his great-grandfather "was but a Waterman, looking one way and rowing another".

With a zest in which exuberance rather than malice was the chief ingredient, John put into the mouth of Mr. By-ends yet further words which might have been spoken by William Foster, "I always had the luck to jump in my judgment with the present way of the times, whatever it was, and my chance was to get thereby." But it was Edward Fowler of Northill who supplied the example of the Minister, described by Mr. Money-love, who became "extraordinary zealous in some points of Religion, that he meddled not with before".

> "Suppose a Minister, a worthy man, possessed but of a very small Benefice and has in his eye a greater, more fat and plump by far; he has also now an opportunity of getting of it; yet so as by being more studious, by preaching more frequently, and zealously, and because the temper of the people requires it, by altering of some of his principles, for my part, I see no reason but a man may do this . . . and yet be an honest man."

Before John invented this company of adaptable turncoats for his own entertainment, he carried Christian and Hopeful over the "delicate Plain called Ease", which "was but narrow", and wore the smiling face of Flitwick Moor with its summer adornment of stitchwort and saxifrage. Near by, on a "little hill" rising from the smooth ground, stood the village of Pulloxhill, where the prevalence of shining yellow talc suggested gold to the credulous. The Rev. Thomas Cox, writing between 1711 and 1717, actually reported that a gold mine had been discovered there "about twenty years ago".

Avoiding temptation from the hill called Lucre and the silver mine of Demas, Christian and Hopeful passed the old monument in the shape of a woman significantly inscribed "Remember Lot's wife", and found themselves at rest beside "the River of the Water of Life".

This "pleasant River", and the meadow "curiously beautified with Lillies" which "was green all the year long", embodied for John his earliest memories of afternoons spent fishing with Margaret on the banks of the Ouse. But he could not allow Christian and Hopeful to linger there long; all too soon they were straying down the track which led past the "Ould Ruines" to By-path Meadow and the mound of Bedford Castle, which was also the habitation of Giant Despair.

This time the Ouse betrayed the Pilgrims by its disconcerting winter habit of rising suddenly and flooding its banks; "the waters rose amain", and caused Christian and Hopeful to be captured by Giant Despair and trapped in the dungeon of Doubting Castle. But thanks to Hopeful's optimism and the key called Promise which Christian plucked from his bosom, they escaped "out of his Jurisdiction", and were compensated by reaching, at long last, the Delectable Mountains seen from Ampthill House.

The Chilterns, soaring to their full height immediately south of Dunstable, were bare of the gardens and orchards which stretched at their feet. But "fountains of water" gushed in vigorous streams from their chalky slopes where the anemone pulsatilla, or Pasque flower, blossomed in spring, and in autumn, when the summer orchids were over, the bellflowers and gentians grew.

At Tottenhoe, east of Dunstable, the quarries of brown sandy stone beneath the lower chalk formed a door in the side of a hill, "very dark and smoaky" within. This John recognized immediately as the By-way to Hell, "that Hypocrites go in at" and "such as sell their Master with Judas". Not far away were the "tombs" which Christian and Hopeful perceived from the Mountain named Caution. John had known from his boyhood those wind-swept tumuli or buried mounds of an older civilization, where walked the blind victims of Giant Despair.

On the descending slopes of the mountains, after their dazzling glimpse of the Celestial City through a "Perspective Glass" from the top of the high hill called Clear, John had left his Pilgrims when he was released from prison in 1672. He had dismissed them in a brief phrase, "So I awoke from my Dream", but again and again during that interval of perilous freedom, he had turned back to reconsider the early stages of their progress.

Now he realized that, if his allegory was ever to be finished, their journey must end. It must also end quickly, with less attention to detail than he had been able to give to the story during the long months of his first imprisonment, since plans were already on foot for his release.

In London his good friend, Dr. John Owen, had promised to approach the Bishop of Lincoln on his behalf. There were other colleagues, such as George Cokayn of Cotton End, now preacher to an Independent community in Red Cross Street within the parish of St. Giles, Cripplegate, who would help him to fulfil the formalities required by the law. They would find two Nonconformist sympathizers who would undertake to go to the Bishop and offer a cautionary bond, on the strength of which John could be set free.

"And I slept," he wrote, "and dreamed again, and saw the same two Pilgrims going down the Mountains along the High-way, towards the City."

Here they encountered Ignorance, that deadly foe of John's tumultuous youth, who came upon the highroad from "a little crooked Lane". When they had shaken him off they passed along the very dark track in which they met the man whom seven Devils had bound with seven strong Cords, and were carrying to the door in the side of the hill at Tottenhoe. Close to this place was Dead-man's Lane, where Little-Faith encountered the misadventure which Christian related to Hopeful; the name came into John's head with the memory of Deadman's Corner close to Deadman's Cross, at the top of Hanger Hill on the highroad from Bedford to London.

On the Delectable Mountains the shepherds had warned them to avoid the toils of the Flatterer, a false Apostle, but they turned once more from the way, and received severe chastisement from Evangelist for becoming entangled in his net.

John remembered that lesson to the end of his life. In London, shortly before his death, a friend complimented him after a service on the "sweet sermon" which he had delivered.

"Aye," said John. "You need not remind of that, for the Devil told me of it before I was out of the pulpit."

This encounter and the meeting with Atheist, whose features bore a remote likeness to John's former Elstow friend Harry, were the last of the Pilgrims' severe trials until they reached the banks of the River. A long theological discussion carried them over the Enchanted Ground, in which the air of the plain, after the sharp, clean atmosphere of the heights, seemed as heavy as the air of the Enchanted Garden belonging to the Magician Ormandine in the story of the Champion, St. David.

Their method of keeping themselves awake seems strange to the twentieth-century traveller, but in John's day it was a customary form of diversion. In his Introduction to the 1898 edition of *The Pilgrim's Progress*, Sir Charles Firth referred to the autobiography of Ellwood, the Quaker, who described how he and his friend Ovy made a journey to Stokenchurch to learn the principles of Quakerism from Isaac Pennington, and "having taken some refreshment and rest at Wycombe, went on cheerfully in the afternoon, entertaining each other with grave and religious discourse which made the walk easier".

During their own conversation, Hopeful related to Christian the story of his conversion, which owed much to the author's experience.

> "One day I was very sad, I think sadder than at any one time of my life, and this sadness was through a fresh sight of the greatness and vileness of my Sins: And as I was then looking for nothing but hell, and the everlasting damnation of my Soul, suddenly, as I thought, I saw the Lord Jesus look down from Heaven upon me, and saying, Believe on the Lord Jesus Christ, and thou shalt be saved.
>
> But I Replied: Lord, I am a great, a very great sinner. And he answered, My Grace is sufficient for thee . . ."

So talking of their spiritual adventures they came through the Enchanted Ground into the land of Beulah, where they were within sight of the City. Here they heard continually the singing of birds, as John had heard them in childhood in the Ellenbury Woods; they saw every day the flowers appear in the earth, as the violets and celandines had appeared in past Aprils beside the spring at the end of the field outside Thomas Bunyan's cottage.

Now they had passed beyond the Valley of the Shadow, for in that country the sun shone night and day, and the Shining Ones commonly walked there because it lay upon the borders of Heaven. But though they were near the gates of the City, the dark River of Death stretched between.

How often John had crossed the facsimile of that river, mist-ridden and black in the deep nights of winter as he walked home to his cottage after preaching at Haynes or Cotton End! But he had come over it by the Great Bridge; Christian and Hopeful must struggle through the cold engulfing flood which his own soul would traverse in the final stage of its journey. By those waters the chapel where Offa, King of Mercia, lay buried had been swept away, but John knew that in the end, like Christian and Hopeful, he would pass through them and inherit eternal life within the walls of the City where his Pilgrims now stood.

He wrote of that City one Sunday evening in late spring, with the watchman's horn sounding from the Bridge, and the bells of St. Paul's chiming so loudly that their melody seemed to pour like liquid music through the narrow window of his cell. The watchman was the Trumpeter who "saluted Christian and his Fellow with ten thousand welcomes from the World", and the sound of the bells accompanied the Heavenly Host which came out to meet the Pilgrims with harps and crowns, saying "Holy, holy, holy is the Lord."

John laid down his pen and listened, but the Bedford streets outside the gaol were silent. Afterwards he never knew whether the chimes of St. Paul's had really echoed through the quiet town, or whether, like Christian, he had escaped from prison into his dream, and heard all the bells of the Celestial City ringing for joy.

In the manuscript which John Bunyan had just completed, he had made Bedfordshire's homely villages and peaceful streams shine with the light of heaven itself, and had turned the life of an ordinary man struggling to overcome his daily temptations into a journey as heroic as Jason's quest for the Golden Fleece.

He had finished the first half of a task which later generations were to acclaim as the supreme example of unconscious achievement, for he neither knew nor cared that at a single step he had created the English novel, with its long history and infinite variety. Still less did it matter to him that, in time to come, he would be an honoured member of those "English Men of Letters" whose contemporary representatives were either to remain genuinely unaware of him or to display ostentatious indifference.

His sole purpose was to bring sinners to repentance; to conduct "the weak and tempted people of God", for whose benefit he had already published *Grace Abounding*, on a pilgrimage through the wilderness of this world to the glory of that which is to come. A naturally tolerant man living in an age of intolerance, he might have written, like his successor, William Morris, in "An Apology" for *The Earthly Paradise*:

> Dreamer of dreams, born out of my due time,
> Why should I strive to set the crooked straight?

But in fact he would never have written it. To set the crooked straight was exactly what he regarded as his job. The dreaming of dreams was a side-track, a by-product, a way of enduring the tedium of prison. Not until the end of his life, when practice had made him an adept in the art that he never realized he had mastered, was the sheer delight of telling a story to run away with him, and cause him, in the second part of *The Pilgrim's Progress*, occasionally to forget his moral intentions.

None the less, as he wrought that unrecognized miracle in his cell above the gateway of the County Gaol, his creative mind subconsciously obeyed the simple inspired rules laid down for themselves by the artists of all generations. Later he described his instinctive obedience to them in lines claiming confidence in his powers of expression:

> thine only way
> Before them all, is to say out thy say
> In thine own native language, which no man
> Now useth, nor with ease dissemble can.

The charm of that "native language", as he employed it, lay in simplicity of writing combined with wealth of imagery.

Disraeli called John Bunyan "the Spenser of the people", but Macaulay insisted with truth that *The Pilgrim's Progress*—unlike *The Holy War*—was completely free from the tediousness which pervaded *The Faerie Queene*.

In the long involved allegories which preceded John Bunyan's, the characters—Justice, Temperance, Courtesy, and the rest—were bloodless abstractions arousing no response in the reader. But for John these characters lived and breathed, pulsating with energy and emotion because he had known them in his own experience. Faithful, Discretion, Talkative, Hate-good, Hopeful, were universal types embodied in particular persons who became as real to his readers as the neighbours they met in the street.

It was this linking of religious allegory with realistic character-drawing which made John Bunyan what Rudyard Kipling called him,

> The Father of the Novel,
> Salvation's first Defoe,

and caused Macaulay to perceive as the highest miracle of genius "that things which are not should be as though they were". John gave, he said, "to the abstract the reality of the concrete".

The temptations of his Pilgrims were as audible and visible as his own temptations described in *Grace Abounding*; Satan had been experienced as a hand plucking at his garments, just as the Old Adam tweaks Faithful's flesh. Their hope and faith, symbolized by the Delectable Mountains and the Celestial City, were as concrete as the salvation which he had once seen as adorned with golden seals. Even their capacity for exhorting each other in homiletic idiom was a human attribute; the idiom, like the opportunity, changes, but our belief that we can improve our neighbour by treating him as a public meeting does not.

John Bunyan took the vocabulary of the common people and made it into the language of the literary artist, who says exactly what he wants to say in words which all readers can understand. Like Dante in fourteenth-century Italy and Hu Shih in twentieth-century China, he transformed the strong, homely speech of everyday life into a vehicle of superlative art.

That art, unlike the work of lesser writers with one eye on the main chance, was always passionately sincere, with the sincerity of those to whom the conviction is everything and the consequences are nothing. It moved with the simple and lovely power of the Authorized Version of the Bible, which itself had embodied the language of the humble at its best.

John's work was to remain significant for generations to come because it could be accepted, not as the product, in Bernard Shaw's words, "of a Tinker's theology", but as the testimony of a Christian whose blindness was the blindness of his age, but whose human insight, which deepened as he grew older, was determined by values that made it true for all time.

In the phraseology of a contemporary judgment, he was "accomplished with an excellent discerning of persons", and also with the ability to assess the significance of spiritual experience. His journey was the journey of all seekers after righteousness, who cry, in John Masefield's words,

> Friends and loves we have none, nor wealth nor blessed abode,
> But the hope of the City of God at the other end of the road.

It is ironic to reflect that, if the story of that journey were published today, one school of critics would probably regard it as unworthy to enter the literary category which it created. Their repudiation would not have troubled John Bunyan. His sense of mission was so strong that, as Professor J. W. Mackail has shown, it made him forego a happy ending to his story, since he had to dispose of Ignorance who, however plausible, is the root of all sin.

In getting rid of him to his own satisfaction, John would neither have been flattered by Professor Mackail's description of this conclusion as "tremendous", nor disturbed by the contrary criticism that the episode comes as an anti-climax after the piling up of tension and exaltation.

John Bunyan resembled the draughtsman who designs a poster for a propagandist organization, and is found to have produced, by accident, a work of genius. So compelling is that genius, and so unfashionable today the idea that art and moral purpose can effectively be combined, that the fundamental truth of his "message" is easy to overlook.

Yet it stands, a part of our religious heritage, the same

yesterday, today, and for ever. In the story of the Pilgrim, whether we call him Christian or John Bunyan, the Puritan struggle for freedom of worship merges into the eternal struggle of man to find unity with God, and becomes, in the widest and deepest sense, the epic of the soul.

On 21 June, 1677, a cautionary bond was drawn up on John Bunyan's behalf and offered to Dr. Thomas Barlow, Bishop of Lincoln. The two sureties in whose name it was drawn were London Nonconformists living in the parish of St. Giles, Cripplegate.

One, Thomas Kelsey, had been present in Hitchin on 29 March that same year, when John Wilson was established as pastor at the Tilehouse Street Chapel. The other, Robert Blaney, was a former associate of Oliver Cromwell, and from 1654 to 1662 had acted as Clerk to the Haberdashers' Company.

These two colleagues entertained no illusions that John Bunyan, who had refused to conform for nearly twenty years, would do so in six months; nor would they have wished that he should. They merely assumed that he would not strain toleration to its utmost limits, and believed that, if he behaved as reasonably as he had always done towards the members of other denominations, nothing further was likely to happen.

In this belief they were justified. The authorities had grown weary of their failure to regulate John's conscience by Act of Parliament, and Bedford Corporation contained influential members who shared, or at least sympathized with, his opinions. He was destined, too, for an early and swift success which would eclipse even the impression made by *Grace Abounding*. For one reason or another, no one cared to attack him again after his second imprisonment.

The triumph of *The Pilgrim's Progress* had not been, however, a foregone conclusion. Before his release, John read the manuscript to some of his fellow prisoners. Amongst them, as usual, were several Nonconformists; they included John Wheeler from Cranfield, and a young man from Kensworth, Thomas Marsom, who was later to become pastor of the Park Street Church at Luton.

Joseph Middleton
1784

THE

Pilgrim's Progreſs

FROM

THIS WORLD,

TO

That which is to come:

Delivered under the Similitude of a

DREAM

Wherein is Diſcovered,
The manner of his ſetting out,
His Dangerous Journey; And ſafe
Arrival at the Deſired Countrey.

I have uſed Similitudes, Hoſ. 12. 10.

By *John Bunyan.*

Licenſed and Entred according to Order.

LONDON,
Printed for *Nath. Ponder* at the *Peacock*
in the *Poultrey* near *Cornhil*, 1678.

Title-Page of *The Pilgrim's Progress*, First Edition.

When John had finished reading there was a difference of opinion, one or two listeners maintaining that it was unbecoming and dangerous in a Christian to reduce religion to the level of a romance. At first young Marsom agreed with the critics, but he asked John if he might borrow the manuscript and read it by himself. By the time that he finished it he had changed his mind, and strongly advised John to publish the story.

In his "Authors Apology for his Book", John subsequently recorded this conflicting counsel and his own decision.

> Well, when I had thus put my ends together,
> I shew'd them others, that I might see whether
> They would condemn them, or them justifie:
> And some said, let them live; some let them die:
> Some said, John, Print it; others said, not so:
> Some said it might do good; others said, no.
> Now was I in a straight; and did not see
> Which was the best thing to be done by me:
> At last I thought, since you are thus divided,
> I print it will, and so the case decided.

And print it he did. After a rapid revision in the midst of his renewed pastoral duties, he put his allegory into the hands of his publisher, Nathaniel Ponder, at the Peacock in the Poultry. This colleague subsequently acquired the nickname of "Bunyan Ponder" owing to the great prosperity which the manuscript brought him.

It was registered at Stationer's Hall on 22 December, 1677, licensed on 18 February, 1678, and forthwith published in a small octavo volume of 328 pages at 1*s*. 6*d*. Its success was immediate, astonishing no one so much as John himself. A second edition appeared the same year, and a third in 1679. Eleven editions, amounting to 100,000 copies, an enormous sale for the seventeenth century, had been issued by the time of John's death in 1688.

In the second and third editions he added not only Mr. Worldly Wiseman and Mr. By-ends, but Christian's explanation of his reasons for leaving his wife and children. Some seventeenth-century readers, like certain twentieth-century poets, had not perceived the difference between an allegorical and a real departure; they had failed to distinguish the fear of physical danger from the dread of spiritual death. Threatened by the one, we stay with our beloved; driven by the other, we are compelled to part company with them if their perception of truth falls short of our own.

Other later additions included the confession to Goodwill at the wicket gate, the discourse with Discretion and her companions at the Palace Beautiful, Apollyon's oath "by my infernal Den!" and the provision of a wife called Diffidence for Giant Despair. To make the work more serious, John removed some of his trenchant marginal comments—"O brave Talkative!" "Christian snibbeth his fellow"—which the editors of later generations were to replace.

In July 1926 one of the only four known copies of the first edition was sold by public auction for £6,800. By that time John Bunyan, who never owned one hundredth part of such a sum, had graduated through two-and-a-half centuries into the company of the immortals.

And there, despite the resurrection of Giant Pagan, he seems likely to remain.

CHAPTER XVI

THE YEARS OF TRIUMPH

"O! that I could mourn for England, and for the sins that are committed therein . . . It is the duty of those that can, to cry out against this deadly plague, yea, to lift up their voice as with a Trumpet against it. . . . Now God Almighty give his people Grace, not to hate or malign Sinners, nor yet to choose any of their wayes, but to keep themselves pure from the blood of all men, by speaking and doing according to that Name and those Rules that they profess to know, and love; for Jesus Christs sake."

JOHN BUNYAN: *The Life and Death of Mr. Badman.*

WHEN John was released for the last time from Bedford Gaol, he faced ten more years of life which, in contrast to the half-century that he had already seen, were to be as tranquil and satisfying for himself as they were to prove ominous and stormy for England.

That last decade had its ups and downs, of course. It was to bring forth individuals who, like the rascally John Wildman of his own Bedford congregation, again sought to scandalize his name. Its political conflagrations were also to break out into new flames of persecution, short-lived but as intense as any that he had known, which would again intermittently cast the shadow of prison across the autumn sunshine of his closing days.

But taken as a whole, those years, illumined by the instant success of *The Pilgrim's Progress* and the demand that it created for his other work, were marked by a rising crescendo of triumph. His fame had spread far beyond Bedford; at least annually he made long visits to London, and went on perpetual circuit to other parts of England. He travelled on horseback over roads which, though they were still muddy and full of potholes, took him across a countryside whose face had gradually but perceptibly changed in the five decades that he remembered.

Large areas of heath and moorland which had been wild in

his youth were gradually coming under cultivation; the thick forests were slowly shrinking as more trees were felled to provide new buildings for scattered but steadily developing towns. The gardens of the wealthy landowners grew more formal and exotic as the long carriage-drives bordered with native oaks and elms were replaced by the avenues of limes and horse-chestnuts which had become fashionable under Charles II. The severity of the churchyards, with their grey tombstones beneath dark implacable yews, softened as the newly planted cedars and sycamores sprang from the mould to share the vigil of the older trees.

John's colossal energy had never stirred him to any ambition for worldly possessions. Like the shepherd-boy whom Christiana and her fellow-pilgrims were to meet in the Valley of Humiliation, he was content with what he had. His first biographer wrote of him, "He was not a man that preached by way of bargain for money, for he hath refused a more plentiful income to keep his station." When he was not preaching, teaching and travelling, his time was spent upon activities which, in all centuries, have brought gain to others rather than their performers.

Though letter-writing had not yet become general, his correspondence was so large that the disappearance of all his letters apart from those recorded in the Church Book has puzzled his biographers. Many of these letters dealt with the needs of Nonconformists outside Bedford and the reconciliation of differences between "Professors" of the Gospel.

To this correspondence were added the supervision of his own community, the keeping of Minutes, the constant preparation of sermons, and the transcription of the best as books or pamphlets. During his final decade John produced, in one form or another, thirty-six pieces of publishable writing, of which only two have apparently never been printed.

Not all these publications were works worthy of remembrance. Perhaps only one, the Second Part of *The Pilgrim's Progress*, was a great work of literature, and only two others were to join the miscellaneous and unpredictable ranks of the classics; but each made its contribution to that task of soul-salvation which in John's eyes was so much more important than literary achievement. His mind was a flood-tide perpetually overflowing with ideas; his energy sprang from the vitality common to most men and women of genius, who find pleasure in nothing so much as in work, and relax only with reluctance.

After the publication of *The Pilgrim's Progress*, this quality of genius was recognized by discriminating representatives of the book trade, whose judgment, in those days as in these, is often sounder than that of circles which would now be called "high-brow". One such bookseller and printer, John Bagford, born in 1650, collected books on commission and hunted up title-pages and lost sections to restore imperfect copies. In the diary of the antiquary, Thomas Hearne, a paragraph recorded how John Bagford once walked "into the country, on purpose to see the study of John Bunyan".

When he came, continued the diarist,

> "John received him very civilly and courteously, but his study consisted only of a Bible and a parcel of books, *The Pilgrim's Progress*, chiefly, written by himself, all lying on a shelf or shelves."

Though John was never a politician, concentration upon these books now became difficult owing to the panic excitement which swept the country twelve months after his final release from prison. England had hardly made peace with Holland, where Spinoza had died in 1677, and Charles II signed his sixth secret treaty with Louis XIV, who was now at the height of his glory, when Titus Oates let loose upon the Privy Council the lurid fantasy of the Popish Plot.

Titus Oates was the son of a Baptist Puritan Chaplain. A congenital liar, who had tried various denominations and in 1677 announced his reconciliation with Rome, he belonged to the sorry race of informers whom John Bunyan was shortly to hold up to public obloquy in *The Life and Death of Mr. Badman*. By announcing to the Privy Council that on 24 April the Jesuit Congregation had met in the White Horse Tavern and made a plot to murder the King, Oates brought an element of wild melodrama into his sordid profession.

To a generation which had seen its contemporaries die in the Great Plague and its houses reduced to ashes by the Great Fire, Oates's colossal hoax did not appear fantastic. We who have witnessed the pursuit of Nazi and Communist Fifth Columnists can understand the reign of terror that it initiated better than our grandparents who lived in sedater times. When the Middlesex magistrate before whom Oates's depositions had been taken, Sir Edmond Berry Godfrey, was found murdered in the fields near Primrose Hill, London and the rest of the country became frantic with passion against "the Papists" who were supposed to have done the deed.

On 17 November, 1679, men and women brought up on stories of the Gunpowder Plot organized a Pope-burning pageant which made its way by torchlight through the autumn twilight to Temple Bar. There, beneath the eyes of the Whig aristocracy who awaited their arrival on the balconies of the Green Ribbon Club, they burned the Papal effigy at the foot of Elizabeth's statue with shouts and incantations which suggested to the authorities that a new revolution had begun.

The Opposition party led by Anthony Ashley Cooper, Earl of Shaftesbury—who were actually to be christened "Whigs" in 1680—had regarded Oates's "disclosures" as a gift from God, and did nothing to check the ensuing panic. Under its influence they became leaders of the House in the final session of the Cavalier Parliament which had sat since 1661, and the King, who knew that the Plot was fictitious, was compelled by the country's representatives to call out the militia and enforce the penal laws against the Catholics.

Until the announcement of the Plot, Catholic peers had sat in the House of Lords and a few lesser Catholics had quietly retained their seats in the Commons. Now a new "Disabling Act" was passed to exclude all Catholics, though James, Duke of York, was exempted by name from its provisions. Five Catholic peers were thrown into the Tower; papers implying that James intended to further the interests of Catholicism were found in the possession of his wife's secretary, Coleman, who was tried and executed.

To add to the tension, Ralph Montague, the English Ambassador in France, revealed the secret agreement between Charles and Louis to the House of Commons, which immediately impeached the King's chief Minister, the Earl of Danby, under the impression that he was the person responsible. To save both Danby and himself, Charles dissolved Parliament on 24 January,

1679. After more than seventeen years, England was plunged into the new excitement of a General Election.

The furore of the anti-Papal panic, spreading from London to Bedford, subsequently elicited from John Bunyan one of his few but indubitably sincere expressions of loyalty towards the occupant of the English throne, however lamentable the royal conduct.

> "Our days indeed had been days of trouble, especially since the discovery of the Popish plot, for then we began to fear cutting of throats, of being burned in our beds, and of seeing our children dashed to pieces before our faces. But looking about us, we found we had a gracious king, brave parliaments, a stout city, good lord-mayors, honest sheriffs, substantial laws against them, and these we made the object of our hope, quite forgetting the direction in this exhortation—let Israel hope in the Lord."

While the country feared the renewal of Civil War, and Bedfordshire, like the rest of England, prepared for the General Election, John began to wonder whether he had exaggerated the decrepitude of Giant Pope. He was already contemplating a sequel to *The Pilgrim's Progress*—

> But If thou shalt cast all away as Vain,
> I know not but 'twill make me dream again,

he had written at the end of Part I—and in the continuation, the Church of Rome was to appear as the "very rampant" child-devouring monster living in the woods near the town of Vanity.

Meanwhile, during those opening months of 1679, the polling brought electors who had never voted before into Bedfordshire towns, where, unable to find accommodation, they slept huddled together for warmth round the market crosses. Almost everywhere the Country Party, as the Whigs were called, defeated the Court Party.

In Bedfordshire alone the election cost them £6000, but they had the satisfaction of defeating Lord Bruce and the Court Party by 500 votes. Lord William Russell, son of the Duke of Bedford, was returned with Sir H. Monoux for the county, while the borough repudiated Sir William Beecher, one of John's judges, and sent to Westminster Sir William Franklyn and William Paulet St. John.

In spite of these political diversions and the new struggle over the Exclusion Bill to prevent the succession of James, Duke of York, which followed the Election, John managed during 1678 and 1679 to produce two more books. Both of these were derived from sermons; *Come and Welcome to Jesus*, based on John vi, 37, "Him that cometh to me I will in nowise cast out", was a new commentary on salvation. *A Treatise of the Fear of God* contained a discourse on the words "Blessed is everyone that feareth the Lord", and was adorned by a frontispiece showing a woodcut reproduction of John asleep from an engraving by Robert White.

Though he was often away from Bedford in the years following his release, John's congregation remained, as usual, his chief concern. In spite of discouragement, persecution, and his own frequent absences, a religious census initiated by Archbishop Sheldon in 1676 showed that, in the five parishes of the borough alone, the thirty Nonconformists of 1669 had grown to 121.

Unfortunately, they were not all impeccable Nonconformists. The Church Book recorded that, while John was in prison, the congregation had withdrawn from Edward Dent of Gamlingay for mismanaging his sister's affairs. On 24 July, 1678, John himself noted an admonition given to Mary Fosket for scandalmongering against "Brother Honylove"; and in February 1679, John Stanton was reproved for beating his wife.

To the misdemeanours of recalcitrant members was added the loss of valuable supporters by death. In November 1681, "our aged and much honnered Brother John Sewster departed this life", and two days later the Church lost one of its Elders, John Bunyan's old friend Samuel Fenn. Another aged member, Anthony Harrington, to whom John had written his official letter in 1669, continued to survive; when John Bunyan and John Fenn sent another official communication to George Cokayn in December 1681, he also signed it.

During the remainder of his pastorate, John's care of the records became more and more haphazard. Continually pressed for time as he was, his vigorous untidy entries appear only at long intervals, and for the last five years of his life cease altogether. Nevertheless it was during his prolonged leadership of the Bedford Church that the methods of discipline were developed which his successor, Ebenezer Chandler, was to continue and amplify.

John Gifford had established his community on the broadest of principles which John Bunyan firmly maintained. Members of the Church leaving Bedford were not allowed to join new communities unless these were equally tolerant in their outlook. New members found acceptance only after an examination as careful as that given to would-be Friends by Quaker Elders today. Disorderly members were first admonished, then "withdrawn from", and, if their recalcitrance persisted, finally cast out. Neither drunkenness nor dishonesty, gambling nor Sabbath-breaking was permitted; scandalmongering was severely condemned, and private cruelty, such as wife-beating, proscribed.

The high domestic standards demanded of the Church by its pastor and Elders derived their inspiration from St. Paul's admonitions to the early Christian community. They were also a response to the laxity and corruption permeating society from the lustful, extravagant Court. The little Bedford Church which, with few failures, kept itself under John Bunyan unspotted from the world, conveys to modern minorities struggling against the corruptions of paganism and the cruelties of war an assurance that light may be cast by the smallest of candles into the Valley of Shadows.

A rare instance of persistent misbehaviour in the Bedford Church may have been responsible for the long periods which John spent in Essex after his release from prison. Between the note on 24 July, 1678, recording the misbehaviour of Mary Fosket, and a letter sent from the Elders in 1681 "to Sister Hauthorn by way of reproofe for her unseemly language", no entry by John appeared in the Church Book. Local tradition in the adjoining Essex towns of Bocking and Braintree insists that he wrote one of his major works in this district during those years.

His friends John Tabor and John English, at whose comfortable homes he is said to have stayed, were both Elders of Bocking Independent Meeting, one of the earliest Nonconformist communities in England, which had sixty members as far back as 1550. In John English's farm at Bocking End, John Bunyan worked in a "little quiet chamber upstairs" on a book which was probably either *The Life and Death of Mr. Badman* or *The Holy War*. When he was not writing, he preached to hundreds of Essex Nonconformists in the great barn of the farm or on the Square outside the White Hart Inn.

The man whose conduct contributed to these long absences from Bedford was a member of the Meeting named John Wildman, who had been admitted in 1669. Whatever the psychological explanation for his sudden animosities after years of peaceful discipleship, the Church Book records that, at a meeting in Cotton End on 2 November, 1680, he made charges against the congregation in which "he was found extriordinary guilty of a kind of railery and very great passion".

Passing from the general to the particular, Wildman made scandalous accusations of financial misbehaviour against John Bunyan, for which he was described as "an abominable lyer and slanderer", and warned that, failing repentance, he would be cast out of the Church. Repentance of a kind evidently occurred, since the casting-out process was postponed for three years. But the entry in the Church Book for 2 November, 1680, though it expresses indignation, does not indicate surprise.

The strained relations between John Bunyan and this unruly brother were evidently a long-standing form of tension, from which he escaped whenever he had some exacting work to finish. He also hated divisions, and was ready to make any sacrifice to achieve reconciliation; he did, in fact, ultimately lay down his life for its sake. He may well have believed that his prolonged absence would mend the breach, though the last entry that he ever made in the Church Book showed that this hope was disappointed.

> "1683. A church meeting at Cotton-end the 20 of April for breaking of bread where there was also a frothy letter of John Wildman's presented to the congregation, wherein he counteth our dealing with him for his correction and amendment scuffling and fooling, and so desires a corispondence."

In reply to this effort, Wildman, who had already been "withdrawn from", was told that he could not be readmitted until he had made amends satisfactory to those whom he had abused. The letter conveying this dismissal was signed by John Bunyan and sixteen other members, one of these being "Jo. Whitbread", who was presumably the son or brother of the argumentative William.

Even then, the Church had not heard the last of Brother Wildman. In the midst of the distress which followed John Bunyan's death five years later he endeavoured to get himself reinstated, but his case was "deferred". Soon afterwards he left Bedford, but reappeared in 1699 and again asked to be admitted. His efforts were vain; one or two Church members talked with him, but eventually decided against his readmission, "y[t] being very bad things reported of him as w[t] were acted by him in Barkshire".

John Wildman's obscure and inauspicious name would not be worthy of remembrance but for his traditional connection with the book that ranks fifth among John Bunyan's sixty works, *The Life and Death of Mr. Badman,* published in 1680 by Nathaniel Ponder.

In his sixteen-page Introduction, "The Author to the Reader", John explained that this study of a scoundrel who exuberantly fulfilled all the lurid possibilities of Original Sin was intended to be a companion-piece for *The Pilgrim's Progress*.

> "As I was considering with my self, what I had written concerning the Progress of the Pilgrim from this World to Glory; and how it had been acceptable to many in this Nation: It came again into my mind to write, as then, of him that was going to Heaven, so now, of the Life and Death of the Ungodly, and of their travel from this world to Hell."

The belief that such a story could be equally acceptable to his readers was a failure of judgment on John's part; Robert Browning showed a better understanding of human nature when he wrote in *Rabbi Ben Ezra:*

> What I aspired to be
> And was not, comforts me.

Since mankind, however delinquent, consistently prefers the idealism of things as they might be to the realism of things as they are, *The Life and Death of Mr. Badman* never approached the success of *The Pilgrim's Progress*. It was nevertheless a lively and readable story, varied with miscellaneous anecdotes which occasionally reached Grand Guignol levels, of a rogue who "swarmed with sins, even as a Beggar does with Vermin".

Mr. Badman was the Universal Spiv. He was also the particular spiv, a vicious swindling tradesman who may or may not have been the counterpart of John Wildman, but whom John Bunyan evidently numbered amongst his Bedford acquaintances.

Comfortably unimpeded by libel laws, Mr. Badman's creator acknowledged with a frankness enviable to his more handicapped literary successors that he had

> "as little as may be, gone out of the road of mine own observation of things . . . all the things that here I discourse of . . . have been acted upon the stage of this World, even many times before mine eyes."

As he described how Mr. Badman robbed his master, consorted with "loose companions" who were first cousins to John's riotous contemporaries at Elstow, borrowed and cheated, married a virtuous orphan for her money and then ill-used her, turned informer in order to distress her, defrauded his creditors by going bankrupt, emerged more prosperous than ever, and finally lost everything through a second marriage with a woman as worthless as himself, John revealed his lifelong memory of the two books which had been the only dowry of his young wife Mary.

In *The Plain Man's Pathway to Heaven*, four characters kept up a dialogue "of heavenly matters" throughout a long spring day. Similar in its dialogue form, *The Life and Death of Mr. Badman* emerged from a leisurely discourse between two elderly gossips, Mr. Wiseman and Mr. Attentive. Mr. Wiseman, whose own experiences often coincided with those of John's converted self, began the dialogue by sighing deeply. Upon being asked, as he had obviously hoped to be, for the explanation of his distress, he launched himself and his listener into the story of the man "for whom the Bell tolled at our Town yesterday", and "who is not dead only, but damned".

John told his moral tale with a gusto which reached the heights of credulous enjoyment in descriptions of the awful punishments meted out by divine justice to informers, who fell from steeples, died from scepticaemia after dog-bites, and were smitten down by apoplectic strokes. One of them, described by John as "one W. S., a man of a very wicked life", can be identified from the Quaker records as William Swinton, the sexton of St. Cuthbert's Church. For all its humour both conscious and unconscious, this book does not merit comparison with John's major works. After the artistry and humanity of *The Pilgrim's Progress*, it inevitably conveys that sense of anti-climax which comes from leaving the Celestial City for the next street.

In the story of his Pilgrim, John escaped from his century into the universe. Through the medium of a dream, he freed himself from the shackles of time and environment. He was John Bunyan detached from his circumstances, using his imagination and proclaiming his values with a freedom which caused his Nonconformist friends to entertain misgivings about the wisdom of publication.

With *Mr. Badman* he returned to the contemporary Puritan world of sin, judgment, and punishment; guilt was guilt, for which he sought neither motive nor explanation. In fact he did give the explanation, which his modern readers can recognize though he did not; he described in detail that over-pious upbringing against which, in the terminology of today, Mr. Badman "reacted". Apparently it never occurred to John—perhaps in that century it could not have occurred to him—that excess of piety defeats its own ends.

Yet even here the open-minded John Bunyan who belonged to eternity put in, despite the seventeenth-century John Bunyan, an occasional appearance. It was the affectionate and forgiving parent of a young and sometimes rebellious family who made Mr. Wiseman describe with approval the attempts of Mr. Badman's father to help his erring son. And it was the deep insight of religious genius which conferred on Mr. Badman the gaudy prosperity of successful vice and the "lamb-like death" of "a Chrisom child".

John knew that the real victim of suffering is the person who inflicts it; that the true punishment of sin lies in what it does to the sinner. Hell was an actual place to him, but he was also aware that we carry it in ourselves. Just as surely he understood the cost of everlasting life; his most heroic pilgrims had the hardest time crossing the River. Mr. Badman, the perpetual adolescent, excluded himself for ever from that fellowship of suffering in which saints and martyrs bought maturity with pain, and thus accomplished their eternal day.

When John wrote *The Life and Death of Mr. Badman*, English literature, influenced by France, was yearly growing smoother, politer, and more polished. His book represented the rough, simple, unsophisticated writing still read by the common people. Like all his work, it resembled a vigorous wild-flower from field or forest growing amid the short-lived exotic plants of a formal garden.

He could have written, as Winifred Holtby wrote in the final years of life which produced *South Riding*,

> "My herbs are plain, but their stems are all the stronger."

His Mr. Badman might well have been the ancestor of Alderman Snaith of the South Riding County Council, the man who corrupts others while avoiding the consequences for himself.

But whether he saw his composite villain as John Wildman, or his unconverted self, or the typical scheming tradesman of the town that he knew, John made him the symbol of Restoration England. Mr. Badman exemplified that corrupt era as the Puritans saw it, a matter for deep mourning and regret. The fact that darkness comes before dawn is seldom convincing to those still in darkness.

"They are bad men that make bad times," Mr. Wiseman remarks to Mr. Attentive; "if men therefore would mend, so would the times." In "The Author to the Reader", John explained the relationship between Mr. Badman and contemporary evils.

"That which has made me publish this Book is,

1. For that wickedness like a flood is like to drown our English

world: it begins already to be above the tops of mountains; it has almost swallowed up all; our Youth, our Middle age, Old age, and all, are almost carried away of this flood. O Debauchery, Debauchery, what hast thou done in England! Thou hast corrupted our Young men, and hast made our Old men beasts; thou hast deflowered our Virgins, and hast made Matrons Bawds. Thou hast made our earth to reel to and fro like a drunkard; 'tis in danger to be removed like a Cottage, yea, it is, because transgression is so heavy upon it, like to fall and rise no more."

John had good reason to deplore the state of England, for in the year following the publication of *Mr. Badman,* reaction at Whitehall became grave enough to eclipse his always limited sense of personal triumph. During the previous eighteen months, political tension had centred round the Exclusion Bill brought forward by the Whigs. Charles, determined that it should not pass, dissolved Parliament three times between 1679 and 1681.

To his fifth and last Parliament, summoned to Oxford, the Whigs went armed, while the nation began to fear a new Civil War even more than a Catholic successor to the throne. Within eight days this Parliament too had been dissolved by a King secretly fortified with promises from Louis XIV of three years' monetary supplies, and the disconcerted Whigs, taken unawares, fled on horseback or by coach to their country homes.

To avoid summoning any more Parliaments, Charles became yet again the pensioner of Louis XIV. Resolving, like his father, to govern alone, he took all possible measures to crush the scattered Whigs; these included changes among the magistrates and in the Militia, and a new enforcement of the Clarendon Code. While loyal addresses rolled up to Whitehall from members of the High Church Party all over the country, including a "Humble Address of the Lieutenant, Deputy-Lieutenant, Justices of the Peace, Military Officers, Clergy, Gentlemen, and Freeholders of the County of Bedford", the gaols again became crowded with persecuted Nonconformists.

In the midst of the consternation caused by this fresh onslaught, an alarming new comet filled the people with the characteristic dread which John Evelyn had expressed in 1680:

"We have had of late several comets, which though I believe appear from natural causes and of themselves operate not, yet I cannot despise them. They may be warnings from God, as they commonly are forerunners of his animadversions."

Sir Isaac Newton's friend, Edmund Halley, who in 1687 helped Newton to secure the publication of his great work, *The Mathematical Principles of Natural Philosophy*, approached comets in a more scientific spirit. Collecting all the observations available to him, he calculated that this particular traveller had visited the earth in 1607 and 1531. His successors would recognize it as the "flaming sword" which Josephus saw over Jerusalem before its destruction by Titus, and the strange phenomenon observed in England before the landing of William the Conqueror. Its reappearance, after several more visits, in 1910 gave a disturbing plausibility to its alleged indication of disastrous wars.

But when John Bunyan saw the incandescent streamers of Halley's Comet invade the heavens above Bedford in 1682, it heralded only a local and limited war by Charles II upon the Corporations of English towns.

CHAPTER XVII

UNHOLY POLITICS AND *THE HOLY WAR*

"For here lay the excellent wisdom of him that built Mansoul, that the walls could never be broken down nor hurt by the most mighty adverse potentate, unless the townsmen gave consent thereto."

JOHN BUNYAN: *The Holy War.*

THE Life and Death of Mr. Badman was an animated presentation of existing national and local evils, the national picture being symbolised by the local portrait. In his next book, *The Holy War*, which was surpassed only by *The Pilgrim's Progress* and *Grace Abounding*, John Bunyan dealt prophetically with a national form of unholiness that soon became local.

So accurately did this book, published in 1682, forecast with its elaborate symbolism a series of events which occurred in Bedford during 1684, that some of John's biographers have been deceived by the apparent coincidence. One of the most devoted actually states that "a new Charter to suppress Dissenters, given to Bedford by Charles the Second, *led to* Bunyan's satire on the new corporation of the town of Mansoul in *The Holy War*".

This assumption underrated John's shrewd ability to put two and two together, and through his imaginative understanding to relate the ensuing sum to the trend of national events. It also ignored his memory, going back to his 'teens, of similar practices at an earlier period.

One of the chief characters in *The Holy War* is Mr. Conscience, the Recorder of the "fair and delicate town, a corporation, called Mansoul", in the "gallant country of Universe". When John published this book, which in Macaulay's opinion would have been England's greatest religious allegory if *The Pilgrim's Progress* had never been written, the Recorder of a town was a far greater personage than the legal expert who now presides at Quarter Sessions.

He was the patron of the Borough, the controller of its politics, and the intermediary between the Government and the Corporation. He also acted as the confidant of the Royal Court, who kept a wary eye on local events. His office carried the right to nominate Burgesses and Freemen, and thus enabled him to control Parliamentary elections. Because Bedford returned two Members to the House of Commons, its political importance was out of all proportion to its population and size.

At the beginning of the Civil War the Recorder of Bedford was the Earl of Bolingbroke, and his deputy a Royalist lawyer named Taylor. Owing to the influence of Sir Samuel Luke these two officials were replaced, and under the Commonwealth the distinction between Burgesses and Freemen was abolished. The Common Council, formerly composed of all the Burgesses and thirteen Freemen, consisted at various times of fifteen to eighteen Common Councilmen, together with the Mayor and Bailiffs. These changes were intended to extinguish the semi-hereditary form of government in the town, and to substitute a more democratic authority.

The fact that local government reflected national developments was therefore within John's knowledge when he began to write *The Holy War*. His prophetic perspicacity, embodied in the story, is best understood by describing national and local events first, though they came second.

Charles II dissolved his last Parliament at Oxford on 28 March, 1681. The proscription of the Whigs in the public service followed, and in November came the trial of their leader, the Earl of Shaftesbury. Shaftesbury could not be legally tried outside London, and in London, controlled by the Whigs as it had formerly been dominated by the Parliamentarians, no jury would convict him. Enraged by his acquittal and flight to Holland, Charles and the Royalists decided to remodel the Corporation of London and other cities in order to secure a Tory Government.

The attack on London's self-government began in June and July 1682, with the election of two Tory Sheriffs, who were forced by a combination of fraud and violence upon the reluctant Whig majority. Since the sheriffs appointed the juries, which could deal trenchantly with every person anathema to the Court, the leading Whigs started to discuss a general insurrection while their subordinates planned the assassination of the King. But they were too weak and disintegrated to carry through such a scheme before London passed, with the new Mayor and Sheriffs, into the hands of the Tories at the end of September.

This easy success encouraged Charles to make a systematic onslaught on the municipal charters of the old Corporations, which under even Charles I had never suffered such interference. These old Corporations had considerable influence on the election of Members of Parliament; the Burgesses selected the Members, but the Corporations selected the Burgesses. If, therefore, the King secured control of the Corporations, he would automatically acquire control over Parliament.

The attack on Bedford had its subtle beginnings even earlier than the attack on London. In 1681, when John Bunyan was writing *The Holy War*, the Recorder of Bedford was Robert Bruce, first Earl of Ailesbury, a member of the Court Party in whose "House Beautiful" the visiting tinker had practised his trade. Soon after the dissolution of the Oxford Parliament, an Order in Council was made to inquire whether all Bedford's Corporation officials had complied with the Corporation Act by taking the Sacrament in church.

Although the Corporation had been effusively loyal at the time of the Restoration, its sympathies were mainly with the "Country Party" controlled by the Whigs. In opposition to the Court Party, this political group favoured Protestantism, Dissent, and the succession of Charles's natural son the Duke of Monmouth, rather than that of James, Duke of York. It was not therefore surprising that the town Chamberlains, Miles Wade and Andrew Freebody, had omitted to take the Sacrament within twelve months of their election.

The Recorder declared their places void. The following December he turned his attack upon the Deputy-Recorder, Robert Audley, whose tombstone, recording his death in 1702, can still be seen on the floor of the Chantry Chapel in Welbourn Church, Lincolnshire. At the council in Whitehall the Earl accused Robert Audley of being "an enemy to the Government and to the Church of England, and a great countenancer of conventicles and phanaticks in the town of Bedford". He therefore suggested that, under the Corporation Act, Mr. Audley and other Aldermen should be displaced.

The ageing Deputy-Recorder appeared at the Council table,

protested that he had served as an officer under the King's father, had suffered the sequestration of his estate after the War, and had never attended a conventicle in his life. Paying an unsolicited tribute to his neighbour John Bunyan, he added that if conventiclers preached as well as they were reputed to do, and churchmen as badly, he might easily go to a conventicle yet.

At this first interchange Robert Audley had won a temporary victory, but this did not long postpone the Recorder's determination to "tune" and "purge" the Corporation. In this resolve he had the support of Paul Cobb, who was still Clerk of the Peace, and in September 1683 replaced John Paradine as Mayor. By the end of that year, Robert Audley had been displaced, and a total of seventy-six new Burgesses, selected from "safe" families such as the Fosters, Dyves, Chesters, and Wingates, added to the Burgessdom of Bedford.

Almost as though he had watched these events taking place in a "prospective glass" which altered the proportions of time rather than space, John Bunyan had prophetically recorded detail after detail in his book published the previous year. Even though he had no law of libel to contend with, it seems doubtful whether John would have ventured to identify his Diabolus with either the King or the Earl of Ailesbury. The fact remains that the behaviour of Diabolus at Mansoul bore a peculiar resemblance to the conduct of the Recorder at Bedford.

> "Now, having got possession of this stately palace or castle, what doth he but makes it a garrison for himself, and strengthens and fortifies it with all sorts of provision, against the King Shaddai, or those that should endeavour the regaining of it to him and his obedience again. This done, but not thinking himself yet secure enough, in the next place he bethinks himself of new modelling the town; and so he does, setting up one and putting down another at pleasure. Wherefore my Lord Mayor, whose name was my Lord Understanding, and Mr. Recorder, whose name was Mr. Conscience, these he put out of place and power."

With seventy-six new Burgesses whose loyalty to the Court could be guaranteed, it was not difficult for the Earl of Ailesbury to arrange for the surrender of the existing municipal Charter. Under date 8 January, 1684, the Minute Book of Bedford Corporation recorded the voluntary surrender of those liberties which, as John had already reminded his fellow-citizens in *The Holy War*, could not be taken from them "unless the townsmen gave consent thereto".

> "It is agreed, consented, concluded, and ordeyned unto, by and with the consent of ye Maior, Alldermen, Bayliffes, Burgesses, and Comonalty in this present Councell, That ye charter of this Corporacon bee surrendered and given up to His Majestie, and that the Maior of this Corportion doe take and carry up the Charter to doe the same: And that His Majestie bee humbly petitioned to grant the town a new one with like privileges as the former was, or such other priviledges as hee shall be pleased to grant."

With this measure of latitude the King's task was easy, though a feeble last-moment attempt by the substitute-corporation to retain some of the borough's privileges had to be countered by subtle suggestions of municipal economy and individual pickings in a letter to the Mayor from the Earl's son, Lord Bruce:

> "I can give you some perfect assurance that very small fees will be expected as things are ordered, so that you may surrender the wholle charter at a cheaper ratte, then you might doe as you proposed for the surrendering of ye governing part. You should have an Attorney or Sollicitor in town to manage the thing . . ."

Paul Cobb, who appears in a quarter of a century to have added the personalities of Mr. Worldly Wiseman and Mr. Money-love to his original rôle of Mr. Legality, was himself a solicitor, and immediately perceived the personal possibilities of surrendering the Charter. It was, therefore, without any further misgiving that he set off by coach from Bedford Bridge for London on a fine spring day, carrying the Town Charter and dreaming agreeably of financial and social advancement as reward for his efforts.

On 19 July the Earl of Ailesbury brought the new Charter from London himself. A municipal deputation of several hundred horse met him beyond Elstow. At the Guildhall the new Charter was read aloud, the Earl made a triumphant speech, and a "splendid entertainment" followed. But when the cost of all this rejoicing had been met by the dubious device of mortgaging the town's charity-lands in Holborn, and the Mayor, with a brother-lawyer, Thomas Christie, had been recompensed for the legal cost of yielding up ancient liberties, the members of the Corporation studied their new Charter with the same sense of dismay as the Burgesses of the sixty other boroughs who shared their experience.

It appeared that there were several "strings" to the "more ample liberties and privileges" so verbosely emphasized in the first paragraph recording "the improvement of Our Boro' or Town of Bedford". The first was the nomination, in the Charter itself, of the "good and discreet men" who were initially to hold the various municipal offices.

These ranged from "our well-beloved Paul Cobb the elder gentleman", who was inevitably to be Mayor, to "our Well Beloved William Foster", the first named of nine Common Council men. They concluded with "Our well beloved Paul Cobb the younger", appointed to be "the first and present Coroner of the said Boro'."

It is tempting to speculate how the author of *South Riding* would have dealt with Bedford Corporation and the Cobb family, had she been there to observe the situation with John Bunyan.

The selected Recorder, "Our right well beloved and right trusty Cousin and Councellor Robert Earl of Ailesbury", could of course point out to the discomforted Councillors that by the new Charter they had been granted the right to hold two fairs or markets annually, but what really troubled them was the concealed pill so dubiously sweetened by this privilege. For, ingeniously wrapped up in the verbal intricacies characteristic of Charters at this period, there followed a threat:

> . . . "*Provided always* and We do reserve unto Us Our heirs and successors by these presents full power and authority from time to time and at all times hereafter the Mayor Recorder Steward Common Clerk Coroner and any or some of the Aldermen Bailiffs Chamberlains or Common Council

of the Boro' or Town aforesaid for the time being at Our will and pleasure or of Our heirs or successors made in Privy Council and signified to them respectively under the seal of the Privy Council to amove and declare him or them amoved And so often as We Our heirs or successors by any such Order made in Privy Council shall declare such Mayor Recorder Steward Common Clerk or any or some of the Aldermen Bailiffs Chamberlains or Common Council of the Boro' or Town aforesaid for the time being amoved that then he or they so declared amoved from his or their several and respective offices by that fact and without any other further process indeed and to all intents and purposes whatsoever shall be amoved and that so often as the case may happen . . ."

The well-beloved and discreet gentlemen over whose cherished heads the fear of being "amoved" at the whim of the sovereign would perpetually hover, were also required, before exercising any of their rights, to take "the corporal oaths called the Oathes of Allegiance and Supremacy, and all other oaths appointed by Statute of this Our realm of England for such offices and persons upon the holy Evangelists of God".

This interesting document concluded with a reminder that the privilege of holding a Charter—even such a Charter—involved "yielding and paying to Us Our heirs and successors yearly so much so great such the same and such kind of rents services sums of money and demands whatsoever as for the premises or any or some of them ought to be yielded and paid Notwithstanding", etc.

It is hardly surprising that John Bunyan, the shrewd peasant-preacher who had more confidence in "the holy Evangelists of God" than in Kings and Recorders, refused to have anything to do with the "great one" who came to Bedford, after a reversal of the political machine three years later, to offer him an official position under the Government of King James II.

John was never a politician. *The Holy War* suggests that he always saw too clearly through the manœuvrings of rulers and governments to trust his message and reputation to the shifting cross-currents of political expediency.

His theme was implicit in the full title of his book, published in 1682 by Dorman Newman at the King's Arms in the Poultry, and by Benjamin Alsop at the Angel and Bible in the Poultry: "*The Holy War, made by Shaddai upon Diabolus For the Regaining of the Metropolis of the World. Or, The Losing and Taking Again of the Town of Mansoul.*"

This allegorical history was intended to portray the fall and redemption of mankind, told as the saga of a besieged city. The city once belonged by right to Shaddai or God, but was betrayed by a Fifth Column which admitted the besieging giant Diabolus through Ear Gate and Eye Gate. After this catastrophe, Lord Understanding ceased to be Mayor, Mr. Conscience was dismissed from the post of Recorder, and Lord Will-be-Will became a species of local commissar working for the alien government. The tale might be a story of modern Europe, though John—for whom Mansoul was sometimes an individual soul, and sometimes the collective soul of the Christian community—set out to describe the struggle between God and the Devil for the control of humanity.

In his rhymed Introduction, he told the reader with his customary directness that here also he had incorporated his own spiritual experience.

> Then lend thine ear to what I do relate,
> Touching the town of Mansoul and her state;
> How she was lost, took captive, made a slave;
> And how against him set, that should her save;
> Yea, how by hostile ways she did oppose
> Her Lord, and with his enemy did close.
> For they are true: he that will them deny
> Must needs the best of records vilify.
> For my part, I myself was in the town,
> Both when 'twas set up, and when pulling down.

Four different ingredients composed the story, the first being, as usual, John's memory of his unconverted state, and the second his recollection of the Civil War. The geography of Universe never became so concrete as the scenes of *The Pilgrim's Progress*, but Mansoul was definitely a garrison town. Though his fighting men used the armour of timeless fable in addition to their seventeenth-century weapons, John clearly remembered Newport

Pagnell as he wrote of Mansoul's walls, its "old castle", and its five gates corresponding to the five senses.

His third ingredient was his shrewd estimate of political tendencies both national and local; only in the fourth place came the influence of books that he had read. Amongst these Milton's were conspicuous, for *The Holy War* put together the themes of both *Paradise Lost* and *Paradise Regained.*

John also owed a possible debt to Thomas Fuller's straightforward story of the Crusades, *A History of the Holy War*, published in 1639; to *The Purple Island* of Phineas Fletcher, cousin to John Fletcher the dramatist; and finally, once again to Richard Bernard's *The Isle of Man.* This "Isle" had a county town called "Soule", and the rascally thief Sin often wandered along its four main streets, Sense Street, Thought Street, Word Street, and Deed Street, which may have suggested the Ear-Gate, Eye-Gate, Mouth-Gate, Nose-Gate, and Feel-Gate of Mansoul.

Today this long involved allegory is interesting only if it is read in connection with the political machinations which it foresaw and interpreted. In so far as the book had a human hero, he was the Recorder of Mansoul, Mr. Conscience, the recognizable first cousin of Robert Audley, Deputy-Recorder of Bedford. But John was not thinking of Robert Audley alone.

For him Mr. Conscience represented all the Seven Champions of Christendom rolled into one. He was a British super-champion who in his thousands had died at the stake, suffered exile, languished in prison, endured the distraint of his goods, lost his job, and confronted the scorn or hostility of his fellows. All through the ages he had appealed from adverse contemporary judgments to the Christ of the Gospels, who had crowned and enthroned him in the words of the Eighth Beatitude which John quoted on the title-page of *A Relation of the Imprisonment of Mr. John Bunyan*:

> "Blessed are ye when men shall revile you, and persecute you, and shall say all manner of evil against you falsely for my name's sake."

The Holy War never won the popularity of *The Pilgrim's Progress.* John wrote *The Pilgrim's Progress* to please himself, *The Holy War* to improve his readers; and readers have an obstinate habit of deciding for themselves what is going to improve them. A second edition was not demanded until 1696, eight years after the author's death. There is a so-called second edition in the Bodleian Library dated 1684, but it is probably pirated.

Though the book was conceived on a larger scale than any of its predecessors and in some ways showed a maturer psychological insight, its characters never sprang to life with the same determination as the pilgrims and their guides or assailants. Mr. Anything is obviously a near relative of Mr. By-ends, and Mr. Carnal-Security of Mr. Worldly Wiseman; but we do not meet Lord Will-be-Will and Captain Boanerges in the local High Street where we so often encounter Talkative and Ignorance, nor do we number Captain Credence with Faithful amongst our personal friends.

Emmanuel himself is seldom recognizable as the Christ of the Gospels; Diabolus has more personality than Shaddai's Son, but less than Apollyon. John regarded Diabolus with an evident contempt very different from the awed respect shown to Christian's terrible adversary. At the beginning of the story he refers to his villain as "this bramble", and at the end makes him desert his Army, which falls defenceless into Emmanuel's hands.

In his Introduction to the 1887 Edition of *The Holy War*, Dr. John Brown referred to an essay by Professor Gustave Masson which compared the three Devils of Luther, Milton, and Goethe.

Luther's Devil was not a mere literary creation, but a real personal enemy, author of all the evil in life. Milton's Satan was a ruined archangel with the grandeur of fallen greatness; Goethe's Mephistopheles represented Milton's Satan after centuries of wickedness. Dr. Brown likened Diabolus to Luther's Devil; he is a hideous but contemptible creature who lacks both the sublimity of Satan and the guile of Mephistopheles.

Two-and-a-quarter centuries after the publication of *The Holy War*, Rudyard Kipling carried the prophetic qualities which had enabled John Bunyan to forecast intrigues within Bedford Corporation forward into the war-distraught world of 1917. In a famous seven-verse poem to which he gave the same title as John's book, he narrowed the struggle between good and evil for the soul of man down to the contemporary conflict between England and Germany.

A tinker out of Bedford,
A vagrant oft in quod,
A private under Fairfax,
A minister of God—
Two hundred years and thirty
Ere Armageddon came
His single hand portrayed it
And Bunyan was his name!

These verses were first published in the Christmas number of *Land and Water* for 1917, and are now included among Kipling's collected poems.

In an inscription beneath *The Holy War* Memorial Window, companion to *The Pilgrim's Progress* Window in Elstow Church, Kipling's transition from the universal to the particular is quietly reversed:

TO THE MEMORY OF BUNYAN
AND TO REMIND ALL CHRISTIAN PEOPLE
OF THE HOLY WAR THEY SHOULD BE ENGAGED IN
ON THE SIDE OF EMMANUEL.

The unholy politics which John Bunyan satirized in *The Holy War* did not finish with the new Bedford Charter. Nothing less than the end of the Stuarts could have ended them.

Two days after the sham privileges conferred upon Bedford Corporation had been accepted with short-lived rejoicings, one of Bedfordshire's Members of Parliament, Lord William Russell, was executed in Lincoln's Inn Fields. The heir of the first Duke of Bedford, he had been deeply implicated in the underground Whig activities which led to the abortive Rye House Plot.

From the time of the election of the London Tory sheriffs in the summer of 1682, the subterranean intrigues of the disorganized Whigs had rumbled peevishly on until the spring of 1683, when the makers of the Assassination Plot decided to attack Charles on his return from Newmarket. The place chosen was Rumbold's Rye House, which commanded the road. Charles passed the Rye House several days earlier than he had been expected and the plot misfired; but its makers were arrested, and the Whig combination against the King was discovered.

Lord Russell was not the exemplary saint that some writers on this period have depicted. He had relentlessly pursued old Lord Stafford, the last victim of the Titus Oates panic, to his execution in 1680, and had been in close communication with William of Orange when he visited England in 1681. Although he had taken no part in the plot to kill the King, he had been involved in a conspiracy which the conspirators regarded as legitimate constitutional agitation and the King and his party as preparation for rebellion.

When the conspiracy was unveiled, those who were incriminated reacted according to their characters. Lord Howard turned King's evidence; Essex committed suicide in prison; Algernon Sidney, contemptuous in death as in life of royal tyrants and the fickle mob, followed Russell to the scaffold. In prison Russell, visited by two liberal-minded clergymen, Tillotson and Burnet, refused with courteous dignity to purchase his life by a declaration that it was always unlawful to resist the Sovereign.

He stood his trial as a traitor and, in accordance with current practice at treason trials, was not allowed the help of a lawyer. No objection, however, was taken to the presence of a friend who would make notes of the evidence and assist his memory. His wife, Lady Rachel, volunteered her services, and played her part with stoic efficiency though she could not save him from death.

It is unlikely that Lady Rachel and Elizabeth Bunyan ever met, but both belong to the noble army of wives who have won a niche in history by the gallant support of a husband's lost cause.

An outburst of Tory loyalty followed the Rye House Plot, not least in Bedfordshire which was anxious to prove its non-complicity with its erring Member. On 9 September, appointed as a day of thanksgiving for the King's escape, the Earl of Ailesbury's chaplain, Thomas Pomfret, Vicar of Luton, preached at Ampthill a sermon of effusive congratulation which he afterwards printed and dedicated to the Earl. Two months later the Earl himself, accompanied by his son, presented an address to His Majesty which contained some words of ominous import to John Bunyan and his congregation.

> "We think our selves bound in Duty, to the care we ought to have of His Majesties Safety, and the security of the Government, as now by Law established in Church and State, to Present all Conventicles and pretended Religious-Meetings, and all Clubs and Cabals of such whose Religion or Loyalty is much and justly to be doubted."

Throughout the following year the Earl, as Lord-Lieutenant of Bedfordshire, proceeded to put his policy into practice. The Rye House Plot brought much the same trouble to innocent Nonconformists as the Popish Plot had brought to innocent Catholics. Amongst existing Bedfordshire documents, the constables' presentments for 1684 are the longest for many years. The spelling and handwriting also compare unfavourably with those of earlier constables, thereby testifying to the growing reluctance of intelligent persons to harry the Nonconformists.

In January 1685 the Earl of Ailesbury arbitrarily ordered the General Sessions of the Bedfordshire magistrates to be held at Ampthill instead of Bedford, so that he might the more effectively pursue his campaign. At these sessions the Court, over which the Earl presided, passed a long resolution "that all such Laws as had been provided for the reducing all Dissenters to a thorow Conformity shall be forthwith put into a speedy and vigorous execution".

Fate, however, temporarily interrupted the "vigorous execution", for within three weeks of the General Sessions Charles II, smitten by an apoplectic stroke, lay dead. On his death-bed, he was, at last, formally received into the Catholic Church. Before the end of the year, the Earl too had departed from the earthly scene of his political intrigues.

The brother who followed Charles on the throne was not, to all appearances, a better exchange. England's liberties were saved because he was in fact much worse, being handicapped by poorer judgment and an obstinate, precipitate temperament. Throughout his short reign he suffered from the illusion that the Anglican

Church could be persuaded to favour Catholicism owing to its energetic denunciation of Protestant Dissent.

After judges anxious to gain the new King's favour had sentenced Titus Oates to a flogging so severe that it would have killed anyone less tough, James and the Church united in ferocious persecution of the Nonconformists. Once more men and women who had desired only to worship God in their own way were fined, imprisoned and ruined while the country gave itself up to the excitement of another General Election.

On 19 May, 1685, the new Parliament met with an enormous Tory majority to which Bedfordshire contributed its full quota. The borough returned Sir Anthony Chester, whose father had dealt so severely with Elizabeth Bunyan in the Swan Chamber, and Thomas Christie, who had helped Paul Cobb to surrender the historic liberties of the Corporation. From the county also went two Tories, Sir Villiers Chernocke of Hulcote and William Butler of Biddenham.

The House met with a determination both to resist Catholicism and to harass the Nonconformists. Its ability to concentrate on these objectives was soon limited by the necessity of dealing with Argyle's insurrection in the north and Monmouth's rebellion in the west. While Judge Jeffreys harried the rebels to the scaffold through the legal travesty of the Bloody Assize, many English families atoned for the national policy towards Nonconformists by receiving the Huguenots fleeing from France after the Revocation of the Edict of Nantes.

To John Bunyan and his friends it seemed unlikely, amid the turbulent passions of the time, that he would long remain out of prison. Once again the members of the Bedford Church were holding their meetings at dead of night, omitting hymns, reaching their pulpits through trap-doors, and posting sentinels to guard against the newly encouraged spate of informers. Magistrates and clergy sought offenders to present; fines and excommunications kept the Ecclesiastical Courts perpetually occupied; the prisons were again filling up. Even old and honoured Puritan leaders, such as Richard Baxter, did not escape.

It was the last period of systematic religious persecution to be experienced in England; but its victims, as usual, did not know how soon they were to pass from menacing darkness into reassuring light.

If the authorities were determined to suppress John again, his now established reputation as writer and preacher might well be an incentive rather than a deterrent. The forthcoming marriage of his youngest daughter Sarah to William Browne increased his resolve to safeguard in advance his modest possessions for Elizabeth and their family.

He therefore decided to draw up a Deed of Gift which would confer upon his "well-beloved wife, Elizabeth Bunyan" all his worldly goods, so that if he were taken again she would not be penniless. This Deed, in John's handwriting—small, strong, yet always sprawling as though in a tremendous hurry to reach the end of the line—covered almost one side of a strong folio page, and was drawn up on 23 December, 1685. In the opening sentence, in spite of *The Pilgrim's Progress* and *The Holy War*, he still described himself as a practitioner of his original trade.

> "To all people to whom this present writing shall com, I, John Bunyan of the parish of St. Cuthbirts, in the town of Bedford, in the county of Bedford, Brazier, send greeting. Know ye that I, the said John Bunyan, as well for and in consideration of the natural affection and love which I have and bear into my well-beloved wife, Elizabeth Bunyan, as also for divers other good causes and considerations me at this present especially moueing, have given and granted . . . all and singular my goods chattels, debts, ready money, plate, Rings, household stuffe, Aparrel, utensills, Brass, pewter, Beding, and all other my substance whatsoever . . ."

After a silver twopenny-piece had been attached to the seal, four members of John's congregation witnessed the document. One was John Bardolph, whose malt had been distrained by "old Battison" after William Foster's raid in 1670, and another William Hawkes, the Church deacon whose wife Martha was the youngest daughter of John Gifford, born after her father's death. When the Deed was completed, John hid it so carefully that even Elizabeth never found it, and was obliged after John's death to administer his estate as that of an intestate person.

The document was discovered only in 1838, when the house which the Bunyan family had occupied was pulled down. It had never, in the end, been required, for hardly more than a year after John signed it, the King had changed his policy.

At the beginning of his reign, James had believed that with the support of the Established Church he could violate the Test Act, and gradually Romanize English institutions. Early in 1686 he had achieved an initial success when the Bench of Judges, packed with his own supporters, decided in the case of Sir Edward Hales, a Catholic army officer who had refused to take the test, that the King could dispense with the law.

In virtue of this dispensing power, James gave authority to avowed Romanists amongst the clergy to retain their benefices. The Master of University College, Oxford, Obadiah Walker, who had set up a press for printing Roman Catholic tracts and openly celebrated Mass in the College, was permitted to keep both his Catholic allegiance and his post. Massey, an avowed Roman Catholic, was made Dean of Christ Church, and Parker, a secret Roman Catholic, appointed Bishop of Oxford.

The Protestant clergy retaliated by preaching openly against the errors of Rome. After Dr. Compton, Bishop of London, had refused to suspend Dr. Sharp, Dean of Norwich, for his anti-Catholic sermons, James set up an Ecclesiastical Commission Court, and put Judge Jeffreys in charge. Its first act was to suspend the Bishop of London for his refusal to suspend the Dean of Norwich.

The English people, who had become civilized enough to suffer from a sense of suppressed outrage after the atrocities of the Bloody Assize, now realized with dismay that the King had conferred on himself sufficient power to suppress all the religious teachers in the country. When members of the Franciscan and Carmelite Orders began to walk openly through the London streets, riots broke out, celebrations of the Mass were interrupted, and the trained-bands refused to put down the rebels.

Even the obstinate consciousness of the King, so reluctant to assess the meaning of experience, was impressed by the quality of this resistance. Since neither the Church nor its adherents would support him, he ingeniously resolved to purchase the goodwill of the Dissenters by adopting a general policy of toleration. So on

4 April, 1687, he issued on his own authority a new Declaration of Indulgence, suspending the penal laws against Catholics and Nonconformists alike, dispensing with all religious tests, and permitting public worship for both communities.

The Churchmen, seriously alarmed, now endeavoured to persuade their former victims that, after a period of yet further patience, toleration more reliable than the King's particular brand might be legally assured to them by a new Parliament. A strange situation arose in which Church and King contended for the favour of the once-despised Nonconformists, each trying to blame the other for the long story of persecution.

Anxious to obtain Parliamentary sanction for his Declaration of Indulgence, James dissolved the existing Parliament and took steps to ensure that the next would give him greater support. Like his father, he determined to "new-model" the Corporations, but this time the well-beloved officials were to be selected on a different basis. Preference was to be given to Catholics and Dissenters who would support the policy of the Court.

Each Lord-Lieutenant was required to go down to his county and put to his deputies and the county magistrates a series of questions designed to ascertain what policy they would pursue at a General Election. To their credit half the Lord-Lieutenants in England promptly refused their co-operation, but amongst those who gave it was Thomas, the new Earl of Ailesbury, who as Lord Bruce had so often helped his father to harry the Bedfordshire Nonconformists.

Summoning the deputies and justices to the Chapel of Herne, he put to them the questions which were being circulated throughout the country:

> "1. If in case you shall bee chosen Knight of the Shire or Burgess of a Towne, when the King shall think fitt to call a Parliament, will you be for taking off the Penall Laws and the Tests?
>
> 2. Will you assist and contribute to the Election of such Members as shall be for takeing off the penall Laws and Tests?
>
> 3. Will you support the King's Declaration for Liberty of Conscience by living friendly with those of all perswasions, as subjects of the same Prince and good Christians ought to do?"

On the whole the country gentlemen gave respect-worthy answers, which have been preserved among the Rawlinson manuscripts in the Bodleian Library at Oxford. Sir William Gostwick of Willington, for instance, maintained his stubborn convictions in a courageous if somewhat contradictory reply.

> "First, he never designs to stand, but if he be chose, he cannot part with the Penall Laws and tests.
>
> Second, that he cannot contribute to ye election of any such as will.
>
> Third, he was ever for Liberty of Conscience, and submitts it to ye law to support or not to support the same, and is desirous to live friendly with all persons of what perswasion soever, as becomes a good Christian."

Benjamin Conquest, of Houghton Conquest, equally desired "to live peacably and frendly with those of all perswasions", but insisted that, as his principles were those of the Church of England, he would feel obliged to "vote for such as in his conscience he believes are most fitt to serve the King". Sir Anthony Chester could not agree to the repeal of the penal laws, but had the same peaceable inclinations as the other magistrates. Sir George Blundell, one of the justices who sent John Bunyan to prison in 1660, "submissively answers that occurrences are so variable in future contingencies by the order of Divine providence, that he cannot pretend to a capacity of determining beforehand what his thoughts and actions will be".

Among the replies of these men who in language of varying frankness subscribed to their prejudices, there was one flagrant answer which commanded none of the esteem that we feel for those who, contrary to their interests, defend opinions at variance with our own. William Foster, Doctor of Laws, justified John's portrait of him as Mr. By-ends in one significant sentence:

"He submitts all to his Majesties pleasure."

For a quarter of a century Dr. Foster had arrested Nonconformists at conventicles and pursued them in and out of the Ecclesiastical Courts, but he remained the only man on the Bedfordshire Bench who was willing, at the King's behest, to forget the principles on which he had presumably acted. He was prepared to go even further, and to stand for Parliament as the colleague of a Nonconformist, John Eston, son of the older John Eston, now dead, who had helped John Gifford to found the Bedford Church.

This oddly assorted candidature did not, however, prosper. When the Lord-Lieutenant, as part of the process of "regulating" the Corporations so that they would elect tolerationists to the next House of Commons, wrote to Bedford Corporation on behalf of Eston and Foster, he received from the Mayor a guarded and unwelcome reply:

> "In obedience to your Honour's comands, I this day Sumoned a Councill, and did acquaint them with what your Lordship Said that . . . Dr. Foster and Mr. Eston were fit person's to serve for Burgesses of this Borrough in the next Parliament: And may it please your Lordship to give leave to acquaint your honour that the eleccion for this Towne is not in the Corporaceon alone but that every Inhabitant (not taking Collection nor being a Sojourner and noe Freeman) hath a Vote therefore they cannot give assurance how the Majority of Voices will determine. But all who were present in Councell did declare that when his Majestie shall be pleased to Issue forth his Writts to Summon a Parliament they will endeavour the Elec'ion of such member's as they shall beleive to be of undoubted loyalty and that shall be serviceable to the King and Kingdome."

Thomas, Earl of Ailesbury, of course knew perfectly well that the members of the Town Council controlled the elections, and meant to convey by their wary answer that they did not intend to elect the suggested candidates. When the matter was brought before the Privy Council, the measures which seemed best to the King's princely wisdom were two Mandatory Letters, dismissing first one half and then the other of the Bedford Corporation. The expelled members were replaced largely by Nonconformists, five of whom had to be voted into Burgessdom.

In the end the response from the whole country was so unreliable that the King abandoned his attempt to obtain a subservient Parliament by local manœuvres. But by that time Paul

Cobb and his colleagues, who four years earlier so exuberantly accepted the new Charter which gave the King power to "amove" them, had been eliminated from Bedford Corporation by the very instrument that they helped to create.

In his biographical sketch written shortly afterwards, Charles Doe put on record John Bunyan's reaction to the Royal experiments in Bedford.

"When Regulators went into all cities and towns corporate to new-model the magistracy, by turning out some and putting in others," John, he related, worked hard with his congregation

> "to prevent their being imposed on in that kind. And when a great one in those days, coming to Bedford upon some such errand, sent for him (as was supposed) to give him a place of public trust, he would by no means come at him, but sent his excuse.
>
> "He advised his brethren 'to avail themselves of the sunshine by diligent endeavours to spread the Gospel, and to prepare for an approaching storm by fasting and prayer' . . . He foresaw all the advantages that could redound to the Dissenters would have been no more than Polyphemus, the monstrous giant of Sicily, would have allowed Ulysses—to wit, that he would eat his men first, and do him the favour of being eaten last."

John, in other words, quietly refused to be made a "stooge"; he saw through the King's policy of temporarily favouring the Puritan sects in order to reduce the power of the Protestant Church to resist the Catholics. One of his last works, left unpublished at his death and printed as No. 56 in Charles Doe's Folio, was a treatise against the Church of Rome, called *Of Antichrist and his Ruin*, or *The Slaying of the Witness*.

In his book, *The Holy City*, written in Bedford Gaol, John had embodied his vision of a universal Church. But he had now come to understand, through his widening circle of knowledgeable friends, the reactionary continental forces with which the Catholicism of Charles II and James II was so closely linked.

Had he been asked at that time to sum-up the lessons that his vicissitudes had taught him, John might have replied in the words of Bernard Shaw's *Man and Superman*:

> "This is the true joy in life, the being used for a purpose recognized by yourself as a mighty one; the being thoroughly worn out before you are thrown on the scrap heap . . . And also the only real tragedy in life is the being used by personally minded men for purposes which you recognise to be base."

The pursuit of those base purposes caused the reign of James II to end in a series of resounding explosions. In April 1688 the King ordered a Second Declaration of Indulgence to be read in the Churches, but when the day came hardly a clergyman obeyed. From a London pulpit Samuel Wesley, the father of John, preached a sermon on the text: "Be it known unto thee, O King, that we will not serve thy gods, nor worship the golden image which thou hast set up."

When seven Bishops—including Sancroft, Archbishop of Canterbury—petitioned against the Indulgence, James ordered their trial on a charge of seditious libel. They were tried and acquitted amid the rejoicings of the populace, shared by the soldiers stationed on Hounslow Heath to protect the King against the mob. Throughout that summer some significant figures travelled perpetually between England and the Continent, their journeys accelerated by the belated birth of a Prince on 10 June, and the consequent threat of a Catholic dynasty.

Not the least active of these emissaries was Edward Russell, nephew of the Duke of Bedford, who saw in the Prince of Orange and the coming Revolution a constructive revenge for the execution of his cousin, Lord William. When the conspiracy succeeded and the Dutch Prince landed at Torbay, James, deserted by courtiers and soldiers alike, fled to France. With him, the last Stuart monarch, travelled those spectres of despotism and intolerance which had haunted England for nearly a hundred years.

John Bunyan did not survive to witness the logical conclusion of these reverberating events. Before the end of that summer he had reached the final stage of his journey by way of the London which had so long read his writings and listened to his words.

CHAPTER XVIII

BUNYAN'S LONDON

"In those days we were afraid to walk the Streets, but now we can shew our Heads. Then the name of a Professor was odious, now, specially in some parts of our Town (for you know our Town is large) Religion is counted Honourable."

JOHN BUNYAN: *The Pilgrim's Progress.* Part II.

DURING the last years of the Commonwealth, John Bunyan had begun to visit the friends that he and the Bedford Church were making in London. These included relatives of its members; others were drawn from the pastors of London congregations with whom the Church was in correspondence.

To the end of his life John never lost the capacity for wonder which is the basis of reverence; it was with amazement that he first saw the great city where nearly half a million people were now gathered. No urban settlement in England compared with that agglomeration of congested humanity and crowded dwellings, picturesque in their haphazard inflammable squalor. Norwich and Bristol, next in importance, each held fewer than thirty thousand inhabitants. For all the self-conscious dignity of its Corporation officials, John saw Bedford afresh as little more than a glorified village.

Through wide marshy meadow-lands wound the Thames, its muddy banks carrying their water birds and vigorous plant life from silent country fields into the heart of the City. Within sight of St. Paul's, the bearded tits plunged in and out of pink valerian and white water-hemlock. Narrow streams, such as the Fleet, the Westbourne, and the Tyburn, threaded their way through the small valleys which bisected this rich garden land. From its damp mellow green, the red gables of houses and leaden spires of churches thrust sharp silhouettes towards the sky.

Their roofs hugged the protecting shadow of the ancient wall, which extended north and east in a series of deep zigzags crowned by the white fortifications of the Tower. Beyond the water-meadows stretching west from London, a terra-cotta outcrop of dwellings clustered round the grey Abbey Church in the separate colony of Westminster.

John soon learned that this habitation of the King and Court was linked with the mercantile City of London by a road running behind the great houses, with their halls, courts, and gardens, which faced the Thames from the causeway known as The Strand. When first he passed that way in spring, jackdaws were chattering on the ornamented roofs, and the rooks cawed loudly in the Temple rookery beside the river.

During one of his earliest visits, he stayed with friends who lived on London Bridge. Its mussel-encrusted piles supported the turreted Nonesuch House which was a show-piece of London, giving to its humbler neighbours above the water an ancient grandeur rivalling that of the Ponte Vecchio in Florence. John's hosts satisfied his youthful country appetite with a good supper of fish caught in the town ditch under the City walls, and salted eels taken from the river between Hammersmith and Kew. With these they served a salad garnished with the wild herbs which grew at the edge of the City roads.

Like other young Londoners, the junior members of this family spent much of their time in catching the pike, perch and bream which were so plentiful in the Thames, together with the salt-water fish—turbot, sole, and plaice—which came up the river from the Estuary. Sometimes they went to the country instead, and once took John with them. He was reminded of his own activities as an angler in the Ouse when he watched the boys fishing in the River Lea, which above Limehouse ran through lovely pastoral country jewelled with bright villages.

From his leaded window-panes above London Bridge, John could see the road on the south side of the river rambling between tin-yards and built-up alleys. Here the houses of mariners and chandlers clustered side by side between wharves and warehouses on the river-bank. He soon learnt that these congested areas outside the walls were known as "the Liberties", in which half the population of London lived.

No other great English city was surrounded by these sprawling slums, where a vagrant population brought filth and disease right up to the homes of reputable workers. From Lambeth, Stepney, Whitechapel, and Cripplegate sprang the plagues which periodically menaced London, and were to kill 100,000 Londoners in 1665.

Beyond the slums stretched the flat expanse of South London, with its stagnant pools where snipe and spotted crane abounded. The inhabitants of "the Liberties" found an escape from their misery by hunting ducks through the soggy marshes with the help of spaniels, and afterwards foregathering at The Dog and Duck in Southwark or some other favourite inn.

At the other social extreme were the great squares being laid out for well-to-do residents by enterprising landowners with country property adjacent to London or Westminster. One to the north of the Strand, known as Covent Garden, had a great piazza in the Italian style, designed for the fourth Earl of Bedford in the 1630s by Inigo Jones. His influence was also recognizable in another close by, where fine red-brick houses ornamented with pilasters surrounded Lincoln's Inn Fields.

Setting out one day south-west from the City to see the market gardens in the villages of Chelsea and Fulham, John made a deviation northward to inspect the long low mansion which the fourth Earl of Southampton had built on one of his Bloomsbury fields. In front of it, builders were laying out a square of plain brick houses; the first leases, they told him, would be granted about 1661, and the area would be known as Bloomsbury Square.

John walked south through the meadows to Piccadilly, where wild bugloss still grew on the dry banks above the ditches. On the north side great classical palaces had arisen, and paths planted with trees were laid out beside them. Between Piccadilly and Chelsea stretched the water-logged swamp known as the Five Fields.

Succeeding generations would drain this area, and carve out new building sites with strange urban names such as Hyde Park Corner, Grosvenor Place, and Sloane Street. They would even direct the Westbourne, which flowed through the marsh, into a conduit pipe to carry it across Sloane Square Underground Station into the Thames. But now snipe and woodcock inhabited the flowering rushes in summer, and in autumn the wild traveller's joy trailed over the hedges like tangible smoke. Only to the south, in St. James's Fields, were signs of development which suggested the beginnings of yet another aristocratic square.

During his prison years John tried to recall those early impressions of Commonwealth London, but the sense of wonder and excitement had vanished. It was eclipsed in his memory by the anxieties of that fruitless journey on which, a year after the Restoration, he had discussed with London friends how best to secure his release from gaol.

The capital of Charles II's England had then seemed to him to be hostile and intimidating, though externally it was gayer than Cromwell's London. A garish change had passed over it, resembling another which would come two centuries and a half later, when the lush splendours of the Edwardian Court would succeed the austere widowhood of Victoria.

Through the streets of Westminster paraded the Lifeguards which the new King had formed for his protection; their scarlet coats adorned with gold lace, and broad-brimmed hats massed with drooping white feathers, symbolized a transition from sober restraint to reckless extravagance. The eye of the countryman from Bedford observed their long-tailed, beautifully groomed horses with an appreciation which was not extended to the ornamental riders. Their broad white collars, scarlet sashes, and high boots of jacked leather inspired him with the same misgivings as the companies of players starting to perform again at the Red Bull, where frivolities under the Commonwealth had been limited to rope-dancing and "drolls".

All over London coffee-houses were springing up, to supply not only coffee but the new "China Drink" which was sometimes called tea. When John looked tentatively inside, he saw gaily-dressed girls with abundant ringlets, and older women whose curled wigs stood high above their heads. Girls and matrons alike wore peaked bodices and full sleeves, open in front and caught together by jewelled clasps. Their large hooded cloaks fell back to reveal wide skirts of materials so rich that to a Puritan their cost seemed incalculable.

Not less frivolous were the escorts of these women, with their dandified shoes and stockings taking the place of the leather boots which at least suggested action. Some of them even carried muffs in the street, and wore their breeches edged with deep frills and rosetted at the knee.

John returned with relief to the sobriety of Bedford, even

though return meant prison and the wrath of authority with his jailor and himself. This meretricious London was the outward and visible sign of the changed national values which had been responsible for his imprisonment; a new age was beginning whose architects sought to eliminate him and his kind.

Years passed over Bedford and London. From "the Liberties" outside the City walls, the laden carts carried their dead. Beneath lowering smoke clouds, scarlet tongues of flame devoured the spireless central tower of old St. Paul's. The Great Plague and the Great Fire came and went.

John Bunyan did not see London again until six years after the Fire had destroyed the City.

With his preaching-license in his pocket, he went up during the summer of 1672 to visit Nonconformist congregations as the newly appointed pastor of the Bedford Church. He had always been welcome, but now he was honoured, not only for his official position but for his book *Grace Abounding*, which had given many members of his congregations a true understanding of his character. Above all, he was respected for the twelve years' imprisonment with which he had paid the price of his integrity.

To the raw new London now slowly rising from the ashes of the old, John brought his new philosophy of constructive acceptance. It responded at the deepest levels to the pioneer spirit of Christopher Wren and his army of builders; John's eyes which had looked on squalor and tragedy without losing their vision of the Holy City could also see the future London whose foundations were taking shape under his eyes.

At present the ruins were still dominant; in restless flight the undaunted jackdaws circled above spectral chimneys of brick and stone. But after six years their stark ugliness had been softened by the small yellow petals and lance-shaped leaves of the London rocket, which resembled the treacle mustard familiar to John in Bedfordshire lanes. It covered the rubble in a delicate profusion only to be surpassed three centuries later by the rose-bay willow-herb, which was to perform the same healing function after London's next epoch of devastation.

Everywhere building seemed to be in progress; it was not

confined to the City, where Wren's white Renaissance Churches were ousting the Gothic ghosts of their predecessors and creating London's new silhouette for the admiration of future centuries. Order was now beginning to replace the picturesque jumble swept away by the Fire; regular rows of red-brick houses lined the streets where pavements for pedestrians were separated from the cobbles by a series of small posts.

After the old buildings covered with wall-rocket and rue-leaved saxifrage, these new houses looked bare, but their standard pattern had a pleasing precision. Four-storied buildings with balconies flanked the six principal streets. In the less-important roads the houses were three storeys high, and one only in the by-lanes. A few big mansions with courtyards and gardens spread over the spaces behind the streets. Altogether, in that year 1672, over 1200 houses had been started, and of these 1000 were under scaffolding.

Towards the west, where many of the homeless had fled, new dwellings were springing up with the jaunty freshness of April flowers. Many of these already stood side by side in the cobbled streets surrounding Covent Garden, Lincoln's Inn, and St. James's Square. A new building centre had started at Seven Dials; the flood-tide of small red houses was inundating the old imposing palaces of the Strand.

In Soho and Gray's Inn Fields the patterns of two more embryonic squares were visible, while Lord St. Albans, who in 1660 had obtained a sixty-year lease from the Crown to build a few large mansions for the best families in St. James's Square, had changed his policy in response to the rush of aristocratic householders and luxury traders from east to west.

Not only had he increased the number of his building plots to twenty-two; he intended to establish a market and put up a church. Designed by Wren except for its tower and built in 1683, St. James's, Piccadilly, was destined to encounter its own Apollyon in the shape of a 1940 land-mine.

Its scaffolding would soon be visible from St. James's Park, newly stocked with the red, white and spotted deer which had disappeared during the Commonwealth, and lively with wild-fowl which included pelicans and white ravens. Under Charles II the Park itself was growing more formal, though herds of cows still grazed there; the French landscape gardener Le Notre had made a canal to flow through it, and was planting lime-trees.

Active all over London, too, was Nicholas Barbon, son of that "Praise-god Barebone" who gave his name to the Little Parliament of 1653. Barbon had established himself as the speculative builder of the 1670s, who erected small houses on ground which he sold to workmen at so much per foot of frontage. Westminster was now the fashionable place to live, but Barbon's customers preferred comfort to fashion. They kept him fully occupied in building the Essex House Estate south of the Strand, and Red Lion Square north of Holborn.

By the time that John's second imprisonment had ended, the City was closely built up with narrow-fronted houses on sites stretching back to more than twice their width. The larger dwellings had two heavily panelled parlours on the ground floor beneath their huge iron-work shop-signs, and wide oak staircases leading to the bedrooms. Behind their toy gardens decked with little fountains were coach-houses or stables, which cut them off from a new inner maze of courtyards and alleys.

The February of 1678 in which John came up to supervise the publication of *The Pilgrim's Progress* saw a London utterly changed from the remembered city of his young manhood. The new St. Paul's was slowly emerging from the site of the old Gothic building; it had been designed to support a great dome of which river travellers would have an uninterrupted view, since a huddle of mean houses and cottages alone divided it from the Thames.

Only the women selling daffodils in the new Cheapside seemed to John to be unaltered, and the boys whistling tunes in the streets. As the 70s turned into the 80s, their favourite melodies came from the music of young Henry Purcell, the infant prodigy who in 1680, at the age of twenty-two, succeeded his master, Dr. Blow, as organist of Westminster Abbey. Two years later he added to this major honour his appointment as organist at the Chapel Royal.

One of the new features of resurrected London which most impressed John was the Green Ribbon Club which the Whigs had founded in 1675 and named for their Party colours. This Club represented the first official headquarters of a political party; it was the centre of the modern propaganda machine which the Whigs had invented. With the Earl of Shaftesbury as its President, it had been established in the King's Head Tavern on the west side of Chancery Lane, opposite the Inner Temple.

In their organizing power and influence over the mob, the members of the Green Ribbon Club resembled their distant successors who founded the Jacobin Club of the French Revolution. They included representatives of the Lords and Commons, City Aldermen, veterans of the Parliamentary Army, and professional intriguers whose precise function eluded definition. Hired poets and pamphleteers, such as Shadwell and Blount, moved in and out of the tavern; even Titus Oates belonged to the Club for a time, and was cultivated as an electioneering mascot by junior lawyers and young men from country mansions.

The Club's banqueting-room, so often heady with smoke, wine, and eloquence, opened on to long balconies from which members could lean and address the populace. Crowds assembled beneath these balconies, as today they wait outside the Houses of Parliament and Buckingham Palace, to see the owners of those names which were then the current coinage of conversation. Sometimes the Duke of Monmouth came there to enjoy a crowded hour of the pseudo-glorious life which was to end on the scaffold after Sedgemoor. Toasted and flattered by his fellow-members and cheered by the fickle mob, he was an incongruous colleague for Titus Oates, though both were soldiers of fortune.

Like John Bunyan himself, this strange cradle of progressive opinion contributed its quota to the essentially British export known as personal freedom.

The London of the Green Ribbon Club was becoming a modern city, closely in touch with the Continent of Europe. Already, in 1681, a London penny post had been founded; ten years later, mails would go twice a week to France, Italy, Germany, Spain, the Netherlands, Denmark, and Sweden.

Only old-fashioned people now used Sedan chairs; the young and enterprising, who appreciated the speeding-up of life, travelled along the Thames in boats which were gloriously apparelled on State occasions, or crossed the City in new wooden coaches, leather-covered and nail-studded, with attractive domed roofs. Sometimes the horses were driven with coloured reins, and the coaches had windows fitted with glass; Samuel Pepys had owned such a coach as early as 1669.

Unlike his elegant contemporary, John Bunyan preferred to travel through London on foot, though after the publication of *The Pilgrim's Progress* his fame as writer and preacher carried him into the best-known pulpits of the London Nonconformists. Some of these were to be found in the Halls of the great City Companies, which the Dissenters used before they possessed chapels of their own. Their favourite Meeting Houses included Pinners' Hall, Girdlers' Hall, and Salters' Hall, architectural treasures standing back from the street behind the courtyards and gardens which had saved them from the Fire.

Pinners' Hall had been built by the Pinmakers' Company in 1636, on land leased from Sir Christopher Clitherow who had been Lord Mayor of London the previous year. It stood in Old Broad Street next to Winchester House, the home of the Paulets who were Marquesses of Winchester. The Guild had declined in importance, and after the Restoration let their building to a group of Independents.

In the year that John Bunyan was released from his first imprisonment, a famous institution known as the "Merchant's Lecture" had been founded at Pinners' Hall. From that year until 1694, this lecture was given on a Tuesday morning by outstanding Independent and Presbyterian divines. In 1677, just before Richard Wavel became pastor, the Independents remodelled the Hall, though it was to survive only for another twenty-two years. It was here that John preached one of his best-known sermons, on "The Greatness of the Soul", which he enlarged into a book in 1683.

Returning to his lodging after delivering this address, John hardly heard the congratulations of the friends who accompanied him home. He had been moved deeply by the effort he had made to save the souls of his congregation, and somehow, that day, the greatness of the soul seemed to identify itself with the greatness of the city in which his passionate words had been spoken.

In thirty years he had seen the linked cities of London and Westminster grow into one large metropolis stretching along the

Thames, which enclosed the satellite villages of Chelsea and Fulham in its deep south-westward curve. When he first observed London's river its water had been almost as clear as Cardington Brook, but now its deep stream was becoming polluted as the population increased. Garbage not thrown into the river was still deposited on the streets, in which kites were the unofficial scavengers. The smell of the City in summer reminded John of the Saffronditch at the point where, loaded with Bedford refuse, it joined the Ouse.

London was also becoming more smoky. Like other City-dwellers, the friends with whom he stayed on London Bridge had used charcoal from the Great North Wood to cook their food, or furze from Wimbledon Common. By the 1680s the sea-coal brought in ships from the north-east coast had begun to displace the swiftly burning wood. It lasted longer, but its smoke cast a thin veil of black soot over the trees in the Parks, and spoiled the growth of the roses in City gardens.

John never realized that this first mild onslaught of unregulated smoke-dust was symbolic of London's anarchic growth. Its free development, like that of the people whose capital it was, had resisted, and would continue to resist, all attempts at planning. It had grown, not steadily, but in spasmodic surges, due partly to the increase of population, but also to political changes.

The most spectacular period of its growth had been the one which John had witnessed, following the Great Fire. But even after the ancient squalid city which had defeated the modernizing schemes of Charles I had been swept away, Charles II and his scientific friends were never able to impose upon its citizens any large-scale design for its future.

London was unashamedly a commercial capital, whose practical merchants and speculative builders looked with suspicious eyes upon the exotic architectural luxuries created by Inigo Jones and his pupils. The City's conglomeration of gables and mullioned windows was the work of organized carpenters and masons who were craftsmen rather than artists. They belonged to a race which, when it was not resisting its monarchs, treated them with good-humoured tolerance rather than respect.

The men and women of London were not interested in providing their rulers with a political capital designed to impress foreigners, like the Paris of Louis XIV, or nineteenth-century Berlin. They liked their royal symbolism, but preferred it to be economical; even in 1947, when Princess Elizabeth was married, they were still arguing about the financial value of royalty in terms of Parliamentary appropriations.

If London's character was not political, it was still less ecclesiastical. In spite of all the attempts of Anglicanism to dominate policy, church interests and property exercised little influence. The combination of commercial architecture and Nonconformist preaching witnessed by large congregations in the Halls of the City Companies expressed, more appropriately than the Cathedral ceremonies of the Established Church, the spirit of that people which was a nation of shopkeepers long before Napoleon described with ineffectual contempt its obstinate source of power and pride.

From the early beginnings of the Puritan Revolution, the City in which John Bunyan's mortal body was soon to lie had been a stronghold of Nonconformity. His most eminent London friend, Sir John Shorter the goldsmith, was actively interested in Nonconformist teaching, though in order to fulfil his official functions he occasionally conformed.

In 1687, when Sir John became Lord Mayor of London, the Guildhall Chapel was closed, so he established a conventicle in Grocers' Hall where he had his official residence. Here, from time to time, he invited well-known dissenting Ministers to preach. Some of John Bunyan's few treasures which in later years were to be canonized as "relics"—his ivory-headed staff, for instance, and the small inlaid cabinet with a curious design of the musical instruments that he loved on the inside of its door—were probably gifts from this wealthy friend. His connection with Sir John and the Grocers' Hall Conventicle became so well known that, after his death, the author of *The Pilgrim's Progress* was mistakenly described by an uninformed letter-writer as "his lordship's teacher or chaplain".

But the level proletarian head of John Bunyan—who refused both the overtures made to him to work in London, and the offer of a position in a London business for his son Joseph—was never turned by the attentions of the great. At least as much as Sir John's friendship he valued that of Charles Doe, the loyal and kindly comb-maker from Southwark who came to know John Bunyan only during the last three years of his life.

Other London friends included Dr. John Owen, the Nonconformist divine who had intervened with Bishop Barlow of Lincoln to procure John's release from his second imprisonment. Dr. Owen, his senior by twelve years, shared with John the fortunate publisher of *The Pilgrim's Progress*; not long before Nathaniel Ponder issued this best-seller, he had brought out a theological work for John Owen entitled *The Reason of Faith*. Sometimes Dr. Owen, who died in 1683, invited John Bunyan to address his congregation in White's Alley, Moorfields; it was he who told Charles II that he would be glad to exchange his own erudition for the tinker's eloquence.

Another London minister whom John often visited was his old friend from Bedfordshire, George Cokayn, one of the teachers ejected after the Restoration, who was now pastor of a congregation in Red Cross Street within the City. George Cokayn owned a house at Cotton End, and a license to preach there had been granted to John Whiteman, an elder of the Bedford Church, in 1672. His London congregation included a young grocer named John Strudwick, with whom John Bunyan had become friendly. Occasionally during his London visits he stayed at John Strudwick's house, the Sign of the Star, on Snow Hill beside Holborn Bridge.

It was especially to Charles Doe and George Cokayn that posterity would owe its knowledge of John Bunyan's later years. George Cokayn was almost certainly responsible for one of the anonymous early biographies which recorded the chief events of John's life; he also took charge of the manuscript entitled *The Acceptable Sacrifice*, which was in the press when John died. In 1689 he published it with an introduction by himself, dated 21 September, 1688.

Charles Doe atoned by devotion for his lack of scholarship; in modern idiom he would be called a "fan". He himself described, in some memoirs entitled *A Collection of Experience* and published in 1700, how he came to know John Bunyan through hearing him preach at the time of the Nonconformist persecution under James II, when "because of his fame, and I having read some of his books, I had a mind to hear him".

Owing to the new opportunities given to informers, this meeting was held at a private house. John preached on a text from Proverbs x, verse 24: "The fear of the wicked, it shall come upon him: but the desire of the righteous shall be granted." This sermon was one which he subsequently expanded as a treatise found among his papers at his death, *The Desires of the Righteous Granted*.

At first Charles Doe, greatly preferring the New Testament to the Old, was prejudiced against John by his choice of text, but he soon realized that, though the words might come from Proverbs, the spirit behind them was that of the Gospels.

> "Mr. Bunyan went on and preached so New Testament-like that he made me admire, and weep for joy, and give him my affections. And he was the first man that ever I heard preach to my unenlightened understanding and experience, for methought all his sermons were adapted to my condition and had apt similitudes, being full of the love of God and the manner of its secret working upon the soul, and of the soul under the sense of it, that I could weep for joy most part of his sermons; and so, by a letter, I introduced myself into his acquaintance, and, indeed, I have not since met with a man I have liked so well. I was acquainted with him but about three years before he died, and then missed him sorely."

After James II's Declaration of Indulgence two years later, these Nonconformist meetings again became public and were held in a variety of halls and chapels. One of John's preaching-places was a strange little wooden shanty in King's Court, Great Suffolk Street, with a yawning open baptistry immediately inside the door where adults were immersed, and three galleries running round the building. Next door a tumble-down old dwelling house contained several low garrets or cupboards in the roof, where the preacher could hide if the populace showed signs of hostility.

In 1687, towards the end of John's life, a new chapel, under the control of Bishop Barlow, was erected for Presbyterian worship on ground leased for the purpose in Zoar Street, a small alley off Gravel Lane in Southwark. Here, by the Bishop's permission, John gave one of his last sermons to a packed congregation.

Wherever he preached crowds came to hear him, for his

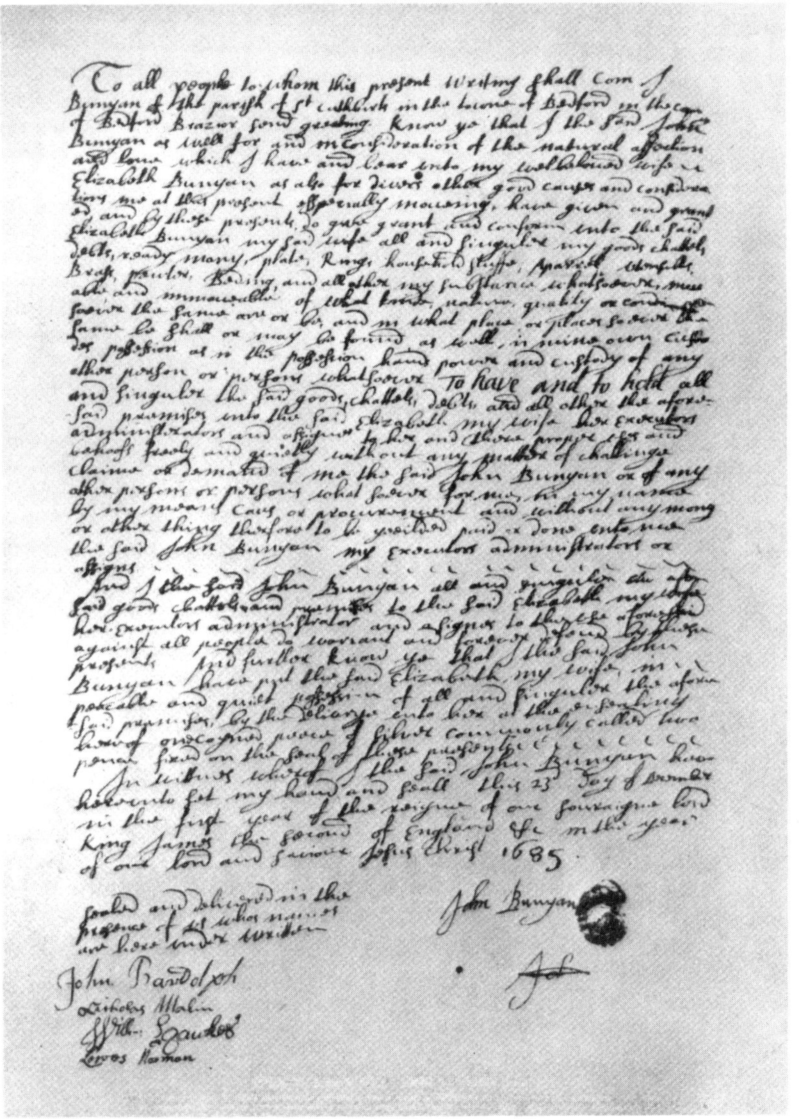

To all people to whom this present Writing shall Come I John Bunyan of the parish of St Cuthberts in the towne of Bedford in the County of Bedford Brazier send greeting. Know ye that I the said John Bunyan as well for and in Consideration of the natural affection and love which I have and bear unto my welbeloved wife Elizabeth Bunyan as also for divers other good causes and considerations me at this present especially moveing, have given and granted and by these presents do give grant and confirm unto the said Elizabeth Bunyan my said wife all and singuler my goods chattels debts, ready mony, plate, Rings, household stuffe, Apparrell, utensills, Brass, pewter, Bedding, and all other my substance whatsoever, moveable and immoveable of what kinde, nature, quality or condition soever the same are or be, and in what place or places soever the same be shall or may be found as well in mine own custody possession as in the possession hands power and custody of any other person or persons whatsoever To have and to hold all and singuler the said goods, chattels, debts and all other the aforesaid premises unto the said Elizabeth my wife her executors administrators and assignes to her and theire proper use and behoofe freely and quietly without any matter of challenge claime or demand of me the said John Bunyan or of any other person or persons whatsoever for me in my name by my means cause or procurement and without any mony or other thing therefore to be yeilded paid or done unto me the said John Bunyan my executors administrators or assignes.

And I the said John Bunyan all and singuler the aforesaid goods chattels and premises to the said Elizabeth my wife her executors administrators and assignes to the use aforesaid against all people do warrant and defend by these presents. And further know ye that I the said John Bunyan have put the said Elizabeth my wife in peaceable and quiet possession of all and singuler the aforesaid premises, by the delivery unto her at the ensealing hereof one coyned peece of silver commonly called two pence fixed on the seale of these presents.

In witness whereof I the said John Bunyan have hereunto set my hand and seale this 23 day of December in the first year of the reigne of our Soveraigne lord King James the second of England &c in the year of our Lord and Saviour Jesus Christ 1685.

John Bunyan

Sealed and delivered in the presence of us whose names are here under written

John Bardolph
Nicholas Malin
Willi: Hawkes
Lewes Harmon

BUNYAN'S DEED OF GIFT

Drawn up in his own handwriting in 1685. The original is at the Bunyan Meeting, Bedford. It was found 150 years after his death.

ZOAR STREET CHAPEL, SOUTHWARK

Here Bunyan is said to have preached in the last few months of his life. From an old print.

appearance—anonymously described by Charles Doe or George Cokayn—was now as remarkable as his vigorous manner and eloquent message. Though a tall, powerfully built man with the large bones of peasant stock, he had always been too energetic to grow corpulent in middle-age. His reddish hair, sprinkled with grey, still grew abundantly above his high forehead and penetrating blue eyes; his nose was large but straight, and his mouth generous beneath a short moustache. The pallor of imprisonment had long given way to his normal ruddy complexion, but the severity of that ordeal remained written in a sternness of countenance which made the mild affability of his normal conversation a disarming surprise.

Usually reticent in private company, John became vehement in both language and delivery the moment that he reached the pulpit. In his sermons he was most apt to reveal his prejudices, especially against the Book of Common Prayer, but his utterances were usually illumined with a charity and tolerance far beyond his time. To the end of his public life, which continued until ten days before his death, he deplored "personal disputes, heats and bitter contentions", and insisted that, if his followers wanted to label him, they must call him "a *Christian*" and nothing more.

> "And as for those factious titles of Anabaptists, Independents, Presbyterians, or the like, I conclude that they came neither from Jerusalem, nor from Antioch, but rather from Hell and Babylon; for they naturally tend to divisions. You may know them by their fruits."

Though it is usually the majority which subscribes to prejudices and minorities which seek to discard them, the minority that was ready to accept the doctrine of Toleration was now large enough to give John a powerful following. Soon—far sooner than he and his colleagues imagined—it would be representative enough to turn Intolerance off the English throne. Charles Doe recorded the enthusiasm of that minority with a vividness enhanced by his own:

> "When Mr. Bunyan preached in London, if there were but one day's notice given, there would be more people come

together to hear him preach than the meeting-house could hold. I have seen to hear him preach, by my computation, about twelve hundred at a morning lecture by seven o'clock on a working day, in the dark winter-time. I also computed about three thousand that came to hear him one Lord's Day at London, at a town's-end meeting-house, so that half were fain to go back again for want of room, and then himself was fain at a back-door to be pulled almost over people to get up-stairs to his pulpit."

In his eager affection, Charles Doe went on to describe John Bunyan as "a second Paul". His estimate was exaggerated, but not wholly inappropriate. Paul was a tent-maker and John a tinker; both men experienced conversion through the consciousness of divine displeasure, the one on the road to Damascus and the other on Elstow Green. Both, after a period of apprenticeship, were encouraged by a heavenly vision, Paul at Corinth and John at Stevington Cross; both suffered persecution and imprisonment, sought comfort in prison from "books and parchments", and contributed the story of their spiritual odysseys to sacred literature.

Through "our light affliction, which is but for a moment", each, in his own day, followed his Master to the Celestial City, and at long last added the palm of mankind's retrospective reverence to the golden crown of abounding grace.

After publishing *The Holy War* in 1682, John Bunyan produced six short books before he began, in the midst of these triumphant London years, to write the second part of *The Pilgrim's Progress*.

The Barren Fig-Tree, or *The Doom and Downfall of the Fruitless Professor*, an exposition of the parable in the thirteenth chapter of St. Luke, followed immediately after *The Holy War*. Next came, in 1683, the published version of the sermon on *The Greatness of the Soul and the Unspeakableness of the Loss Thereof*, which John had preached at Pinners' Hall.

During the same year, in *A Case of Conscience Resolved*, he turned aside from general principles to advise a group of London women who had consulted him regarding the propriety of meeting separately for prayer, "without their men". After giving his judgment against this practice on the ground that it would encourage masculine idleness, he published as a half-sheet broadside in April 1684, a sixteen-stanza poem, *A Caution to stir up to watch against Sin*, which appealed especially to male Christians to practise the principles that they professed.

On similar lines was *A Holy Life the Beauty of Christianity*, also written in 1684 and published early in 1685. John's triumphant vitality, despite the renewal of persecution and fresh threats to his freedom, led him to produce a third book in this crowded year. *Seasonable Counsel*; or, *Advice to Sufferers*, was essentially a tract for the times; it was both a statement of loyalty to the King and his Government, unjust though they might be, and a challenge to the persecuted to trust in God and face their sufferings in a mood of constructive acceptance.

These short pieces were mere preliminaries to the greater work, planned ever since the success of *The Pilgrim's Progress*, which John had been writing, mentally and on paper, for the past two or three years. When he finished his most popular book in 1677, he had suggested in the last line of his Conclusion that he might be prepared to "dream again". The fulfilment of this half-defined intention was soon precipitated by the attempts of some writers to deprive him of credit for his work, and of others to do his dreaming for him.

In "An Advertisement To The Reader", published at the end of the Introduction to *The Holy War*, he had countered his detractors with typical directness:

> Some say the "Pilgrim's Progress" is not mine,
> Insinuating as if I would shine
> In name and fame by the worth of another,
> Like some made rich by robbing of their brother.
> Or that so fond I am of being sire,
> I'll father bastards; or, if need require,
> I'll tell a lie in print to get applause.
> I scorn it: John such dirt-heap never was
> Since God converted him.

The imitators were less easy to deal with, particularly when —like one who signed himself T. S.—their supplements claimed to improve upon the original by methods which "may prevent that lightness and laughter which the reading of some passages occasions in some vain and frothy minds". Since no copyright laws existed to protect him, there was nothing for John to do but write, as his thirty-fourth book, the promised sequel before other "improvers" stepped into the field, and as vigorously as possible relegate their counterfeit productions to the obscurity that they deserved.

Introducing his own sequel with eight pages of rhymed couplets entitled "The Authors Way of Sending forth his Second Part of the Pilgrim", John tackled the parasites who battened on his fame.

> 'Tis true, some have of late, to Counterfeit
> My Pilgrim, to their own, my Title set;
> Yea others, half my Name and Title too;
> Have stitched to their Book, to make them do;
> But yet they by their Features do declare
> Themselves not mine to be, whose ere they are.

When the Second Part was ready for publication early in 1685, John appended, on 1 January, a firm note on the reverse of the title-page:

> "I appoint Mr. Nathaniel Ponder, But no other, to Print this Book."

Like Cervantes' continuation of *Don Quixote*, but unlike the majority of sequels, this narrative, which showed Christian's family following his footsteps through a landscape now well-known to thousands of readers, was an immediate success. It soon became almost as popular as Part I, and six editions had been published by 1693.

In common with the adventures of Christian and the complex allegory of *The Holy War*, the Second Part of *The Pilgrim's Progress* sprang from the essence of John's own life, combined with detailed observation, recollections of the books that he had read, and statements of his dreams for humanity and himself. The story of Christiana, her children, and her young companion

Mercy, named after the daughter of John's old friend William Dell, was a moral rather than a theological tale. It also resembled a modern picaresque novel even more closely than its dramatic but less discursive predecessor.

Repeatedly, as in the account of the boy Matthew's illness, the description of Mercy's love-affair with Mr. Brisk, and Mr. Great-heart's long narrative of Mr. Fearing, "one of the most trouble-some Pilgrims that ever I met with in all my days", the story ran away with both the allegory and the author. It was held in check only by the geographical framework, based upon the familiar Bedfordshire countryside.

The action of the book was less tense and vivid than the drama of Christian's pilgrimage, but John's handling of his characters had become freer. Incidents were more numerous, personalities more varied; the pilgrims, gathering accretions until they resembled a small village on the march, moved in a more leisurely fashion, and breathed a gentler air.

Their journey was less frightening even when giants were encountered, for the reader knew in advance that these enemies would be slain. Conversation was affectionate and hospitality agreeable; the Interpreter addressed Mercy as "dear heart", and the House Beautiful provided her, in a lengthy sojourn, with "Musick in the House, Musick in the Heart, and Musick also in Heaven". When the Pilgrims departed, agreeable gifts of wine, corn, figs, raisins, and pomegranates were sent to them by the Lord of the Way to make their pilgrimage easier.

In his Prefatory lines, John dwelt upon these amiable episodes with evident satisfaction.

> Go, tell them also of those dainty things,
> That Pilgrimage unto the Pilgrim brings,
> Let them acquainted be, too, how they are
> Beloved of their King, under his care;
> What goodly Mansions for them he provides,
> Tho they meet with rough Winds, and swelling Tides.
> How brave a calm they will enjoy at last,
> Who to their Lord, and by his ways hold fast.

On leaving House Beautiful, Christiana and her companions found this brave calm in the Valley of Humiliation, which they entered to the melodious notes of "Countrey Birds" whose singing recalled the words of the hymn "All people that on earth do dwell". The Valley had become a memorial garden, like the transformed battlegrounds of the Somme after the First World War, with an inscribed pillar recording Christian's victory over Apollyon. It was a green and fruitful place, "beautified with Lillies", where "labouring Men" received "good Estates", and the pilgrims encountered nothing more frightening than the shepherd boy singing one of John's best Elizabethan-style lyrics:

He that is down, needs fear no fall,
He that is low, no Pride:
He that is humble, ever shall
Have God to be his Guide.

Even Vanity Fair, where the travellers made a long stay at the house of Mr. Mnason who kept "a very fair Dining-Room", turned out to be, in the words of American municipal advertisements, "a good place to live". The martyrdom of Faithful had made the unruly citizens "more moderate than formerly".

"I think," reported Mr. Contrite, who lived there, "the blood of Faithful lieth with load upon them till now; for since they burned him, they have been ashamed to burn any more. In those days we were afraid to walk the Streets, but now we can shew our Heads."

This Second Part of *The Pilgrim's Progress* reflects John Bunyan with a soul completely adult. The old narrow Puritanism which caused so many of his early conflicts has developed into a mellow toleration of music, dancing and gaiety if they are accompanied by inward grace, and a deep human understanding of folly, weakness and error. Not least interesting, in the light that it throws upon his own progress, is his treatment of the spiritually impaired. Not one fails to reach the Celestial City, though Mr. Ready-to-halt gets to the River bank on his crutches, and Mr. Despondency and his daughter, Mrs. Much-afraid, have to be rescued by Mr. Great-heart from Giant Despair.

Mr. Great-heart, Mr. Standfast, and Mr. Valiant-for-Truth represent both the Puritan warriors whom John had admired during his obscure activities as a young soldier, and his conception of his own ideal self. But in contrast to their heroic portraits, Mr. Fearing and other minor characters are portrayed with a spiritual comprehension which is equally tender and true.

They have, indeed, their place in any text-book on modern psychology; Mr. Honest is a staunch curmudgeon, Mr. Despondency a characteristic melancholic, and Mr. Fearing a typical example of anxiety neurosis. John showed his deepest insight in his description of this troublesome pilgrim; he recalls the wartime behaviour of our own neurotic acquaintances, who found bombs and other actual calamities a drastic medicine for the self-manufactured obsessions which frightened them so much more.

"Difficulties, Lyons, or Vanity-Fair, he feared not at all," wrote John. " 'Twas only Sin, Death and Hell, that was to him a Terror; because he had some Doubts about his Interest in that Celestial Countrey."

Throughout the lovely narrative of Mr. Fearing's pilgrimage, John's merciful New Testament God, unlike his old wrathful Jehovah, tempers the wind to the shorn lamb. The Slough of Despond is dry on a "Sun-shine Morning"; there is "a kind of a Sympathy" between him and the Valley of Humiliation, where he lies on the ground and kisses the flowers. The Valley of the Shadow of Death, though he approaches it "ready to dye for Fear", is "as quiet while he went thorow it, as ever I knew it before or since". And when he finally stands on the River brink, shivering with terror lest after all he should not see the Face of his Lord, "the water of that River was lower at this time, than ever I saw it in all my Life; so he went over at last, not much above wet-shod".

After John had brought the rest of his miscellaneous company to the banks of that River, he described their separate departures in response to the celestial summons with a poignancy which suggests his intuitive awareness of his own approaching end. Unlike Christian and Hopeful, these pilgrims do not confront their ordeal alone; those that survive accompany them to the River brink, just as he himself, only three years later, was to be accompanied there by his London colleagues.

As "the Day drew on that Christiana must be gone . . . the Road was full of People to see her take her Journey. But behold all the Banks beyond the River were full of Horses and Chariots, which were come down from above to accompany her to the City-gate". Following her, one after another, the halt, lame and despondent throw away their fears and their crutches, and plunge into the water.

For Mr. Valiant-for-Truth and Mr. Standfast, the last to be summoned, death has no sting and the grave no victory. In the words of Mr. Standfast's farewell, John conveyed a prophetic message to his family and friends:

> " 'I see my self now at the end of my Journey, my toilsome Days are ended. I am going now to see that Head that was Crowned with Thorns and that Face that was spit upon for me.
>
> 'I have formerly lived by Hear-say, and Faith, but now I go where I shall live by sight, and shall be with him, in whose Company I delight my self.
>
> 'I have loved to hear my Lord spoken of, and wherever I have seen the print of his Shooe in the Earth, there I have coveted to set my Foot too . . . He has held me, and I have kept me from mine Iniquities; Yea, my Steps hath he strengthend in his Way.'
>
> Now while he was thus in Discourse his Countenance changed, his strong men bowed under him, and after he had said, Take me, for I come unto thee, he ceased to be seen of them."

Mr. Standfast ceased to be seen of them because, though John Bunyan's imagination could now compass nearly all human vicissitudes, one universal experience remained unknown to him. He had passed so often through the deeps of affliction, but still there was one more river to cross. At the brink of its dark waters, he had now almost arrived.

GROCER'S HALL IN THE CITY OF LONDON

Sir John Shorter, when Lord Mayor of London in 1687, established a Conventicle here at which Bunyan and other leading Dissenters preached.

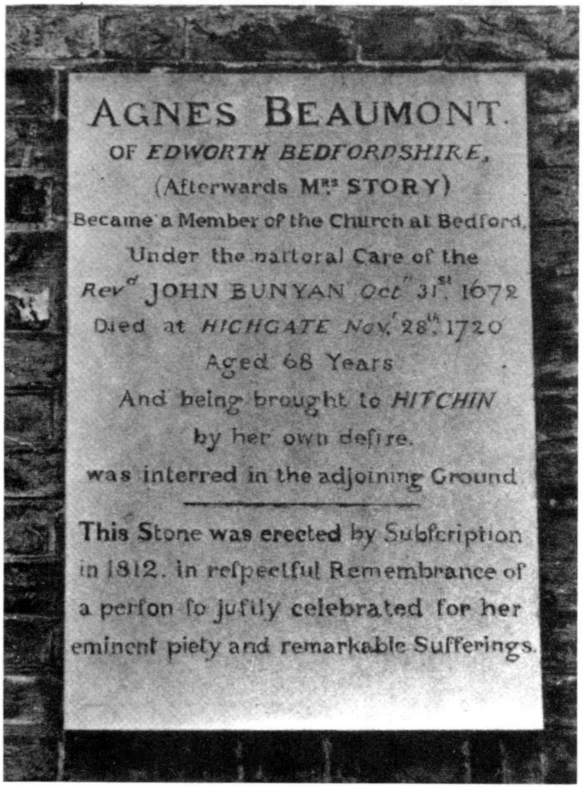

THE AGNES BEAUMONT MEMORIAL
On the outer wall of Tilehouse Street Baptist Church, Hitchin, facing the graveyard.

JOHN STRUDWICK'S HOUSE ON SNOW HILL, LONDON
The house where John Bunyan died, reproduced from

CHAPTER XIX

ONE MORE RIVER

"Many have spoke of it, but none can tell what the Valley of the shadow of death should mean, until they come in it themselves."
JOHN BUNYAN: *The Pilgrim's Progress.* Part II.

IN the middle of August 1688, John Bunyan set out from Bedford on a typical mission.

He was due in London the next day, but had decided to make a circuitous journey by way of Reading in order to reconcile a young Bedford neighbour with his father. The son had incurred the father's displeasure, and was much perturbed because he had been told that he would be disinherited.

When the young man approached him, John characteristically agreed to act as peacemaker. He regarded the work of reconciliation, whether public or private, as an important part of his Christian profession. To his youthful petitioner he had repeated the words which he so often used: "It is love that edifieth, but division pulleth down."

Though John was so ready to undertake this personal service, Elizabeth wished with anxious concern that he had relegated it to someone else. She knew that he was tired, for his health had been poor ever since the spring, when he had suffered from an attack of the sweating-sickness which his successors were to call by the equally unscientific name of influenza.

John smiled cheerfully and caressed her hair with more than usual tenderness before he mounted his horse, for she had bidden him farewell as though she were saying good-bye for ever instead of for only a fortnight.

After all, he thought with rueful affection, as he waved his hand and rode off towards the Bridge, her loving anxiety was only natural. In two months' time he would be sixty, and his life had been hard from his childhood onwards. He could not expect to ride so fast, or to fit so much into a day, as he had been able to do at twenty-seven when he first started preaching in the Bedfordshire villages.

Sometimes the thirty-three years that he had lived since then seemed very long, especially when he reflected that the whole life of Jesus had been no longer, or recalled the endless months in prison. But when he thought in terms of what he had done and still hoped to do, those three decades seemed very short.

How strange it was that a man's life should be so vulnerable, when the fruit of his mind and spirit, if preserved and cherished, could last almost for ever!

As John rode south-west, the cloud-masses which heralded stormy weather piled up all over the sky. He did not notice them, for he was thinking with satisfaction of how much his own mind had produced during the last two or three years. It had been especially active during the past eight months, for in that short period he had sent no less than five books to the press. The manuscript of a sixth, *The Acceptable Sacrifice* or *The Excellency of a Broken Heart*, he was carrying with him to London; it brought the number of his publications up to forty-three.

In 1685 he had followed the Second Part of *The Pilgrim's Progress* with a short book entitled *The Perpetuity of the Seventh-Day Sabbath*, and a treatise on the parable of *The Pharisee and the Publican*. These had been issued by a new publisher, John Harris, "over against the Church in the Poultrey".

The current discussion in clerical circles of the possible alternative use of the Jewish Sabbath was not, John knew, a question of more than temporary interest, but it seemed to him to cause the very kind of doctrinal controversy which so unnecessarily divided the Church of God. In his work on the subject he made one of his few references to economic inequality, for his book, he stated, "being little, may best suit such as have but shallow purses, short memories, and but little time to spare, which usually is the lot of the mean and poorer sort of men".

John Bunyan was no seeker after wealth and place; the London preaching position which he refused would have given him more comfort than the pastorship of the Bedford Church. What did move him to occasional anger was injustice—"one law for the rich and another for the poor". He had sometimes reflected that, if he had been a wealthy man, he could probably have bought himself out of prison without violating his conscience by undertakings to give up preaching. From Bedford Gaol he had written with some bitterness in *Grace Abounding* of the "crackt-groats and four pence-half-pennies" which rich men carried in their purses to bestow on the poor, "when their Gold is in their Trunks at home".

Of all the nine works that he contemplated as he rode, the one which had given him most pleasure to write had been his *Book for Boys and Girls*, or *Country Rhimes for Children in verse on seventy-four things*, published in May 1686. He often thought, as he composed his swift unpolished verses, of Quarles' *Emblems* which had pleased him so much in his own youth; from memory and experience he finally produced a species of moral *Aesop's Fables*. Today we appreciate their informality better than John's nineteenth-century critics, just as we prefer the brick-and-timber of the seventeenth century to the intricate decorations on the Albert Memorial.

After the little initial reading lesson for children, the affectionate father of six sons and daughters, now grown up, explained that his verses were meant for readers of all ages.

> They're Boys and Girls of all Sorts and Degrees,
> From those of Age, to Children on the Knees.
> Thus comprehensive am I in my Notions;
> They tempt me to it by their childish Motions.
> We now have Boys with Beards, and Girls that be
> Big as old Women, wanting Gravity.

Having contributed this characteristic description of the perennial non-adult, John plunged eagerly into his homely rhymes. As though approaching death brought back his earliest memories with peculiar vividness, he wrote, usually with graphic joy, of birds and beasts in their relation to each other and to man; of the flint in the water, the swallow in the air, the sinner caught "like a fly in a Spider's web"; of the bee, the "cuckow", the mole in the ground, the fruitfulness of a tree, the frog, the candle, the horse in the mill, the whipping of a top. Even the penny loaf, the looking-glass, the lanthorn, and a pair of spectacles, provided themes for his fancy.

The lines *Upon the Boy on his Hobby-Horse* showed a parent's tender observation of the children for whom he wrote:

Look how he swaggers, cocks his Hat and rides,
How on his hobby-horse, himself he prides:
He looketh grim, and up his Head doth toss,
Says he'll ride over's with his Hobby-horse.

They were strangely off-set by the only bitter verses in the book, which embodied the universal protest of disillusioned fathers and mothers against *The Disobedient Child*:

They snap, and snarl, if Parents them controul,
Tho but in things, most hurtful to the Soul.
They reckon they are Masters, and that we,
Who Parents are, should to them Subjects be!
They'll by wrong doings, under Parents, gather
And say, it is no Sin to rob a Father.
They'l jostle Parents out of Place and Pow'r
They'l make themselves the Head, and them devour.

This utterance is so unlike John's habitual geniality that even he must sometimes have endured the exasperation eternally aroused in the older generation by its arrogant juniors. There may be more than coincidence in the fact that John's eldest son, also a brazier, joined the Bedford Church only in 1693, though he was a man of thirty-two when his father died. Possibly this younger John Bunyan typified the "disobedient child" who, like so many disobedient children, became reconciled with his parent in spirit only when the elder John was no longer there to benefit by the change.

The remainder of John Bunyan's nine new books were less gaily attractive than his rhymes for children, but each one possessed some feature that made it memorable. Their publication followed James II's second Declaration of Indulgence; John had worked on first one and then the other during the two preceding years.

Amongst these five the most significant was *The Jerusalem Sinner Saved*, or *Good News for the Vilest of Men*, for it provided further evidence of John's transformation from an Old Testament to a New Testament type of Christian. He had long outgrown the youthful tendency to sit in judgment which had wrought *A Few*

[London News Agency Photos, Ltd.

BUNHILL FIELDS, 1948

The bomb-damaged cemetery in the City of London where John Bunyan is buried.

[*London News Agency Photos, L*

BUNYAN'S TOMB, 1948

Beneath the plane trees in Bunhill Fields, at the end of the path.

Sighs from Hell; the keynote of *The Jerusalem Sinner Saved* was not condemnation but comfort.

"I have been Vile myself, but have obtained Mercy," he wrote, "and I would have my Companions in Sin partake of Mercy too." The latter part of the book was addressed particularly to the victims of despair.

"There is nothing like Faith to help at a Pinch," he advised them. "Faith dissolves Doubts, as the Sun drives away the Mists."

This message of consolation was evidently acceptable to many remorseful Christians, for forty years after John's death his expanded sermon had gone through ten editions and been translated into several languages. Its immediate successor, *The Work of Jesus Christ as an Advocate*, dealt with the similar theme of Christ's intervention for sinners.

In *A Discourse of the Building, Nature, Excellency, and Government of the House of God*, John turned for the last time to verse, and in a pocket volume of sixty-three pages wrote a metrical rendering of the "House Beautiful" theme in *The Pilgrim's Progress*. *The Water of Life* and *Solomon's Temple Spiritualiz'd* were again both sermons, describing the divine grace and glory.

While John contemplated his recent books on his long fifty-mile ride, the sultry day had grown heavier until the clouds seemed to press down upon his head like a low ceiling in an airless room. Preoccupied though he was with pleasant thoughts of achievement, he became conscious as he rode through Aylesbury that his head and limbs were aching. Pressing on beneath the ridge of the Chilterns, he passed the villages of Marlow and Henley.

When the russet-hued roofs of Reading came in sight, he packed up his meditations and prepared for the interview before him.

On one or two previous occasions, John Bunyan had visited Reading. Once, when the fire of persecution blazed fiercely, he came to the Thames-side town disguised as a carter holding a whip, and preached to the people. Now he was able to ride openly through the streets and deliver his sermon without fear of informers. King James's Declaration, however specious, had some concrete advantages for travelling Dissenters.

The Baptists' Meeting House was situated in Mill Lane;

during times of trouble a back door enabled the congregation to escape across the bridge which spanned a branch of the River Kennett into a boat-house where they sometimes met. Nearby stood the Bear Inn, a few hundred yards from the top of Pigney Lane. At the time of John Bunyan's visit, the Reading pastor was John Rance. John spent the night with him after preaching, and called next morning upon the irate father of his Bedford friend.

He found the interview less troublesome than he had feared; the father, perhaps secretly hoping for a way of reconciliation, eventually proved amenable to John's plea for love and forgiveness.

"I will ask the boy to come here and talk things over," he said. "I shall surely be glad to see him."

John left the house thankfully assured that his mission had succeeded, but the talk had lasted longer than he expected and it was nearly midday when he started on the forty-mile ride to London. Yesterday's clouds had returned, and now covered the sky. A dull stillness, like the interval of silence before thunder, hung over the fields where the elms, overburdened with their summer leaves, stood motionless as sentries, and the ripe purple of elderberries darkened the dividing hedges.

The thunder did not come, but when John was half-way to London a heavy storm of rain broke, and continued to descend with pitiless intensity. The raindrops blinded his horse, which slowed down and stumbled perpetually. Before he started, he had already been fatigued from the previous day's long journey; now, soaked and shivering, he rode stoically on through the moist, steaming lanes. As the late summer afternoon darkened, the drenched leaves of the thick woods dripped cold water on to his head and shoulders.

John arrived totally exhausted at the home of his friend John Strudwick, where he was staying for this London visit; he was hardly able to alight from his weary horse when he reached the four-storeyed house with the gabled roof near the Church of St. Sepulchre. Strudwick and his wife, who hurried out to help him, were distressed by John's pale face and uncertain gait.

The beloved pastor, who had always seemed to them the quintessence of energy and vigour, looked suddenly old and broken. They hastened to put him to bed, rubbed him down with warm towels, and gave him a hot potion of herbs to drink while they dried his saturated garments before the kitchen fire.

"Crossing the River of Death"
(From the Chinese translation of *The Pilgrim's Progress*)

John slept with the heaviness of extreme fatigue, and next morning felt better, though his limbs still ached. The following day or two he stayed quietly in John Strudwick's house, preparing for the press his latest book, *The Acceptable Sacrifice*, which George Larkin was to publish.

Its theme, based upon the seventeenth verse of Psalm 51 —"The sacrifice of God is a troubled spirit: a broken and contrite heart, O God, shalt thou not despise"—was similar to that of *The Jerusalem Sinner Saved*. Besides emphasizing God's readiness to accept a contrite heart, John also tried to show how the process of repentance could be induced. A man, he insisted, could not be reclaimed from sin "but by the wounding, breaking, and disabling of the heart that loves it".

On Sunday, 19 August, John had promised to preach to the congregation of his friend John Gammon, in Petticoat Lane, which was later to be rechristened Middlesex Street. This Whitechapel meeting-house stood close to the eastern entrance to the city, a "spacious fair street and somewhat long". Being the road into Essex it was already a great thoroughfare, with houses growing up on either side.

John Bunyan walked the mile to the meeting with John Strudwick. He had not previously been out since his exhausting ride, and the short walk seemed to him enormously long. His feet and body felt heavy, and for the first time in many years he wondered apprehensively how he was going to acquit himself in the pulpit. But when he stood there looking upon the customary crowd of listeners, his energy temporarily returned, and he preached with unimpaired passion upon his text from the first chapter of St. John, verse 13:

"Which were born, not of blood, nor of the will of the flesh, nor of the will of man, but of God."

This sermon also was subsequently published, though not from John's manuscript. A member of the congregation reconstructed it from his notes, in which he had carefully copied the preacher's concluding words:

> "Be ye holy in all manner of conversation. Consider that the holy God is your Father, and let this oblige you to live like the children of God, that you may look your Father in the face with comfort another day."

That "other day" was now fast approaching for John Bunyan. Two days after his sermon, on 21 August, the symptoms of pneumonia began to appear, and he retired to bed in a high fever. The storm which drenched him on his ride from Reading had conveyed his summons to cross the River. Though he was not yet old, his physique had been undermined by years of prison and his phenomenal energy sapped by persistent overwork. The sufferings which he had survived when others sank under them took their toll at last.

He grew delirious and a doctor was summoned, but his acute illness was now too deeply established to respond to treatment. Occasionally he became conscious of his closest friends—George Cokayn, Charles Doe, John Strudwick—moving quietly in and out of his darkened room, and accepted with patient gratitude their anxious attempts to mitigate his discomfort. But his mind continually wandered, and his thoughts travelled far from the London bedroom in which he lay dying.

He did not know how ill he was or he would have asked for Elizabeth to be summoned, and his friends did not realize until too late that this was indeed the end. But he thought of her constantly, and of his blind Mary, that beloved eldest child whose death during his prison years had deepened the shadows of his night.

Sometimes, in the haphazard roaming of his feverish thoughts, Mary and his sister Margaret, the playmate of his childhood, fused into one. Again he and she sat fishing together on the banks of the Ouse where the August fields were white with meadow-sweet, or wandered hand-in-hand looking for the dark-blue, pink-tipped buds of the early autumn gentians on the Chiltern Hills.

He had always thought of those chalk downs as the Delectable Mountains, and now they seemed more desirable than ever; he longed for their fresh winds to cool his hot forehead and burning limbs. When John Strudwick's wife brought a bowl of water and laved his face and hands, he dreamed that he stood beneath the crystal streams which flowed like fountains down the steep slopes where the chalk showed white through the short dry grass.

The day before John died, an old friend joined him on the River brink. Passing Newgate on his return from St. Bartholomew's

Fair, which he had proclaimed open according to custom, Sir John Shorter was thrown from his horse a few minutes' walk from John Strudwick's house. John Bunyan was too ill to be told that his friend had been mortally injured so close to the spot where he lay. The former Lord Mayor survived him only by four days; he died on 4 September, and was buried in the Lady Chapel of Southwark Cathedral.

On the morning of 31 August a shower of rain moistened the dry streets of the City, though later the sky cleared and the sun came out. John Bunyan's fever had now left him, but the strain on his tired heart had been too great for recovery. His life of dynamic energy, with its rich joys, deep sorrows, prolonged endurance, and gradual garnering of wisdom, was over all too soon.

Throughout that day he lay with closed eyes, instinctively fighting for breath. From time to time George Cokayn or Charles Doe wiped the moisture from his face; it was all, now, that they could do for him. Towards evening he became conscious and tried to sit up; this last effort revealed to him his extreme weakness, and he realized that he was dying. To George Cokayn he spoke in a whisper; he desired nothing more, he said, than to be with Christ. He did wish he could have seen Elizabeth and the children once more, but if he must leave them without a word of farewell, that too was the will of God . . .

Again he relapsed into unconsciousness, and his dreams took flight to the place which throughout his life as preacher and pastor had been identified with his liberation from the burden of sin. Once more he came up the winding road from the Holy Well in the valley to "a place somewhat ascending", and knelt for the last time at Stevington Cross. Its base was deep in shadow, but the golden light of the setting sun illumined its head until the outlines of the ancient stone were lost in glory.

Suddenly, as he finished his prayer and looked up, the heavens opened above the cross-roads. Through the fiery clouds he thought that he saw the walls of the Celestial City, and a host of Shining Ones standing there with crowns on their heads and palms in their hands.

In their midst was a great white throne where a Figure sat with His Face turned away, but even as John waited trembling, the Face looked down from heaven upon the Cross. Immediately its summit appeared to ascend until it vanished into the radiance above his head, and the steps at its base to lengthen until they stretched from the village street to the gates of the City. In a final rapture of recognition, John knew for all eternity that the Lord of the Way was not the wrathful God of his conversion on Elstow Green, but the merciful Jesus who had pardoned his sins and accepted him as His disciple.

Gazing upon that Face in the sunset sky, it seemed to him that he stretched out his hands as he started to climb the steps, and cried aloud in Mr. Standfast's words, "Take me, for I come unto Thee!"

But in the London room where love could not reclaim his worn-out body, the watchers beside the bed only heard him draw his last lingering breath as twilight eclipsed the waning day and "the sun went down upon Christian".

When the letter from London arrived at St. Cuthbert's Street, Elizabeth knew what it contained. With the prophetic intuition of deep love, which functions independently of knowledge or reason, she had known for a fortnight that the news was coming.

After she had read the letter, she went to the window and looked at the autumn fields stretching south to the Ouse where, only the day before his departure, she had walked with John amid the pollen-laden tufts of the long feathery grasses. They would never walk there again, because he had now crossed another River which she too would soon experience.

The many former calamities that she had shared with John had always been bearable because they were due to the operation of external events, and never to any failure in their mutual love. This time, though the disaster still came as a fortuitous happening, it meant the removal of his strong and devoted companionship.

She had lived for him and his children, and the news dealt her a blow as mortal as the rain-storm had inflicted on John. Though she was still under fifty, she survived him only long enough to see his affairs left in order, and the publication of his remaining manuscripts put in hand.

To the members of the Bedford Church, the suddenness of John's end and the fact that he was away from home when he died seemed a tragedy which overwhelmed them. Sorrowfully the record of his death was entered in the Church Book by William Hawkes, the husband of John Gifford's daughter, who in 1685 had been one of the four witnesses to John's Deed of Gift:

> "Wednesday 4th of September was kept in prayre and humilyation for this Heavy Stroak upon us, ye Death of dare (dear) bro: Bunyan. Apoynted also that Wednesday next be kept in praire and humiliation on the same Account."

The stricken Church set aside yet another day, 18 September, "to Humble themselves before God by ffasting and prayre for his Hevy and Sevear Stroak upon us in takeing away our Honoured Brother Bunyan by death". It was three years before they appointed another pastor.

John Bunyan left no worldly wealth; a verse in one of his last books, *The Building, Nature, Excellencies, and Government of the House of God*, indicated that he neither possessed nor valued it.

> Is not each thing we have a-dying?
> My house, my wife, my child, they all grow old,
> Nor am I e'er the younger for my gold;
> Here's none abiding, all things fade away.
> Poor I at best am but a clod of clay.

"By reason," says one of his anonymous biographers, "of the many losses he sustained by imprisonment and spoil, of his chargeable sickness, etc., his earthly treasure swelled not to excess."

A prolonged search failed to locate his Deed of Gift, and the administration of his estate was therefore granted to Elizabeth and two of his Bedford colleagues, Thomas Woodward, Maltster, and William Nicholls, Draper. When the inventory had been taken, the total value amounted to £42 19*s.* 0*d.* John's books had brought him none of the fortune, real or imaginary, which is nowadays attributed to the authors of "best-sellers".

On the sale of these modest goods, and the small profit then available to authors from their publications, Elizabeth lived until she followed him, as Christiana had followed Christian, across the River which bounded the wilderness of this world. But before her death in 1691, she had one more service to render him. Towards the end of 1688, George Cokayn had brought out *The Acceptable Sacrifice* with a Preface by himself, but among John's papers Elizabeth found a number of unpublished manuscripts ready to go to the press. Though her limited means made it impossible for her to issue these herself, she endeavoured through one of John's publishers to find a way of getting them printed.

In the *Mercurius Reformatus* for 11 June, 1690, a relevant advertisement caught the devoted eye of Charles Doe:

> "Mr. John Bunyan, Author of *The Pilgrim's Progress* and many other excellent Books, that have found great acceptance, hath left behind him Ten Manuscripts prepared by himself for the Press before his Death: His Widow is desired to print them . . . which will make together a book for 10s. in sheets, in Fol. All persons who desire so great and good a work should be performed with speed, are desired to send in 5s. for their first payment to Dorman Newman, at the King's Arms in the Poultrey, London."

Through the loyal energy of Doe, these manuscripts—mainly enlarged sermons—were eventually published in a Folio which also contained a circular, entitled *The Struggler*, describing his efforts to produce John's posthumous writings and collect the necessary funds. In *A Collection of Experience*, issued in 1700, Charles Doe described his decision to become a publisher and bookseller after remembering the comfort that John's work had given him.

> "Being under the sense of the peculiar Love of God, it came into my mind as I was upon my Stair-head what work I should do for God, and about the middle of the Stairs I reckoned that to sell books was the best I could do, and by the time I came to the bottom I concluded to sell Mr. Bunyan's, and so I began to sell Books and have sold about 3,000 of Mr. Bunyan's, and have also been concerned in printing the following Books: The works of Mr. John Bunyan in folio, and the 'Heavenly Footman', by John Bunyan."

Charles Doe had intended to produce a companion Folio

containing some of John's greater works, but interested publishers raised objections, and the second Folio did not appear until 1736–37 under other editors. The most important of the sermons published by Doe was *The Heavenly Footman,* which he bought from John's eldest son after Elizabeth's death and produced in 1698. It was addressed to "slothful and careless people", and described the man "who runs for Heaven". Of nine "Directions" given to the runner, the fourth especially recalled *The Pilgrim's Progress*:

> "Beware of by-paths, take heed thou dost not turn into those lanes which lead out of the way. There are crooked paths, paths in which men go astray, paths that lead to death and damnation."

The most valuable of John's works from a biographical standpoint, *A Relation of the Imprisonment of Mr. John Bunyan,* did not appear in Charles Doe's collection. Carefully preserved by John's family or friends for nearly a century, it was published in 1765. The fate of two other short productions, *A Christian Dialogue* and *A Pocket Concordance,* remains unknown.

"Here are Sixty Pieces of his Labours," wrote Charles Doe at the end of his *Catalogue of all Mr. Bunyan's Books,* published with *The Heavenly Footman,* "and he was Sixty Years of Age."

The day before William Hawkes recorded John Bunyan's death in the Book of the Bedford Church, a growing company of mourners followed his sixty-year-old body to its grave in Bunhill Fields.

During the fifteenth century, this City cemetery had been part of the manor of Finsbury Farm. Then known as "Bonhill Field", it was consecrated in 1549 in order that a quantity of human bones removed from the charnel house at St. Paul's might be buried there. In 1665, when the victims of the Great Plague were dying at the rate of eight to ten thousand persons a week, the burial-ground was used again, and later enclosed by a brick wall at the City's expense. Defoe believed that the Great Plague Death-pit was in or near this place.

Robert Southey described Bunhill Fields as the "Campo Santo" of the Dissenters, since it was unconnected with any ecclesiastical building. Though Anglicans and Catholics were occasionally buried there, the Nonconformists had made it their own. John Owen, followed by a long procession of mourners, had preceded John Bunyan in 1683, and George Cokayn was to follow him in 1691.

On 3 September, 1688, George Cokayn conducted John's funeral service beside the new vault which John Strudwick had provided for his dead guest. Beneath a mild autumn sky the small group of friends followed John's coffin from the house on Snow Hill, to be joined by many mourners from his former congregations as they passed through the quiet gardens between Aldersgate and Bunhill Fields.

Standing with bowed heads beneath young plane trees recently planted, the men praying amid the tombs remembered the experiences of prison and persecution which they had shared with the man whose corpse lay at their feet. Suffering had created, as it always creates, a unique fellowship which bound them together, but it had ended John Bunyan's life too early. Who knew what trials still awaited them, in which they would long for his leadership in vain?

Not one of them realized that, throughout the summer, William of Orange had been making preparations to land in England. The politicians and clerics then in contact with him—Shrewsbury, Devonshire, Danby, Russell, and Compton, Bishop of London—kept their secret well. Working in collaboration with them were a number of military rebels, with a young officer named John Churchill at their head.

Two years earlier, the League of Augsburg had been formed against Louis XIV, prototype of all subsequent aggressors. Most English people were ignorant of foreign affairs, but after the Revocation of the Edict of Nantes they knew that the Protestantism of Western Europe was in danger, and were more determined than ever to repudiate Catholic rulers and despotic kings.

"True and saving religion," wrote John Locke, the thinker of the English Whigs, in his *Letters on Toleration* which began to appear twelve months later, "consists in the inward persuasion of the mind, without which nothing can be acceptable to God, and such is the nature of the understanding that it cannot be compelled to the belief of anything by outward force".

John Bunyan, whom outward force never compelled, had given his strength and skill to the inward persuasion of the mind, and was gone only nine months before the right of all minds to freedom of thought and worship was recognized by the law of the land. In the hour of his death, so close to the victory of religious toleration, he became a symbol of hope to all who believe that their unseen objective is still far distant, and die without realizing that their successors will find it at the next bend of the road.

On 31 August, 1948, the two hundred and sixtieth anniversary of John Bunyan's death, I went to Bunhill Fields to find his grave. Today the "Bonhill Field" of Finsbury Farm has become an accessible open-air museum, hardly 100 yards along City Road from Old Street Underground Station on the Northern Line.

It is not a conventional museum, for Nazi bombs have deprived it of order, symmetry, and seclusion. Before the Second World War, lofty warehouses almost surrounded the cemetery; except at its official entrance, the acres of grey tombs remained hidden from view. But in the City fire-raid of 29 December, 1940, several warehouses were burned out and collapsed upon the adjacent tombstones.

Another heavy raid on 9 May, 1941, annihilated many of the buildings which had survived previous onslaughts. Now totally visible, the battered tombs stretch back from the City Road in two large columns, divided by a public footway which runs between locked railings.

The company of the dead is distinguished. John Owen and John Bunyan have since been joined by Henry Cromwell, great-great grandson of Oliver; Susannah Wesley, mother of John and Charles; Daniel Defoe, whose remains lie beneath a grey obelisk erected eighty years ago by the *Christian World News*; and Isaac Watts, the hymn-writer, commemorated by a square box-like sepulchre. The bones of William Blake are here also, brought from a pauper's grave.

On that sultry afternoon the air between Old Street and the cemetery was dense with floating down from the half-faded flowers of the rosebay willow-herb, decorative successor to the London rocket. Owing to its fondness for the sites of burned-out buildings, this plant is known to the City as "the fireweed". Challenged here and there by the bland faces, like tiny dandelions, of yellow nipplewort, the rosebay willow-herb grew in purple patches all over Bunhill Fields.

Fixed in the ruins at the Old Street end of the cemetery I noticed two large hoardings, of which the contents would have astonished John Bunyan. The first advertised "Dreft":

> 5 times more lather. New. Better Than Soap.
> For Fluffier Woollies. Brighter Silks and Undies.

The second presented the passer-by with a picture of two blue screws above a rhymed inscription:

> Some make big stuff
> Some make small;
> More from each is more for all.

Slowly I walked towards the orthodox entrance to the cemetery, though any marauder could now get into it over the ruined walls. On the opposite side of the City Road, the statue of John Wesley stands before Wesley's Chapel with one hand outstretched in blessing, and the words "The World is My Parish" engraved at his feet. He looks with perpetual serene benevolence across the road towards the effigy of John Bunyan, which lies facing him beneath a canopy of plane trees now tall as a cathedral.

The air-raids were kinder to Wesley's Chapel than to Bunhill Fields, though they demolished the grey stone church beside it. Only a few tiles had disappeared from the roof, their deep purple replaced by lighter tiles of the same colour. In front of the Wesley Museum, once Wesley's house, with its blue plaque informing the visitor that "John Wesley (1703–1791) lived here", a small garden glowed with scarlet and yellow dahlias. Perhaps not incongruously, it was the gayest object in the City Road. John Bunyan, I thought, would have appreciated those flowers, which apart from the kindly weeds were conspicuously absent from Bunhill Fields.

On the right-hand gatepost of the cemetery, an inscription tells the visitor that when the burial-ground was closed in 1852, "more than 120,000 Bodies had been interred therein". The inscription on the left-hand gatepost is equally informative:

> This Burial ground of the Nonconformists known anciently as Bunhill in the Fields was enclosed with a Brick Wall at the Sole Charge of the City of London in the Mayoralty of Sir John Lawrence, Knight, Anno Domini 1665 . . .

The custodian of the cemetery, who unlocked the railings which divided me from John Bunyan's tomb, was especially interested in the recorded responsibility of Sir John Lawrence, Knight.

"My namesake, Christian and surname," he told me.

Though the August sun shone with determined cheerfulness upon the ruins, the old grey and white tombstones in the long grass wore a melancholy air, unmitigated by the distant roar of traffic from the City Road. Some of the plane trees, I saw, had been pollarded owing to the shattering effect of age and bombs. Many tombs had suffered damage from vandals other than Nazis.

"Wanton destruction. That's the age we're living in! That's the next generation!" commented the custodian, an ex-member of the London City Rescue Service. Two small high-explosive bombs had fallen, he said, in the cemetery itself, smashing up several tombs; they were responsible for its derelict appearance and the piles of gravestones to be seen here and there. I had already noticed one large heap at the corner nearest to Old Street Station; the grass and weeds growing amongst them gave these relics an air of permanence, as though they were awaiting the Day of Judgment.

Beneath the noblest survivors of the plane trees stands the monument over the tomb which John Bunyan shared with eleven other occupants. John Strudwick followed him there in 1698, and after his death the vault was used for members of his family. No entry of John Bunyan's burial remains in the cemetery register; his name, and the names of those interred with him, were probably first inscribed on the stone when John Strudwick's son-in-law, the Rev. Robert Bragge, was buried beneath it in 1737.

In the publication *Notes and Queries*, a contributor who signed himself H. J. S. reported in 1864 his discovery of the inscription, recording incorrectly the date of death, which first appeared on the Bunyan tomb.

"Here lyes the body of Mr. John Bunyan, author of the 'Pilgrim's Progress', aged 59, who dyed Aug. 17, 1688."

Robert Southey quoted in his biography a verse which was inscribed, he stated, upon John's original gravestone:

The "Pilgrim's Progress" now is finished,
And Death has laid him in his earthly bed.

Whatever form the original inscriptions took, they had long been replaced by the substantial nineteenth-century monument, surrounded by iron railings, which was restored in 1861 when the present recumbent figure by E. C. Papworth was placed there, and repaired again in 1922.

From the general appearance of the blitzed cemetery I expected to find the greyish-brown tomb, with its sculptured pictures of Christian carrying and losing his burden, in need of further renovation. But I was not quite prepared for the damaged stone image, on which a few dry leaves from the plane trees fell as I stood beside it and read the words now carved beneath its feet:

JOHN BUNYAN
Author of the
PILGRIM'S PROGRESS
Obt 31st Augt 1688
Aet 60.

The monument and figure had survived the raids almost unimpaired, but the upper part of the face had vanished. Shrapnel splinters from our guns, said the custodian, had chipped away the nose and eyes.

John Bunyan, it seemed, still speaks to his world congregation from that shell-impaired tomb. In life he issued a perpetual challenge to the conscience of humanity for freedom of worship; in death he cries to that conscience for freedom from fear and from war. A silent protest against cruelty and hatred, his mutilated effigy pleads with the God of Love to bring the perverse children of men through the Valley of Shadows into the way of salvation.

CHAPTER XX

VERDICT OF THE PEOPLE

"To the poor also the Gospel was preached, and what is stranger, by the poor also was it preached. Multiply by tens of thousands that 'man cloathed with rags, with a Book in his hand and a great Burden upon his back', and you have a force of tremendous potency which had been one of the chief elements in the growth of modern England."

G. M. TREVELYAN: *Bunyan's England.*
(*The Review of the Churches,* July, 1928.)

WE have followed John Bunyan's footsteps through his century and his country; we have seen him as a writer of genius, a powerful preacher, and a husband, father, and friend who, in all the personal crises of life, "found himself a man, compassed with Infirmities", yet was also grandly endowed with courage, love and faith. By his writings he has revealed himself as the interpreter not only of his own age, but of the human spirit in all ages.

To complete the picture we must also pursue him through the world of literary opinion, as it has changed and gathered in the course of 300 years. Seeking the impact of his virile personality upon those centuries, we shall find him an extremely controversial figure. Not only have the architects of literary reputations differed amongst themselves regarding his merits; they also differed, until the recent past, from the common people, who accepted him from the beginning and have never changed their verdict.

John Bunyan resembled the type of modern author who goes unsung by the coterie critics until they find, to their dismay, that he has a world-wide following. In his lifetime the majority of the literary pundits remained unaware of him, though the people were reading *The Pilgrim's Progress* in their thousands.

It is improbable that John Milton ever heard of John Bunyan, even within those Puritan circles in which both moved, for Milton was a blind and ailing man of fifty-eight when *Grace Abounding*

[London News Agency Photos, Ltd.

THE SHELL-DAMAGED EFFIGY OF JOHN BUNYAN IN BUNHILL FIELDS

Executed by E. C. Papworth in 1861.

BUNYAN'S STATUE, BEDFORD

The gift of Hastings, ninth Duke of Bedford, executed by J. E. Boehm. Erected in 1874 at the corner of St Peter's Green.

appeared. He died in 1674, four years before the publication of *The Pilgrim's Progress.*

To Evelyn, Vaughan, Aubrey, Baxter, Marvell, Pepys, and Dryden, John's name was certainly as unfamiliar as their names, within his narrower range of literary experience, were unfamiliar to him. *The Holy War* suggests that he read *Paradise Lost*; the possibility that *Hudibras* ever reached him, even though he and Samuel Butler both served in their different fashions under Sir Samuel Luke, is more remote.

In the next century, as the book cherished by the artisans and "petty chapmans" forced its way upwards, conflicting opinions about John Bunyan's place in the selective sphere of literature first began to be expressed.

Had John known of these opinions, they would not have interested him. He was right outside the elegant contemporary world of literary patrons and salons; he neither had, nor wished to have, any knowledge of them. The fact that he produced two of the greatest classics in English literature was quite incidental to his self-ordained task of saving souls and establishing the right of Christians to worship as they chose.

He had, of course, been unaware that he was writing future classics and laying the foundations of the English novel. This achievement would hardly have seemed to him to be worth the effort. His concern was salvation, not literature. The popularity of *The Pilgrim's Progress* pleased him, not as evidence of a welcome given to a great work of art, but as a new means of bringing the souls of the common people to God. He spoke to his own, and his own received him with applause. It was the well-educated, the discriminating, the complacent arbiters of culture, who at first received him not.

He in his turn distrusted these literary practitioners. In the Preface to *The Holy City*, he explained that he had not embellished his material with sentences from the learned fathers because he did not know them, and in any case the Bible was enough. But behind this alleged reason lay another. John shared with Milton the Puritan conception of literary and other gifts as heaven-sent privileges, for which human agencies should not be given the credit that rightly belonged to God.

"I durst not make use of ought thereof," he remarked of the

quotations that he might have included, "and that for fear lest that grace and these gifts that the Lord hath given me, should be attributed to their wits rather than the light of the Word and Spirit of God."

To John, imagination was not a faculty to be used for personal glorification, but a sacred endowment to be dedicated to Christ's service. As Bernard Shaw wrote in *Man and Superman*, he "achieved virtue and courage by identifying himself with the purpose of the world as he understood it".

If John Bunyan were able today to estimate the triumph of his *Pilgrim* in terms of modern calculations, he would not take much pleasure in the status of the literary classic. He would value, above all else, its function as a common human possession uniting world-Christendom in an appreciation of truth. This, he would insist, remains the same however its external manifestations may vary, and is the only road to the City of God.

The Pilgrim's Progress belonged in style and spirit to the great days of Puritanism, which were out of fashion in cultured circles when John wrote his book. Twenty years after the Restoration, when the comedies of Aphra Behn were exceeding Dryden's in voluptuousness, even Samuel Butler, who had exuberantly satirized the Puritans in *Hudibras* and welcomed the new régime, wrote a yet more bitter satire on "The Licentious Age of Charles II":

'Tis a strange age we've lived in, and a lewd,
As e'er the sun in all his travels viewed.

The aristocratic profligacy of the Court dominated both science and literature; the intellectuals whose decrees established or withheld reputations had no use for Puritanism and moral enthusiasm, which seemed to them both sentimental and vulgar. But this cynicism hardly touched the majority of the people scattered over the country. At the time that John Bunyan was writing, Puritanism still dominated Bedfordshire.

In conscious protest against corruption in high places, the Bedford Church maintained its standards. Its members continued to worship in Josias Ruffhead's barn until 1707, when the building with three gabled ridges known in Bedford as "the Old Meeting" was erected on the same site under John Bunyan's successor, Ebenezer Chandler.

Religion itself had become the treasure of the poor; *The Pilgrim's Progress* was revered in modest homes and by humble hearts. Their pious devotion preserved it from oblivion during the century and a half which elapsed before it established itself as a work of literature, and their judgment of its value never altered.

The sale of 100,000 copies during the last decade of John's life represented a huge figure for that day. About 160 editions were issued in the first century after publication; translations, which have now appeared in more than 200 languages and dialects, began almost immediately. Provincial editions came out as early as 1680, though there was none from Bedfordshire until the Sidney Press issued the "Bedford Edition" in 1938.

Three years after Nathaniel Ponder put the book on the market, the Puritan colony in America published their own edition. As a link with the England of their recollection, it came to be so widely read that John wrote proudly of its reception in his rhymed Introduction to the Second Part:

> 'Tis in New-England under such advance,
> Receives there so much loving Countenance,
> As to be Trim'd, new Cloth'd & deckt with Gems,
> That it might shew its Features, and its Limbs,
> Yet more; so comely doth my Pilgrim walk,
> That of him thousands daily sing and talk.

The popularity of *The Pilgrim's Progress* with the unpretentious is easily understood. Religious books were then almost the only serious reading amongst the poor, and this one represented their struggles, ideals, and emotions in the form of a story vivid in colour and enthralling in action. The widely held conception of life as a pilgrimage derived its images from the Bible rather than from the various books suggested as John's possible models.

"These all died in faith," wrote St. Paul in the eleventh chapter of his Epistle to the Hebrews, "not having received the promises, but having seen them afar off, and were persuaded of them, and embraced them, and confessed that they were strangers and pilgrims on the earth".

Pilgrims travelling to the Holy Land or visiting the shrine of St. Thomas at Canterbury were familiar medieval sights, of which the tradition had survived; they had also been known at obscurer places, such as Stevington's Holy Well. Raleigh, Quarles, George Herbert and other writers had helped by their work to perpetuate the idea of a pilgrim life.

John's readers had been brought up, like himself, on emblem books, and fables of giants and dragons; they still half-believed that these legendary creatures could be encountered by their acquaintances, of whom John wrote and whose workaday language he used. They also knew their Bible by heart, and could not only follow his references, but share the imaginative force which the study of the Scriptures had conferred on the English people.

Giving unity to the whole narrative, whether pathetic, humorous, satirical, realistic, romantic, or tragic, was the Puritan ideal of conduct, a system of values not confined to John's century which every seeker after righteousness recognizes as his own. To say, as Sir Charles Firth has said, that *The Pilgrim's Progress* is the prose epic of English Puritanism does not limit its application, but makes it the common possession of a world-fellowship of Christians.

The story appealed to John's contemporaries, as it still appeals to our own, because it represents the Christian's conflict as never finished until he reaches the Celestial City; it is a continuous series of unpredictable conquests which keep the reader in suspense. John recognized that the same spiritual battles have to be fought again and again, not only through the centuries, but in personal lives.

Popularity, however, is one thing, and prestige quite another. John soon achieved the one, but, except within his own circle of friends and followers, he never experienced the other. The fact that his readers ran into thousands even stirred, as it so often stirs, contempt in the self-appointed dictators of literary standards. An estimate of him by the Rev. Thomas Cox, writing on

Bedfordshire's personalities as an appendage to its geography, probably represented current opinion in those orthodox circles which considered themselves educated.

> "John Bunnyan, Author of the Pilgrims Progress, and several other little Books of an Antinomian Spirit, too frequently to be met with in the Hands of the common People, was, if we mistake not, a Brasier of Bedford."

In such eyes as these, John remained merely a Dissenting preacher with some small reputation as an author amongst Nonconformists. The fame of a book is always more easily established than that of its writer, and the growth of John's literary reputation was as slow as the success of *The Pilgrim's Progress* had been swift.

It is true that his work had its discriminating admirers even amongst his immediate literary successors. Jonathan Swift, who was twenty-one when John died, said that he had been better entertained and more informed by a few pages in *The Pilgrim's Progress* than by a long discussion upon the will and the intellect. Samuel Johnson, forty-two years younger than Swift, inquired in a comment recorded by Mrs. Piozzi whether there was "ever anything written by mere man that was wished longer by its readers, excepting *Don Quixote, Robinson Crusoe*, and *Pilgrim's Progress*"?

But lesser writers than these giants continued to be scornful or condescending for over a century. Addison, born sixteen years before John's death, is reputed to have said disparagingly that he never knew an author who had not his admirers, since Bunyan and Quarles pleased as many readers as Dryden and Tillotson. In a lecture on *The Pilgrim's Progress*, delivered at the Royal Institution in March 1924, John W. Mackail, Professor of Poetry at Oxford from 1906 to 1911, stated that this passage was wrongly attributed to Addison, but no one disputes that in the next century the highbrow Mrs. Montagu called Bunyan and Quarles "those classics of the artificers in leather".

Her contemporary, William Cowper, admired John Bunyan, but lacked the courage which enabled Dr. Johnson to fly in the face of accepted judgments. Cowper's lines from *Tirocinium*, written in 1784, have often been quoted. Though one of his Olney hymns was entitled *The Valley of the Shadow of Death*, and referred to "fierce Apollyon" as being at the head of the author's foes, these lines damned John with tepid praise:

> Oh thou, whom, borne on fancy's eager wing
> Back to the season of life's happy spring,
> I pleas'd remember, and, while mem'ry yet
> Holds fast her office here, can ne'er forget;
> Ingenious dreamer, in whose well-told tale
> Sweet fiction and sweet truth alike prevail:
> Whose hum'rous vein, strong sense, and simple style,
> May teach the gayest, make the gravest smile;
> Witty, and well employ'd, and, like thy Lord,
> Speaking in parables his slighted word;
> I name thee not, lest so despis'd a name
> Should move a sneer at thy deserved fame;
> Yet e'en in transitory life's late day,
> That mingles all my brown with sober gray,
> Revere the man, whose PILGRIM marks the road,
> And guides the PROGRESS of the soul to God.

Cowper's patronizing timidity was not effectively challenged in literary circles until Robert Southey became, in 1830, the first author of repute who thought John Bunyan worthy of the considerable biography which he wrote for a new and sumptuous edition of *The Pilgrim's Progress*. But John's status had evidently been quietly ascending for the previous half century, since Southey remarked that "forty years ago" he was "even then in high repute". His fame, he added,

> "may literally be said to have risen; beginning among the people, it has made its way up to those who are called the public. In most instances the many receive gradually and slowly the opinions of the few, respecting literary merit . . . But here the opinion of the multitude has been ratified by the judicious."

In that same year Coleridge endorsed Southey's opinion in his *Table Talk* and, according to H. N. Coleridge, also inscribed his admiration on the flyleaf of his copy of *The Pilgrim's Progress*:

> "I know of no book, the Bible excepted as above all comparison, which I, according to *my* judgment and experience, could so safely recommend as teaching and enforcing the whole saving truth according to the mind that was in Christ Jesus, as the Pilgrim's Progress."

Lord Macaulay went even further; in his Essay on *The Pilgrim's Progress and John Bunyan,* written as a review of Southey's edition in December 1831, he wound his approval up to portentous enthusiasm, and castigated the well-intentioned Southey for displaying Anglican prejudices:

"His attempts to excuse the odious persecution to which Bunyan was exposed have sometimes moved our indignation."

With Macaulay's classification of John Bunyan and John Milton as "the only two great creative minds" of the seventeenth century, the period of contempt mingled with lukewarm praise definitely ended. When J. A. Froude published his *Bunyan* in 1880, John was at last included among English Men of Letters—that proud, captious, and exclusive set of which no one would have been more surprised than Bedfordshire's peasant preacher to find himself a member.

Had he known, he would probably have exclaimed in distress that he hoped he was not regarded *only* as that—a reaction which Froude appreciated.

> "It was not a dignity that he ever desired, and he would probably have classed most of his associates with Talkative the son of Saywell, who dwelt in Prating Row."

Since that official acceptance by Literature only seventy years ago, a complete library of books, essays, articles and pamphlets has gathered round John Bunyan's name. From the mass a few publications stand out as landmarks; they include Dr. John Brown's painstaking and comprehensive biography, first published in 1885; Sir Charles Firth's illuminating Introduction to the 1898 edition of *The Pilgrim's Progress*; the short inspired volume of William Hale White ("Mark Rutherford") in 1905; Professor Mackail's lecture, afterwards published as a brochure, in 1924; and Sir G. M. Trevelyan's noble essay, *Bunyan's England,* first delivered as a Bunyan Tercentenary commemorative address at Cambridge on 19 January, 1928, and printed in *The Review of the Churches* the following July.

None of the volumes on John Bunyan written for or since his Tercentenary has the same status as these books and essays. Appreciation reached its peak with George Bernard Shaw, who declared in the *Saturday Review* during 1896 that Bunyan was "better than Shakespeare".

In spite of Southey and Macaulay, the growth of John Bunyan's fame was relatively slow during the first half of the nineteenth century. Even in Bedford nobody thought, when the County Gaol was pulled down in 1801, of making a sketch or keeping a stone in John's memory. Nor was any relic retained of his St. Cuthbert's Street cottage when it was demolished in 1838 to make room for the two uninspiring little houses that stand there today.

"I wonder," wrote the Rev. C. F. Farrar in *Old Bedford* (1926), "what the hearth-stone of the room where *The Pilgrim's Progress* was written would fetch today at Messrs. Sotheby's?"

As late as 1845 the voice of disdain was still audible; a certain Professor Craik, who published in that year a survey of *Literature and Learning in England*, dismissed John Bunyan in three contemptuous lines. It was the Evangelical movement, reaching its height in the 1840s, which finally established John among the great men and women of mankind. Because it represented a new manifestation of the Puritanism so deeply rooted in the English character, that movement exalted him as much as he had formerly been debased, and justified Southey's statement that the educated minority had come over to the opinion of the common people.

The high reputation at last endorsed by the tiny cultured circles that alone knew what was really happening in their contemporary world had long been a matter of simple acceptance in the religious sects which especially claimed John Bunyan as their own. Their desire to honour him now accorded with national sentiment, and soon took shape in Bedford.

In 1849, at the height of the Evangelical revival, a new meeting house was built to replace the old three-ridged structure

THE BRONZE DOORS OF BUNYAN MEETING, BEDFORD

The work of Frederick Thrupp, inspired by Ghiberti's doors in Florence. The ten panels show ten scenes from *The Pilgrim's Progress*.

PERSONAL RELICS OF JOHN BUNYAN

This collection, showing his chair, fiddle, staff, table, anvil, lacquer cabinet and prison door, was specially assembled for this picture at Bunyan Meeting.

of 1707. Still standing on the land which had once been John Eston's garden, it was opened in 1850, and is there today.

A substantial oblong building in dark red brick which is universally known as "Bunyan Meeting", it has weathered the storms of 100 years and looks capable of resisting them for at least another century. Inside the vestibule door hangs a stone tablet, commemorating pastors of the Bedford Church from John Gifford to John Brown. The monuments within include one to Hannah Bunyan, John Bunyan's great-grand-daughter through his eldest son John.

When Charles Doe published his Folio in 1692, he had prophesied that his friend would one day be known "over the European and American world . . . and in process of time to the whole universe". This expression of faith by a simple devotee reached almost its highest point of fulfilment when, thanks to the initiative of the ninth Duke of Bedford in 1874, evangelical appreciation overflowed into a Bunyan Festival.

Francis Charles Hastings Russell, cousin of the former Duke, had long been a Bunyan enthusiast. As a relatively poor man who never expected to inherit the title, he promised that if he ever possessed enough money he would make a presentation to Bedford in John's memory. The unexpected death of his cousin in 1872 gave him his opportunity. In 1861, a Committee of which the Earl of Shaftesbury was President had placed E. C. Papworth's monument over John's tomb in Bunhill Fields, and the new Duke now decided that Bedford also must have a statue.

This memorial was duly executed by J. E. Boehm, and set up at the corner of St. Peter's Green. Its unveiling on 20 June, 1874, brought together a great assembly of men and women from many denominations. Lady Augusta Stanley performed the ceremony, and her husband, Dean Stanley, at the Duke's request, chose the subjects for the bas-reliefs on the pedestal. The Press attended in force, and *Punch* decided to honour the occasion with a long poem which concluded by applauding the verdict of the common man:

The People are weary of vestment-vanities,
Of litigation about inanities,
And fain would listen, O Preacher and Peer,
To a voice like that of the Tinker-Seer;

Who guided the Pilgrim up, beyond
The Valley of Death, and the Slough of Despond,
The Doubting Castle, and Giant Despair,
To those Delectable Mountains fair,
And over the River, and in at the Gate
Where for weary Pilgrims the Angels wait!

Today the stripling trees planted round the statue seventy-five years ago have grown so tall that their drooping boughs cast deep shadows over John's face, and make a good photograph obtainable only in winter. Larger than life-size in bronze, he contemplates Bedford's High Street from his pedestal, his face half-turned towards the site of his old home the County Gaol. At his feet are engraved the sentences from *The Pilgrim's Progress* which the sculptor sought to materialise:

It had eyes lifted up to heaven,
the best of books in his hand, the
law of truth was written upon his
lips . . .

It stood as if it pleaded
with men.

These Bedford and Bunhill Fields memorials were followed by others, the first being another gift from the Duke of Bedford. In 1876 he presented to Bunyan Meeting the bronze doors inspired by Ghiberti's doors in Florence, which now stand at its entrance. For two years the sculptor, Frederick Thrupp, had worked upon the ten panels, representing ten scenes from *The Pilgrim's Progress,* without any idea where they were ultimately going. A fellow-artist who brought them to the Duke's notice was indirectly responsible for their appropriate use.

At the restoration of Elstow Church in 1880, two windows illustrating *The Pilgrim's Progress* and *The Holy War* were put in at the east end of the north and south aisle. Close to *The Pilgrim's Progress* window stands Christopher Hall's pulpit, and a pew door more dubiously associated with John. Twenty years afterwards a number of young people in Southwark, "delighting in the Great Allegory, *The Pilgrim's Progress*", subscribed for a Memorial

Window to be placed in the Cathedral where John's friend, Sir John Shorter, lies buried.

In 1912, a Bunyan Memorial Window was unveiled on the west side of the north transept in Westminster Abbey. The Harlington Church window, in the "Bunyan country" followed in 1929. A London statue of John now looks down upon Southampton Row from the corner of the Baptist Church House.

Meanwhile, a hunt for Bunyan letters, Bunyan signatures, and Bunyan relics began, chiefly in the East Midlands. Though none of John's correspondence has yet emerged apart from the specimens in the Church Book, the recent discovery of the bond at Aylesbury suggests that letters may still be found within the pages of old books or amongst unsorted documents. Two lines of his handwriting are preserved in the John Rylands Library in Manchester.

Bunyan signatures still exist, some questionable, but four undoubted. The original copy of John's Deed of Gift may still be seen at Bunyan Meeting, and the Baptist College, Bristol, owns Vavasour Powell's "Concordance" with John's signature on the title-page. The Public Records Office contains John's application made in 1672 for a licence to preach. Another signature, on a deed drawn up in 1653, belongs to the London Society of Antiquaries.

The "relics" of John's life showed a tendency to increase as his fame expanded; Bunyan pulpits and chairs are displayed in several Bedfordshire villages. The Bunyan Meeting in Bedford possesses, in addition to the Church Book, many genuine memorials of his life and work. Amongst them may be seen a prison door from Bedford County Gaol; it stands below the list of pastors in the vestibule of the Meeting and is reputed to have been the door of John's cell.

In the small "Museum" behind the Chapel are other possessions which John used and handled. The inlaid cabinet probably presented to him by Sir John Shorter is there, with its set of small drawers and the decorated lid which suggests that even late in life his youthful fondness for music and games persisted. Preserved also by the Trustees of the Bunyan Meeting are John's iron fiddle and inscribed anvil, his ivory-handled Manilla cane, and the oak table and chair which he used during his pastorate. The old chair, with its worn green velveteen cushion, now lives in a glass case; it appears very low for a man as tall as John Bunyan because its legs were shortened for a diminutive successor.

The documents at the Meeting include a fragment of a bill-head from John Strudwick's shop on Snow Hill, showing a picture of the house where John died; and a copy of the Warrant issued for his arrest in 1675. In a Bedford bank, for greater safety, is the jug with the zigzag design made of Old English Slip Ware which Elizabeth Bunyan used for carrying soup to John in prison.

Also in the Museum, two other fragments of the past stand side by side; these are the "wicket gate" and the belfry door, taken from Elstow Church at the time of its restoration. The pale tough old wood, hard as metal, seems destined for as long a life as the grey tombstones which surround the green square of lawn in the Garden of Remembrance. On its east side, now occupied by the caretaker of the Meeting, is the creeper-covered eighteenth-century house of John Howard, the prison reformer, who lived here at week-ends in order that he might attend the Sunday services without violating his Sabbatarian principles by travelling.

In the centre of the lawn a white Memorial Sundial commemorates the Bunyan Tercentenary in 1928, when British writers and readers combined to give the once despised tinker a literary canonization. Books, articles, and pamphlets whirled from the Press like leaves in an autumn gale; sermons were preached and addresses given; devout admirers held services on the site of John's birth and in other places associated with his memory; the *Bedfordshire Times* published an illustrated Tercentenary Supplement.

Seldom indeed, as Sir G. M. Trevelyan remarked in his commemorative address at Cambridge, had there been such an exaltation of the humble and meek.

That exaltation was the work of the common man—and woman. Between the second, almost unnoticed, centenary of John's birth, and the third which acknowledged him as one of "the splendours of the firmament of time", the people had come into their own. It was more than a coincidence that the year 1928 also saw, with the enfranchisement of women at twenty-one, the last instalment of universal suffrage in Britain.

Few are the men and women whose names remain familiar to the contemporary public 100 years after their birth. Those known to mankind 300 years afterwards can be counted in tens. The Bedfordshire tinker is one of them and one he seems likely to continue, in spite of occasional attempts to diminish his stature by critics who bark at him like petulant poodles yapping at a large unruffled sheep-dog.

The little debunkers will always be with us; they have their day and cease to be. It is genius allied with integrity which finds its appointed place and stays there, competing for permanence with the Rock of Ages.

John Bunyan in part answers to Shaw's description of him as a force of Nature with a tinker's theology. Amongst a people living so close to the soil, prudery was rare—another matter which some of John's modern detractors seem imperfectly to have understood. Those who call him "coarse", and deplore or ignore his references to gripes, purges, vomiting, pregnancy, and delivery, might as well expect the thunderstorm to wait until we have shut the windows, or the pains of childbirth to come upon us only when the fire is lit and the bed nicely made.

John Bunyan has the same inevitability as these events. He overpowers his readers, just as he once overpowered his hearers, with the primitive force of copulation and parturition, sickness and sleep and death.

He would have been surprised and probably amused by the refined preachers who have found some of his passages embarrassing. The contrary critics who say that his writing has naturalness but no vulgarity endeavour to whitewash him in a manner that he would neither have understood nor appreciated. He is frequently vulgar, but never sordid. The furtive snigger is unknown to him because, unlike his enlightened admirers, he saw no shame in natural processes.

If the literary assessors conditioned by the Victorian era were most disconcerted by the quality that they called his "frankness", it is his vigorous unashamed Christianity, and his conception of literature as the mere ally of his moral purpose, which clashes more profoundly with certain tendencies of modern criticism.

What would happen if *The Pilgrim's Progress* were published for the first time today?

It is not difficult to imagine. By some conspicuous reviewers, the book would be ignored altogether. Other critics would dismiss its author in "Shorter Notices" as a tendentious tract-writer having no connection with literature, and his allegory as religious propaganda masquerading as a story.

And this, in fact, is exactly what it was, except that it did not even masquerade. It had other qualities too, but they were there by accident—the accident of a native capacity for style and characterization belatedly perceived by a posterity anxious to perceive them. Yet the "tracts" of John Bunyan stand among the great classics of English literature, though his learned contemporaries did not put them there. It was, and is, the people of England who gave them their place.

The Pilgrim's Progress tells us, with no uncertain voice, that literature enters a period of decline as soon as its self-appointed exponents seek to narrow its boundaries to exclude this or that. When Kipling called John Bunyan "Salvation's first Defoe", he thereby affirmed that Salvation is as legitimate a theme for the novel as Robinson Crusoe. Whatever, he implies, a writer wants to say, and can say effectively, is literature.

To make it less comprehensive than this means boycotting the Miltons, the Bunyans, the Tolstoys, the Shaws, and a host of lesser writers whose work "speaks to the condition" of men and women in their day. A literature which refuses to accept them becomes cynical, devitalized, and tenuous.

In the course of three centuries, John Bunyan reconciled Puritanism with English letters, and proved that the alleged antithesis between art and moral idealism is unreal. A few men and women of genius will always succeed in creating a synthesis, and thereby produce the greatest art of all.

For them, as Trevelyan has stated, it is life, rather than art, that counts; and life is an eternal reality in which antithetical elements fuse and are made one. It is life, too, which matters to the people, who value art only in so far as it interprets life. That is why it is they who decide, in the last resort, which writers shall wear the crown of immortality, and they who always will.

POSTSCRIPT

THE RELEVANT PILGRIM

"Men are too lofty, too proud, too wild, too devilishly resolved in the ways of their own destruction. Nothing will hinder them from ruining their own precious and immortal souls but the breaking of their hearts."

JOHN BUNYAN: *The Acceptable Sacrifice.*

IN July 1948, when the two hundred and fiftieth birthday of the Society for the Propagation of Christian Knowledge was celebrated by the performance of *The Pilgrim's Progress* for two weeks at Covent Garden, a member of the audience overheard a conversation between two women.

One could not accept the idea of the great Puritan allegory being enhanced by the Covent Garden Choir and Ballet.

"If Bunyan knew, he would turn in his grave!" she exclaimed indignantly.

"But perhaps, my dear," responded her companion soothingly, "he has moved with the times."

We who have followed John Bunyan through his century, and have shared with him the music and dancing which enlivens the Second Part of *The Pilgrim's Progress*, know that he "moved with the times" much faster than the majority of his fellow Puritans. He moved, indeed, so effectively that within his lifetime he passed through the whole gamut of opinion from Calvinistic intolerance to the larger charity which carried England into an era of religious toleration.

His progress in his own age gives him a peculiar relevance for the present century, which is also revolutionary and transitional.

"Bunyan as an author has no 'times'," wrote R. Ellis Roberts in *The Bookman* for December 1927. "We value him first not for what he tells us of his own day, his own religion or his own society, but for what he tells us of ours."

Twenty years later, writing in *The Friend* for 20 August, 1948, on another seventeenth-century figure, the Quaker thinker

Robert Barclay, Dr. D. Elton Trueblood likewise emphasized the relationship between those days and these.

> "At this juncture of the world's history, when the mood of urgency is dominant, most of us feel that we have little time or energy for pointless historical curiosity. Our purpose is not to glorify the past, but rather to rescue from oblivion and neglect a set of ideas which have vital bearing on the problems of the present day. If there are any ideas of a former generation which can give direction to our distressed and perplexed time, we ought to pay close attention to them."

Though obvious contrasts, theological and material, divide the seventeenth from the twentieth century, there remain some striking resemblances.

Each followed the age, gathering retrospective prestige as subsequent shadows lengthened, of a famous Queen; Elizabeth died in 1603 and Victoria in 1901. The seventeenth century saw Central Europe devastated between 1618 and 1648 by wars of religion; the twentieth has witnessed its reduction to a shambles by wars of ideology.

The international conflicts in each period were followed by the descent of civilization into a deepening inhumanity, which produced, in an endeavour to arrest spiritual deterioration, its prophetic apostles of peace. Hugo Grotius set himself, in the seventeenth century, the task which first the League of Nations and then the United Nations Organization have endeavoured to fulfil in the twentieth. In both centuries, the majority of outstanding writers and thinkers failed to give effective support to the ideal of world unity.

But the profoundest resemblance lies in the apocalyptic quality of each age, in which immemorial structures were shaken to pieces as internal conflicts came to the surface. The religious and political strife brought by the Protestant Reformation, one of the great revolutionary periods of human thought, finds its counterpart in the modern struggle of democracy against totalitarianism. Monarchical dictators established themselves in the earlier century, and Fascist or Communist dictators in the later; Louis XIV in France played a similar rôle to that of Hitler in Germany and Stalin in Russia.

The men and women of the seventeenth century, like ourselves in the twentieth, perceived only dimly whither they were being carried by the swift currents of their time. In each age their uncertainty was intensified and their danger increased by scientific development, which has caused "progress" to be falsely identified with material civilization and technical knowledge.

So far has this process now advanced that such knowledge may lead our own age to annihilation unless, like John Bunyan and his seventeenth-century contemporaries, we can counterbalance it with new forms of spiritual development.

For these reasons we are mentally closer to the seventeenth century than our predecessors of the nineteenth, who believed in continuous progress and British domination, and regarded England as safe for ever from the threat of despotism and the shadow of medieval barbarity. Having lived for a decade and a half upon the edge of totalitarian night, with conscription at home replacing the press gang and cries assailing our ears from concentration camps abroad, we can no longer boast that our society has outgrown the savagery of our ancestors.

In a different guise we fight the same battles against the same Apollyon, whether we call it the totalitarian State, or describe it, like John Bunyan, by the simpler name of sin. And now, as then, our most reliable armour is a national Christian tradition which has no connection with power, and a great deal with resistance to power.

It was established for us by such men and women as the seventeenth-century Nonconformists, whose only power was the power of the spirit. They bought our freedom at the price of their own, and driven by conscience repeatedly broke oppressive laws which finally yielded to their fearless opposition.

The liberty which they created, often with their blood, made their country the moral leader of Europe. When the Continent was setting up its self-styled "enlightened" despots, England through her religious and political struggle became both architect and symbol of spiritual emancipation and western democracy.

During the past thirty years the hearts of British men and women have repeatedly been broken by calamity, but their spirit, like John Bunyan's, has never been defeated. Unlike their nineteenth-century ancestors they have passed through the Valley of Humiliation, and have grown strong in the strength of those qualities which function neither by power nor by might.

If this story of John Bunyan and his struggle for spiritual freedom illustrates the better part played in history by the great people of whom he was typical, then there is justification for one more study added to the many which have already been made. And if it shows that, for all their readiness to compromise and their ability to adapt themselves to changing circumstances, the tough moral fibre of the British race is unchanged and unchangeable, then John Bunyan, moving with the times, proves in our day as in his own that Britain has not only a past, but a future.

Wherever *The Pilgrim's Progress* is read, there the men and women who spring from the same stock as its author confront the challenge of the human crisis. Their place, now as then, is in the van of the struggle for those Christian values which carry the pilgrims of every century through the River of spiritual death to the Celestial City.

THE END

BIBLIOGRAPHY

Author's Note.

From the vast literature on John Bunyan and the seventeenth century, I have selected the few books which seem likely to be most useful to the general reader. These short lists include many of the publications which I have found helpful.

The list of books by John Bunyan himself I have endeavoured to make complete and chronological. For an exhaustive bibliography by a lifelong expert, the interested reader is referred to *A Bibliography of the Works of John Bunyan,* by Frank Mott Harrison (Oxford University Press, for the Bibliographical Society, 1932).

The would-be student of Bunyan and his times can obtain from the Borough Librarian, Public Library, Bedford, the Catalogue, price 1*s*., of the John Bunyan Library (Frank Mott Harrison Collection). This gives the titles of about 850 publications, most of which, with some others, are also obtainable at the British Museum Library. They include a number of books published in the sixteenth, seventeenth and eighteenth centuries, together with first editions of several of John Bunyan's works.

THE HISTORICAL BACKGROUND

James Harvey Robinson: *History of Western Europe.* (Ginn & Co. 1903.)

Mary A. Hollings: *Europe in Renaissance and Reformation.* (Methuen. 1909.)

A. H. Johnson: *The Age of the Enlightened Despot.* (Methuen. 1909.)

G. N. Clark; *The Seventeenth Century.* (Oxford University Press. 1929.)

J. W. Allen: *English Political Thought,* 1603–1660. (Methuen. 1938.)

G. M. Trevelyan: *England Under the Stuarts.* (Methuen. 1904.)

G. M. Trevelyan: *English Social History.* (Longmans, Green. 1944. U. S. A. 1942.)

H. S. Skeats and C. S. Miall: *History of the Free Churches of England,* 1688–1891. Chapter I. Review of Ecclesiastical History from the Reformation to the Revolution. (Alexander & Sheppard. 1891.)

J. R. Green: *A Short History of the English People.* 1874. (Dent. Everyman's Library.)

S. R. Gardiner: *A Student's History of England.* Vol. II. 1509–1689. (Longmans, Green. 1905.)

S. R. Gardiner: *Constitutional Documents of the Puritan Revolution.* (Clarendon Press, Oxford. 1906.)

C. Grant Robertson: *Select Statutes, Cases, and Documents,* 1660–1832. (Methuen. 1904.)

Edward Hyde, Lord Clarendon: *History of the Rebellion in England.* (Clarendon Press. 1888.)

Charles H. Firth: *Cromwell's Army.* (Methuen. 1921.)

F. W. Bull: *A History of Newport Pagnell.* (W. E. & J. Goss, Kettering. 1900.)

Rev. C. F. Farrar: *Old Bedford.* (F. W. Hockliffe, Bedford, and Simpkin Marshall. 1926.)

Rev. S. R. Wigram: *Chronicles of the Abbey of Elstow.* (Parker & Co. 1885.)

John Howard: *State of the Prisons in England and Wales.* (Third Edition, 1785.)

M. and C. H. B. Quennell: *A History of Everyday Things in England.* Vol. II. 1500–1799. (Batsford. 1942.)

ARTICLES, ETC.:

G. M. Trevelyan: *Bunyan's England. Review of the Churches,* July 1928.

W. M. Wigfield: *Recusancy and Nonconformity in Bedfordshire.* Bedfordshire Historical Record Society. Vol. XX. 1938.

William Raabe: *Elsa of the Fir.* Story of the Thirty Years' War. (Trans. R. G. L. Barrett. 1943.)

BOOKS BY JOHN BUNYAN

(Major Works are shown in heavy type)

Some Gospel-Truths Opened. (J. Wright, London, and M. Cowley, Newport Pagnell. 1656.)

A Vindication of . . . Some Gospel-Truths Opened. (London and Newport Pagnell. 1657.)

A Few Sighs from Hell. (M. Wright, London. 1658.)

The Doctrine of the Law and Grace Unfolded. (M. Wright, London, and M. Cowley, Newport Pagnell. 1659.)

Profitable Meditations. **Verse. (Francis Smith, London. 1661.)**

I will pray with the Spirit and with the Understanding also, or A discourse Touching Prayer. (Second Edition, London. 1663. First Edition unknown.)
Christian Behaviour. (Francis Smith, London. 1663.)
A Map, shewing the order and causes of Salvation and Damnation. Broadside. (?1663.)
One Thing is Needful: or Serious Meditations upon the Four Last Things. Verse. (? 1664.)
Mount Ebal and Gerizim. Verse. (? 1664.)
The Holy City. (Probably Francis Smith, London. 1665.)
The Resurrection of the Dead, and Eternal Judgment. (Francis Smith, London. 1665.)
Prison Meditations. Verse. (1665.)

GRACE ABOUNDING TO THE CHIEF OF SINNERS. (George Larkin, London. 1666.)

A Confession of my Faith. (Probably Francis Smith. 1672.)
A Defence of the Doctrine of Justification by Faith in Jesus Christ. A reply to Edward Fowler's *The Design of Christianity.* (Francis Smith, London. 1672.)
Differences in Judgment about Water-Baptism no Bar to Communion. (John Wilkins, London. 1673.)
Peaceable Principles and True. (1674. First edition unknown.)
Light for them that sit in Darkness. (Francis Smith, London. 1675.)
Instruction for the Ignorant. (Francis Smith, London. 1675.)
Saved by Grace. (1675. First edition unknown.)
The Strait Gate. (Francis Smith, London. 1676.)

THE PILGRIM'S PROGRESS. Part I. (Nathaniel Ponder, London. 1678.)

Come and Welcome to Jesus Christ. (B. Harris, London. 1678.)
A Treatise of the Fear of God. (Nathaniel Ponder, London. 1679.)

THE LIFE AND DEATH OF MR. BADMAN. (Nathaniel Ponder, London. 1680.)

THE HOLY WAR. (Dorman Newman, London. 1682.)

The Barren Fig-Tree. (1682. First edition unknown.)
The Greatness of the Soul. (Ben. Alsop, London. 1683.)
A Case of Conscience Resolved. (1683.)
A Caution to Stir up to Watch against Sin. Broadside. (1684.)

Seasonable Counsel; or, Advice to Sufferers. (Ben. Alsop, London. 1684.)
A Holy Life the Beauty of Christianity. (Ben. Alsop, London. 1684.)

THE PILGRIM'S PROGRESS. Part II. (Nathaniel Ponder, London. 1685.)

Questions about the Nature and Perpetuity of the Seventh-Day Sabbath. (Nathaniel Ponder, London. 1685.)
A Discourse upon the Pharisee and the Publican. (Jo. Harris, London. 1685.)

A BOOK FOR BOYS AND GIRLS. Verse. (Nathaniel Ponder, London. 1686.)

Good News for the Vilest of Men. (Subsequently known as *The Jerusalem Sinner Saved.*) (1688.)
The Work of Jesus Christ as an Advocate. (Dorman Newman, London. 1688.)
A Discourse of the Building, Nature, Excellency, and Government of the House of God. Verse. (George Larkin, London. 1688.)
The Water of Life. (Nathaniel Ponder, London. 1688.)
Solomon's Temple Spiritualiz'd. (George Larkin, London. 1688.)
The Acceptable Sacrifice. (George Larkin, London. 1689.)
Mr. John Bunyan's last Sermon at London. (1689.)

POSTHUMOUSLY PRINTED IN CHARLES DOE'S FOLIO, 1692:

An Exposition on the Ten First Chapters of Genesis.
Of Justification by Imputed Righteousness.
Paul's Departure and Crown.
Of the Trinity, and a Christian.
Of the Law, and a Christian.
Israel's Hope Encouraged.
The Desires of the Righteous Granted.
The Saints Priviledge and Profit.
Christ a Compleat Saviour.
The Saint's Knowledge of Christ Love.
Of the House of the Forest of Lebanon.
Of Antichrist, and his Ruin.

BELIEVED PRINTED, BUT NO COPIES KNOWN:

A Christian Dialogue.
A Pocket Concordance.

PRINTED BY CHARLES DOE, 1698:

The Heavenly Footman.

PRINTED IN 1765:

A Relation of the Imprisonment of Mr. John Bunyan.

NOTE.—A useful Omnibus volume of John Bunyan, containing *Grace Abounding, A Relation of the Imprisonment,* and *The Pilgrim's Progress,* Parts I and II, was published by the Cambridge University Press in 1907. The 1898 edition of *The Pilgrim's Progress,* published by Methuen, contains an excellent Introduction by Sir Charles Firth.

The Life and Death of Mr. Badman was published in "The World's Classics" by the Oxford University Press in 1929, with an Introduction by Bonamy Dobrée.

A good edition of *The Holy War,* with an Introduction by Dr. John Brown, was issued by Hodder & Stoughton in 1887. Frederick Warne & Co. published a later edition (undated) in the "Chandos Classics".

A facsimile of the First Edition of *A Book for Boys and Girls,* with an Introduction by Dr. John Brown, was published in 1889 by Elliott Stock.

BOOKS ON BUNYAN

(Short Selected List in Chronological Sequence)

Joseph Ivimey: *The Life of Mr. John Bunyan, Minister of the Gospel at Bedford.* (Booth & Co. 1815.)

Robert Southey: *Cromwell and Bunyan.* (1830.) (John Murray. 1846. Select Biographies.)

Thomas Babington Macaulay: *The Pilgrim's Progress and John Bunyan.* (December 1831.) Critical and Historical Essays, Vol. II. (Dent. 1907.)

Robert Browning: *Ned Bratts.* A Poem on Bunyan. In *Dramatic Idylls.* (Smith, Elder. 1879.)

J. A. Froude: *Bunyan.* (English Men of Letters Series.) (Macmillan. 1880.)

John Brown, D.D.: *John Bunyan: His Life, Times and Work.* (William Isbister, London. 1885.) Tercentenary Edition revised by Frank Mott Harrison. (Hulbert Publishing Co., London. 1928.)

C. H. Firth: *Introduction* to *The Pilgrim's Progress*. (Methuen. 1898.)

G. Bernard Shaw: Epistle Dedicatory to *Man and Superman* (1901–03). In *Prefaces*. By Bernard Shaw. (Constable. 1934.)

William James: *The Varieties of Religious Experience*. (Gifford Lectures on Natural Religion, 1901–02. Lecture VIII.) (Longmans, Green. 1937.)

William Hale White (Mark Rutherford): *John Bunyan*. (Hodder & Stoughton. 1905.)

Cambridge History of English Literature. Vol. VII. *Cavalier and Puritan*. Chapter VII. *John Bunyan, Andrew Marvell*. By the Rev. John Brown, D.D. (Cambridge University Press. 1911.)

J. W. Mackail: *The Pilgrim's Progress*. A Lecture delivered at the Royal Institution of Great Britain, 14 March, 1924. (Longmans, Green. 1924.)

Gwilym O. Griffith: *John Bunyan*. (Hodder & Stoughton. 1927.)

G. B. Harrison: *John Bunyan*. A Study in Personality. (Dent. 1928.)

M. P. Willcocks: *Bunyan Calling*. (Allen & Unwin. 1943.)

Henri A. Talon: *John Bunyan* (1628–1688) *L'Homme et L'Oeuvre*. (Crépin-Leblord, Éditeur, Moulins Allier, Paris, 1948.)

ARTICLES ON BUNYAN

W. T. Whitley: *Bunyan's Imprisonments: A Legal Study*. (*Transactions of the Baptist Historical Society*. Vol. VI. No. 1. 1918.)

A. St. John Adcock: *Bunyan's Progress*. (*The Bookman*. December, 1927.)

Augustine Birrell: *John Bunyan*. (*The Bookman*. December, 1927.)

Robert Lynd: *John Bunyan To-day*. (*The Bookman*. December, 1927.)

R. Ellis Roberts: *Bunyan and His Times*. (*The Bookman*. December, 1927.)

Hensley Henson (Bp.): *An Anglican's Reflections on Bunyan's Career*. (*Review of the Churches*. July, 1928.)

Alfred Hills: *Bunyan at Bocking*. (*The Essex Review*. January, 1929.)

Joyce Godber: *The Imprisonments of John Bunyan*. (*Transactions of the Congregational Historical Society*. April, 1949.)

NOTE.—Numerous articles on John Bunyan, his contacts, and his contemporaries have appeared in the *Transactions of the Congregational Historical Society* and the *Transactions of the Baptist Historical Society* (*Baptist Quarterly*) from 1900 onwards. These reviews can be consulted at the Library of Friends' House, Euston Road, London; or borrowed from Dr. Williams Library, Gordon Square, London.

The Publications of the Bedfordshire Historical Record Society, many of which contain material relevant to Bunyan, can be consulted in the County Record Office, Shire Hall, St. Paul's Square, Bedford.

RELEVANT WORKS BY BUNYAN'S PREDECESSORS AND CONTEMPORARIES

Martin Luther (1483–1546): *Commentary upon the Epistle of St. Paul to the Galatians.* (Thomas Vautroullier. 1595.)

John Foxe (1516–1587): *Actes and Monuments of matters most speciall* . . . (Book of Martyrs.) Eighth edition. (London. Company of Stationers. 1641.) (The copy in the John Bunyan Library belongs to the same edition as that which Bunyan had in prison.)

Nathaniel Bacon: *A Relation of the Fearful Estate of Francis Spira in the year 1548.* (London. Christopher Meredith. 1649.)

Edmund Spenser (1552–1599): *The Faerie Queene.* (Macmillan. 1906.) (Globe Edition.)

Michael Drayton (1563–1631): *Poly-Olbion.* (1612.)

Richard Johnson (? 1573–1659): *Famous Historie of the Seaven Champions of Chrisendom.* (? 1596, with Second and Third Parts 1608 and 1616.)

Francis Quarles (1592–1644): *Emblems, Divine and Moral.* (1635.)

James Shirley (1596–1666): *Death the Leveller.* (*Oxford Book of English Verse.* 1910.)

Edmund Calamy (1600–1666): *The Souldier's Pocket Bible.* (1643.) (Elliott Stock, London. 1895.)

Robert Ram: *The Souldier's Catechism.* (? 1643.) (Elliot Stock, London. 1900.)

William Dell (? 1607–1669): *Christ's Spirit a Christian's Strength.* (E. Huntington. 1816.)

William Dell: *Right Reformation.* (R. White for Giles Calvert, London. 1646.)

William Dell: *Theological Works.* (Giles Calvert. 1652.)

N.B.—The entry on William Dell in the *Dictionary of National Biography* is incorrect. It confuses him with the quite different secretary to Archbishop Laud, and inaccurately gives his death as 1664. The date correctly given in the "Bishop's Transcript" of Yelden Parish Register is 1669.

John Milton (1608–1674): *Poetical Works*. Oxford Complete Edition. (Oxford University Press. 1908.)
John Milton (1608–1674): *Areopagitica* (1644). (Dent, 1927. Everyman's Library.)
Samuel Butler (1612–1680): *Hudibras*. (1663–1678.)
Lewis Bayly: *The Practice of Piety*. (1612.)
Jeremy Taylor (1613–1667): *Holy Living and Dying*. (1650–1651.)
Richard Baxter (1615–1691): *The Saints Everlasting Rest*. (Religious Tract Society. 1650.)
John Evelyn (1620–1706): *Diary*. (Cassell's National Library. 1904.)
Andrew Marvell (1621–1678): *An Horatian Ode upon Cromwell's Return from Ireland*. (*Oxford Book of English Verse*. 1912.)
George Fox (1624–1691): *Journal*. (1694.)
John Locke (1632–1704): *Letters on Toleration*. (1689.)
Samuel Pepys (1633–1703): *Diary*. (Macmillan, 1906. Globe Edition.)
Agnes Beaumont (?1654–1720): *The Narrative of the Persecution of Agnes Beaumont in 1674*. (Constable's Miscellany of Original and Selected Publications in Literature. Introduction by G. B. Harrison.)
Arthur Dent: *The Plain Man's Pathway to Heaven*. (W. H. for G. Latham, London. 1654.)
Edward Fowler: *The Design of Christianity*. (1671.)
Edward Fowler: *Dirt Wip't Off*. (1672.)
Charles Doe: *A Collection of Experience*. (1700.)
John Walker: *The Sufferings of the Clergy*. (1714.)
The Church Book of the Bunyan Meeting. Facsimile Edition 1928, with Introduction by G. B. Harrison.

TRAVEL, TOPOGRAPHY, AND NATURAL HISTORY

THE JOHN BUNYAN COUNTRY:

Victoria County History of Bedfordshire.
Victoria County History of Buckinghamshire.
Victoria County History of Hertfordshire.
Victoria County History of Cambridgeshire.
William Camden: *Bedfordshire*. (Part of his Survey of the British Isles, *Britannia*, first published 1586, with later editions.)
Rev. Thomas Cox: *Bedfordshire*. (Part of his *Magna Britannia et Hibernia*, 1720–1731, originally published in monthly numbers as supplement to the five volumes of *Atlas Geographus*, 1711–1717.) Can be seen at the John Bunyan Library.

Charles Abbot: *Flora Bedfordiensis*. 1798. (Abbot was a Bedfordshire naturalist and Vicar of Oakley Raynes, Bedfordshire.) Can be seen at Bedford Public Library.

Daniel and Samuel Lysons: *Magna Britannia*. Vol. I. Part I. *Bedfordshire*. (London. T. Cadell and W. Davies. 1813.)

John Brown, D.D.: *Bunyan's Home*. Illustrated by Alan Barraud. (Ernest Nister, London. Undated. About 1891.)

Albert J. Foster: *Bunyan's Country. Studies in the Bedfordshire Topography of The Pilgrim's Progress*. (H. Virtue & Co. 1901.)

Albert J. Foster: *The Ouse*. (S.P.C.K. Undated.)

Arthur Mee (Editor): *The King's England*. (Volume on Bedfordshire and Huntingdon.)

Beauchamp Wadmore: *The Earthworks of Bedfordshire*. (Bedfordshire Standard Newspaper Co. 1920.)

W. R. Davidge: *Bedfordshire Regional Planning Report*. (Prepared for the Bedfordshire Advisory Joint Town Planning Committee.)

LONDON:

Victoria County History of London.

Alfred W. Light: *Bunhill Fields*. (C. T. Farncombe & Sons. 1913.)

R. S. R. Fitter: *London's Natural History*. (Collins. 1945.)

John Summerson: *Georgian London*. (Pleiades Books, Ltd. 1947.)

GUIDES, PAMPHLETS AND ARTICLES

C. Bernard Cockett: *Bunyan's England*. A Tour with a Camera in the Footsteps of the Immortal Dreamer. (Leagrave Press, Luton. 1948. 2*s*.)

S. V. Hartley: *An Illustrated Guide Book to the Abbey Church of Elstow*. (Bedford. W. T. Baker. Undated.)

D. A. Bungey: *The Church and Parish of St. Mary, Bedford*. (Booklet obtainable at St. Mary's Church.)

F. W. K.: *A Visitor's Guide to the Parish Church of St. Paul, Bedford*. (Leaflet obtainable at St. Paul's Church.)

Rev. E. P. Higham: *Resurgo Splendide*. The Story of Eaton and her Church. 1*s*. Booklet obtainable at the Church of St. Mary the Virgin, Eaton Socon, Bedfordshire (near St. Neots).

Mary S. F. George: *Millbrook: Village in the Hills*. (*Bedfordshire Magazine*. Summer. 1947.)

Mary S. F. George: *The Story of Houghton House.* (Three articles in the *Bedfordshire Magazine.* Summer, Autumn and Winter. 1948.)
"Fenrod": *Angling in Bedfordshire.* (*Bedfordshire Magazine.* Autumn. 1947.)
J. G. Dony: *Wild Flowers in Bedfordshire.* (Luton Museum. 1948.)
J. G. Dony: *Wild Orchids in Bedfordshire.* (*Bedfordshire Magazine.* Spring. 1948.)
Keith Piercy: *Bedfordshire Birds in Early Spring.* (*Bedfordshire Magazine.* Spring. 1948.)
Henry A. S. Key: *Wildfowl in Bedfordshire.* (*Bedfordshire Magazine.* Summer. 1948.)
Bernard West: *Butterflies of the Bedfordshire Woodlands.* (*Bedfordshire Magazine.* Summer. 1948.)

INDEX

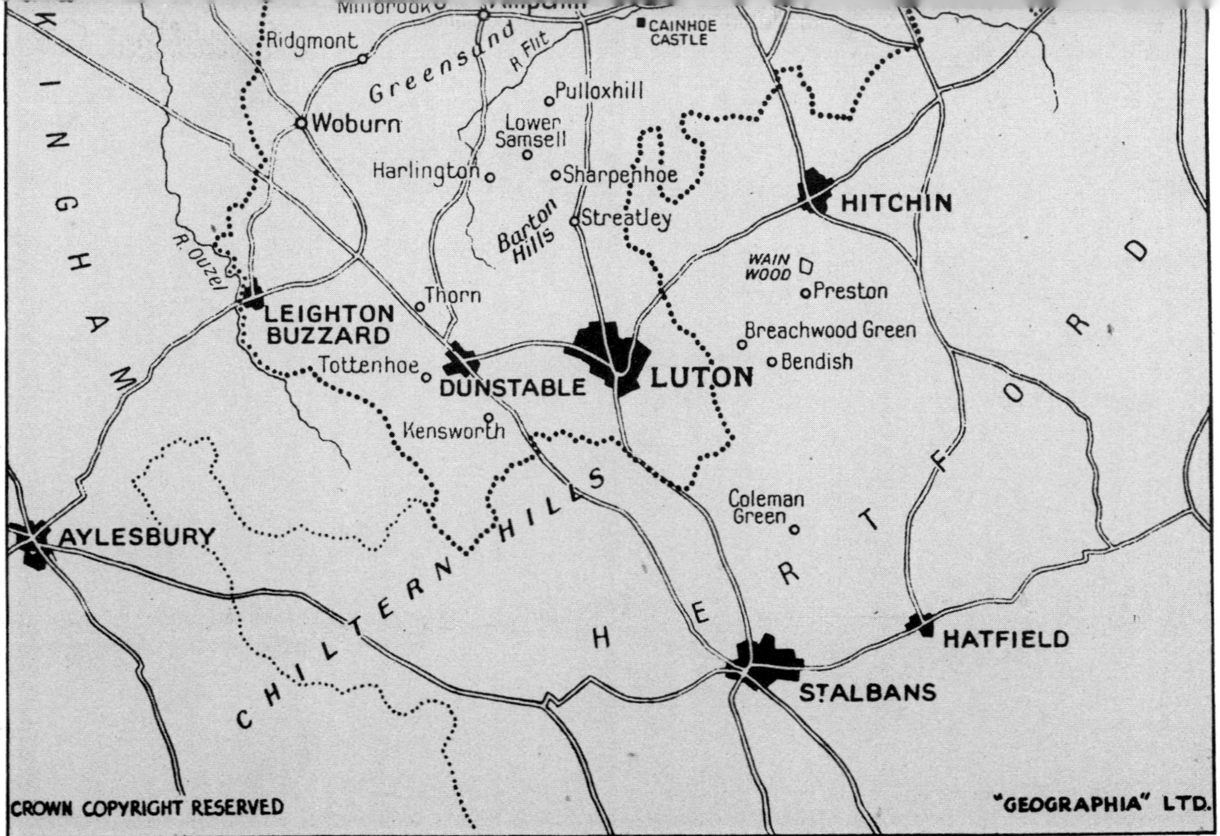
KINGHAM
Ridgmont
Greensand
R. Flit
CAINHOE CASTLE
Pulloxhill
Woburn
Lower Samsell
Harlington
Sharpenhoe
Barton Hills
Streatley
HITCHIN
R. Ouzel
WAIN WOOD
Preston
Thorn
LEIGHTON BUZZARD
Breachwood Green
Tottenhoe
DUNSTABLE
LUTON
Bendish
Kensworth
Coleman Green
AYLESBURY
CHILTERN HILLS
HERTFORD
HATFIELD
ST. ALBANS
CROWN COPYRIGHT RESERVED
"GEOGRAPHIA" LTD.